Multifaceted Explorations of Consumer Culture and Its Impact on Individuals and Society

David J. Burns
Kennesaw State University, USA

A volume in the Advances in Marketing, Customer Relationship Management, and E-Services (AMCRMES) Book Series

IGI Global
DISSEMINATOR OF KNOWLEDGE

Published in the United States of America by
IGI Global
Business Science Reference (an imprint of IGI Global)
701 E. Chocolate Avenue
Hershey PA, USA 17033
Tel: 717-533-8845
Fax: 717-533-8661
E-mail: cust@igi-global.com
Web site: http://www.igi-global.com

Library of Congress Cataloging-in-Publication Data

Names: Burns, David J., 1958- editor.
Title: Multifaceted explorations of consumer culture and its impact on individuals and society / David J. Burns, editor.
Description: Hershey : Business Science Reference, [2018]
Identifiers: LCCN 2018001829| ISBN 9781522561200 (hardcover) | ISBN 9781522561217 (ebook)
Subjects: LCSH: Consumption (Economics)--Social aspects. | Marketing--Moral and ethical aspects. | Advertising--Moral and ethical aspects.
Classification: LCC HC79.C6 M858 2018 | DDC 306.3--dc23 LC record available at https://lccn.loc.gov/2018001829

This book is published in the IGI Global book series Advances in Marketing, Customer Relationship Management, and E-Services (AMCRMES) (ISSN: 2327-5502; eISSN: 2327-5529)

British Cataloguing in Publication Data
A Cataloguing in Publication record for this book is available from the British Library.

For electronic access to this publication, please contact: eresources@igi-global.com.

Advances in Marketing, Customer Relationship Management, and E-Services (AMCRMES) Book Series

Eldon Y. Li
National Chengchi University, Taiwan & California Polytechnic State University, USA

ISSN:2327-5502
EISSN:2327-5529

Mission

Business processes, services, and communications are important factors in the management of good customer relationship, which is the foundation of any well organized business. Technology continues to play a vital role in the organization and automation of business processes for marketing, sales, and customer service. These features aid in the attraction of new clients and maintaining existing relationships.

The Advances in Marketing, Customer Relationship Management, and E-Services (AMCRMES) Book Series

addresses success factors for customer relationship management, marketing, and electronic services and its performance outcomes. This collection of reference source covers aspects of consumer behavior and marketing business strategies aiming towards researchers, scholars, and practitioners in the fields of marketing management.

Coverage

- Mobile services
- CRM strategies
- Telemarketing
- Database marketing
- Mobile CRM
- Social Networking and Marketing
- Online Community Management and Behavior
- CRM and customer trust
- B2B marketing
- CRM in financial services

IGI Global is currently accepting manuscripts for publication within this series. To submit a proposal for a volume in this series, please contact our Acquisition Editors at Acquisitions@igi-global.com or visit: http://www.igi-global.com/publish/.

The Advances in Marketing, Customer Relationship Management, and E-Services (AMCRMES) Book Series (ISSN 2327-5502) is published by IGI Global, 701 E. Chocolate Avenue, Hershey, PA 17033-1240, USA, www.igi-global.com. This series is composed of titles available for purchase individually; each title is edited to be contextually exclusive from any other title within the series. For pricing and ordering information please visit http://www.igi-global.com/book-series/advances-marketing-customer-relationship-management/37150. Postmaster: Send all address changes to above address.

Titles in this Series

For a list of additional titles in this series, please visit: www.igi-global.com/book-series

Marketing Techniques for Financial Inclusion and Development
Dhiraj Jain (Symbiosis International University (Deemed), India) and Adya Sharma (Symbiosis International University (Deemed), India)
Business Science Reference • copyright 2018 • 311pp • H/C (ISBN: 9781522540359) • US $215.00 (our price)

Diverse Methods in Customer Relationship Marketing and Management
In Lee (Western Illinois University, USA)
Business Science Reference • copyright 2018 • 333pp • H/C (ISBN: 9781522556190) • US $215.00 (our price)

Handbook of Research on Social Marketing and Its Influence on Animal Origin Food Product Consumption
Diana Bogueva (Curtin University, Australia) Dora Marinova (Curtin University, Australia) and Talia Raphaely (Curtin University, Australia)
Business Science Reference • copyright 2018 • 453pp • H/C (ISBN: 9781522547570) • US $325.00 (our price)

Analyzing Attachment and Consumers' Emotions Emerging Research and Opportunities
Giuseppe Pedeliento (University of Bergamo, Italy)
Business Science Reference • copyright 2018 • 308pp • H/C (ISBN: 9781522549840) • US $185.00 (our price)

Building Brand Identity in the Age of Social Media Emerging Research and Opportunities
Amir Ekhlassi (University of Tehran, Iran) Mahdi Niknejhad Moghadam (Sharif University of Technology, Iran) and Amir Mohammad Adibi (University of Tehran, Iran)
Business Science Reference • copyright 2018 • 189pp • H/C (ISBN: 9781522551430) • US $145.00 (our price)

Neuromarketing and Big Data Analytics for Strategic Consumer Engagement Emerging Research and Opportunities
Joana Coutinho de Sousa (Unlimited-Hashtag, Portugal)
Business Science Reference • copyright 2018 • 200pp • H/C (ISBN: 9781522548348) • US $165.00 (our price)

Holistic Approaches to Brand Culture and Communication Across Industries
Sabyasachi Dasgupta (O.P. Jindal Global University, India) Santosh Kumar Biswal (Symbiosis International University, India) and M. Anil Ramesh (Siva Sivani Institute of Management, India)
Business Science Reference • copyright 2018 • 281pp • H/C (ISBN: 9781522531500) • US $225.00 (our price)

Multi-Platform Advertising Strategies in the Global Marketplace
Kenneth C. C. Yang (The University of Texas at El Paso, USA)
Business Science Reference • copyright 2018 • 377pp • H/C (ISBN: 9781522531142) • US $205.00 (our price)

IGI Global
DISSEMINATOR OF KNOWLEDGE

701 East Chocolate Avenue, Hershey, PA 17033, USA
Tel: 717-533-8845 x100 • Fax: 717-533-8661
E-Mail: cust@igi-global.com • www.igi-global.com

Table of Contents

Detailed Table of Contents

Self-construction is a process by which a person exercises self-governing agency and fashions his or her own identity, creatively weaving together the various values, beliefs, loves, and aesthetic tendencies that ultimately make a self. Though consumer culture seems to provide the raw materials necessary for self-construction using the meaning-making and signaling capabilities of products and brands, consumption-based projects of self-creation will likely falter because of structural features of desire-formation in that setting. For projects of self-creation to be meaningful, the choices about what kind of identity to form must (1) flow from reflective processes and (2) be based on grounds that the agent him or herself can endorse—two conditions necessary for self-governing agency. Yet desires in consumer culture are often hardened into what Kant calls "passions," a kind of desire that precludes and overcomes reflective processes thus undermining the self-governing agency that is required for self-construction.

Fetishism is the attribution of value to an object. To understand fetishism, therefore, requires a grasp of the value which is attributed to an object. More dynamically, it points to the need to comprehend the mechanisms—the processes—by which value is attributed to a product. The purpose of this chapter is to offer a new conceptualization of consumer value. The chapter begins by presenting a brief review of the consumer value literature, situated within the broader context of axiology. It then summarizes research which explored the concept of consumer values (plural) in the specific social context of the high-fidelity audio culture—those people for whom high-fidelity audio has been fetishized. The chapter continues by offering and explaining the new conceptualization of consumer value, and suggesting future research directions. Finally, it discusses the new conceptualization of consumer value with respect to consumer culture in general, and to fetishism in particular.

Building on the sociocultural dimension of consumption, this chapter sees consumption as the interaction between individuals, products, and meanings. One of the frameworks within consumer culture theory, symbolic interactionism, further explains this co-creation of meaning, building on the idea that people are creating their reality when interacting with one another. A theory providing us with greater detail in how people interact with one another is role theory, according to which people play various roles in their lives, some with greater and some with lesser importance, and each one of them is accompanied with certain expected behaviors. One of the roles we play in contemporary societies is that of a consumer, providing us with an explanation of why the things we expect from consumption change over time. In this, the above will be analyzed parallel to the identification of constructs from the marketing literature for the proposed framework.

Individuals' participation in the marketplace has exceeded all projections. As opposed to a leisure-based utopia that was predicted by many, even with most basic needs being satisfied, most individuals continue to strive to obtain more and more income to participate in the marketplace at progressively higher rates. This chapter examines this seemingly counter-intuitive reality. Specifically, this phenomenon is explored within the theories of Rene Girard, where the concept of mimetic desire is discussed and advanced as a primary motivation behind most present-day consumption. The movie, The Joneses, is the used as an avenue to illustrate the theories of Rene Girard. Several conclusions are drawn.

Tatzel proposed a theory of money worlds and wellbeing comprised of four prototypical consumer patterns based on whether consumers are high/low on materialism and simultaneously tight or loose with money. Tatzel proposes that the four prototypes (value-seekers, non-spenders, big-spenders, and experiencers) differ strikingly along many values, attitudes, and behaviors. This study uses data from 1,016 U.S. student consumers to test empirically the typology and differences. A cluster analysis confirmed that a four-cluster solution best represented the data, supporting Tatzel's model. Subsequent ANOVAs showed that two of the four groups differed predictably in the hypothesized directions. Significant differences between big-spenders and non-spenders appeared in levels of price sensitivity, status consumption, generosity, brand engagement, worry about debt, and spending. The other two groups, value-seekers and experiencers, fell between them. The findings partially confirm Tatzel's theory and suggest that "money worlds" are one way of conceptualizing consumer culture.

Preface

INTRODUCTION

When one views the developed world today (along with large segments of the developing world), the pervasiveness of consumer culture is readily seen. In a consumer culture, the value of virtually everything is determined in the marketplace – few things have intrinsic value. Physical possessions are the primary focus of life for most individuals and become the basis upon which individual success is measured. The pervasiveness of the consumer culture is such that even individual identity becomes a commodity that is developed and maintained in the marketplace.

The omnipresence of the consumer culture, however, is such that is it often difficult for many within such cultures to understand it or to grasp what life would be like in an alternative culture. It is similar to the proverbial fish trying to understand what it is like to be wet. Without an alternative frame of reference, it is often difficult to understand the environment one is in.

Consumer culture has been receiving attention as the effects of consumer culture become more and more apparent. When one takes a "logical" look at the activities and choices of individuals in a consumer culture, at first, it is difficult to understand or make sense of it. Why, for instance, do individuals repeatedly purchase products they do not want or need? Why do individuals work increasingly long hours and often go into debt to acquire products that they do not have the time or the ability to enjoy? This manuscript examines aspects of the meaning behind individuals' choices and activities within consumer culture. Most examinations of consumer culture, however, have been one-dimensional, examining only selected ramifications. This work looks at consumer culture from a number of perspectives – taking a multifaceted approach. The contributors come from a variety of areas and reflect a number of different perspectives.

First, the historical development of consumer culture will be explored. Then, the contents of this work will be introduced.

CONSUMER CULTURE: HISTORICAL ORIGINS

Arguably, the presence of a consumer culture is not new. Archeological evidence, Biblical record, etc. all provide evidence that a consumer culture has existed for millennia. What has changed, however, is its pervasiveness. Until relatively recently, consumer culture was limited only to those at the very top of society. Typically, only these few individuals had the means and the ability to pursue a life dominated by possessions. It has only been relatively recently that a consumer culture has been available to the masses. What follows is a quick and, arguably, overly simplistic overview of the rise of consumer culture among the masses. Included in this discussion is an introduction to the relationship between consumer culture and individual identity, an issue that plays a central role in consumer culture and which arises in several of the chapters included in this book.

Premodernism

For most of human history, most individuals have lived their lives from a premodern mindset. Premodern societies are characterized by traditionalism, with individuals experiencing relatively minimal change through their lives (Koppl, 1996). Subsistence farming is the most common activity. In fact, 60-80 percent of individuals' time is typically spent either raising food for personal consumption or raising the income necessary to acquire food for personal consumption. The lack of income, however, is insufficient in and of itself to explain the lack of widespread involvement of individuals in the marketplace. In premodern societies, when households acquire surplus financial resources, the resources are typically not used in the marketplace to buy additional products even when products to acquire are available (McKendrick, 1982). Instead of spending the surplus, the surplus is either saved or is used to acquire leisure time (Perkin, 1969). Individuals living within premodern societies generally view possessions from a utilitarian perspective. Little meaning is ascribed to possessions other than the direct physical benefit they provide. Hence, there generally is little reason to acquire more possessions beyond those relatively few needed for subsistence.

Key to understanding individuals' behavior toward possessions in premodern societies is to examine the basis of individuals' identities. For individuals in premodern societies, their identities, or their selves, are developed and have their bases in the relatively permanent relationships of family, community, and religion. The family into which one is born typically determines one's social status, occupation, etc. often with little opportunity for change. Furthermore, most individuals rarely stray far from their community in the absence of any specific hardship (e.g., warfare, climate change). Moreover, religion tends to play a significant roles in the lives of most premodern individuals. Key to religion is the identification of who God is and how one relates to Him and to others. In other words, for most premodern individuals, their identities are relatively fixed at birth – they have relatively little opportunity to personally affect their identities, but they possess freedom to operate within these "given" identities.

Modernism

Modernism prompted a rethinking in the nature of life. A number of major movements drove the rise of modernism, including the industrial revolution, the enlightment, and the reformation. For the purposes of this discussion, primary attention will be placed on the effects of the industrial revolution to illustrate some the changes that occurred in individuals' lives. First, the industrial revolution provided individuals with a level of choice that was not available previously. The industrial revolution required large concentrations of individuals to staff new industrial complexes. Consequently, the industrial revolution prompted a significant migration from the countryside to the cities as individuals had the choice to change occupations and places of residence, leading to significant urban growth. The migration and the changing occupations, in turn, significantly weakened individuals' relationships with their family and community (Lyon, 1999). In addition to leaving family members behind in the move to urban centers, in the city, the family was no longer the unit of production. Consequently, family members often found themselves separated from each other the majority of time as they pursued various occupations outside of the home. Furthermore, with the rise in science, religion became less influential in the lives of many individuals (Venkatesh, 1999). This allowed individuals to question the meaning of life and how they relate to the physical world.

As the consequence of the industrial revolution, then, the role played by the relatively permanent bases of individuals' identities in premodern societies (family, community, and religion) significantly declined (Lyon, 1999). Consequently, individuals' identities came to be more likely to be based on transient, physical realities instead of items with greater permanence. As a result, individuals began to play an active role in the construction of their identities. Indeed, the masses gained control of their identities to a degree never before possible – individuals selves were no longer a relatively unchangeable given. Instead, individuals' selves became something that individuals could have have input into.

Products often play integral roles in the self-construction process. Products became to be imbued with images – images paired with products often through marketing activities (Waide, 1987). The pairing of products with images became a channel through which an individual could build their own self by purchasing the products associated with the desired image (Ahponen, 1990). By acquiring products associated with specific images, the images are "acquired" and come to represent the person that one desires to be.

Postmodernism

Questions began to appear during the 20th century in many societies challenging whether reality is truly a rational, unchanging commodity as it is assumed to be within modernism (Ferguson, 1996). Consequently, the existence of concrete reality or objective truth, a critical foundation of modernism, is rejected under postmodernism. Instead, attention is placed on hyper-reality – the idea that socially constructed reality can be more real than reality itself (Fullerton, 1998). Within postmodernism then, the modernist hallmarks of the supremacy of logic and rationality fall, but there were few replacements.

With the rejection of objective reality, the presence of relatively permanent anchors upon which to base the self did not just weaken as they did in modernism, but have virtually vanished in postmodernism (Cova, 1996). Instead, the self exists merely to display – to display the articles which portray a desired image. The mass media has become the means through which images are created and presented – images that become the building blocks for individual self-formation. Shopping, in turn, becomes an exercise in self construction.

Consequently, within postmodernism, marketing has achieved an unforeseen level of societal significance. Instead of focusing on identifying and meeting consumer wants and needs, the focus is on providing consumers with the building blocks necessary to build personal images and to construct desired realities (Panigyrakis & Zarkada, 2014; Venkatesh, 1999). "The image is the substance" (Cova, 1996, pp. 496). The consumer culture, a key characteristic of postmodernism, consequently, achieves a level of significance never before observed. The marketplace is no longer merely a source of products to fulfill physical needs, but instead, the marketplace becomes the source of life itself – the source of happiness, the measuring stick of success, and, most importantly, the reservoir of images from which one's very self can be constructed. It is within this reality that this book exists.

The Threat

Unquestionably, consumer culture has brought a level of affluence to the masses that was unforeseen and unimagined. Today, the level of convenience afforded the typical individual in consumer culture surpasses that enjoyed by the all but the very most wealthy in times past. From this perspective, consumer culture has delivered much more than it promised.

Arguably, consumer culture is redefining the focus of life. Instead of relationships with others being the primarily goal in life, in consumer cultures, the primary focus of life involves products and their acquisition. Products are viewed as the end-all in life and as the primary source of happiness through their ability to be used to define one's identity. Is this true? Do products bring happiness and joy?

Perceptions that possessions bring happiness are widespread and are ingrained in most individuals in consumer cultures. The success of consumer culture in transforming lives has led to a widespread belief that one's quality of life is a function of the quantity of things that one possesses (Roper Starch Worldwide, 1994). This mentality is most easily observed by exploring the relationships between happiness and income, where income is used as a proxy for ability to purchase more products. As would be expected, a widespread belief exists in consumer cultures that happiness is based on one's income, or one's ability to acquire possessions and experiences without hindrance (O'Shaughnessy & O'Shaughnessy, 2002). Additional income provides individuals with increased ability to acquire products for enjoyment, but more importantly, increased freedom to define one's own specific identity. Is income able to bring happiness? Empirical research does not support the existence of this relationship. Indeed, once an individual's subsistence needs are met, additional income and the things that can be acquired through its use have not been found to positively affect an individual's level of happiness (Kottler, 1999; Myers, 2000). Allen concludes "We have no proof that more material goods such as more cars or gadgets has made anyone happier – in fact, the evidence seems to point in the opposite direction" (Packard, 1980, p. 246). It appears, therefore, that consumer culture, along with all of its apparent benefits, is not without potentially very serious problems.

Although consumer culture has been examined from a number of different perspectives, much remains unknown. That is the focus of this book – to further understand consumer culture and its affects on individuals.

CONTENTS OF THE BOOK

This work contains several papers addressing a number facets of consumer culture and how it affects individuals and society. The papers arise from several different disciplines and reflect a number of different perspectives.

In the first set of papers, the focus is on exploring the meaning and manifestations of consumer culture.

In Chapter 1, "Consumerism and Self-Construction," Hadaway explores the role that the self plays in individuals' activities in the marketplace. Self-construction is arguably the primary activity of individuals in consumer culture and provides the basis for understanding this phenomenon.

In Chapter 2, "Fetishism and Consumer Value," Branch explores the issue of value within a consumer culture. In his analysis, he explores the relationship between fetishism and how value is attributed to products.

In Chapter 3, "The Consumption Performance: Applying Role Theory," Koronaki and Panigyrakis explore the multiplicity of roles that individuals play within a consumer culture. As a result of self-construction activities, individuals are not limited in the number of roles that they can develop, a reality that has important implications.

In Chapter 4, "Mimetic Desire as Illustrated in The Jones," Burns examines the role of desire and illustrates the role that marketing plays in the production of desire in individuals. Given that the needs of most individuals in consumer cultures are met, there is a need for something else to be the primary driver of purchasing activity.

The second set of papers focuses on the effects of consumer culture on individuals, families, and society.

In Chapter 5, "'Money Worlds' and Wellbeing: An Empirical Test of Tatzel's Model of Consumption," Flynn, Goldsmith, and Brusco explore individual differences in materialism and the degree to which one is loose with their money to provide increased understanding of individuals' activities in the marketplace.

In Chapter 6 and Chapter 7, "Youth Consumer Practices: A Sense of Not Belonging" and "Adolescent Self-Consciousness and the *En Fusion*," Wilson explores the effects of consumer culture on the lives of adolescents. Probably more so than and other demographic group, consumer culture has transformed the role and lifestyles of adolescents.

In Chapter 8, "Waste and Efficiency in a Consumer Economy," McMullen discusses the issue of waste as it relates to a consumer economy. The chapter examines some proposed solutions to economic wastefulness, as well as some alternative visions of economic progress.

The third set of papers explore religious aspects of consumer culture.

In Chapter 9, "The Spirit of Capitalism vs. the Spirit of Consumerism: A Comparative Typology," Van Til explores possible theological ties in the transition from the Protestant work ethic (which focuses on industry and thrift) to the consumerism common in consumer culture. He particularly notes the transition in the role of identity in individuals' activities.

In Chapter 10, "Consumer Persona: Segmentation Scheme Based on Buddhist Temperaments for Digital Marketing," Chaisuwan, Chantamas, and Prasongsukarn explore consumer culture in light of the Buddhist temperaments and examines how the temperaments relate to marketing strategy.

In Chapter 11, "Consumerism, Violence, and Dehumanization: The Vicious Dynamic Circle," Lambert explores the detrimental effect that living in a consumer culture has on individuals' selves and the ultimately on the human condition.

The fourth set of papers explore consumer culture from a global perspective.

In Chapter 12, "Turkey's Experience of Modern Consumer Culture," Kiran examines the rise of consumer culture in a nonwestern country that has been traditionally opposed to consumption and short-term enjoyment.

In Chapter 13, "Advertising and Consumerism in Nigeria," Endong explores anti-consumer activities used by telecom operators in Nigeria. In doing so, the potential for exploitive activities in a less-regulated environment is raised.

Finally, the last set of papers, explores alternatives to consumer culture.

In Chapter 14, "Waking Up: Consumerism and Plato's *Republic*," Ragland discusses how consumers are blinded to the effects of consumer and explores the role that education can play in overcoming consumerism. Using Plato, he explores ways that individuals can reject consumer culture and its effects.

In Chapter 15, "A Producer Mindset as an Alternative to a Consumer Mindset," Warren and Stratford extend this conversation by exploring a producer consciousness as an alternative to consumer consciousness. They explore tools individuals can use to prompt this reorientation of one's approach to life.

CONCLUSION

Taken together, the perspectives introduce and develop various aspects of consumer culture that illustrate the pervasiveness of consumer culture and its infiltration into every walk of life. It is hoped that this multifaceted investigation will prompt discussion and further interdisciplinary research into consumer culture. Consumer culture can only be understood when it is examined simultaneously from multiple perspectives.

The manuscript is the outgrowth of a seminar comprised of university professors from a variety of disciplines from colleges and universities from across the U.S. supported by the Lilly Fellows Program (Eli Lilly and Company). The participants of the seminar are the authors of several of the chapters included in this book.

David J. Burns
Kennesaw State University, USA

REFERENCES

Ahponen, P. (1990). Signifying the signs – Simulating cultural political subjectivity in postmodernity. *Acta Sociologica*, *33*(4), 341–357. doi:10.1177/000169939003300406

Cova, B. (1996). What postmodernism means to marketing managers. *European Management Journal*, *14*(5), 494–499. doi:10.1016/0263-2373(96)00043-6

Ferguson, H. (1992). Watching the world go round: Atrium culture and the psychology of shopping. In R. Shields (Ed.), *Lifestyle shopping: The subject of consumption* (pp. 21–39). London, UK: Routledge. doi:10.4324/9780203413074_chapter_2

Fullerton, G. L. (1998). The marketing concept in a post-modern era. In P. J. Gordon & B. J. Kellerman (Eds.), *Enhancing knowledge development in marketing* (pp. 198–203). Chicago, IL: American Marketing Association.

Koppl, R. (1996). Man has fallen and he can't get up: An essay on postmodernism and advertising. In M. Cross (Ed.), *Advertising and culture: Theoretical perspectives* (pp. 75–84). Westpoint, CT: Praeger.

Kottler, J. A. (1999). *Exploring and treating acquisitive desire: Living in the material world.* Thousand Oaks, CA: Sage Publications.

Lyon, D. (1999). *Postmodernity*. Minneapolis, MN: University of Minnesota Press.

McKendrick, N. (1982). Commercialization and the economy. In N. McKendrick, J. Brewer, & J. H. Plumb (Eds.), *The birth of a consumer society: The commercialization of eighteenth-century England* (pp. 9–194). Bloomington, IN: Indiana University Press.

Myers, D. G. (2000). *The American paradox: Spiritual hunger in an age of plenty*. New Haven, CT: Yale University Press.

O'Shaughnessy, J., & O' Shaughnessy, N. J. (2002). Marketing, the consumer society and hedonism. *European Journal of Marketing*, *36*(5/6), 524–547. doi:10.1108/03090560210422871

Packard, V. O. (1980). *The hidden persuaders*. New York, NY: Pocket Books.

Panigyrakis, P., & Zarkada, A. (2014). A philosophical investigation of the transition from integrated marketing communications to metamodern meaning co-creation. *Journal of Global Scholars of Marketing Science*, *24*(3), 262–278. doi:10.1080/21639159.2014.911494

Perkin, H. (1969). *The origins of modern English society, 1780-1880*. New York, NY: Routledge.

Roper Starch Worldwide. (1994). *Survey of America's inner financial life*. New York, NY: Roper Starch Worldwide.

Venkatesh, A. (1999). Postmodernism perspectives for macromarketing: An inquiry into the global information and sign economy. *Journal of Macromarketing*, *19*(2), 153–169. doi:10.1177/0276146799192006

Waide, J. (1987). The making of self and world in advertising. *Journal of Business Ethics*, *6*(2), 73–79. doi:10.1007/BF00382020

Section 1

The Meaning and Manifestations of Consumer Culture

Chapter 1
Consumerism and Self-Construction

Bradford S. Hadaway
Georgetown College, USA

ABSTRACT

Self-construction is a process by which a person exercises self-governing agency and fashions his or her own identity, creatively weaving together the various values, beliefs, loves, and aesthetic tendencies that ultimately make a self. Though consumer culture seems to provide the raw materials necessary for self-construction using the meaning-making and signaling capabilities of products and brands, consumption-based projects of self-creation will likely falter because of structural features of desire-formation in that setting. For projects of self-creation to be meaningful, the choices about what kind of identity to form must (1) flow from reflective processes and (2) be based on grounds that the agent him or herself can endorse—two conditions necessary for self-governing agency. Yet desires in consumer culture are often hardened into what Kant calls "passions," a kind of desire that precludes and overcomes reflective processes thus undermining the self-governing agency that is required for self-construction.

INTRODUCTION

The kind of consumerism that finds expression in affluent, advanced capitalist societies like the U.S. certainly has its critics. Such critics challenge its cheap, quickly obsolete, mass-culture outputs, its environmental consequences, its promotion of North/South inequalities and economic injustice, or its tendency to turn everything into a commodity, including the laborers who toil to produce the goods and services of consumer culture (Camacho, 1998; Crane, 2010; Daly, 1998; Lee, 1993; Pogge, 1998). Whatever goods consumer culture musters are often met step for step with accompanying difficulties that are just as damaging to modern life as the goods are palliative. It is difficult to celebrate the "advances" of the latest smart phone technology without worrying over what humans will become when they are constantly wired, mediating social contact through devices, and communicating in shorter and shorter bursts (some of which disappear ten seconds after access).

DOI: 10.4018/978-1-5225-6120-0.ch001

Yet there is one area where consumerism seems to offer a more hopeful and interesting positive contribution to a modern world where traditional sources of meaning have lost much of their natural force and pull. Much of the success of consumerism has been built on the manipulation of the symbolic meanings of the things people own, making them more than just bundles of utilities portrayed in the advertising of an earlier age (Baudrillard, 1981; Bordo, 2000; Goldman & Papson, 2000). Modern consumers consume meanings along with the physical commodities, and for selves that had been robbed of key sources of identity in a disenchanted modernity, this could provide welcome relief. Projects of self-creation and meaning-making could proceed apace in the vast arena of the marketplace, with almost unlimited resources that not only help to tell the agent's own best story but also to communicate that story to others. Self-constructors in the marketplace can exercise creativity and weave together meanings expressively to buttress the thin, wavering identities left in postmodernism's wake.

Such self-constructors can grant the central premise of nihilism that life has no intrinsic meaning or value and still find hope in the newfound freedom to construct meaning for themselves by what they purchase, use, and display. Camus might depict life as a meaningless and perpetual Sisyphean exercise in boulder-rolling, but consumeristic self-constructors can transform Sisyphus' boulder-rolling into a Nike-style ad celebrating the heroic pursuit of an elusive ideal (Camus, 1955). Beckett might depict life as an absurd meandering from one episode to another searching for some pitiable comfort (1954). Yet for the consumeristic self-constructor, the barren site where Vladimir and Estragon wait in perpetuity for Godot is just another opportunity for a dilapidated, shabby exterior to be transformed into a location with curb appeal during the "big reveal." In other words, against the backdrop of nihilistic anxiety, perhaps there is some value in using consumer culture to create self-narratives which are creations of real inspiration and beauty, cheerfully stealing whatever still has resonance from the old meta-narratives.

This chapter will explore this heroic ideal of self-construction in consumer culture to find out whether it really can hold out the promise of identity-formation to a culture having trouble finding itself (Taylor, 1989; Taylor, 2000).[1] It begins by piecing together a working definition of self-construction as expressed in its practical rather than theoretical context. Then the conception of self-governing agency presupposed by the self-construction projects one might undertake in the marketplace is examined. And finally, the chapter will show that those who attempt to practice self-construction through ordinary consumptive practices in consumer culture are forming their desires in ways that destabilize the self-governance necessary for self-construction. Contrary to its own best hopes and dreams, then, self-construction in consumer culture is a practice that contradicts or undermines itself.

BACKGROUND

A sustained, careful analysis of commonly-expressed contemporary problems of the self is obviously beyond the scope of this paper, but some account of these problems is needed to show what motivates consumers when they attempt self-construction in the marketplace. One frequently invoked malaise of modernity is the loss or diminishment of powerful, stable, often-monolithic, "horizons of meaning" which in a former age may have served to situate individuals and allow them to discover a given identity somewhere within that horizon (Taylor, 1991). As grand narratives about the meaning of life have become increasingly fragmented and disempowered, so have the selves that used to rely upon those grand narratives for self-integration and meaning (Taylor, 1989; Taylor 1991). Since the horizons of meaning are no longer functioning without significant crises of legitimation, more responsibility for the creation of new narrative sources for identity is in the hands of each individual.

Attitudes towards this modern reality may, of course, differ. While many will lament the loss of a stable horizon and grope towards new sources of the self to replace the old only out of regretful necessity, some may experience the wiping of the horizons as a kind of liberation from undesirable roles, externally imposed. As Taylor suggests, modernity has both its knockers and its boosters (1991). Both of these attitudes provide a powerful incentive for individuals to look for new sources of meaning, new senses of self-worth, and new sources of coherence and self-integration. Consumer culture has increasingly become an outlet where it is thought that this kind of work can be done (Bauman, 2001; Featherstone, 1991; Firat & Venkatesh, 1995).

The loss of stable and widely-shared horizons of meaning not only impacts the individual's ability to maintain a coherent, stable, and meaningful self, it also impacts how the self operates in social space. Modernity has, for example, created new prospects and challenges for individualism understood as differentiation and distinction. The prospects for a more comfortable embrace of the Romantic ideal of individuality initially seem better given the more open space for meaning-making, but this newfound openness has been launched against the backdrop of a mass culture that can inhibit just as easily as promote the creative formation and expression of a self. The very individuals who would like to tout their unique place in the world must do so while wearing roughly the same clothes as their peers, using the same technology as their peers, enjoying the same entertainments as their peers, and so on (Newholm & Hopkinson, 2009). To avoid the loss of a sense of self by an immersion in utter sameness, individuals must look for ways to differentiate within mass culture. Consumer culture has adapted to provide the sources for some levels of differentiation through processes like product innovation, niche-marketing, and counter-branding.

The other challenge for the self in the modern age is to find this kind of distinctiveness or individuality without completely undermining chances for affiliation and connection. Without stable and widely-shared horizons of meaning, it becomes more difficult for people to find in others the kind of widely-shared identity-conferring values and beliefs which can provide something more than fleeting or tenuous connections based purely on ephemeral shared interests. If Michael Sandel is right in claiming that thick, constitutive communities are only possible when people see in others their own identity-conferring values, then once religious convictions and civic-mindedness and other traditional sources of identity have less of a hold, the self of modernity risks more isolation (Sandel, 1982). There is a need to explore new sources for community and affiliation, and self-construction seems at least one method by which one could take charge of the process. As one builds a self, it will be done with the restoration of ties of connection and affiliation in mind, and just as consumer culture provides resources for differentiation, it also provides resources for connection through processes like common brand affiliations, product affinity groups, and general symbolic signaling that helps agents present stories about themselves which others may accept as grounds of meaningful connection (Elliot & Wattanasuwan,1998).

The fact that modern individuals are met with challenges of both differentiation and affiliation suggests that the road to self-construction will seemingly pull in two opposite directions, but there may be a common thread running through both of these strands of modernity that allows for a thoughtful melding of the disparate ideals. In both cases, what people may be really seeking out is some sense of recognition (Taylor, 1991). The desire for differentiation may be a way for people to rise above the sea of sameness to be recognized as individuals, and the desire for affiliation may be a way for people to secure group recognition. People want to matter, not only to themselves, but also to others.

These and other problems of the self naturally serve as the overarching practical context when people undertake projects of self-construction, and thus the problems will also establish the general contours of what self-construction will mean when it is the proposed solution to the problems. What understanding of self-construction, then, is operative when consumers believe that they are buying to build a self that is a coherent and stable bearer of meaning, a seat of both individuality and affiliation, and a ground of recognition? The next section of the chapter unpacks the idea of self-construction in its practical context, ultimately arriving at a working definition that will be evaluated for practical contradictions at the end of this chapter.

SELF-CONSTRUCTION IN CONSUMER CULTURE

Defining Self-Construction

Though other approaches are possible, this chapter will explore self-construction as it shows up in ordinary practices and discourse—particularly in the practices and discourse of contemporary consumerism. If it is true that one of the explanations for the allure that consumption has in the contemporary world is that it has become a crucial vehicle of self-construction, replacing the increasingly-impotent, traditional sources of the self, then some subset of consumers marches out into the marketplace mulling some version of the thought, "I will buy to shape who I am." There is significant value in capturing what the consumers themselves could mean by such a statement—i.e., what clusters of ideas are being presupposed—even without any expectation that what they mean is necessarily capable of being wrangled into a fully coherent and wholly defensible theory.[2] Such clusters of ideas can carry immense *practical* power even when the ideas themselves are theoretically messy, confused, and inchoate. Ideas need not be clear and theories need not be sound to move people to act. Thus they are worth exploring in themselves to determine what the prospects might be for their use in solving the problems of the self in the modern age.

At bottom, modern self-constructors are those who attempt to fill the voids left by traditional sources of conferred-identity by adopting or fashioning any particular elements that they, themselves, take to be central to their own identities. These elements might include core beliefs, values and attitudes, emotional proclivities, desires and affections, human excellences, bodily appearances, identity-conferring possessions, aesthetic tastes, and so on. Determining the list of things that is conceived of as central to identity is itself part of the self-construction process, and thus lists will vary for different individuals. Some may think that beliefs and values are the chief building blocks of identity, while others may think that desires and affections are closer to the root of human identity. What matters is that in all cases, the goal of self-construction is to bring what the agents themselves perceive as the relevant identity-conferring elements into line with some vision they have of a more fully-realized self (Howe, 2008; McAdams, 1996; Schectman, 1996).

In addition, perceptions about what elements are malleable enough to warrant attention may differ. Some may believe that the whole self can be overhauled or systematically rebuilt one plank at time like the ship of Theseus, but more often people will likely have an appropriately tempered set of expectations about what can really be changed or adopted, and will thus focus on less herculean efforts. They will strive to cultivate a self that represents just enough of a firm platform to allow the agent to remain standing when it is hit with the various aftershocks of modernity.

Self-constructors might also operate with the assumption that some portions of their identities should be off-limits to revision. Here the point is less about whether the feature of identity is malleable and more about whether all the old horizons of meaning have really been obliterated as some have taken Nietzsche to suggest.[3] If self-construction is to be meaningfully in the hands of the constructing agent, part of the process may amount to an assessment that at least some of the traditional foundations of the self remain sound, regardless of what the loudest critics of modernity might say. For example, a Christian might accept that he or she has a basically untouchable core identity, set as a result of God's indwelling presence, while still believing that he or she has an outer, peripheral identity that must be constructed, primarily to better express and reflect the inner identity that's established by God (Luther, 2003; Merton, 1966).[5]

It is not surprising that the emerging picture of self-construction leaves much up to the individual, and the principles of choice dictating certain outcomes of the construction process follow suit. While each individual will make choices for reasons, the exact character of those reasons is not specified. Some will choose targets they take to be good from a prudential point of view. The identity they construct will aim at the increase of their own long term happiness. Others will work to bring the self into line with some moral vision that they endorse; environmentalism, social justice, and hands-off libertarian self-sufficiency all can be used to structure a self. And while there may be other grounding values (the choices may be aesthetically pleasing or even just needed for consistency, all of the choices will fit into the intentionally broad categories of "good" or "authoritative" to the individual him or herself. What appears good or best to individuals will likely be established as partial answers to the problems of meaning-making and self-worth mentioned above. If self-construction is mainly about securing some sense of meaning for life, then it follows naturally that those elements of an identity that will appear good to choose will be the ones that the individual him or herself takes to be most likely to confer meaning.

No specific theory of rational choice or moral reasoning is presupposed by this vision of self-construction, and the view is also agnostic about whether one's search for reasons for building this self rather than that self is an entirely subjective affair or whether there may be objective constraints upon choice such that one cannot rightfully consider the adoption of the identity of a sociopathic egoist as "good" or "authoritative." This agnosticism is not an implicit nod to skepticism about objective conceptions of the good or the possibility of a common, universally binding morality. Instead, the agnosticism is simply an acknowledgement that when explored in its practical context, self-construction will be undertaken both by those who see it as a complete freedom to self-create without any fetters and by those who are genuinely looking for a best version of themselves relative to standards they think all should be able to ascertain, at least in roughly similar ways.

To admit that the conception of self-construction is consistent with broadly subjectivist accounts of value, is not, however, to say that there are no reasonable constraints upon the way that meaningful choices can be made, even in that context. Charles Taylor argues convincingly that the attempt to build an identity is an inherently dialogical process (1991, p. 33). Though the older, traditional, monolithic horizons of meaning may have lost their hegemony as sources of the self, people still must choose who they want to be in dialogue with some horizon of meaning (regardless of whether that horizon is itself grounded in any kind of objective reality). One cannot, for example, simply stipulate that it is a meaningful fact about him or herself that there are 3,732 hairs on the head. Such a fact could only take on genuine meaning if there was some broader story presented by others perceived as significant to the agent (one's family, or peer group, or nation, or religious tradition, etc.) about why that particular number of hairs is valuable --e.g., 3,732 is a sacred number, valued by the gods (Taylor, 1991, pp. 36-7). It is important to note just how limited this conclusion is, perhaps in spite of appearances. The only thing the dialogical character of self-constitution rules out is the idea that one can create meaning or value by mere exertions of monological choice or will or preference. And what it rules in is perhaps even more important. As one enters dialogue with significant others in some horizon of meaning about what is or is not worth doing or being, reasoning and judgment are required to determine how those dialogues should be resolved. The inherently dialogical character of determining what is meaningful or valuable dictates a need for a deliberative process (even when the interlocutors are or must be imagined) about what should or should not be done to build a self.

Yet it remains self-construction only if the final judgment is, in some significant sense, up to the individual him or herself after the engagement with the significant others (present or imagined). This point shines a light on the final and most important feature of the conception of self-construction. Self-construction requires the possession and use of self-governing agency. The purpose of self-construction is to serve as a contrast both to the idea of a conferred identity, where one's identity is set definitively by nature or God or the dictates of a social order, and to the idea of an accidental identity, where people are formed unreflectively, tossed hither and yon by social force and circumstance (as would be the case in early socialization processes). In both cases, the relevant species of control is missing, and that is precisely what the idea of self-governing agency adds. The meaning of self-governing agency will be explained in some detail in the following section, but completing the final definition of self-construction only requires acknowledgement that one's choices are self-governed when those choices are made reflectively without undue inhibition or interference from external or internal factors. And one's choices are self-governed only when based on grounds that the agent him or herself has found to be good or even authoritative.

It is important to note that the problems of the self to which self-construction is the alleged antidote cannot be adequately addressed without the assumption that self-governing agency is operative. For those who look to self-construction as a form of liberation from traditional horizons of meaning, it hardly makes sense to imagine self-construction as a process governed by something other than the self. And even for those who have undertaken self-construction under duress in light of the disempowerment of traditional sources of the self, if the construction process were not the product of one's self-governing agency, the result will still be disempowerment of the self.

All the foregoing considerations lead to a working definition of self-construction as it might be used in its current practical context. In practice, then, *self-construction is, in attempt or actuality, for reasons that, given uninhibited reflection, the person him or herself takes to be good or even authoritative, an adopting or fashioning of all those things about a person that he or she might take as constituting identity—e.g., core beliefs, values, emotional proclivities, desires and affections, human excellences, attitudes, bodily appearances, identity-conferring possessions, aesthetic tastes, etc.* The next section explores in greater depth the role that self-governing agency plays in this conception of self-construction. This will allow the reader to determine whether or not the self-governing agency required for self-construction is sustainable when individuals attempt to self-create through typical consumptive habits in consumer culture.

Self-Governing Agency

The notion of self-governing agency is complex and complicated, the subject of a vast literature in philosophy and a variety of other disciplines. A grasp of the full substance of the concept of self-governing agency is not, however, required to evaluate its role in self-construction. What is needed, instead, is to pick out and briefly explain two conditions which must be satisfied for an act of self-creation to express self-governing agency. These are conditions which have already shown up in the account of self-construction set out above, so the main job in the remainder of this section is to make those conditions explicit and clear, thus completing the account of self-construction.

This task begins with the assumption that the threshold capacity of self-governing agency has been met by self-constructors working out their identities in consumer culture. But with that said, not all choices made by those who meet the threshold capacity reflect that fundamental capacity. The conditions described below represent an attempt to distinguish between particular decisions that are most clearly reflective of self-governing agency, and others which lack, to some degree, the features which would make one confident that the resulting actions were genuinely self-governed. As opposed to "basic autonomy," which sets the threshold conditions necessary to call one a self-governing being, here the focus is on decisions that, more or less, reflect "ideal autonomy" (Christman, 2003; Hill, 1991, pp. 50-1). For example, imagine a person who meets whatever threshold conditions are required to be treated as a fully self-governing agent, yet who also, for whatever reason commonly makes choices in a particular area of life which cannot properly be attributed to the agent him or herself. Perhaps the person, James, is a personnel director constantly at the mercy of a manipulative supervisor. The supervisor feeds false information which steers the director's decisions away from those that would have been selected without the interfering influence. James is generally capable of choosing a breakfast cereal, a television program, or even a spouse, but the range of personnel decisions are infected with a form of consistent interference which means that desire to fire Bob and Sally is not really James's own in a significant sense. And that sense grows increasingly strong if James simply adopted the supervisor's viewpoint without sensitivity to its truth, without reflecting on the quality of the reasons embedded in the viewpoint, and so on.

Self-government in the relevant sense, then, is only evaluated at the level of decisions, and these decisions are evaluated on a continuum where one end represents those decisions which meet the conditions for self-governing agency without question or qualification, and the other end represents those decisions where it is just as obvious that the conditions are not being met. The toughest cases reside in the middle, but attempts to make judgments about such cases will always refer to the degree to which the conditions of self-governing agency are met. In the case above, the mere presence of systematic, manipulative deceit might have been enough to proclaim that the resulting action was not self-governed in a meaningful sense, but when the absence of any reflective action from James is added, the decision falls further away from the end of the continuum reflecting full self-governing agency.

With this background in place, it is important to examine more closely the two conditions which are associated with self-governing agency and which may be undermined in subtle ways when an individual undertakes self-construction through consumptive behavior. The first condition holds that actions that express self-governing agency presuppose an "uninhibited self-reflective process" which allows for internal deliberations about appropriate courses of action and about the appropriate desires, attitudes, beliefs, and character traits which might be behind those courses of action (Christman, 1991).[4] The main obstacles to the fulfillment of this condition, then, would be things that inhibit reflection, and the inhibitions might be external or internal. External factors might include severe and malicious cases where one's control over another allows for the constant interruption of conditions needed for reflection. Examples might include a prisoner being tortured, a child systematically deprived of the necessary educational grounds of reflection, or a brainwashed spy conditioned to believe untruths. But such factors might also be more ordinary and innocuous as when one friend distracts another from examining some course of action with some array of entertaining diversions at the point when reflection might otherwise take place. Internal factors could range from laziness to a paralyzing fear of any self-analysis to a steadfast belief that ignorance is bliss.

The reason why uninhibited reflection seems a necessary constituent of self-governing agency might be best captured in a thought experiment involving a person who never enjoys the reflective space to deliberate. In a Kafka-esque world, some unfortunate soul has gotten into the clutches of a brilliant malevolent manipulator who has a brain scanner that registers all impending beginnings of reflection and deliberation. At each moment where the person might consider whether this or that desire is itself worthy of embracing or acting upon, the manipulator has programmed a device to crank Metallica songs at 100db. No matter what the person does to try to consider whether some action is worth doing, the constant distraction prevents it, and thus the proposed action is simply done or not done according to the particular whim most present at the time. After years of this, the conditioning is complete, and even without the burst of distracting music, a strong internal aversion prevents any significant deliberation about action. Because all agents have desires which they might disavow or resist given the chance to do so, one cannot simply assume that the presence of some desire that is his or hers being realized in action is consistent with self-governing agency. And without any deliberation at all, one might rightly wonder whether there is any meaningful sense in which the manipulated individual is really living his or her own life. If it turned out that there was some way to determine that the acted-upon values and beliefs were in line with the manipulated person's own most basic values and beliefs, the consistency would merely be accidental. The behaviors and the associated desires are happening to the person rather than being adopted or endorsed by the person. Thus, the actions that reflect the most completely realized self-governing agency will presuppose a deliberative space in which actions can become or become recognized as one's own.

The successful fulfillment of the condition of uninhibited reflective processes is not, however, contingent upon a requirement that every single decision, no matter how small or how large, must be preceded by careful, thorough deliberation in order to count as self-governed. The very idea of a character or a self presupposes some stability and continuity in judgments about action-generating desires and values. But one also should not assume that the stability that grounds character is immutable or should be untouchable. On the contrary, human frailty, finitude, and susceptibility to self-deception suggests that there must be some mechanism in place by which even the most stable grounds of character may be subjected to a re-examination, if only to come away with a stronger sense of how central they are to the self (Kymlicka, 2002). At least one way of meeting the condition requiring deliberative space could be the maintenance of a kind of openness to details of prudential and moral salience in ordinary life, such that one is readily alerted to matters which could realistically call one's currently-endorsed values and desires into question (Herman, 1993). This, in turn, would prompt the thicker processes of reflection and deliberation which are more traditionally invoked as conditions of self-governing agency.

The second condition of self-governing agency states that actions that express self-governing agency are based on grounds that the agent him or herself has found to be good or even authoritative. While the preservation of deliberative space mentioned in the first condition is a kind of capability requirement—i.e., one is not capable of making a self-governed decision when one has no meaningful chance for deliberation or reflection—the second condition is an authenticity requirement. Even if space for reflection were given and taken, if the resulting choices do not reflect the person's own value system in some meaningful way, the choices are not self-governed (Dworkin, 1988).

There are stronger and weaker versions of this second condition. A very strong (and thus more controversial) version might suggest, for example, that to be self-governed the decisions have to pass some individually sanctioned, internal test of prudence or morality. In such a view, the goal would always be an authoritative choice. For example, when considering whether to purchase a deep fat fryer or a year-long gym membership, the individual might consider whether a moral or prudential principle would demand one or the other, allow neither, or allow both, and once the outcome of those moral and/or prudential considerations is made clear, then the person would only be self-governed if acting in accordance with the outcome of those considerations, for to do otherwise would be acting contrary to one's own authoritative rules. In spite of a the ways that such a view insures the coherence between action and the agent's own value system, it is deeply problematic because it would mean that any action that one completes that is contrary to one's own principles lacks the relevant type of self-governing agency. Since it is the case that moral responsibility is typically only ascribed to individuals in conditions when they are indeed self-governing, this view would have as a consequence that no one is responsible for the things that they do contrary to their own principles.

To avoid this problem, weaker versions of the authenticity condition are to be preferred. There are a variety of options from which to choose, but the unifying characteristic is that the particular decision and its grounding desires must be endorsed as "the thing to do" in some given situation, regardless of whether the decision is taken to be the best of all alternatives or the morally required action, etc. Frankfurt's well-known version of agency simply requires that first order desires grounding some action be approved by second order desires—desires that one have the relevant first order desires (Frankfurt, 1971). For example, one may have a first order desire for the deep fat fryer and all the delicious things it might produce. But the self-governing agent is able to stand back from the first order desire and reflect on whether or not this particular desire is itself desired. On the continuum ranking the self-governing agency of decisions, the most fully realized agency would be in those whose second order desires correspond well with their first order desires.

Still weaker versions of the condition leave the specific mechanism open and just require that the decisions and their grounding desires emerge in some way from the agent's own evaluational system. Even this wide open formulation allows one to rule out the oversimplified view that one is acting with self-governing agency as long as he or she is acting on some particular desire. The authenticity condition recognizes that not all desires are indicative of the agent's "real self" or the agent's most fundamental self-perceptions or even the agent's set of desired-desires. Thus the agent's acting on whatever desire seems most pressing at any given time is not always consistent with the purest forms of self-governing agency.

This last, open formulation is adequate for the purposes of this chapter. It will be made clear in what follows that it is the first necessary condition, the requirement of deliberative space, which is most challenged as people are formed in particular ways in consumer culture, so it is less important to have a specific understanding of what it means for one to own the actions in some kind of authenticity condition. It is enough to know that regardless of how one's actions are reconciled with their value system, deliberative space will be required to find the relevant grounds from which to act. With the relevant notions of self-construction and self-governing agency clarified, the next task is to consider the ways that consumers might try to express that agency in the construction of selves in the marketplace.

Constructing a Self in Consumer Culture

Building a self in consumer culture is an extremely complicated affair, both because of the dizzying array of sources for the self available in the marketplace and because of the difficulty of stitching together a reasonably coherent and meaning-bearing story for oneself out of that same dizzying array. These factors conspire against those who would seek to maintain self-governing agency in projects of self-construction in consumer culture. There will always be pressures to construct selves unreflectively and without authenticity.

The fundamental building blocks of the process seem to be fairly straightforward--the purchasing of products that have symbolic meanings rich enough to contribute to the individual's self-understanding while also successfully signaling to others messages which increase recognition in the sense described above—sometimes by differentiating the individual from others and sometimes by offering points of possible connection with others (Elliot & Wattanasuwan, 1998; Burns, n.d.). In addition, the objects themselves become part of an extended self with the result that the loss of the object would be perceived as a loss of part of the self (Belk, 1988). Apple electronic devices serve as examples of products with consumable meanings that also signal a kind of distinctive taste to others and provide resources for affiliation. And the only thing that might offset the feeling of loss, if one of those products were to be misplaced or destroyed, would be the thought of its imminent replacement.

But the example oversimplifies things because the symbolic meanings are not precise, and they are always somewhat in flux due to changes in marketing plans and competition. There are no exact symbolic meaning labels parallel to nutrition labels which enable consumers and self-constructors to make simple choices in comparison to all the other objects out there which purport to offer the same basic benefits to the self. When the very self is at stake, information must be sought, interpretations must be clarified, and judgments must be made in thicket of options.

The complexity of this process is ratcheted up considerably with the realization of just how expansive the terrain of consumer culture has become. So far, only the single consumptive activity of buying a product has been considered. Though this remains a common activity of self-construction in consumer culture, advanced capitalism presents one with several other ways to build a self. Many consumptive activities are better characterized as spending rather than buying, because the end result is not necessarily a product with any kind of lasting presence, at least in terms of tangibility. For example, modern consumers spend a good bit of money on experiences rather than products—entertainment, cruises, seminars on gardening—and the experiences themselves serve some of the same functions as more traditional products. The ongoing technological revolution also insures that consumption occurs not just with visits to stores (online or otherwise), but with each click, swipe, or touch. Each time one browses a site, sends a text, checks email, watches a movie, pokes a friend, tweets, or engages in one of the million other distractions that are out there, one consumes in the sense described here. With these and other forms of expansion of consumer culture, the sources of the self found in the practices of consumerism have increased exponentially.

With such complex terrain to cover, one can see why some see self-construction in the marketplace as both a kind of liberatory process (Firat & Venkatesh, 1995) and a heroic process. Those who rise to the challenge of constructing a meaningful self, given the competing messages and the endless sources of meaning, have, in effect, conquered the labyrinth or cleaned the Augean stables. A simple collage of arbitrary identity elements collected in consumer culture might be easy to produce, but this will not be anything close to the self for which the disenchanted modern souls may pine. The successful self-constructor requires both careful thought, strength of determination, and a kind of artistry when taking all the disparate elements and finding a story to tell about them that is as compelling to the one doing the telling as it may be to one who hears it from the outside. And for these reasons, it seems likely that many, if not most, who attempt this process will struggle mightily and often end up simply being formed as an unreflective mirror of various facets of the culture. When the levels of choice seem crushing rather than freeing (Schwartz, 2004), and when it is not at all clear how the consumptive activities might actually fit together into some semi-coherent story, an identity is still being formed, but one without the liberatory and unifying elements sought (Burns, n.d.). The constant danger is that the passivity of unreflective formation will replace the kind of control and direction that should be a central feature of self-construction as described above.

Given this array of circumstances which will have a tendency to promote passivity it should be obvious why self-governing agency is especially important when doing self-construction in the marketplace. First, as noted earlier, when working towards an understanding of self-construction in its practical context, the process of self-construction is always dialogical, not monological (Taylor, 1991, p. 33). Even though some of the traditional horizons of meaning have been disempowered, there will always be *some* horizons of meaning, set by significant others, which serve up the range of options for self-understanding which are then engaged dialogically by the self-constructor. In consumer culture, there are many micro-horizons of meaning, and they present themselves through marketing processes. One of the distinctive markers of consumer culture in advanced capitalism is that the corporations and their messaging have become what Taylor calls significant others for those looking to establish an authentic identity. They offer up their own horizons of meaning or, more frequently, they co-opt the older horizons and adapt the messaging to their own ends The Marriott chain of hotels has, for example, recently adopted Jesus' golden rule as a slogan (Marriott TV Commercial, 2017). The self-constructors who have openly embraced consumer culture as an appropriate resource for self-cultivation will assume that significant meaning can be mediated by the world of things, but the dialogical character of the encounter means that they will need an uninhibited reflective space to question the proposed meanings, to weigh their relative value compared with other competing values, and to determine the overall fit with the narrative unity that's emerging as an identity. In other words, they will need to meet the first condition of self-governing agency described above. Otherwise, the people working towards self-construction become the passive receptacles of some subset of meanings and values from the various horizons of meaning vying for hearts and minds.

Second, the symbolic meanings transmitted by brands through marketing processes can be nearly as totalizing and powerful as the meanings were from the old traditional horizons of meaning. Think about how successful the smart phone industry has been at making it an unassailable norm that connection in the contemporary world must be mediated by the devices and their apps. To be off the smartphone grid is practically the same as being disconnected entirely. Those who see connectedness as a central plank in their identity, then, might have a difficult time thinking beyond or outside of a limited range of options, and not even know that their choice of this mode of self-definition was insufficiently their own. The deliberative space might be there, but it is not sufficiently employed because the choice of that way of being connected has the feel of self-evidence. In this case and others like it, the second condition of self-governing agency described above is invoked. Whatever reasons are offered for choices made in the process of marketplace self-construction have to be tied in some way to the agent's own evaluational system. Acting on the basis of a powerful desire for a particular choice is not, by itself, sufficient to fulfill that second condition.

The foregoing considerations should make clear the significant role that self-governing agency must play in self-construction when that process is carried out in practices related to consumer culture. What was shown first in this chapter is that self-governing agency is conceptually required for a meaningful, practical account of self-construction. What has now been shown is just how practically important self-governing agency is, given the difficulty of self-construction in the consumer mode and given the myriad ways that individuals can slide back into more passive kinds of formation in consumer culture. The final question to address in this chapter is whether self-governing agency can actually be sustained well or at all when self-constructors try to accomplish their aims through ordinary consumptive activities in a consumer culture. The chapter argues that there are structural features of desire formation in consumer culture that will consistently undermine the conditions required for decisions that reflect self-governing agency.

Unstable Self-Construction in Consumer Culture

So far, little has been said about how desires may be involved in the process of self-construction, but there are several reasons to focus attention there. First, desires are prominent features of the ordinary understanding of identity. Second, in consumer culture, it is crucial for those trying to move products to appeal generally to the affective and appetitive side of the human, and so it is not surprising to learn that the affective side of human life is influenced by almost every facet of the consumptive process in advanced capitalism (Campbell, 1987; Galbraith, 1958/1998). When confronted by constant messages about what to love, it would be surprising if human loves were not being shaped in significant ways. Third, and most importantly, desires interact in complex ways with the human ability to live as self-governing agents.

The current section of the chapter will investigate a certain species of desire (what Immanuel Kant and others have called a passion) and show how typical consumptive practices in consumer culture may cultivate them. Since the presence of passions in people undermines self-governing agency, it follows, then, that those who seek to practice self-construction through ordinary consumptive practices in consumer culture are likely forming their desires in ways that destabilize the self-governance necessary for self-construction. Self-construction in consumer culture is a practice that contradicts or undermines itself.

To advance from this point, it will be necessary to dabble a bit in Kant's moral psychology.[5] Kant's account of the affective side of human life includes a number of elements which show how humans could be formed in ways that subvert the proper exercise of self-governing agency. His understanding of inclinations and passions serves to explain how the consumptive lives of humans shrink deliberative space and thereby make it impossible for them to truly own many of the choices that would otherwise be self-defining in the sense described in this chapter. In what follows, it will be argued that while inclinations, as such, constitute no serious threat to human self-governance, passions do.

Inclinations are, for Kant, "habitual desires" (Kant, 1998, p. 29).[9] They typically direct humans towards need-fulfillment, self-preservation, and happiness (Kant, 1978, p. 267). Humans may have inclinations as widely disparate as stable desires to enjoy high-quality, well-cooked food, and others to engage in philanthropic concerns as often as possible. As will be made clear, inclinations may run amok and contradict generally positive purposes, but their fundamental function in human life is constructive (Kant, 1998, p. 58). So while some particular inclinations may need to be subdued entirely or adopted only under the guidance of other principles individuals hold dear, inclinations *as such* do not constitute a pervasive or intractable threat to one's own dignity as a bearer of capacities for self-governance. Such is not the case, however, with respect to passions.

A passion is a "sensible desire that has become a lasting inclination" (Kant, 1996, p. 408), and one that the subject "can subdue only with difficulty or not at all" (Kant, 1978, p. 251). Since inclinations are, by definition, desires that are "habitual" it seems reasonable to assume that passions are desires that by some mechanism (to be explored briefly below) have become even more deeply rooted, pervasive, and intractable than mere habit. Some of Kant's more metaphorical descriptions of passions in the Anthropology reinforce this idea. A passion is a "stream which burrows deeper in its bed," or "a madness that broods over an idea which settles in ever more deeply" (Kant, 1978, pp. 251-2). Passions, by definition, exhibit character-like stability, regularity, and predictable consequences. They are calmly taken up over time, and one who lives with a passion lives as though it is an organizing principle, a piece of the furniture of daily life.

As a mere inclination, ambition may routinely influence one to pursue those ends which would advance his or her status or perceived success. As a passion, ambition becomes such a dominant motivating force that it can only be uprooted by the most persistent character-transforming exertions. The passionately ambitious person does not just regularly act in ambitious ways. The passionately ambitious person finds it exceedingly difficult to do anything else, including, in the most severe cases, considering and pursuing other complementary ends beyond ambition--even those necessary for human happiness. For those who are passionately ambitious, the inclination to ambition has gradually hardened into a rigid and irremediable fixture of character just as a slow acting poison gradually settles into a person's system making a subsequent cure more difficult or impossible.

It is worth drawing attention to the fact that the substance of the passion (the object of the deeply rooted desire) is not the primary source of Kant's complaint. Though the sharpest rebukes are reserved for passions which have as their aim something which is consistently evil (betrayal or dishonesty, e.g.), passions with aims that are commonly perceived as morally neutral (personal ambition) or even morally praiseworthy (acts of compassion) are also inconsistent with problematic for self-governing agency. Kant claims that "the most good-natured desire, even when it aims at what (according to matter) belongs to virtue, for example, beneficence, is still (according to form) not merely pragmatically ruinous but also morally reprehensible as soon as it turns into passion" (Kant, 1978, p. 267).

Before shifting to the ways in which a passion can subvert self-governing agency, there is a puzzle to solve about passions—a puzzle that emerges when one considers passions alongside the rest of Kant's basic account of moral psychology. Kant rejects the idea that any inclinational forces can independently have weight capable of determining the agent's action directly without that agent taking the inclinations as reasons for acting. In other words, it is not as if all the various desires present at any given time have various strengths and the strongest one automatically wins by issuing in action (Herman, 1993). Instead, the inclinations present the agent with incentives to act, but the agent is only motivated to act when he or she adopts, by an act of the will, that inclination as a true interest of the agent him or herself. What this means is that it is not possible to understand the absence of control over a passion simply as a sign of the strength of the desire. Yet if the mere strength of the passion is not sufficient to explain its power to produce action and resist reason's control, what is?

The main clue offered by Kant about how this happens is given in the fact that "a passion always presupposes a maxim on the part of the subject, to act according to an end prescribed to him by his inclination" (Kant, 1978, p. 256). The power of a passion to prompt action without easy control by reason is not about the particular strength of some desire--some urgency in the way that it is felt--but instead the automatic and habitual adoption of the inclination as a reason for acting without subjecting the end of the inclination to any other process of evaluation (e.g. by prudential or moral reasoning). Once the inclinations have been given a sort of free pass from the constraints that might emerge from careful comparison of this inclination with the totality of all inclinations (as is frequently the case in prudential deliberations) or from a careful assessment of a proposed course of action by one of the formulations of the Kant's fundamental moral principle (the categorical imperative), a habit is formed. It is not the habit to act in a certain way, but a habit of selective deafness to certain kinds of considerations which might otherwise complicate the ready pursuit of one's infatuations, and thus the inclination is given a kind of sovereignty that refuses to be corrected. The problem is automaticity and the lack of what might called deliberative space--the separation between inclination and action where the representation of one's duty or thoughts of happiness might have the chance to move the agent to forego what the inclination prescribes, given that it conflicts with duty or one's long-term self-interest.

This helps makes clear the central reason why passions and self-governing agency are not compatible. When a passion is in place, both conditions of self-governing agency that have been discussed are challenged. There is no uninhibited deliberative space in which the course of action prescribed by the passion is evaluated, with a decision that is reflective of the agent's own evaluative system. Instead, the agent has been habituated to act on the inclination whenever it presents itself without reflection, and as a result the agent becomes less and less attuned to issues of prudential or moral salience that might otherwise prompt a second thought about the kinds of actions the inclinations prescribe. In sum, a passion is a habituated avoidance of reflection, and without reflection, the agent's choices are not authentic in the sense described above.

All that remains to make the argument complete is to posit a way in which self-construction practices in consumer culture might cultivate passions of various sorts. Kant said little about how passions might be formed, instead focusing his attention on the problems for moral agency that emerge when passions are already in place. So a basic model must be constructed that explains how ordinary desires might become inclinations (habitual desires) and ultimately harden into passions. Then consumptive practices in consumer culture can be checked to see if they match the model.

The first thing that the model needs is a method by which ordinary desires may be generated and then habituated into inclinations. Contemporary marketing practices have proven to be remarkably successful at generating and/or providing outlets for the practice of desires. The presence of intractable passions towards getting and spending may very well begin as the result of a complex interplay between fundamental human needs and a culture which presents pervasive and powerfully influential models of fulfillment in the pursuit of material aims. Kasser et al. (2003) have explored the psychological causes and ramifications of consumer culture, and their compelling research indicates that those with the highest scores on a materialistic values orientation scale exhibit proportionately lower scores with respect to their own sense of fulfillment in key areas of need: needs for a sense of competence, rich relationships, and a sense of autonomy (Kasser, Ryan, Couchman, & Sheldon, 2003, pp. 13-21). As insecurities and dissatisfactions with life mount, people perform a kind of consistent self-medication with acquisitive desire. Though it is quite clear from several studies that there is limited correlation between overall satisfaction with life and the satisfaction of material desires (above the baseline necessary to be out of the reach of poverty's own insecurities), one finds people again and again returning to the well of materialism for a drink (Myers, 2003). Kant would likely claim that baseline psychological needs, coupled with a cultural model which touts (through advertising and general socialization) materialism as a cure-all has trained a kind of character that perpetuates its own entrenched desires, even in several cases where the acquisition of goods is not delivering the goods.

If those pursuing self-construction through consumptive activities are trying to addresses the malaises felt as a result of the loss of traditional horizons of meaning and traditional sources of the self, then it is not difficult to see why desires might be raised and habituated in consumer culture. For those who experience a crisis of the self (whether acutely or in a more diffused sense of *ennui*), the structure of acquisitive desire in consumer culture might mirror the theory of Kasser et al. (2003), above. A loss of a sense of integration, conferred senses of meaning, and recognition are more than sufficient to promote desires to try out the market's solutions to these problems.

For those who experience the wiping of the old horizons as liberation, a different mechanism might be in play, but it is just as tied to desire formation. The impulse to freedom and independence is itself a fundamental drive in the human story, and so if consumer culture promises fulfillment of such an ideal, the desires will be just as habit-forming in that context as they would be when the self-constructor is trying to correct a powerful deficiency or absence. And regardless of whether the ground of self-construction is crisis or liberation or both, the pervasiveness of marketing and the ubiquity of consumptive choices mean that the self-constructor gets more than enough practice to cultivate habits of desire.

So far the model has only explained the cultivation of various inclinations in consumer culture. A passion, however, is a more deeply entrenched inclination that is no longer attentive to possible alteration in light of the demands of other moral or prudential principles of the agent him or herself. The model needs to show how consumptive practices could cultivate such inattentive, and thus largely invulnerable desires, and two different pathways will be explored. First, there is a biological component to consider in tandem with the cognitive pursuit of various ideals. In the mid-50's, two researchers, Olds and Milner made discoveries about the brain's reward system by allowing lab rats to stimulate with tiny pulses of electricity the parts of their own brains that release dopamine (McGonigal,2012, pp, 107-33).[7] The rats were placed in a so-called "Skinner Box" which contained a lever that would control the shocks to see if the rat would self-stimulate. It did--up to 2,000 shocks in an hour. The rat was seemingly insatiable as he plied the lever, and the only thing that stopped it was exhaustion. They even electrified a part of the floor to see if the rat would endure self-torture in order to get to the lever, and no amount of pain was too much with the lever in sight (McGonigal,2012, pp, 107-33).

Though Olds and Milner had been calling their little patch of heaven in the brain, the pleasure center, it is likely *not* the case that bliss was motivating the rat to pull the lever so many times. Instead, one recent popular theory, based on work done by Kent Berridge and others is that something more akin to wanting (incentive salience is the official term) or anticipation of reward or arousal is the driving force (Berridge, Robinson, & Aldridge, 2009). This is a species of desire that is pleasant enough in itself (roughly speaking), but rather than serving as a kind of satisfaction (or liking as Berridge et al. (2009), puts it), it instead makes one alert to the possibility of satisfaction, making it more likely that the organism will seek out those things that are good for it. The little shock was stimulating a neurotransmitter called dopamine that keys one's attention to the prospect of some reward. In this case, because there was no tangible reward, no satisfaction came, but what is interesting and troubling about this all at the same time is that the mere presence of the dopamine was enough to keep pulling the lever to exhaustion. The anticipation of reward was sufficient.[8]

What has all this to do with consumptive habits? Promise of reward is powerful, even if it never connects with anything truly rewarding. When habits are formed through conditioning by the satisfaction of consumptive desire, the arousal becomes a sufficient reason to act. There is no need for a deliberative process that tries to determine whether some genuine reward might follow in terms of self-construction. The structure of desiring in consumer culture tends towards arousal for its own sake, so once one employs that mechanism routinely for the purposes of some significant task like self-construction, tripping all the levers available to get the job done, the desires begin to take on the character of passions—enchantments which refuse to be corrected. And when the passions are in full force, the agent makes it a kind of policy to act on the desires whenever presented, without consideration of their genuine value or standing relative to other concerns.

One may object that even the people most seemingly in the deep throes of materialism enjoy a kind of deliberative or reflective process about the objects they desire and which they hope will provide additional links of meaning in their emergent selves. They mull which thing would truly be best, given the full range of options available. They may shop aggressively for better deals or just the right thing. But none of this is the kind of deliberation that truly matters. Kant noted that deeply rooted passions still allowed for people to form principles on the basis of those passions and think carefully about how they should be fulfilled (Kant, 1996). One who hates as a passion likely has a number of plans for how to best manifest that hatred. The kind of deliberation missing is about whether or not the grounding inclination and the ends to which it directs one deserve pride of place in the agent's own larger evaluational scheme. And when the allure of wanting has itself become a sufficient reason to act, deliberation in this sense is rendered otiose. The processes of desire formation and hardening in consumer culture take on a life of their own. Though the initial pull to consume may be driven by projects of self-construction, the number of "dopamine levers" in a society where consumption is the dominant mode of existence will promote a habituated and unreflective pursuit of arousal for its own sake and largely divorced from the very projects which must be reflectively engaged to have any meaning.

The second pathway towards passions to explore has to do with the presence of disincentives to deliberate that can arise naturally in the process of consumptive self-construction. In order to give hegemony to a set of desires, one need only sense that there might be difficulties of various sorts if those desires are subjected to scrutiny. Those difficulties might be sufficient to deter deliberation frequently enough to habituate a passion and guarantee the inclination at its heart free reign. A number of these difficulties were explored previously when explaining why self-governing agency is in high demand when one attempts self-construction in the marketplace. Self-construction must be heroic in that arena because the array of choices can be paralyzing, the ambiguity of meanings can be an exercise in perplexity in some cases, and in other cases the hegemony of other culturally dominant meanings can make it unclear what really belongs to the self-constructor and what is a cultural "given." And through all of this, hard-to-come-by excellences of thought and self-determination are required to see the projects of self-construction through to the end. Self-construction is hard, and as a result, the constant need to deliberate with care and determination may not look attractive, even when the overall context of the crisis of the self may push one towards self-construction. As a result, the very conditions that demand such rigor from the choices made in behalf of self-construction also push the self-constructors towards the formation of passions. The more difficult it is to deliberate about and own one's decisions in self-construction, the more likely that the one attempting self-construction will simply cultivate habitual desires in familiar patterns that merely passively reflect culture rather than use its elements in individualized projects of meaning and self-interpretation.

FUTURE RESEARCH DIRECTIONS

The model above serves as a theoretical framework which indicates plausible pathways by which passions might be formed in consumer culture. Other pathways could be suggested and explored. And like all philosophical frameworks which refer to empirically testable phenomena, relevant studies could be constructed to challenge or affirm the efficacy of the empirically testable aspects of the model. Finally, the creation of passions in consumer culture will have significant moral implications from a Kantian perspective. Such moral implications are worthy of additional study.

CONCLUSION

Consumer culture becomes the dominant culture, in part, because it is so effective at producing passions which replicate spending and buying patterns without sufficient reflection. And this is exactly the feature of consumer culture which becomes problematic for self-constructors. From one side, consumers have the allure of "wanting" pushing them towards passions when they try to self-construct in consumer culture. From the other side, consumers have the avoidance of the challenges maintaining a stable and self-validated self through reflective processes pushing them towards passions. If the model suggested above gets things basically right, then passion formation will be the constant partner to self-construction in consumer culture. Because passions are inimical to the kind of self-governance required for true self-construction, self-construction undertaken through ordinary consumptive practices in consumer culture will likely end up defeating itself.

REFERENCES

Baudrillard, J. (1981). *For a critique of the political economy of the sign* (C. Levin, Trans.). Candor, NY: Telos Press Publishing.

Bauman, Z. (2001). Consuming life. *Journal of Consumer Culture*, *1*(1), 9–29. doi:10.1177/146954050100100102

Beckett, S. (1954). *Waiting for Godot*. New York, NY: Grove Press, Inc.

Belk, R. W. (1988). Possessions and the extended self. *The Journal of Consumer Research*, *15*(2), 139–168. doi:10.1086/209154

Berridge, K. C., Robinson, T. E., & Aldridge, J. W. (2009). Dissecting components of reward: 'Liking,' 'wanting,' and 'learning.'. *Current Opinion in Pharmacology*, *9*(1), 65–73. doi:10.1016/j.coph.2008.12.014 PMID:19162544

Bordo, S. (2000). Hunger as ideology. In J. B. Schor & D. B. Holt (Eds.), *The consumer society reader* (pp. 99–114). New York, NY: The New Press.

Burns, D. (n.d.). *Identity through consumption activities: A review and critical analysis*. Unpublished manuscript.

Camacho, L. A. (1998). Consumption as a topic for the north-south dialogue. In D. A. Crocker & T. Linden (Eds.), *Ethics of consumption: The good life, justice, and global stewardship* (pp. 19–27). Lanham, MD: Rowman and Littlefield Publishers, Inc.

Campbell, C. (1987). *The romantic ethic and the spirit of modern consumerism*. Cambridge, MA: Blackwell.

Camus, A. (1955). *The myth of Sisyphus and other essays* (J. O'Brien, Trans.). New York, NY: Vintage Books.

Christman, J. (1991). Autonomy and personal history. *Canadian Journal of Philosophy*, *21*(1), 1–24. doi:10.1080/00455091.1991.10717234

Christman, J. (2003). Autonomy in moral and political philosophy. In E.N. Zalta (Ed.), *Stanford encyclopedia of philosophy*. Retrieved November 21, 2015 from http://plato.stanford.edu/archives/fall2003/entries/autonomy-moral/

Crane, D. (2010). Environmental change and the future of consumption: Implications for consumer identity. *Anuario Filosofico, 43*(2), 353–379.

Daly, H. E. (1998). Consumption: Value added, physical transformation, and welfare. In D. A. Crocker & T. Linden (Eds.), *Ethics of consumption: The good life, justice, and global stewardship* (pp. 19–27). Lanham, MD: Rowman and Littlefield Publishers, Inc.

Dworkin, G. (1988). *The theory and practice of autonomy*. Cambridge, UK: Cambridge University Press. doi:10.1017/CBO9780511625206

Elliot, R., & Wattanasuwan, K. (1998). Brands as symbolic resources for the construction of identity. *International Journal of Advertising, 17*(2), 131–144. doi:10.1080/02650487.1998.11104712

Featherstone, M. (1991). *Consumer culture and postmodernism*. London, UK: Sage Publications Limited.

Firat, A. F., & Venkatesh, A. (1995). Liberatory postmodernism and the reenchantment of consumption. *The Journal of Consumer Research, 22*(3), 239–267. doi:10.1086/209448

Frankfurt, H. (1971). Freedom of the will and the concept of the person. *The Journal of Philosophy, 68*(1), 5–20. doi:10.2307/2024717

Galbraith, J. K. (1958/1998). The affluent society (40th anniversary ed.). New York, NY: Mariner Books.

Goldman, R., & Papson, S. (2000). Advertising in the age of accelerated meaning. In J. B. Schor & D. B. Holt (Eds.), *The consumer society reader* (pp. 99–114). New York, NY: The New Press.

Herman, B. (1993). *The practice of moral judgment*. Cambridge, MA: Harvard University Press.

Hill, T. E. Jr. (1991). *Autonomy and self-respect*. Cambridge, UK: Cambridge University Press. doi:10.1017/CBO9780511609237

Howe, L. A. (2008). Self and pretence: Playing with identity. *Journal of Social Philosophy, 39*(4), 564–582. doi:10.1111/j.1467-9833.2008.00443.x

Kant, I. (1978). *Anthropology from a pragmatic point of view*. Carbondale, IL: Southern Illinois University Press.

Kant, I. (1996). *The metaphysics of morals* (M. Gregor, Trans. & Ed.). Cambridge, UK: Cambridge University Press. doi:10.1017/CBO9780511809644

Kant, I. (1998). *Religion within the boundaries of mere reason* (A. Wood & G. di Giovanni, Trans. & Eds.). Cambridge, UK: Cambridge University Press.

Kasser, T., Ryan, M., Couchman, C. E., & Sheldon, K. M. (2003). Materialistic values: Their causes and consequences. In T. Kasser & A. D. Kanner (Eds.), *Psychology and consumer culture: The struggle for a good life in a materialistic world* (pp. 11–28). Washington, DC: American Psychological Association.

Kymlicka, W. (2002). *Contemporary political philosophy: An introduction* (2nd ed.). Oxford, UK: Oxford University Press.

Lee, M. (1993). *Consumer culture reborn: The cultural politics of consumption.* London, UK: Routledge. doi:10.4324/9780203359655

Luther, M. (2003). *On Christian liberty* (W. A. Lambert Trans. & Ed.). Minneapolis, MN: Augsburg Fortress.

Marriot T. V. Commercial. (2017). *Human: The golden rule.* Retrieved March 31, 2018 from https://www.ispot.tv/ad/w6rw/marriott-human-the-golden-rule

McAdams, D. P. (1996). Personality, modernity, and the storied self: A contemporary framework for studying persons. *Psychological Inquiry, 7*(4), 295–321. doi:10.120715327965pli0704_1

McGonigal, K. (2012). *The willpower instinct: How self-control works, Why it matters, and what you can do to get more of it.* London, UK: Avery.

Merton, T. (1966). *Raids on the unspeakable.* New York, NY: New Directions Publishing.

Myers, D. G. (2003). Wealth and happiness: A limited relationship. In D. Doherty & A. Etzioni (Eds.), *Voluntary simplicity: Responding to consumer culture* (pp. 41–51). Lanham, MD: Rowman and Littlefield.

Newholm, T., & Hopkinson, G. C. (2009). I just tend to wear what I like: Contemporary consumption and the paradoxical construction of individuality. *Marketing Theory, 9*(4), 439–462. doi:10.1177/1470593109346896

Nietzsche, F. (2001). *The gay science* (B. Williams, Trans. & Ed.). Cambridge, UK: Cambridge University Press. doi:10.1017/CBO9780511812088.005

Pogge, T. W. (1998). A global resources dividend. In D. A. Crocker & T. Linden (Eds.), *Ethics of consumption: The good life, justice, and global stewardship* (pp. 19–27). Lanham, MD: Rowman and Littlefield Publishers, Inc.

Sandel, M. (1982). *Liberalism and the limits of justice.* Cambridge, UK: Cambridge University Press.

Schectman, M. (1996). *The constitution of selves.* Ithaca, NY: Cornell University Press.

Schwartz, B. (2004). *The paradox of choice: Why more is less.* New York, NY: Harper Collins.

Taylor, C. (1989). *Sources of the self: The making of the modern identity.* Cambridge, MA: Harvard University Press.

Taylor, C. (1991). *The ethics of authenticity.* Cambridge, MA: Harvard University Press.

Taylor, R. (2000). The meaning of life. In E. D. Klemke (Ed.), *The meaning of life* (2nd ed.; pp. 167–175). Oxford, UK: Oxford University Press.

ADDITIONAL READING

Baxley, A. M. (2010). *Kant's theory of virtue: The value of autocracy*. Cambridge, UK: Cambridge University Press. doi:10.1017/CBO9780511779466

Buss, S., & Westlund, A. (2018). Personal autonomy. In E.N. Zalta (Ed.), *Stanford encyclopedia of philosophy*. Retrieved March 21, 2018 from http://plato.stanford.edu/archives/spr2018/entries/personal-autonomy/

Cross, G. (2000). *An all-consuming century: Why commercialism won in modern America*. New York, NY: Columbia University Press.

Douglas, M., & Isherwood, B. (1979/1996). *The world of goods: Towards an anthropology of consumption*. London, UK: Routledge.

Elgin, D. (1993). *Voluntary simplicity: Toward a way of life that is outwardly simple, inwardly rich* (2nd ed.). New York, NY: Quill.

Engstrom, S. (2002). The inner freedom of virtue. In M. Timmons (Ed.), *Kant's metaphysics of morals: Interpretive essays* (pp. 289–315). Oxford, UK: Oxford University Press.

Frierson, P. (2003). *Freedom and anthropology in Kant's moral philosophy*. Cambridge, UK: Cambridge University Press. doi:10.1017/CBO9780511498121

Twitchell, J. B. (1999). *Lead us into temptation: The triumph of American materialism*. New York, NY: Columbia University Press.

KEY TERMS AND DEFINITIONS

Deliberative Space: An allotment of adequate time and care for reasoned reflection about key decisions.

Dialogical Character of Identity: A conceptual requirement of identity formation or discovery. It stipulates that meaningful building blocks of an agent's identity be formed or uncovered in dialogue with frameworks of meaning that cannot be reduced to mere products of individual choice.

Horizons of Meaning: Narrative or theoretical frameworks of interlocking and more or less coherent beliefs that present accounts of a life worth living or a character worth having Inclination: habitual desire.

Passion: A lasting inclination which is not easily susceptible to change or correction by an agent's own reason.

Self-Construction: An adopting or fashioning of all those things about a person that he or she might take as constituting identity (e.g., core beliefs, values, emotional proclivities, desires and affections, human excellences, attitudes, bodily appearances, identity-conferring possessions, aesthetic tastes, etc.).

Self-Governing Agency: Decision making that proceeds from uninhibited reflection with choices that reflect the agent's own values.

ENDNOTES

1. Both sources rely on historical and philosophical to explain why crises of identity might be more prevalent now than in the past.
2. Even though this chapter does not attempt to construct a complete and coherent theory of self-construction in this paper, it is indebted to those who have done this kind of work for providing some of the key elements of a process that may be involved when self-construction is "tried" in its practical context. See, e.g., Schectman (1996).
3. In the famous madman passage where the death of God is proclaimed, the madman asks those who "killed" God, "Who gave us the sponge to wipe away the entire horizon?" (Nietzsche, 2001, p. 120).
4. The language of "uninhibited self-reflective processes" is from Christman, but the idea is used in a narrower sense in this chapter.
5. It is important to note that one need not embrace Kantian ethics, metaphysics, or epistemology in order to accept the concept of a passion set out in what follows as an obstacle to agency.
6. Following a common convention in Kantian scholarship, the page numbers will correspond to the appropriate page numbers of *Kant's gesammelte Schriften, herausgegeben von der Deutschen Akademie der Wissenschaften*. (1902). Berlin: Walter de Greyter. These page numbers are found in the margins of the editions included in the reference list.
7. The details about Olds and Milner's experiment are from McGonigal (2012, pp, 107-33).
8. These tests were extended to humans. Though methodological concerns about these experiments are likely to call the results into question, the outcomes in the human experiments were strikingly like those recorded with the rats in the Skinner Boxes.

Chapter 2
Fetishism and Consumer Value

John Branch
University of Michigan, USA

ABSTRACT

Fetishism is the attribution of value to an object. To understand fetishism, therefore, requires a grasp of the value which is attributed to an object. More dynamically, it points to the need to comprehend the mechanisms—the processes—by which value is attributed to a product. The purpose of this chapter is to offer a new conceptualization of consumer value. The chapter begins by presenting a brief review of the consumer value literature, situated within the broader context of axiology. It then summarizes research which explored the concept of consumer values (plural) in the specific social context of the high-fidelity audio culture—those people for whom high-fidelity audio has been fetishized. The chapter continues by offering and explaining the new conceptualization of consumer value, and suggesting future research directions. Finally, it discusses the new conceptualization of consumer value with respect to consumer culture in general, and to fetishism in particular.

INTRODUCTION

In the everyday, fetishism might be conflated with eroticism, conjuring the entry for 'sexual fetishism disorder' in the American Psychiatric Association's (2013) *Diagnostic and Statistical Manual of Mental Disorders* which defines sexual fetishism as a sexual excitement which is derived from an inanimate object or non-genital body part. According to Mulvey (1993), however, fetishism is a broader social phenomenon, involving "the attribution of self-sufficiency and autonomous powers to a manifestly 'man' derived object" (p. 7). Indeed, fetishism entails a kind of Cartesian relationship between an object of interest (the fetish) and the person who has an interest in the object (the fetishist).

The term fetish is thought to be derived from the Portuguese term *feitiço*, meaning spell, superstition, or even witchcraft (Pietz, 1987). It arose in the 17th century when Portuguese explorers noted the significance which the various native peoples of West Africa whom they encountered vested in the amulets, charms, and talismans which they wore. The notion of *feitiço* "stressed its use as an instrument to achieve a concrete, material effect, while its status as an object of worship was central to the idea of *idolo* [idolatry]" (Pietz, 1987, p. 36).

DOI: 10.4018/978-1-5225-6120-0.ch002

Karl Marx introduced the term *warenfetischismus* (commodity fetishism) in his book *Capital: Critique of Political Economy* (1867). Marx argued that in an economy of independent producers and buyers, commercial activity adjusts according to the changing values of the goods and services (the commodities) which are produced and exchanged. Social interaction, therefore, is expressed and mediated through two things: 1. money and 2. commodities. The intrinsic worth of any commodity, however, Marx theorised, is denoted by the value which buyers in the market attribute to it.

It is this idea of attributed value which was likewise captured by Hekma (2007) who defined fetishism as the attribution of value to an object. Two fundamental ideas are central to this definition. First, an object is not inherently valuable. Indeed, its worth is not a given *prima facie*. On the contrary, an object only becomes valuable when value is attributed to it...when it becomes imbued with value. When this object is a product—a commodity in the language of Marx—fetishism ought to be considered as an aspect of consumer culture.

Second, fetishism occurs within a specific social context. That is to say, an object is not universally a fetish, but instead a fetish only to a group of people for whom the object has been fetishised. As underlined by Mulvey (1993), "fetishes are supremely culturally specific, so...one man's divine may be another man's lump of wood" (p. 7). Again, therefore, when fetishes are products, fetishism ought to be considered as an aspect of consumer culture.

To understand fetishism in consumer culture (*à la* Hekma and Marx), therefore, requires a grasp of the value which is attributed to a product. More dynamically, it points to the need to comprehend the mechanisms—the processes—by which value is attributed to a product. To understand fetishism in consumer culture also requires an emic approach, which seeks to understand meanings from the 'native's perspective' (Holt, 1994) in his or her own terms and conceptual categories. An emic approach also assumes that a co-constituting relationship exists between these meanings and one's existential stance within a specific culture (Thompson, Locander, & Pollio, 1989). In simple terms, an emic approach means making sense of a fetish within its cultural context.

Value—consumer value, more specifically—however, is not well-understood by most marketers. This is ironic, considering that consumer value is perhaps the foundational concept in the discipline of marketing. As suggested by Holbrook (1999),

[g]iven the importance of this topic, one might expect that a vast marketing-related literature would be devoted to exploring the nature and types of consumer value...Yet my impression is that such emerging attempts have thus far failed to investigate the nature and types of consumer value with anything like the degree of comprehensiveness and systematization needed to make telling conceptual inroads into the issues of concern (p. 3).

The purpose of this chapter, therefore, is to offer a new conceptualisation of consumer value. The conceptualisation stems from research which explored the concept of consumer values (plural) in the specific social context of the high-fidelity audio culture—those people for whom high-fidelity audio has been fetishised. The research initially sought to address the weaknesses of Rokeach's conceptualisation of values which has come to dominate the discipline of marketing. In doing so, however, it ultimately led to a new conceptualisation of consumer value (singular). The chapter begins by presenting a brief review of the consumer values literature, situated within the broader context of axiology. It then summarises the research within the high-fidelity audio microculture. The chapter continues by offering and explaining the new conceptualisation of consumer value. Finally, it discusses the new conceptualisation of consumer value with respect to consumer culture in general, and to fetishism in particular.

THE CONSUMER VALUES LITERATURE

Discussions of value have existed for millennia (Bahm, 1993). Plato and Aristotle, for example, placed good above all else in their ethical philosophies (Aschenbrenner, 1971). Christianity and other world religions are essentially value-oriented, occupied with dilemmas of good and evil (Werkmeister, 1961). And early economic theories reflect the notion of value (See Smith (1816) for example.).

It was the German philosopher Hermann Lotze, however, who first proposed the idea of a general philosophy of value—*axiologie*, or axiology in English—as distinguished from ethics, religion, law, politics, economics, and all other disciplines of the social sciences (Lemos, 1995), which, "disregarding particular value [disciplines], would yet be foundational to them all and would be concerned with the valuational aspects of human experience as a whole" (Werkmeister, 1970a, p. xxvii).

As a scientific pursuit, axiology seeks to address a wide array of questions about value. Chief among these is the fact/value debate. As summarised by Alicke (1983), "twentieth-century value theory has been dominated by the question of whether values can be treated like any other scientific proposition or fact, or whether they constitute a realm of experience that cannot be accounted for in terms of description, empirical propositions of science" (p. 14). A second key question about value centres on the object/subject debate (Walsh, 1998). Do values exist independent of humans, for example, or are values brought into existence through the human act of valuation? Other questions about value include: What are the characteristics of value? What are its origins? Does value entail affective, cognitive, or conative components, or a combination of all three (Meddin, 1975)? Does it have an appetitive dimension (Alicke, 1983)? Does value have a normative dimension (Lovejoy, 1950)? And how are values related to other concepts such as beliefs, attitudes, norms, and ideals (Albert, 1968)? In general, however, these and other questions about value can be categorised into three axiological problems: 1. the epistemological status of value, 2. the nature of value, 3. the criterion of value (Angeles, 1992).

Consumer Value

Despite the obvious lessons which axiology can teach marketers, there is a conspicuous lack of reference to axiology in the marketing literature. Indeed, the majority of conceptualisations of consumer value have been influenced by, if not altogether derived from, the discipline of economics—specifically, the notions of exchange, use, utility, and trade-off. For Smith, Ricardo, and other eighteenth century economists, value was an intrinsic part of commodities (McKnight, 1994), predicated on the cost and scarcity of a commodity. It was essentially the accounting aspect of an exchange which, in effect, amounted to 'what could be got' for the commodity.

Economists then latched onto the Aristotelian notion of use, arguing that value ought to be viewed in terms of the consequences which are derived from the commodity in use (Smart, 1891). Value, therefore, is a utility function of the consequences of the intrinsic economic properties of the commodity. Bernoulli added that people, by nature, are utility-maximisers (Chung, 1994), and consequently a value 'calculus' was born. Later refinements to this utilitarian approach were based on the works of Bentham and Mill, who suggested that utility is primarily hedonistic, and that pleasure can never be had without pain. Value, therefore, took on the idea of a trade-off between benefits and costs.

These economic notions of exchange, use, utility, and trade-off are more than obvious in the consumer value literature. Indeed, Kotler, the father of modern marketing, wrote that "[a] transaction is the exchange of values between two parties" (1972, p. 47), where value to the consumer is defined as the ratio of benefits to costs. More recently, Zeithaml (1988), for example, suggested that value (or perceived value as she called it) is a combination of the intrinsic and extrinsic attributes of a product, of the perceived quality of the product, and of the perceived sacrifice which the individual must make to acquire the product. And Woodruff (1997) intimated that "[c]ustomer value is a customer's perceived preference for and evaluation of those product attributes, attribute performances, and consequences arising from use that facilitate (or block) the customer's goals and purposes in use situations" (p. 143).

One deviation from the pure economics-oriented conceptualisations of consumer value is by Holbrook (1999), which contends that consumer value is a preference for a specific product from among a set of alternatives. Holbrook's conceptualisation of consumer value replaces exchange and use with experience. Indeed, Holbrook argued that value arises as the result of a transaction, but at the moment of the product's use—that which he calls the experience. Additionally, he suggested that value "resides *not* in the product purchased, *not* in the brand chosen, *not* in the object possessed, but *rather* in the *consumption experience(s)* derived therefrom" (p. 8). Utility for Holbrook is conceived as the services which are provided by the product to the consumer. These services, therefore, are the sources of utility; products are merely the vehicles.

The main difference in Holbrook's conceptualisation of value, however, is with the economic notion of trade-off. In other conceptualisations of consumer value, it is claimed that consumers create accounting like T-tables of benefits and costs for different products, the results of which are profit-like totals. Choice among products, therefore, is explained by utility maximisation—the most profitable product as perceived by the consumer is chosen. For Holbrook, however, value is the choice. Indeed, mimicking the micro-economic theory of choice behaviour, valuation becomes synonymous with preference-ordering, involving the cognitive ranking of alternatives.

THE RESEARCH

The research on which this chapter is based explored the phenomenon of consumer values (plural) in the high-fidelity audio microculture. The research was premised on the notion that the concept of consumer values has been accorded a position of great importance by marketers, the result of which is an extensive consumer values literature in the discipline of marketing. A critique of this literature, however, concluded that the importance which the concept of consumer values has been accorded has, to a large extent, failed to materialise. This failure is due to the weaknesses of one conceptualisation of consumer values—that of Rokeach (1968). The research initially sought to address the weaknesses of Rokeach's conceptualisation of values, but in doing so, it ultimately led to a new conceptualisation of consumer value (singular). The research was both exploratory and descriptive in nature. It took a decidedly phenomenological perspective, and drew heavily on axiology. It adopted the postmodern notion of consumer microcultures. And it followed hermeneutic data analysis procedures.

More specifically, eleven members of the high-fidelity audio microculture were interviewed several times during an eight-month period. The interviews followed the phenomenological interviewing method and allowed each research participant to articulate the meanings of high-fidelity audio, in the context of his lifeworld. During the interviews, observations were made of the research participants, of their audio equipment, and of their other belongings. Photographs were taken of the research participants' audio equipment and other belongings. Additionally, audio magazines, audio equipment catalogues, and other audio-related documents were collected. Verbatim transcriptions of the interviews, the notes, the photographs, and the other documents were entered into a computer-aided qualitative data analysis software package.

Analysis of the interview transcripts and other data occurred in three separate but inter-related phases. First, individual—or emic—level analyses of the interview transcripts were performed in order to understand the meanings of high-fidelity audio for each of the research participants, in the contexts of their lifeworlds. The second phase moved up to the micro-cultural level; its goal was to understand the distinct pattern of meanings of the high-fidelity audio microculture. And in the third (etic) phase, an explicit effort was made to understand the research participants' emic meanings of high-fidelity audio vis-à-vis a broader theoretical concern—namely, the phenomenon of consumer value. The result was a new conceptualisation of consumer value.

A NEW CONCEPTUALISATION OF VALUE

In summary, value is the degree to which an object satisfies a subject's interest. Object means any conceivable thing, either concrete or abstract. In the context of marketing, object refers to a product which is capable of assuaging a consumer need through a marketing transaction: a good, a service, a destination, an activity, an idea, etc. Satisfaction ought to be thought of in the most general sense (appeasement, mollification, sufficiency, fulfilment, match, etc.), and is the direct result of a comparison between the object and the subject's interest. The subject is a person—in the context of marketing, a consumer. And interest refers to a temporarily-fixed cognitive constraint structure. Consumer value, therefore, is the degree to which a product satisfies a consumer's interest (See Figure 1 for a visual representation.). How can this new conceptualisation of consumer value be explained in terms of the three axiological problems which were identified above?

The Epistemological Status of Value

Epistemology is the philosophy of knowledge (Kvale, 1996). Although some philosophers contend that epistemology is like a continuum, three broad epistemological stances are common. The first epistemological stance, objectivism, is based on the conviction that there is a "permanent, ahistorical matrix or framework to which we can ultimately appeal in determining the nature of rationality, knowledge, truth, reality, goodness, or rightness" (Bernstein, 1983, p. 8). Objectivist conceptualisations of value, therefore, centre on the idea that value is intrinsic to the object—that there is something in the object which makes it valuable to humans. The value of an object is measured by how well it matches the conceptual category to which it belongs. For example, if the intension of 'chair' is 'a knee-high structure with a seat back' then a thing which is called a 'chair' will be more valuable a chair the more of the chair properties it has, and the less valuable a chair the fewer of the chair properties it has. A chair which has no seat is not a *good* chair but a *bad* chair (Hartman, 1973, p. 39).

Figure 1. A visual representation of consumer value

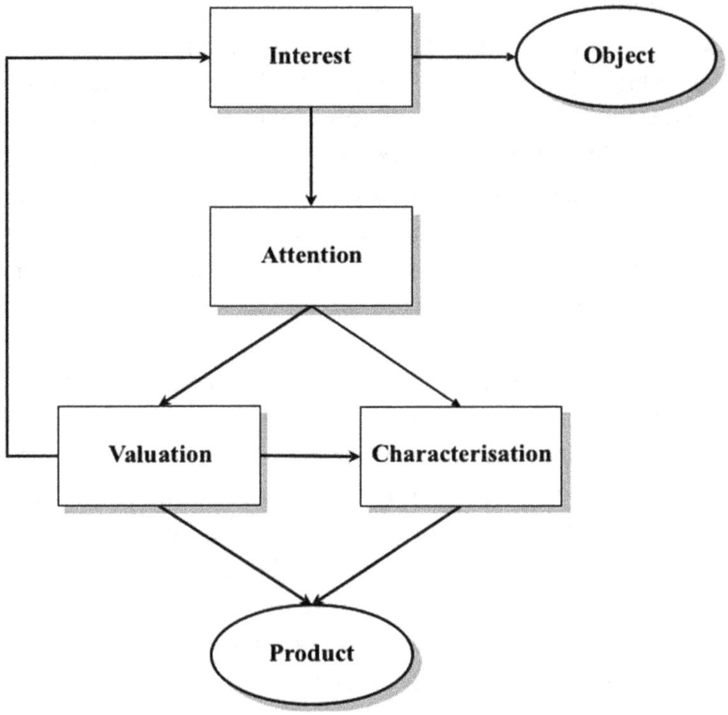

The second epistemological stance, subjectivism, suggests, on the contrary, that "subjectivity is the ultimate reality…that there is no real world that is wholly independent of the 'subject' that knows or experiences the world" (Schwandt, 1997, p. 148). With respect to axiology, subjectivism "entails the belief that the source of value is *within*…the inner world of the agent" (Bond, 1983, p. 138). Value, therefore, inheres not in the object; indeed, objects of the world are valueless. Instead, values arise as the result of human experience. They are considered to be those subjective opinions; preferences; or other affective, conative, or cognitive responses which are projected upon the neutral world (Allen, 1993).

The third epistemological stance, interactionism, posits that knowledge of the world is neither objective nor subjective; meaning does not inhere in the objects of the world, nor do humans create meaning from some netherworld. Instead, interactionism claims that the "objects of the world are indeterminate. They may be pregnant with meaning, but actual meaning emerges only when consciousness engages with them" (Crotty, 1998, p. 43). In interactionist epistemological stance of value, therefore, asserts that value depends on both the object and the subject. As summarised by Frondizi (1971),

[i]f we examine the relationship between the valuable object and the subject that valuates it, we will notice clearly…that the value can exist only in relation to a subject that valuates it…No matter how deep one may go in the analysis, there is no possibility of disconnecting the object from the subject…value is a relational notion requiring both the presence of the subject and the object (p. 146).

It ought to be somewhat obvious, therefore, that the conceptualisation of consumer values which is offered follows an interactionist epistemological stance. Indeed, value defined as the degree to which a product satisfies a consumer's interest points squarely to the concomitance of object and subject for both value and valuation. Only with both an object and a subject does valuation occur and value arise.

Interactionism is advocated here because it responds explicitly to the criticisms of Rokeach's conceptualisation of consumer values. But more apropos, it corresponds to the idea that fetishism is the emic attribution of value to an object. Human consciousness is an "intentional activity, in the sense that intentions are always directed toward objects. In other words, consciousness is always consciousness *of something*. Objects are defined in terms of the practical intentions we have at hand when we encounter them" (Lindlof, 1995, p. 32). Intentionality, therefore, emphasises the interaction between consumer and their fetishes.

Accordingly, valuation is considered an intentional act. To interact with the world consciously is to valuate it. And value is considered the meaningful result of this intentional act. Indeed, it is a conceptual structure (Williams, 1949) which results from the process of valuation—a "cognitive construction emerging from…the interactions of the person in his/her environment" (Veroff, 1983, p. xvii). There is also ample support in the axiological literature for adopting an interactionist epistemological stance. Connor (1992), however, summarised it well in his claim that…

[v]alue is inescapable. That is not to be taken as a claim for the objective existence or categorical force of any values or imperatives in particular; but rather as a claim that the processes of estimating, ascribing, modifying, affirming and even denying value, in short, the processes of valuation, can never be avoided. We are claimed always and everywhere by the necessity of value in this active, transactional sense…we should acknowledge that value and evaluation are necessary as a kind of law of human nature and being, such that we cannot help but enter the play of value, even when we wish to withdraw or suspend from it. (p. 8).

The results of the emic analysis also support an interactionist epistemological stance. Indeed, although the lifeworlds of the research participants vary greatly, the way in which high-fidelity audio is experienced meaningfully is similar, forming a distinct pattern which is not unlike a melody. As suggested by Thompson, Locander, and Pollio (1990), the notes of a melody can be transposed into different keys, but the melody remains the same.

The Nature of Value

In addition to the problem of the epistemological status of value, axiology also identifies the problem of the nature of value—both the property of value and the process of valuation (Runes, 1983). Indeed, it seeks to address such questions as 'What is value?', 'Is it a quality or a relation?', 'Is its presence in a thing dependent on or reducible to the fact that the thing is valued by someone?', 'Is it merely a feeling or desire, or does it involve judgement and cognition?', and 'How and why does value come into existence?'

To begin, the term value and the numerous other value-related cognates and compounds which are used not only in philosophy but also in the other disciplines of the social sciences have resulted in a confusing and often misleading vocabulary (Frankena, 1967). The term value was once relatively transparent, its meaning referring to the worth of an object (Laird, 1929). As such, valuation was the estimation of worth.

With axiology, however, came new uses of the term value which were dramatically different and often conflicting. Four general uses of the term value, however, can be discerned in the axiological literature. The first is value as an abstract noun for all valuative (critical)—that is to say, pro or con—predicates which designate the property of value. An example is 'My car has value.' This use of the term value is often situated in contrast to existential or factual predicates as in 'My car is red.' The second use of the term value is value as a concrete noun which refers to the object which has value. For example, 'These are my values.' designates those objects which a person valuates. The third use of the term value is found mostly in the works of the German philosophers Scheler and Hartman, and refers to a general predicate which subsumes more specific predicates. Just as one might say that an object has colour and, more specifically, that it has the red colour, so one might say an object has pleasure value or courage value. And the fourth use of the term value is value as a verb, as in 'I value your opinion.', for example. With this usage, value is somewhat synonymous with valuate.

The conceptualisation of consumer values which is offered reverts to the original idea of worth. Indeed, it reserves the term value for an abstract noun for all valuative predicates which designate the property of value. The verb valuate, rather than value, is employed for the process of valuation. The third use of the term value—value as a general predicate which subsumes more specific predicates—is intriguing. This colour analogy, however, is a kind of semantic game. Heat, like colour, could also be considered a general predicate of an object, and, according to the same logic, different levels of heat content would be considered specific predicates. It is heat, however, which remains the primary predicate of the object. The second use of the value term—as a concrete noun which refers to the object which has value—highlights a distinction which now pervades the social sciences, but which is problematic. Sociologists (and also marketers) tend to refer to statements about concrete objects as attitudes and reserve the term value for more abstract objects (Alicke, 1983). As suggested by Kilby (1993), however, values and attitudes are related so closely that it ought to be asked if there is the need for the concept of values. Indeed, the more general an attitude, the more it is like a value; the more specific a value, the more it is like an attitude.

Put in a slightly different way, attitudes and values concerned with the same content area can be arrayed along a continuum that ranges from the quite specific to the highly abstract. Since the distinction of attitudes and values is continuous, rather than discrete, an infinite number of levels of abstraction can be imagined, and because of the gradual shading from specific to general, no hard and fast distinction can be made between general attitudes and specific values (Meddin, 1975, p. 890).

Continuing with the nature of value, recall that the conceptualisation of consumer values which is offered suggests that consumer value is the degree to which a product satisfies the consumer's interest. To begin, interest here refers to a temporarily-fixed cognitive constraint structure with respect to a specific object (Valsiner, 1992). This temporarily-fixed cognitive constraint structure is a personal pattern of meanings about the object which are constructed in a cultural context. These meanings guide the person's mental/affective and actional systems (including valuation).

An example here ought to help illustrate this conceptualisation of interest. Imagine that a personal system of meanings included the beliefs that 'Sports cars are cool.', 'Foreign and rare sports cars are especially cool.', and 'If I am cool, people will like me.' This pattern of meanings which is constructed about the object 'sports cars', therefore, will guide mental/affective and actional systems which will be activated or triggered when specific automobiles enter the consciousness.

This conceptualisation of interest and its role in valuation is reinforced by the results of the emic analysis. Indeed, with each research participant, interest in high-fidelity audio equipment was revealed. Consider the research participant Nick as an example. Nick's father was a musician, but only owned 15 vinyl recordings. Consequently, Nick had no interest in high-fidelity early on. Appetence and interest, however, came one day like a revelation, as illustrated in the following excerpt from an interview with Nick.

I remember when...aah...at school. First of all, I went to a boarding school. And generally, people didn't have access to that kind of thing then. But as you got more senior, you had more private space to yourself. And I remember one boy, one day brought in some equipment. I can't remember what it was. I can remember the speakers though being about that. <motions height> Three times as big as I had seen before probably—only about that big <motions again, lower>. Umm...they were Decca—made by Decca, I think, and I just remember thinking, 'You know that was a huge improvement.' I remember the first thing I thought was, 'You know. It makes musicians and people...umm...sound much bigger. You can imagine the people as being proper scale and...umm.' In the early....When would that have been? Early 70s, I suppose. And you know, from then on, I suppose I always realised I wanted something better than the ordinary little Sony, or the ordinary transistor radio. And I realised there was this difference in quality, which I think a lot of people still haven't realised now. Umm....they think that if they see the name Sony on something then it must be the best you can get.

This excerpt also reveals that the interest which Nick developed in high-fidelity became the standard to which he appealed when judging pieces of audio equipment. Indeed, the value which he ascribes the Sony and the ordinary transistor radio are relative to the meaning of high-fidelity which he has constructed. In a dialogue from another interview, this meaning starts to become clearer.

John: *Improvement. Improvement in which ways?*

Nick: *Umm...what sense did I use it in? Improvement in sound quality, I suppose. Yeah, much more life-like—much more kind of involving and...I like to hear the details. I'm not the kind of person who can have the radio on or any kind of music on when I'm doing something else either.*

John: *What about the...umm...design of the equipment?*

Nick: *Not too much...umm...there are limits though. I, I like the look of valve equipment, for example. I like the kind of retro type of look. Umm...I mean I can't see how you can like the look of loudspeakers, quite honestly. And I, well I don't see how you can like the look of any sort of electronic stuff.*

John: *Mmm.*

Nick: *To me, I would, I would be satisfied or I'd be happy if it was all invisible. I'm not interested in impressing people with a number of flashing or anything like that again. It's purely a means to an end.*

Finally, interest as the standard to which he appealed was ubiquitous throughout the interviews with Nick. The following dialogue emphasises this notion.

Nick: *Now...umm...one case in point about looks was that 2 weeks ago, I got a pair of second hand speakers that I tried instead of these B&W 801s which are very good speakers but they were so ugly I wouldn't stand having them in the room. <laughs> They look like....umm. They're a big square box about this high <motions height> with a great big round speaker in the front and a little box on top.*

John: *Yeah.*
Nick: *And then another little box on top of that, like a little eye. It looked sort of like a robot—R2D2 or something.*

Continuing with this notion of interest as standard, according to Gaus (1990), all judgements involve ideals. Indeed, judging, by definition, is the act of referring a particular case (an object, an action, or a decision, for example) to a moral rule, a prescript, a commitment, a guideline, etc. It is an appeal to the standard—a comparison to the benchmark. Valuation, therefore, according to the conceptualisation of consumer values which is offered, is a kind of judgement. It is the act of referring a specific object to the person's interest.

In order to do so, the person must pay attention to the object. Attention here, however, is not the spotlight—in the psychological sense—which a person shines on objects in the world in order to illuminate them. Instead, attention is synonymous with intentionality. As suggested by Brentano and Husserl, it is the meaning which is constructed as a result of a person's 'encounter' with the object.

Attention is concerned in the first instance with characterisation. Indeed, according to Berleant (1973), it is important to distinguish clearly between the existential field of human experience in the first order and the particular cognitive activity of reflective analysis by which people develop their valuative knowledge of that field. Characterisation is achieved through the processes of description ('That ball is red and bouncy.', for example.) and appraisal ('That dress is beautiful but expensive.', for example). Indeed, according to Hall (1952), language "uses both descriptive and appraisive devices in speaking about [objects]" (p. 9). Other social scientists, however, believe that the distinction between description and appraisal is unwarranted, arguing that knowledge of an object—descriptive or appraisive—is always constructed subjectively through judgements which appeal to standards, even with the apparent objectivity of the descriptions 'redness' and 'bounciness.'

Valuation, therefore, is the intentional consideration of this characterisation vis-à-vis interest. It is a meta-level cognitive process which compares the characterisation of a specific object to the 'ideal', as it is defined by the subject. It "is experience dealt with at once removed, so to speak. It results in the formulation of judgements of value" (Berleant, 1973, p. 31). With respect to consumer values specifically, it is the act of referring a product to the consumer's interest.

Returning to the example, an interest in the object sports cars—the personal pattern of meanings which is constructed in a cultural context—guides mental/affective and actional systems. When an automobile is seen on the street or in a magazine or indeed in the mind, a person is activated or triggered to attend to it. An automobile in an advertisement, therefore, comes to exist first as a meaningful characterisation in the mind—"Wow, that is a cool-looking, black Mazda RX-8 with the aftermarket 18 inch polished aluminium wheels and Recaro seats." It is this characterisation which is then considered vis-à-vis interest.

It is the ability of an object to satisfy interest, therefore, which is at the root of value. Indeed, an object has value because a person takes satisfaction in it. According to Werkmeister (1970b), "[o]ur ability to form valid valuational propositions depends on our ability to analyze present decisives, to anticipate what, under given conditions, would satisfy them" (p. 61). Satisfaction, therefore, is not a mode of valuation but its goal.

Satisfaction ought to be defined, however, in the broadest sense. Indeed, it is not just the meeting of hedonic appetites. As summarised by Aschenbrenner (1971), if satisfaction…

...is to serve as the anchor to all our thought about value, we must not confine it to its sensuous modes, to mere stimulation and gratification of the feelings. It must comprise also our most momentous and solemn concerns where something has been possessed, lived through, where it has solved a problem, answered a question. This will include the outcome of agonizing decisions as well as the fulfillment of inclinations, so that we can say not only of food or drink, but even of the outcome of a moral situation that has evoked our judgment, it satisfies (p. 37).

This broad sense of satisfaction finds support in the results of the emic analysis. Indeed, with each research participant, a comparison of the characterisation of his audio equipment with his interest in high-fidelity is revealed. Consider the research participant Mark as an example. In the following dialogue from an interview with Mark, his interest in high-fidelity is first summarised. He then proceeds to characterise some of his equipment. Finally, the comparison of this equipment with his interest becomes evident.

John: *Umm...you said the, the sound is most important to you. What about the sound?*
Mark: *What about it? Umm...*
John: *The sound.*
Mark: *What elements of the sound you mean? Yeah, yeah, I look at it...I'm, I think I'm interested in the end result. It, it's not the buying the product for its own sake, although sometimes the Meridian equipment looks pretty nice. I think it looks nice and that's definitely a factor. But the overall objective is sound more than anything. And unbelievable accurate sound—something that sounds natural.*
John: *Mmm-hmm.*
Mark: *I don't want...It's small and it's great looking. I don't want a big series of black boxes and huge cables. So Meridian seems to strike a balance between...Well, it's some of the best looking stuff and some of the best sounding stuff, I think. That's important.*
John: *Beautiful and clever.*
Mark: *Yeah. You feel sometimes it's a pretty good system. You put something on and it sounds like the vocalist is just there in the room. And I know ex girlfriends and things have commented it sounds pretty accurate. I think that was a good test. Someone who doesn't know...I mean you can be sucked in by the fact that's its expensive. You know what you spent on it. But they just sit down and listen to it and they go "Wow! That sounds really incredible." You know. I remember someone walked past my room in a house here when I was studying here. They were looking for the person playing the guitar. They thought for sure it was a real guitar. It was coming out of the speakers. So that's the kind of sound I'm looking for. Not the house shaking bass. That's always cool, but its not really the main drives.*

Finally, this dialogue with Mark also underlines that satisfaction is not an all or nothing, but a degree. In this way, it is indeed like an interval scale such as temperature. An object can never have negative value, however. Just as an object can be colourless, or it can have colour, so can an object be valueless, or it can have value. To say that an object has negative value is nonsensical. Satisfaction, therefore, ought to be thought of more as the Kelvin scale than the Celsius scale, or as natural numbers in the discipline of mathematics, both of which have an absolute zero which equates to 'absence of.'

Value as the degree of satisfaction was also demonstrated in the results of the emic analysis. Indeed, with each research participant, a comparison of the characterisation of his audio equipment with his interest in high-fidelity resulted in a valuation which was not all or nothing, but a degree. In the following excerpt from an interview with research participant Fraser, the value of his Meridian equipment becomes apparent. Note, however, that another piece of equipment (Krell) which he does not own would be valuated higher in his mind.

It's not particularly inexpensive. But it's not at the high-end of the audio range. It is something...Krell, for example, I would be more happy with...but, but I feel this is perfectly adequate for my, umm...They're stylish—not that I really want a flash system. And as for the audio quality, yes, I do appreciate the audio reproduction of speech and music. But there is better out there.

Similarly, in the following excerpt from an interview with Phil, he discusses the relative merits of the car radio, his current high-fidelity audio equipment, and his old vinyl record deck.

But I think...I said before it's only a means to an end. It's not the be all and end all, the equipment. It's really the music that's important to me. I get to listen to the car radio on the way to work. I get pleasure from that, yeah. But there is a certain other dimension to it. Because I can think of the old days with, umm...LPs. I mean you can't, you know when the scratches come and you're kind of waiting in the music for you, 'Its coming, it's just coming now.' And you have this scratch. Now, you've got CDs without all... That is a breakthrough cause it is distracting.

The Criterion of Value

The third problem of axiology is the criterion of value. As suggested by Frankena (1967), the main question is "whether value judgments are susceptible to being justified or proved" (p. 232). The answer to this question depends largely—if not entirely—on the nature of value (Angeles, 1992). Indeed, how both the property of value and the process of valuation are defined will relate directly to how value is manifest in reality. The criterion of value for hedonic conceptualisations of value, for example, is found in the quantity of pleasure which is derived by the subject. Intuitionists call for preference. And idealists appeal to an objective system of ideals which serve as criteria.

Recall that the conceptualisation of consumer values which is offered suggests that consumer value is the degree to which a product satisfies the consumer's interest. Interest refers to a temporarily-fixed cognitive constraint structure. It is a personal pattern of meanings about an object which are constructed in a cultural context. The attention which this constraint system activates or triggers is synonymous with intentionality. That is to say, it involves the construction of meanings about the object, in terms of both characterisation and valuation. The criterion of value of the conceptualisation of consumer values which is offered, therefore, is meaning.

Meaning here is concerned with that which an object in the world symbolises for humans (O'Shaughnessy, 1992). That is, the construction of meaning is coextensive with the process whereby new symbolic structures come to represent the objects of the world (Klausmeier & Harris, 1966). The vehicles of these cognitive structures are concepts which are organised by cognitive schema (Kamppinen, 1993, p. iv) or narratives (Holt, 1997).

Concepts are linguistic in nature. Indeed, they are terms which are ascribed to objects of the world in order to connote meaning. For example, the characteristic meaning of the object tree is denoted by the word which is spelled t-r-e-e; its connotation is derived from its relations to other concepts, such as leaf, trunk, branch, and bark. The medium of human knowledge, therefore, is language.

According to Durkheim (1974), however, knowledge of an object is not limited to characterisation. Indeed, "there is not one way of thinking and judging for dealing with existence and another for estimating value…Both are aspects of judgement and all judgement involves ideals. The function of some is to express the reality to which they adhere. These are properly called concepts. The function of others is, on the contrary, to transfigure the realities to which they relate, and these are the ideals of value" (p. 95) .

Characterisation and value judgements (valuation), therefore, are overlapping aspects of first-person experience. Indeed, value judgements have the same "logical status…as other empirical judgements pertaining to immediate experience" (Werkmeister, 1967, p. 111). They are "facts, to be described as any other facts" (Urban, 1909, p. 13).

In summary, therefore,

[r]eflection on experience is concerned with valuation, with developing a conceptual framework and arriving at judgements of value which have the abstract generality of all cognitive statements (Berleant, 1973, p. 31).

Value is simply "the meaning of the object for the subject" (Werkmeister, 1970b, p. 38) with respect to interest. In terms of consumer value specifically, consumer value is the meaning of the product for the consumer with respect to interest.

DISCUSSION

This new conceptualisation of consumer value provides a number of insights for consumer culture in general, and for fetishism in particular. To begin, it challenges long-standing assumptions about the phenomenon of consumer values in the discipline of marketing. Principally, it denies the very existence of consumer values as defined by Rokeach's conceptualisation of values, by refuting the logic of universal psychological dimensions. In doing so, therefore, it eschews the distinction between the terms values and value which has been propagated in the discipline of sociology…and in turn adopted by the discipline of marketing. This denial is not without support—in general, the paradigmatic goal in mainstream psychology to understand psychological universals has never enjoyed favour in anthropology or in other culturally-oriented disciplines of the social sciences.

In eschewing the distinction between the terms values and value, therefore, this new conceptualisation of consumer value ends up competing against the economics-oriented conceptualisations of consumer value which have dominated the discipline of marketing. By conceptualising consumer value in this economics-oriented way, marketers have avoided culture. They have made consumer value meaningless. And they have failed to explain why and how value comes into existence. Consequently, this new conceptualisation of consumer value provides a viable alternative to these economics-oriented conceptualisations of consumer value for exploring consumer culture.

Marketers have long been interested in both profiling the values of groups of consumers, and exploring the influence of consumer values on their affects, behaviours, and cognitions. In order to do so, they have adopted an approach which assumes that the rank ordering or weighting of a limited set of universal and largely invariant consumer values can explain differences in consumers.

As suggested by Holt (1994), however, the weight of empirical research and consumer cultural theory suggests that this approach is inadequate for these tasks. Indeed, there is little evidence to suggest that values are satisfactory at discriminating between consumers with respect to behaviour. And only very weak relationships between values and other measures of consumers have been demonstrated.

One of the most prominent values-based tasks in the discipline of marketing is the so-called means-ends chain, which proposes that consumer values are linked to products through product consequences. Products "gain their relevance because they allow the consumer to achieve certain benefits (e.g., reliability or health). A benefit in turn becomes important because the consumer has a higher need for the benefit (i.e., they are related to higher-order personal values such as happiness, security, sense-of-belonging, and achievement)" (Vriens & Hofstede, 2000, p. 5).

In adopting the concept of values as the higher-order need, however, the means-ends chain takes on a nomothetic and reductionist slant—products are assumed to map to a presumably universal set of consumer values. The cultural meanings by which this mapping occurs, however, are largely abstracted out of the elicited chains. Additionally, the meaningful linkages which join products to consequences, and consequences to consumer values, have been supplanted by meaningless arrows (Thompson & Troester, 2002). The phenomenological relevance of the means-ends chain, therefore, might be questioned (See Durgee et al.,1986; Thompson,1997, for example).

Despite these criticisms, the ultimate goal of the means-ends chain—to identify the links between products and consumers' motivations—seems extremely worthwhile. Indeed, a greater appreciation of these product-consumer interactions would enable marketers to develop superior segmentation, more precise positioning, and a more effective marketing mix. It is this very idea which is reflected in Holt's (1994) cultural system of taste.

Holt defined a cultural system of taste as the symbolic system which consumers use to make sense of the universe of products. It is the "ideographic system of tastes which organizes one's understanding of and *evaluation* of consumption objects, and structures one's preferences and actions" (Holt, 1994, p. 182, author emphasis). Among this cultural system of taste is the phenomenon of fetishism.

FUTURE RESEARCH DIRECTIONS

The applied objectives of the means-ends chain might be fulfilled better by aiming to understand—*à la* Holt's cultural system of taste—why a product is valued by a consumer. Indeed, an in-depth exploration of a person's valuation of a product would be far more helpful in understanding the consumer's motivation. Collectively, this would resemble the poststructuralist approach to lifestyles which was advocated by Holt. Methodologically, this would require an approach which combines the new conceptualisation of consumer value with a microcultural analysis like that of the research within the specific social context of the high-fidelity audio culture. It would involve the 'mapping' of consumption practices (including fetishism) of the members of a microculture, with a special emphasis on the valuation processes of these these members.

This approach rests on the critical idea that knowledge of the value which consumers attribute to products is only obtained through consideration of the larger lifeworld in which valuation occurs. Consequently, exploring the context of consumer's daily life experiences is the basis for anticipating the value which they might attribute to different products. As noted by Fournier (1998), moving to this level of ordinary experience is where the meanings which are central to life are indeed constructed.

This approach also intimates that the shared interests of the members of the microculture are that which Thompson and Troester (2002) referred to as the consumer value system. Indeed, their 'network of meaning' theorisation of the consumer value system proposes that consumer values are the meanings of an object which are shared among members of a microculture, and are thereby used as a frame of reference for consumption practices. In other words, consumer value is at the heart of consumer culture (including fetishism).

The methodological challenge of this consumer values/microcultural approach, however, is that it would be most applicable to products which are framed in a microcultural context. Although, with postmodernism and its corresponding fragmentation and decentredness, this requirement is witnessed more and more frequently with consumers. Consider the Ralph Lauren Polo brand 'lifestyler', for example, or the do-it-yourselfer. But the research within the specific social context of the high-fidelity audio culture provides an apt illustration.

An important insight which the new conceptualisation of consumer values provides, for example, is that the meanings which the research participants' ascribe to their high-fidelity audio equipment also includes value. As such, the deeply-rooted self-identities and the emancipating high-fidelity audio microculture are reflected in the value of their high-fidelity audio equipment. That is, value is how they are substantiated. Viewed in this way, therefore, the research participants created their own oasis—their own territory—in society through their consumption. But it is the value of the high-fidelity audio equipment which facilitates this oasis. The new conceptualisation of consumer value, therefore, reinforces the notion of postmodern anarchy which, high-fidelity audio equipment both induces and affords.

CONCLUSION

Fetishism is an aspect of consumer culture. A fundamental idea in fetishism is value. Indeed, a product only becomes a fetish when value is attributed to it. And this attribution of value occurs within a specific social context. This chapter offers a new conceptualisation of consumer value which stems from research which explored the concept of consumer values in the specific social context of the high-fidelity audio microculture—those people for whom high-fidelity audio has been fetishised.

The chapter contributes to the study of consumer culture by adding to the discourse on the phenomenon of consumer value. Indeed, the new conceptualisation of consumer values which is offered improves the understanding of the phenomenon of consumer value, in terms of both the property of value and the process of valuation. This new conceptualisation of consumer values provides a viable alternative to the economics-oriented conceptualisations of consumer value which have dominated the discipline of marketing. And in combination with a microcultural analysis, it constitutes a workable approach for understanding the links between products and consumers' motivating structures.

The research also contributes to the study of consumer culture by lending support to the constitutive relationship between the distinct pattern of meanings of a microculture and the broader historical context of postmodern consumer culture. It affords a richer understanding of how consumers use the distinct pattern of meanings of a microculture as a frame of reference in the valuation of products, and conversely, how this valuation, in turn, helps to shape this distinct pattern of meanings. In very practical terms, it helps to understand the high-fidelity audio fetish…the reasons for which research participant Colin spent more than 10 000 GBP to construct a dedicated listening room which occupies his son's former bedroom, and whose design is based on blueprints of the main sound studio at the BBC headquarters in London, England.

REFERENCES

Albert, E. (1968). Value systems. In D. Sills (Ed.), *International encyclopedia of the social sciences* (Vol. 16, pp. 287–291). New York, NY: Cromwell Collier and Macmillan.

Alicke, M. (1983). Philosophical investigations of values. In L. Kahle (Ed.), *Social values and social change: Adaptation to life in America* (pp. 3–23). New York, NY: Praeger Publishers.

Allen, R. (1993). *The structure of value*. Aldershot, UK: Avebury.

Angeles, P. (Ed.). (1992). *HarperCollins dictionary of philosophy*. New York, NY: HarperCollins.

Aschenbrenner, K. (1971). *The concepts of value: Foundations of value theory*. Dordrecht, The Netherlands: D. Reidel Publishing. doi:10.1007/978-94-010-3093-9

Bahm, A. (1993). *Axiology: The science of values*. Amsterdam, The Netherlands: Editions Rodopi.

Berleant, A. (1973). The experience and judgement of values. In E. Laszlo & J. Wilbur (Eds.), Value theory in philosophy and social science (pp. 24-37). London: Gordon and Breach Science Publishers.

Bernstein, R. (1983). *Beyond objectivism and relativism*. Philadelphia, PA: University of Pennsylvania Press.

Bond, E. (1983). *Reason and value*. Cambridge, UK: Cambridge University Press.

Chung, J. (1994). *Utility and production functions: Theory and applications*. Oxford, UK: Blackwell Publishers.

Connor, S. (1992). *Theory and cultural value*. Oxford, UK: Blackwell Publishers.

Crotty, M. (1998). *The foundations of social research: Meaning and perspective in the research process*. Thousand Oaks, CA: Sage Publications.

Durgee, J. (1986). Richer findings from qualitative research. *Journal of Advertising Research*, *26*(4), 36–44.

Durkheim, E. (1974). Value judgements and judgements of reality. In E. Durkheim (Ed.), *Sociology and philosophy*. New York, NY: Free Press.

(2013). Fetishistic disorder, 302.81 (F65.0). In American Psychiatric Association (Ed.), *American Psychiatric Association. Diagnostic and statistical manual of mental disorders* (5th ed.; p. 700). Washington, DC: American Psychiatric Association Publishing.

Fournier, S. (1998). Consumers and their brands: Developing relationship theory in consumer research. *The Journal of Consumer Research*, *24*(4), 343–373. doi:10.1086/209515

Frankena, W. (1967). Value and valuation. In P. Edwards (Ed.), *The encyclopedia of philosophy* (Vol. 18, pp. 229–232). New York, NY: Macmillan Publishing Company.

Frondizi, R. (1971). *What is value?: An introduction to axiology*. La Salle, CA: Open Court.

Gaus, G. (1990). *Values and justification: The foundations of liberal theory*. Cambridge, UK: Cambridge University Press. doi:10.1017/CBO9780511625046

Hall, E. (1952). *What is value? An essay in philosophical analysis*. London: Routledge & Paul.

Hartman, R. (1973). Formal axiology and the measurement of value. In E. Laszlo & J. Wilbur (Eds.), *Value theory in philosophy and social science* (pp. 38–47). London: Gordon and Breach Science Publishers.

Hekma, G. (2007). Fetishism. In G. Ritzer (Ed.), *The Blackwell encyclopedia of sociology*. London: Blackwell Publishing. Retrieved May 19, 2018 from http://www.blackwellreference.com/public/tocnode?id=g9781405124331_chunk_g978140512433112_ss1-52

Holbrook, M. (Ed.). (1999). *Consumer value: A framework for analysis and research*. London: Routledge. doi:10.4324/9780203010679

Holt, D. (1994). Consumers' cultural differences as local systems of tastes: A critique of the personality/values approach and an alternative framework. *Asia Pacific Advances in Consumer Research*, *1*, 178–184.

Holt, D. (1997). Poststructuralist lifestyle analysis: Conceptualizing the social patterning of consumption in postmodernism. *The Journal of Consumer Research*, *23*(4), 326–350. doi:10.1086/209487

Kamppinen, M. (Ed.). (1993). *Consciousness, cognitive schemata, and relativism: Multidisciplinary explorations in cognitive science*. Dordrecht, The Netherlands: Kluwer Academic. doi:10.1007/978-94-017-1141-8

Kilby, R. (1993). *The study of human values*. Lanham, MD: University Press of America.

Klausmeier, H., & Harris, C. (Eds.). (1966). *Analyses of concept learning*. New York, NY: Academic Press.

Kotler, P. (1972). A generic concept of marketing. *Journal of Marketing*, *36*(2), 46–54. doi:10.2307/1250977

Kvale, S. (1996). *Interviews: An introduction to qualitative research interviewing*. Thousand Oaks, CA: Sage Publications.

Laird, J. (1929). *The idea of value*. Cambridge, UK: Cambridge University Press.

Lemos, R. (1995). *The nature of value: Axiological investigations*. Gainesville, FL: University of Florida Press.

Lindlof, T. (1995). *Qualitative communication research methods*. Thousand Oaks, CA: Sage Publications.

Lovejoy, A. (1950). Terminal and adjectival values. *The Journal of Philosophy*, *47*(21), 593–608. doi:10.2307/2021804

Marx, K. (1867). *Capital: A critique of political economy*. Retrieved May 19, 2018 from https://www.marxists.org/archive/marx/works/download/pdf/Capital-Volume-I.pdf

McKnight, D. (1994). The theory value of the Austrian school. *The Appraisal Journal*, *62*(3), 465–469.

Meddin, J. (1975). Attitudes, values, and related concepts: A system of classification. *Social Science Quarterly*, *55*(4), 889–900.

Mulvey, L. (1993). Some thoughts on theories of fetishism in the context of contemporary culture. *October*, *65*, 3-20.

O'Shaughnessy, J. (1992). *Explaining buyer behaviour: Central concepts and philosophy of science issues*. Oxford, UK: Oxford University Press.

Pietz, W. (1987). The problem of the fetish, II: The origin of the fetish. *Res: Anthropology and Aesthetics, 13*, 23–45. doi:10.1086/RESv13n1ms20166762

Rokeach, M. (1968). A theory of organization and change within value-attitude systems. *The Journal of Social Issues, 24*(1), 13–33. doi:10.1111/j.1540-4560.1968.tb01466.x

Runes, D. (Ed.). (1983). *Dictionary of philosophy*. New York, NY: Philosophical Library.

Schwandt, T. (1997). *Qualitative inquiry: A dictionary of terms*. Thousand Oaks, CA: Sage Publications.

Smart, W. (1891). *An introduction to the theory of value*. London: Macmillan.

Smith, A. (1816). *An inquiry into the nature and causes of wealth in nations*. Philadelphia, PA: D. Hanna.

Thompson, C. (1997). Interpreting consumers: A hermeneutical framework for deriving Marketing insights from the texts of consumers' stories. *JMR, Journal of Marketing Research, 34*(4), 438–455. doi:10.2307/3151963

Thompson, C., Locander, W., & Pollio, H. (1989). Putting consumer experience back into consumer research: The philosophy and method of existential-phenomenology. *The Journal of Consumer Research, 16*(2), 133–146. doi:10.1086/209203

Thompson, C., Locander, W., & Pollio, H. (1990). The lived meaning of free choice: An existential-phenomenological description of everyday consumer experiences of contemporary married women. *The Journal of Consumer Research, 17*(3), 346–361. doi:10.1086/208562

Thompson, C., & Troester, M. (2002). Consumer value systems in the age of postmodern fragmentation: The case of the natural health microculture. *The Journal of Consumer Research, 28*(4), 550–571. doi:10.1086/338213

Urban, W. (1909). *Valuation: Its nature and laws*. London: S. Sonnenschein and Company.

Valsiner, J. (1992). Interest: a metatheoretical perspective. In K. Renninger, S. Hidi, & A. Krapp (Eds.), *The role of interest in learning and development* (pp. 27–42). Hillsdale, IL: Lawrence Erlbaum Associates.

Veroff, J. (1983). Introduction. In L. Kahle (Ed.), *Social values and social change: Adaptation to life in America* (pp. xiii–xviii). New York, NY: Praeger Publishers.

Vriens, M., & ter Hofstede, F. (2000). Linking attributes, benefits, and consumer values. *Marketing Research, 12*(3), 4–10.

Walsh, D. (1998). Subject/object. In C. Jenks (Ed.), *Core sociological dichotomies* (pp. 275–298). London: Sage Publications. doi:10.4135/9781446222041.n18

Werkmeister, W. (1961). *Theories of ethics*. Lincoln, NE: Johnsen Publishing.

Werkmeister, W. (1967). *Man and his values*. Lincoln, NE: University of Nebraska Press.

Werkmeister, W. (1970a). Historical spectrum of value theories: Vol. I. *German language group*. Lincoln, NE: Johnsen Publishing.

Werkmeister, W. (1970b). Historical spectrum of value theories: Vol. II. *Anglo/American group*. Lincoln, NE: Johnsen Publishing.

Williams, R. (1949). Values. *Bulletin of the American Psychoanalytic Association*, *5*(September), 40–51.

Woodruff, R. (1997). Customer value: The next source of competitive advantage. *Journal of the Academy of Marketing Science*, *25*(2), 139–153. doi:10.1007/BF02894350

Zeithaml, V. (1988). Consumer Perceptions of Price, Quality, and Values: A Means-End Model and Synthesis of Evidence. *Journal of Marketing*, *52*(3), 2–22. doi:10.2307/1251446

KEY TERMS AND DEFINITIONS

Axiology: The study of value and valuation.
Epistemology: The theory of knowledge.
Micro-Culture: A societal subgroup with its own language, beliefs, and norms.
Phenomenology: The study of the objects of direct experience.

Chapter 3
The Consumption Performance:
Applying Role Theory

Eirini Koronaki
The American College of Greece, Greece

George Panigyrakis
Athens University of Economics and Business, Greece

ABSTRACT

Building on the sociocultural dimension of consumption, this chapter sees consumption as the interaction between individuals, products, and meanings. One of the frameworks within consumer culture theory, symbolic interactionism, further explains this co-creation of meaning, building on the idea that people are creating their reality when interacting with one another. A theory providing us with greater detail in how people interact with one another is role theory, according to which people play various roles in their lives, some with greater and some with lesser importance, and each one of them is accompanied with certain expected behaviors. One of the roles we play in contemporary societies is that of a consumer, providing us with an explanation of why the things we expect from consumption change over time. In this, the above will be analyzed parallel to the identification of constructs from the marketing literature for the proposed framework.

INTRODUCTION

Lately an increasing number of individuals has been undergoing a shift in how they experience consumption, demanding a more mindful approach to positively evaluate it (Bahl et al., 2016). From the company, a social citizen's behavior is expected (Holt, 2006), while from themselves a brand choice that gives them something real, true and genuinely authentic (Beverland & Farrelly, 2009) and is characterized as a conscious consumption choice, promoting individual, social and ecological well-being is demanded (Mick et al., 2012). Under such a scope, we can see companies increasingly investing in their corporate citizen obligations and brands creating a rhetoric around causes such as gender equality and woman emancipation, political issues, and protection of the environment to name a few. The question naturally

DOI: 10.4018/978-1-5225-6120-0.ch003

emerges: why is it that our expectations from consumption change from time to time and how do those changes affect our consumption experience?

Building on the sociocultural dimension of consumption, we will approach the explanation of the phenomenon described above through consumer culture theory, which sees consumption as the interaction between individuals, products and meanings (McDonald & Wearing, 2013). One of the frameworks within consumer culture theory, symbolic interactionism, further explains this co-creation of meaning, building on the idea that people are creating their reality when interacting with one another (Gusfield, 2003). A theory providing us with greater detail in how people interact with one another is role theory, according to which, people play various roles in their lives, some with greater and some with lesser importance, and each one of them is accompanied with certain expected behaviors (Ward & Robertson, 1973). One of the roles we play in contemporary societies is that of a consumer (Webb, 2000), providing us thus with an explanation of why the things we expect from consumption change over time. Despite the increasing importance that the role of the consumer has in contemporary societies, a framework examining the process of consumption through role theory is still lacking. In this chapter, we will present such a framework, first explaining the relevance of consumer culture theory for interpreting consumption, proceeding with how we can use symbolic interactionism within that theory to understand the role that others can play in this meaning creation process, and concluding with the application of role theory in the role we have as consumers. Finally, we conclude with identifying constructs from the marketing literature that can be used in the proposed framework.

BACKGROUND

Consumer Culture: The Sociocultural Dimensions of Consumption

Leaving behind the classical consumer research viewpoint of a rational decision-making consumer, with decisions as an outcome of the objective comparison of his/her choices, consumption has come to express more than just the evaluation of a range of products over the years. The need for an approach studying the relations between social and cultural patterns of meaning, practice and consumption emerged, studying consumption choices and behaviors from a social and cultural perspective (Appadurai, 1986). This approach is termed Consumer Culture Theory, adopting the viewpoint that meaning is created both in the individual's personal and social lives, through the use of such systems of symbolic interactions (McDonald & Wearing, 2013). Consumption is thus perceived as an active form of relationship, not only to objects, but also to society and to the world, giving individuals the chance to express their personality, values and underlying motivation through its social practices (Baudrillard, 1996). Consequently, it is rendered into a significant parameter of the entire cultural system, helping individuals to understand both their environment and others, through an interconnected system of produced images, texts, and objects that certain groups use either when building their identities, creating meaning or engaging in any type of consumption practice (Kozinets, 2002).

In such a system, marketers are creating ideas and ideals around their brands to which consumers can relate (Emmons, 2005). Consumers leverage on this interconnected system of commercially produced products and images, which they can use as a supplement to construct their identity and determine their relations with others (Moisio et al., 2004).Consumer culture is thus organized around the principle of creating universes of ideas, dreams, visions and beliefs around brands to which consumer would aspire to belong. Two ways of examining consumer culture have been developed (McDonald & Wearing, 2013). The first one is the cultural studies approach, focusing on the meanings of consumption in everyday life and on the ways with which people use consumer signs and symbols for impression management. This is a micro level interpretation and is often free of criticism (Schor, 2007). The critical approach on the other hand, links consumer culture to more superficial relations. It is a macro level approach, and sees that consumers are relatively passive and victims of the prevailing economic system. Despite their different orientation, the interesting key element of both approaches, is their common viewpoint of consumption as central to the individual's self-identity formation (Featherstone, 2007), contradicting the previous relatively fixed and rooted in traditional institutions viewpoint of self-identity and perceiving it as a more fluid entity linked to reflexive individualism and impression management (Elliott & Lemert, 2009).

After having presented how the relationship to consumption has shifted in contemporary societies, clarifying the connections between practice, consumption and meanings, the dependency of consumption on its context became clear. However, whether referring to the micro- or the macro-approach of consumer culture theory, they both examine the relationships in consumption in general, not providing researchers with a generally applicable unifying theory with certain hypotheses to test and rather unifying a group of theoretical perspectives that study the dynamic relations between consumer actions, being the marketplace and cultural meanings. The question emerges: what are the appropriate theoretical perspectives deriving from consumer culture theory and suitable for better understanding consumer behavior?

Symbolic Interactionism: The Importance of Human Interaction

As aforementioned, according to consumer culture theory, consumption is an interaction, not only between the consumer and the object, but also between the consumer and his surroundings. So for a proper understanding of consumption the perspectives of all the participants should be taken into consideration, providing an answer to the question "Why do people behave as they do?" (Stryker, 1980). An appropriate approach for answering this question would be social psychology, involved with research in economics and consumption in psychology, since it examines the ways in which social structures impact persons and interactions and vice versa.

The three major approaches to social psychology are symbolic interactionism, the social structure approach and the group processes approach (Blumer, 1969). Symbolic interactionism mostly emphasizes human interaction (Belk, 1988; Blumer, 1969), defined as an "approach" to and as a "position" for the study of human group life and conduct, which sees reality as a social and developed interaction with others (Gusfield, 2003). According to this, people do not respond to reality directly, rather than to their social understanding of reality, as Goffman states in his influential work "The Presentation of the Self in Everyday Life" (1978).

One of the fundamental perceptions of symbolic interactionism is that every individual is a generator of meaning (Maines, 2001), scanning every interaction, event and even object through a process of interpretation and understanding (e.g., Cicourel, 1973). A multitude of meanings are thus created, which cannot be assumed a priori, and to which individuals respond to in their everyday lives. Chomsky (1959) points out that we cannot presume the emerging meanings from situations anymore, since "the stimulus" is highly dependent on the receiver's perception and way of seeing reality, leading him/her to argue that these stimuli are basically connected to each respective actor and cannot be seen as independent constructs anymore.

Another fundamental aspect of symbolic interactionism is that individuals are not seen as independent of their environments and surroundings, meaning that they cannot be simply or easily described by their fixed characteristics such as age or culture (e.g. Garfinkel, 1969). Their existence is innately related to the relations that form with other individuals, events and objects (e.g. Hewitt, 1976). Consequently, the self can be termed as both a product and a producer of relations with others (Callero, 2003). This means that the self is something constantly changing and evolving, parallel to the individual and his/her surroundings. As a result, the way by which things are lived, experienced and interpreted also change, parallel to the individuals, considering the aforementioned relationship between reality and perception of reality.

The other characteristic of symbolic interactionism is language and symbolism, relating to the fact that people's communication is characterized by high levels of complexity, since differently perceived meanings are created through the language used (Denzin, 1987). The way that individuals respond to the messages they receive depends on what things mean to them in and through symbols, rendering much of human experience dependent on verbal symbols and their interpretations.

In recent years, a revisionist view has risen in importance within the social sciences, represented in the work of Michel Foucault, Harold Garfinkel, and Paul Ricoeur, among others. What they all have in common with symbolic interactionism is a conception of human action as emerging from the relation between subject and object and not as a simple response of the subject to an object. This perspective suggests a creative, emergent, and often unpredictable human being, rendering the humanistic element as the other crucial element of symbolic interactionism.

In summary, through symbolic interactionism meaning is created by each individual, leading to a shifting perception of reality, which is linked to the increased power of language and symbolism and the power of the human element. If we apply the above in the consumption setting, the shifting perceptions around consumption can be more easily understood. Based on this approach each of our customers generates meaning through his/her consumption, based on how he/she perceives reality. This meaning that each of our customers creates is in relation and in response to their environment and how they form their relationships to others, changing according to the language and symbols they use. This leads us toward the conclusion that consumption is something highly dependent on the contextual factor and the relationship we form with others, leading to a clearer explanation of the shifts perceptions regarding consumption go through over time.

However, symbolic interactionism, being a theoretical framework and not a theory, does not provide researchers with specific conceptualizations, lacking thus in rigidness. However, the theories derived from it have clearly defined concepts and relationships between them, allowing for empirical testing and predicting outcomes in social life. One of the most significant theories, deriving from the symbolic interactionism field and suitable for studying consumer behavior, is role theory.

Role Theory: Understanding Behaviour as Socially Defined Positions

According to role theory, the individual develops and evolves within the context of the society he/she lives, forming both the self and its parameters in relation to others. The individual becomes a social entity by taking up one or more of the roles available in society, rendering a person's behavior best understood as the expression of multiple social roles (Ward & Robertson, 1973). What does this mean for the study of human behavior? Roles involve the conduct associated with certain socially defined positions, rather than the particular individuals who occupy them, since they are basically positions or social categories with certain characteristics, a set of patterned, functionally interdependent relations between a social person and a social circle (Linton, 1936; Merton, 1957). These relations involve both duties and personal rights, rendering a role as a cluster of social cues that guide and direct an individual's behavior in a given setting (Lopata, 1991).

This instruction of conduct translates into a learning pattern, according to which social behaviour is learned via observation and imitation of role models who are present in a variety of social systems which the socializee enters throughout the life cycle, including parents, nonfamily adults to coworkers, described as a social learning process (Bandura & Walters, 1977). However, some roles are more central to the individual than others. A role theoretic approach emphasizes the nature of people as social actors who learn behaviors appropriate to the positions they occupy in society, as Goffman (1978) had underlined. A significant point when in a role is the degree to which a particular part is acted appropriately and even though the "actors" in a service setting may be very different individuals when not adopting the role, they must adopt a relatively standardized set of behaviors when they occupy a particular position. In fact, people are often defined by the roles they play, and one is able to generate a profile of this person based on the characteristics that are believed to correspond with this title. One of the most significant dimensions within the role theory field are thus the constructs of role formation and role enactment. All the points during which a role is performed are termed role formation and the level of living up to role is termed role enactment, both fundamental parameters of role theory (Solomon et al., 1985). The level of role enactment is determined by the reactions of fellow actors and observers (the audience) to the role, showing the importance of others in performing a role.

When an individual decides to take up one of those roles and behave as expected from the behavioral protocol, he/she takes on a set of identities (Stryker & Serpe, 1982, 1983). Identities are thus a conception that individuals hold for themselves and refer to what it means for them to be who they are, meaning that they partition a person. Subsequently one can claim that an individual is a sum of all its identities, whereas society is a sum of all its roles (Stryker, 1980). The self can be thought of as a system of identities to which one is more or less committed (Jackson, 1981), and the degree of commitment refers to the concern that one's role enactment is convincing. According to role theory, the self-concept is comprised of a personal identity encompassing idiosyncratic characteristics (e.g., traits, abilities), a social identity encompassing salient group classifications (e.g., religious affiliation, organizational role) (Ashforth & Mael, 1989; Tajfel & Turner, 1985) and a role identity encompassing the characteristics of the particular role. Any stable individual difference can thus impact the way an experience is lived, while simultaneously one's role specific self-concept is formed by the reactions of others to the quality of one's role enactment.

In summary, when the individual takes on a role, a certain identity is adopted. The behavior in that identity, however, can differ depending on one's psychological attributes, social identity and each respective role. From the above, the proposed theoretical framework of this chapter emerges (see Figure 1).

In the next part of the chapter, the proposed framework will be examined in the context of consumer behavior.

The Role of the Consumer: Connecting It to Marketing Literature

It is a widely accepted fact that consumption is a pervasive aspect of contemporary individuals' lives. Within the multitude of roles that people enact, norms and expected behaviors regarding consumption are learned beginning in childhood through the socialization process (Moschis & Churchill, 1978; Moschis & Moore, 1984; Ward, 1974). In the services marketing literature, role theory has been utilized as an

Figure 1. Theoretical framework of the chapter

interpretive framework for the service encounter, whereby consumers are seen to assume a distinct role (Solomon et al., 1985; Webb, 2000).

The relationship between consumption and a person's various identities has been extensively discussed in the context of consumer behavior (Reed, 2002; White & Argo, 2009). Consumers show a strong attachment to anything self-expressive, that is, an object congruent with the self, which reflects the extent of "me-ness" (Kleine, Kleine & Allen, 1995). Under this scope, consumers consider their material possessions parts of themselves (Belk, 1988) and use brands and products that enable creation of their various social identities (Elliott & Wattanasuwan, 1998; Kleine, Kleine & Kernan, 1993). Likewise, in the infant-parent relationship, similarity of personality or temperament increases the extent of emotional bond (Perry, 1998). For example, recent research indicates that consumers construct their self-identity and present themselves to others through their brand choices based on the congruency between brand-user associations and self-image associations (or possible self-image associations; Escalas & Bettman, 2003).

Experimenting with different brands enables consumers to expand and develop a variety of self-concepts, reinforcing and expressing self-identity, allowing one to differentiate oneself and assert one's individuality, and connecting one's self to significant others (e.g., Belk, 1988; Kleine, Kleine & Allen, 1995). The link between consumption and consumers' identities extends far and beyond material goods, as consumption activities can reinstate harmony to unsatisfying self-concepts (Schouten, 1991). Ahuvia (2005) similarly proposes that objects and activities loved by consumers can help structure social relationships and enhance well-being. Consumption basically participates in the construction of an individual's social identity (McCracken, 1986). As aforementioned, contemporary consumers use consumption to make statements about themselves, to create identities and to develop a sense of belonging (Atwal & Williams, 2009). In fact, the symbolic aspect of products has been discussed since the 1950s (Gardner & Levy, 1955; Levy, 1959). As Levy (1959) noted "People buy products not only for what they can do, but also for what they mean" (p.118).

It is perceived as attribution of particular symbolic meanings and values to brands. The goods' value covers not only the economic value grounded by the price, but also the symbolic grounded by the fantasy, emotions, perception and needs of the individual as well. In such a way the goods gain not only the value, but become the value themselves. According to Baudrillard (1996) the commodity becomes the artificial substitute, which is nothing short of the attribute of the spreading narcissist behavior more and more replacing social identification. It is thus intuitively appealing and generally accepted by our society that people use products and brands to create and represent desired self-images and to present these images to others or even to themselves.

Even though the phenomenon of consumption has been examined in conjunction with the role of the consumer, there is an apparent gap in the literature regarding the whole process of the consumer's role, how it is formed and enacted and which factors affect it.

Using role theory as a support theory, the consumers' role formation is modeled as the focal point of this chapter. Accordingly, the consumers' identity is constructed as antecedent, and role enactment as its outcome (see Figure 2).

ROLE FORMATION EXPRESSED THROUGH BRAND EXPERIENCE

As aforementioned, a key aspect of role theory is the formation of the role. We argue that role formation is expressed through brand experience in the context of this framework, considering that role formation is defined as the points throughout which the role is performed and brand experience is defined as every point of interaction with the brand. This basically means that the formation of the consumer's role, which expresses every moment that the role takes place, is actually expressed through brand experience. Thus, one of the key construct to be examined in this research is brand experience.

As a multi-disciplinary concept, definitions on brand experience abound. The interest for brand experience already goes back to the 80's (Holbrook & Hirschman, 1982), but has recently gained an important renewal. Consumers' perception of product quality, for later memory retrieval, is formed through usage after purchase and through learning the product's objective characteristics and its capabilities (Bagozzi & Dholakia, 2006). In this research we adopt the perspective proposed by Brakus et al. (2009), which conceptualizes brand experience as subjective internal consumer responses (sensations, feelings and cognitions) and behavioral responses evoked by brand-related stimuli, that are part of a brand's design and identity, packaging, communications and environments.

Four dimensions of brand experience have been suggested by Brakus et al. (2009), including sensory, affective, intellectual and behavioral. The sensory dimension of brand experience refers to the degree to which the brand appeals to the consumer's senses and whether it makes strong and interesting impressions on them. The affective dimension refers to the degree to which the brand can induce feelings and emotions among consumers. The intellectual dimension is linked to the brand's possibility to stimulate

Figure 2. Variables in proposed conceptual framework

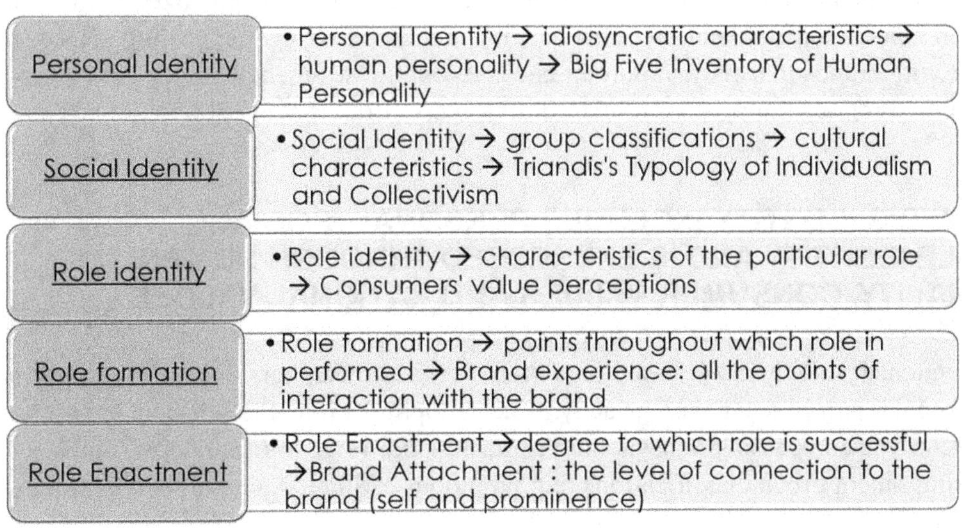

consumer's curiosity, thinking and problem solving. And finally, the behavioral dimension is related to the degree to which the brand is able to engage consumers in physical activities. The importance of brand experience has been underlined by many,, putting forward the idea that brand experience is the real essence of customer brand relationships and thus needs to be thoroughly understood (Chang & Chieng, 2006). In this connection, Brakus et al. (2009) also identified positive influences of brand experience on brand personality, brand satisfaction and brand loyalty.

ROLE ENACTMENT EXPRESSED THROUGH BRAND ATTACHMENT

Another key parameter in the role theory literature is the enactment of the role, which refers to the degree to which the role is enacted appropriately. This part of role theory can be expressed through brand attachment in the branding literature, considering the desired level of connection with a brand is that of attachment. This is justified by the fact that brand attachment refers to the level of connection between the individual and the brand, but also to the prominence of the brand in the individual's mind.

Consumer attachment toward a brand is a strong affective concept (Fournier, 1998). Consumers become attached to a specific brand in the process of defining and maintaining their sense of self (Kleine, Kleine & Allen 1995). The concept of attachment and its formation have been dealt with in the context of infant behavior, as well as in the area of adult relationship, especially romantic relationship behavior (Collins & Read, 1990).

The concept has also been studied in explaining the formation of consumer-brand relationships (Fournier & Avery, 2011). Attachment is basically the process of developing an emotional bond (Collins & Read, 1990), which is facilitated by consistent and repeated experiences between relationship partners. It can be measured on the basis of dependence, anxiety, and closeness (Collins & Read, 1990). Attachment provides psychological comfort and pleasure, and its loss evokes strong distress. Fournier (1998) also describes love and passion as part of the affective attachment involved in the consumer-brand relationship, and reports that attachment is a condition of emotional dependence involving separation anxiety and irreplaceability.

Usually, consumer research postulates an impact of brand experience on the bond connecting the brand with the self, defined as brand attachment (Brakus et al., 2009). Conceptualized with the components of brand-self connection and brand prominence, it is a means to trigger appealing responses. Consumers connect with brands to satisfy important needs through instrumental values and are more prone to remember brand-related impressions of extraordinariness (Brakus et al., 2009).

CONSUMER'S IDENTITY INCLUDES PERSONAL, SOCIAL AND ROLE IDENTITY AND IS EXPRESSED THROUGH HUMAN PERSONALITY, CONSUMER VALUES AND NATIONAL VALUES

As aforementioned, role theory is based on a dramaturgical metaphor, since it examines the degree to which a particular part is acted appropriately. When adopting a role, the self-concept is comprised of a personal identity encompassing idiosyncratic characteristics (e.g., traits, abilities) and a social identity encompassing salient group classifications (e.g., religious affiliation, organizational role) (Ashforth &

Mael, 1989) and a role identity encompassing the characteristics of the particular role. If we transfer this metaphor to consumption, one is led to the following as far as the consumer's identity is concerned.

As far as the personal identity is concerned, it can be related to traits. Traits, referring to dimensions of individual differences in tendencies to show consistent patterns of thoughts (McCrae & Costa, 1997), design the individual's personality. Big Five Model of Human Personality (Goldberg, 1993) has been chosen to represent the consumer's personality in the present framework.

As far as the personal identity is concerned, it can be related to values. Values, operate at multiple levels (Barni et al., 2014), either an individual or a national one, referring to the broad trans-situational, motivational goals, affecting the individual's interpretation of situations, preferences, choices and actions, and to the solutions that groups develop in response to existential challenges and relate to the way social institutions function (Hofstede, 2004) respectively. The centrality of values in consumer research is supported by the stream of research in the field. Values have been characterized as desirable goals, with varying importance, which serve as guiding principles in the individual's life (Schwartz, 1992). Values operate at multiple levels (Barni et al., 2014). They can be examined from an individual and a national perspective, referring on the one hand to the broad trans-situational, motivational goals, affecting the individual's interpretation of situations, preferences, choices and actions (Rohan, 2000), and on the other hand to the solutions that groups develop in response to existential challenges and relate to the way social institutions function (Hofstede, 2004).

Among the individual values two approaches can be taken. The first one refers to human values – the inherent value system of human beings which acts as an independent force influencing consumption attitude. The second one refers to consumer perceived value; the self-reported result of customers who evaluate the product and are affected by factors such as human value, branding and market strategy. This is the perspective relevant in this framework and chosen to represent the role specific identity.

Redding (1990) argues that cultural differences have been one of the influencing factors on consumption of global brands particularly because consumers across cultures buy products and services for different reasons even if they buy the same products. Extant literature drawn from cultural studies emphasizes culture's influence on consumer value perceptions and beliefs. Researchers also suggest that empirically derived cultural domains such as in Hofstede (2004), and Trompenaars and Hampden-Turner (1998) are useful in comparing the effects of consumption across cultures (Wong & Ahuvia, 1998).

Keeping in mind the wide application of cultural frameworks to understand influence of cultural differences in global marketing theory, evaluation of value perceptions of consumers in countries with different national cultures becomes interesting. To measure the cultural orientation towards individualism-collectivism and vertical-horizontal, the 32-item scale developed by Singelis, Triandis, Bhawkuk and Gelfand (1995) is proposed.

Tthe proposed framework, with the related marketing and identity constructs, is presented in Figure 3.

SOLUTIONS AND RECOMMENDATIONS

From the above, the complexity of consumption becomes evident, rendering it highly dependent on the context and on the people participating in it. However, through the role theory approach proposed and the emerging framework, the process through which the role of the consumer is formed can be deconstructed and thus deeper understood.

Figure 3. Proposed conceptual framework with marketing constructs

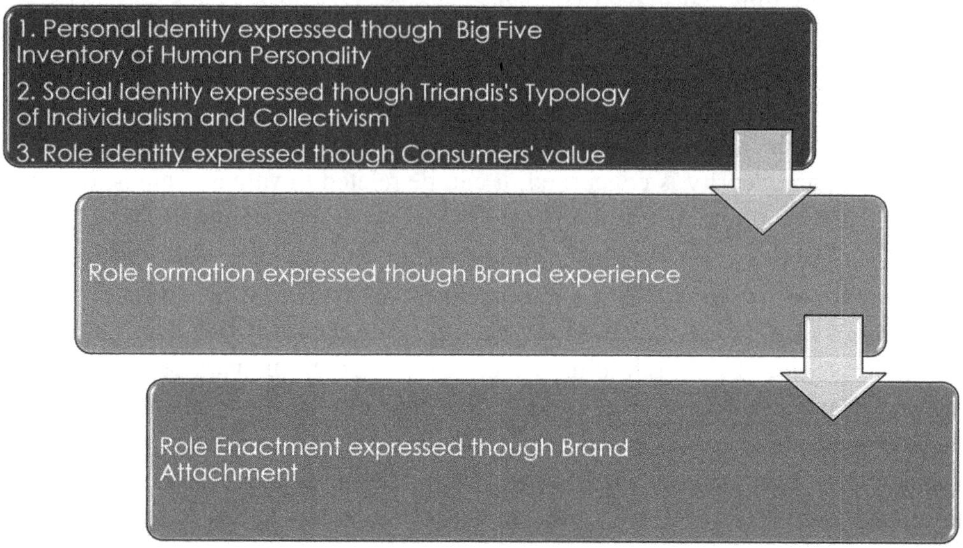

Implications for Consumer Culture Theory

In this part of the chapter, the academic implications of the proposed framework will be discussed. As mentioned in the first part of the chapter, the approach taken to consumption is that it is a relationship that the individual develops to its surroundings and to other individuals, not just towards an object. The ways through which individuals create connections among meanings, objects and texts are under the microscope in such consumer culture studies.

According to such a definition questions that consumer culture theory would pose include: (1) How do images, texts and objects interrelate in consumption? (2) How and through which processes are practices, identities and meanings created when consuming? (3) Through which ways do these interconnected systems help consumers make sense of their environments? To present the contribution of the framework in the consumer culture theory field, the contribution to each of the key research streams will be explained. Consumer Culture Theory studies can be divided into the following subfields such as the fundamental developments in the consumer culture theory field, brands and consumption, identity formation and consumption, cross-cultural issues and consumption, examination of certain subcultures and their consumption motives and critical stance towards consumption.

Under the scope of developments in the field, researchers have long been sought to identify the relationship between subject and object in the Meta modern era (Bettany, 2007). In fact, researchers have been encouraged to look at how consumers perceive their consumption object (Borgerson, 2005). Responding to such an inquiry, this framework proposes a new way of examining the relationship between the consumer and the brand through the application of role theory.

It would be appropriate to emphasize that the importance of brands in contemporary markets. However, Holt (2006) argues that brands have not been studied as much as they deserve in the consumer culture context and encourages the examination of their parameters in contemporary research. Answering to such a call, this framework examines how brands are understood and perceived today and how consumers use them to create their ideal identities, contributing thus to the brands and consumption area of the studies.

Moreover, a more critical stance towards consumption and identity building is needed (Dittmar, 2007). Consumers are asked to become more aware of what is being imposed upon them, this fluid imaginary world termed as "the spectacle" (Dunn, 2000). In such an attempt, this framework contributes towards an understanding of how the consumer perceives "the spectacle" and relates to it. From the above, it can be concluded that the present framework contributes to a variety of areas in the consumer culture theory field, increasing existing knowledge to this key pillar of the study.

Implication for Symbolic Interactionism

Symbolic interactionism is an approach in Consumer Culture Theory, underlining the importance of human interaction and perceptions in everyday life (Blumer, 1969). It supports the viewpoint that an individual's response to their understanding of reality, which is formed and reshaped in accordance to its changing perceptions and beliefs (Gusflied, 2003). The questions to be answered through this approach would include the following (1) How is meaning created from individuals in their everyday lives? (2) How does the self interfere with the interpretation of events and situations? (3) How important is the role of symbols in this meaning creation? (4) How is a relationship created between an object and a subject?

The key areas of research in symbolic interactionism are subjects such as symbolic interactionism perspectives and key points, self through the symbolic interactionism approach, symbolic interactionism in marketing, symbolic interactionism in organizational research and symbolic interactionism as a business research method.

The contributions of this framework can be identified in the self- and marketing-related studies. As far as the self through symbolic interactionism is concerned, Callero (2003) has made some interesting and noteworthy statements. He underlines the significance of power and of the social environment in shaping the self and calls for more sociological-oriented research on the self. He underlines the importance of social and non-humans play in self-construction and encourages other researchers to include them as well. Our framework is based on the principle that the self and its identity within a role, consist of the personal the social and the role-specific elements, and derive from the social surroundings. It also indicates the significant effect that others can have both in the individual's behavior in consumption, andt also in the way that the self is perceived.

The other key are of contribution relates to the application of symbolic interactionism in the marketing field. How brands are used by individuals in their everyday social lives has been underlined in research (Solomon et al., 1985). They have further stated that the way that an individual perceives an experience affects his/her perception of reality, how he sees himself and how he/she behaves. The meanings included in certain products are used as a guide in assessing role performance.

Another contribution lies in the connection between symbols and interactions, a topic calling for further research, according to LaRossa and Reitzes (2009). Researchers were basically asked to examine the ways with which symbolic worlds are created and how those can affect subsequent human behavior. Our framework identifies the significant parameters satisfied through consumption, which can be the avenue for the subsequent symbolic world to be created. Thus, one can argue that the contributions of the proposed framework are significant in the Symbolic Interactionism field as well, as seen from the argument above. This leads us to the following field of our research, the field of Role Theory.

Implications for Role Theory

Role theory, as aforementioned, studies the individual in the context he/she lives in and considers that the individual's personal development takes place when taking up one or more of the roles available in society (Lopata, 1991). This means that understanding a person means understanding the roles he/she is adopting, which are accompanied by certain characteristics and ways of behaving. Naturally, the importance attributed to the various roles adopted throughout one's lifetime varies according to the individuals' personality and social surroundings. As a result, the following questions posed in the role theory approach can be summarized below: (1) How is the consumer's role formed? (2) How is the consumer's role enacted? (3) Which parameters of his/her identity most significantly affect the formation and enactment?

Our framework contributes to role theory on several of its dimensions developed in literature, that include topics such as key concepts in role theory, role theory in managerial studies, role theory in the services setting and role theory and the individual's characteristics.

First of all, role theory has been frequently applied in the service setting and in the management field, when considering the "employee's role". It is only recently, however, that the consumer's role has become a topic of examination (McKeage & Gulas, 2013). These authors call for more researchers to take the role-theoretic approach to study consumer behavior, and find useful insights in trying to understand the consumer when in such a role. They further underline how role theory can be a significant assistant in developing relationship marketing tactics, aiming to create stronger bonds to customers. Our framework contributes in that direction, since it not only adopts the role theory approach to study consumer behavior in such a setting, but also connects it to relational branding elements.

FUTURE RESEARCH DIRECTIONS

Given the lack of empirical research in consumer culture theory, many opportunities exist for researchers to further investigate consumer behavior through this perspective. In this section, recommendations for future research are grouped in two categories, specifically theoretical issues and measurement issues. In terms of theoretical issues, this chapter has focused on brand experience and brand attachment, as well as brand self connection. Future research could use the framework developed in this chapter to other stages in the consumer decision-making process, such as purchase intent and actual purchasing. Such results would not only strengthen the current framework, but also increase its predictive power to other stages of the decision-making process in consumer behavior. As far as the measurement goods recommendations are concerned, both services and products could be included in further research, to examine how consumers relate to them and whether there are any differences between products. Such an examination could further strengthen the proposed framework and the nature of relationship that consumers have to consumption today.

CONCLUSION

From the above the academic and managerial implications of the proposed framework become clear, trying to give more insight into the complex, shifting relationships developed between consumers and their brands. Consumption's dependency on the context and on the role of others was presented through this framework, indicating and answering the shifting perceptions and expectations we have from it. Through the application of such a framework, the way according to which those changes in consumption's perception take place can be better understood and subsequently be better managed and handled.

REFERENCES

Ahuvia, A. C. (2005). Beyond the extended self: Loved objects and consumers' identity narratives. *The Journal of Consumer Research*, *32*(1), 171–184. doi:10.1086/429607

Appadurai, A. (Ed.). (1986). *The social life of things*. Cambridge, UK: Cambridge University Press. doi:10.1017/CBO9780511819582

Ashforth, B. E., & Mael, F. (1989). Social identity theory and the organization. *Academy of Management Review*, *14*(1), 20–39. doi:10.5465/amr.1989.4278999

Atwal, G., & Williams, A. (2009). Luxury brand marketing–the experience is everything! *Journal of Brand Management*, *16*(5), 338–346. doi:10.1057/bm.2008.48

Bagozzi, R. P., & Dholakia, U. M. (2006). Antecedents and purchase consequences of customer participation in small group brand communities. *International Journal of Research in Marketing*, *23*(1), 45–61. doi:10.1016/j.ijresmar.2006.01.005

Bahl, S., Milne, G. R., Ross, S. M., Mick, D. G., Grier, S. A., Chugani, S. K., & Schindler, R. M. (2016). Mindfulness: Its transformative potential for consumer, societal, and environmental well-being. *Journal of Public Policy & Marketing*, *35*(2), 198–210. doi:10.1509/jppm.15.139

Bandura, A., & Walters, R. H. (1977). *Social learning theory* (Vol. 1). Englewood Cliffs, NJ: Prentice-Hall.

Barni, D., Knafo, A., Ben-Arieh, A., & Haj-Yahia, M. M. (2014). Parent–child value similarity across and within cultures. *Journal of Cross-Cultural Psychology*, *45*(6), 853–867. doi:10.1177/0022022114530494

Baudrillard, J. (1996). *The System of Objects*. New York, NY: Verso.

Belk, R. (1988). Possessions and the extended self. *The Journal of Consumer Research*, *15*(2), 139–168. doi:10.1086/209154

Bettany, S. (2007). The material semiotics of consumption or where (and what) are the objects in consumer culture theory? *Research in Consumer Behavior*, *11*, 41–56.

Beverland, M. B., & Farrelly, F. J. (2009). The quest for authenticity in consumption: Consumers' purposive choice of authentic cues to shape experienced outcomes. *The Journal of Consumer Research*, *36*(5), 838–856. doi:10.1086/615047

Blumer, H. (1969). Fashion: From class differentiation to collective selection. *The Sociological Quarterly*, *10*(3), 275–291. doi:10.1111/j.1533-8525.1969.tb01292.x

Borgerson, J. L. (2005). Materiality, agency, and the constitution of consuming subjects: Insights for consumer research. In G. Menon & A. R. Rao (Eds.), *Advances in consumer research* (pp. 439–443). Duluth, MN: Association for Consumer Research.

Brakus, J. J., Schmitt, B. H., & Zarantonello, L. (2009). Brand experience: What is it? How is it measured? Does it affect loyalty? *Journal of Marketing*, *73*(3), 52–68. doi:10.1509/jmkg.73.3.52

Callero, P. L. (2003). The sociology of the self. *Annual Review of Sociology*, *29*(1), 115–133. doi:10.1146/annurev.soc.29.010202.100057

Chang, P. L., & Chieng, M. H. (2006). Building consumer–brand relationship: A cross-cultural experiential view. *Psychology and Marketing*, *23*(11), 927–959. doi:10.1002/mar.20140

Chomsky, N., & Skinner, B. F. (1959). Review of Verbal Behavior by B. F. Skinner. *Language*, *35*(1), 27–58. doi:10.2307/411334

Cicourel, A. (1973). *Cognitive sociology: Language and meaning in social interaction*. Baltimore, MD: Penguin Books.

Collins, N. L., & Read, S. J. (1990). Adult attachment, working models, and relationship quality in dating couples. *Journal of Personality and Social Psychology*, *58*(4), 644–663. doi:10.1037/0022-3514.58.4.644 PMID:14570079

Denzin, N. K. (1987). On semiotics and symbolic interactionism. *Symbolic Interaction*, *10*(1), 1–19. doi:10.1525i.1987.10.1.1

Dittmar, H. (2007). The costs of consumer culture and the "cage within": The impact of the material "good life" and "body perfect" ideals on individuals" identity and well-being. *Psychological Inquiry*, *18*(1), 23–31. doi:10.1080/10478400701389045

Dunn, R. G. (2000). Identity, commodification, and consumer culture. In J. E. David (Ed.), *Identity and social change* (pp. 109–134). Abington, UK: Routledge.

Elliott, A., & Lemert, C. (2009). *The new individualism: The emotional costs of globalization* (rev. ed.). Abington, UK: Routledge.

Elliott, R., & Wattanasuwan, K. (1998). Brands as symbolic resources for the construction of identity. *International Journal of Advertising*, *17*(2), 131–144. doi:10.1080/02650487.1998.11104712

Emmons, R. A. (2005). Striving for the sacred: Personal goals, life meaning, and religion. *The Journal of Social Issues*, *61*(4), 731–745. doi:10.1111/j.1540-4560.2005.00429.x

Escalas, J., & Bettman, J. R. (2003). You are what they eat: The influence of reference groups on consumers' connections to brands. *Journal of Consumer Psychology, 13*(3), 339–348. doi:10.1207/S15327663JCP1303_14

Featherstone, M. (2007). *Consumer culture and postmodernism.* London, UK: Sage.

Fournier, S. (1998). Consumers and their brands: Developing relationship theory in consumer research. *The Journal of Consumer Research, 24*(4), 343–373. doi:10.1086/209515

Fournier, S., & Avery, J. (2011). Putting the relationship back into CRM. *MIT Sloan Management Review, 52*(3), 63–72.

Gardner, B. B., & Levy, S. J. (1955). The product and the brand. *Harvard Business Review, 33*(2), 33–39.

Garfinkel, H. (1969). *Studies in ethnomethodology.* Englewood Cliffs, NJ: Prentice-Hall.

Goldberg, L. R. (1993). The structure of phenotypic personality traits. *The American Psychologist, 48*(1), 26–34. doi:10.1037/0003-066X.48.1.26 PMID:8427480

Gusfield, J. R. (2003). A journey with symbolic interaction. *Symbolic Interaction, 26*(1), 119–139. doi:10.1525i.2003.26.1.119

Hewitt, J. P. (1976). *Self and society: A symbolic interactionist social psychology.* Oxford, UK: Allyn & Bacon.

Hofstede, G. (2004). *Cultures and organizations: software for the mind.* London, UK: McGraw-Hill.

Holt, D. B. (2006). Toward a sociology of branding. *Journal of Consumer Culture, 6*(3), 299–302. doi:10.1177/1469540506068680

Jackson, S. E. (1981). Measurement of commitment to role identities. *Journal of Personality and Social Psychology, 40*(1), 138–146. doi:10.1037/0022-3514.40.1.138

Kleine, R. E. III, Kleine, S. S., & Kernan, J. B. (1993). Mundane consumption and the self: A social-identity perspective. *Journal of Consumer Psychology, 2*(3), 209–235. doi:10.1016/S1057-7408(08)80015-0

Kozinets, R. (2002). Can consumers escape the market? Emancipatory illuminations from burning man. *The Journal of Consumer Research, 29*(1), 20–38. doi:10.1086/339919

LaRossa, R., & Reitzes, D. C. (2009). Symbolic interactionism and family studies. In P. C. Boss, W. J. Doherty, R. LaRosa, W. R. Schumm, & S. K. Steinmetz (Eds.), *Sourcebook of family theories and methods* (pp. 135–166). New York, NY: Springer.

Levy, S. J. (1959). Symbols for sale. *Harvard Business Review, 37*(4), 117–124.

Linton, R. (1936). *The study of man: an introduction.* New York, NY: D. Appleton and Co.

Lopata, H. Z. (1991). Role theory. Social roles and social institutions. In J. R. Blau & N. Goodman (Eds.), *Essays in honor of Rose Laub Coser* (pp. 1–11). New Brunswick, NJ: Transaction Publishers.

Maines, D. R. (2001). *The faultline of consciousness: A view of interactionism in sociology.* New York, NY: Aldine Transaction.

McCracken, G. (1986). Culture and consumption: A theoretical account of the structure and movement of the cultural meaning of consumer goods. *The Journal of Consumer Research, 13*(1), 71–84. doi:10.1086/209048

McCrae, R. R., & Costa, P. T. Jr. (1997). Personality trait structure as a human universal. *The American Psychologist, 52*(5), 509–516. doi:10.1037/0003-066X.52.5.509 PMID:9145021

McDonald, M., & Wearing, S. (2013). *Social psychology and theories of consumer culture: a political economy perspective*. London: Routledge.

McKeage, K. K., & Gulas, C. S. (2013). Relationships, Roles, and Consumer Identity in Services Marketing. *Services Marketing Quarterly, 34*(3), 231–239. doi:10.1080/15332969.2013.798198

Merton, R. K. (1957). Priorities in scientific discovery: A chapter in the sociology of science. *American Sociological Review, 22*(6), 635–659. doi:10.2307/2089193

Mick, D. G., Pettigrew, S., Pechmann, C., & Ozanne, J. (2012). *Transformative consumer research for personal and collective well-being*. New York, NY: Taylor & Francis.

Moisio, R., Arnould, E. J., & Price, L. L. (2004). Between mothers and markets: Constructing family identity through homemade food. *Journal of Consumer Culture, 4*(3), 361–384. doi:10.1177/1469540504046523

Moschis, G. P., & Churchill, G. A. Jr. (1978). Consumer socialization: A theoretical and empirical analysis. *JMR, Journal of Marketing Research, 15*(4), 599–609. doi:10.2307/3150629

Moschis, G. P., & Moore, R. L. (1984). Anticipatory consumer socialization. *Journal of the Academy of Marketing Science, 12*(4), 109–123. doi:10.1007/BF02721803

Redding, S. G. (1990). *The spirit of Chinese capitalism*. New York, NY: Walter de Gruyter. doi:10.1515/9783110887709

Reed, A. (2002). Social identity as a useful perspective for self-concept–based consumer research. *Psychology and Marketing, 19*(3), 235–266. doi:10.1002/mar.10011

Schor, J. B. (2007). In defense of consumer critique: Revisiting the consumption debates of the twentieth century. *The Annals of the American Academy of Political and Social Science, 611*(1), 16–30. doi:10.1177/0002716206299145

Schouten, J. W. (1991). Selves in transition: Symbolic consumption in personal rites of passage and identity reconstruction. *The Journal of Consumer Research, 17*(4), 412–425. doi:10.1086/208567

Schwartz, S. H. (1992). Universals in the content and structure of values: Theoretical advances and empirical tests in 20 countries. Cambridge, MA: Academic Press. doi:10.1016/S0065-2601(08)60281-6

Singelis, T. M., Triandis, H. C., Bhawuk, D. P., & Gelfand, M. J. (1995). Horizontal and vertical dimensions of individualism and collectivism: A theoretical and measurement refinement. *Cross-Cultural Research, 29*(3), 240–275. doi:10.1177/106939719502900302

Solomon, M. R., Surprenant, C., Czepiel, J. A., & Gutman, E. G. (1985). A role theory perspective on dyadic interactions: The service encounter. *Journal of Marketing, 49*(1), 99–111. doi:10.2307/1251180

Stryker, S. (1980). *Symbolic interactionism: A social structural version*. Menlo Park, CA. Benjamin/ Cummings Publishing Company

Stryker, S., & Serpe, R. T. (1982). Commitment, identity salience, and role behavior: Theory and research example. In W. Ickes & E. S. Knowles (Eds.), *Personality, roles, and social behavior* (pp. 199–218). New York, NY: Springer. doi:10.1007/978-1-4613-9469-3_7

Stryker, S., & Serpe, R. T. (1983). Toward a theory of family influence in the socialization of children. *Research in Sociology of Education and Socialization*, *4*, 47–71.

Tajfel, H., & Turner, J. C. (1985). The social identity theory of intergroup behavior. In S. Worchel & W. G. Austin (Eds.), *Psychology of intergroup relations* (2nd ed.; pp. 7–24). Chicago: Nelson-Hall.

Trompenaars, A., & Hampden-Turner, C. (1998). *Riding the waves of culture: understanding diversity in global business*. London, UK: McGraw-Hill.

Ward, S. (1974). Consumer socialization. *The Journal of Consumer Research*, *1*(2), 1–14. doi:10.1086/208584

Ward, S., & Robertson, T. S. (1973). *Consumer behavior: Theoretical sources*. Englewood Cliffs, NJ: Prentice-Hall.

Webb, D. (2000). Understanding customer role and its importance in the formation of service quality expectations. *Service Industries Journal*, *20*(1), 1–21. doi:10.1080/02642060000000001

White, K., & Argo, J. J. (2009). Social identity threat and consumer preferences. *Journal of Consumer Psychology*, *19*(3), 313–325. doi:10.1016/j.jcps.2009.03.007

Wong, N. Y., & Ahuvia, A. C. (1998). Personal taste and family face: Luxury consumption in Confucian and Western societies. *Psychology and Marketing*, *15*(5), 423–441. doi:10.1002/(SICI)1520-6793(199808)15:5<423::AID-MAR2>3.0.CO;2-9

Chapter 4
Mimetic Desire as Illustrated in *The Joneses*

David J. Burns
Kennesaw State University, USA

ABSTRACT

Individuals' participation in the marketplace has exceeded all projections. As opposed to a leisure-based utopia that was predicted by many, even with most basic needs being satisfied, most individuals continue to strive to obtain more and more income to participate in the marketplace at progressively higher rates. This chapter examines this seemingly counter-intuitive reality. Specifically, this phenomenon is explored within the theories of Rene Girard, where the concept of mimetic desire is discussed and advanced as a primary motivation behind most present-day consumption. The movie, The Joneses, is the used as an avenue to illustrate the theories of Rene Girard. Several conclusions are drawn.

INTRODUCTION

In many affluent consumer-based societies today, arguably most physical needs (clothing, food, and shelter) have been met for most of their residents. This was foreseen in many predictions of future life made in the 1950s and 1960s, where the future was viewed as a time of leisure, where the workweek would be halved and much of humanity would be living in a virtual utopia freed from the requirements of employment. Has this utopia arrived? Is a leisure society where life is dominated by recreation and social activities the norm for most today? Clearly, these prognostications could not have been more wrong. In affluent societies where the physical needs of most are more than met, the amount of time spent by individuals in income-producing activities have climbed sharply (Leete & Schor, 1994; Schor, 2004). The amount of time invested in income-producing activities is even more pronounced when the rise of the dual-income household is taken in account (Schor, 1998; Yount, 1997). Indeed, time poverty resulting from spending increasing time in income-producing activities is a characteristic of affluent consumer societies (Schor, 1994).

DOI: 10.4018/978-1-5225-6120-0.ch004

How could the predictions have been so wrong? Interestingly, productivity has increased significantly during this time period, an increase that has been reflected in increasing incomes, particularly among upper-middle income households (Leete & Schor, 1994). The increase in income has been significant. Upper-middle class individuals who were relatively affluent sixty years ago have seen their incomes explode over the past several decades. The increase in income has not come solely as a result of an increasing per-hour pay rate, but as a result of an unprecedented increase in the number of hours worked (Schor, 2004). In other words, the leisure society has not come. Instead, even faced with sharply increasing incomes, most individuals have significantly increased the amount of time devoted to income-producing activities to produce even more income so that they can purchase more. What is the rationale of this counter-intuitive result? The purpose of this paper is to explore the underlying causes of the growth in consumer activities occurring in societies characterized by consumer cultures. First, the role of products in the construction/communication of one's self is examined. Second, the theories of Rene Girard are reviewed. Third, the relationships between Girard's theory and present-day consumption and marketing activities are examined. Finally, the movie, The Joneses, is used as a means to illustrate and explore the ramifications of Girard's theory in present society.

Background

The marketplace in many societies today is characterized by an all-pervasive consumer culture (Easterbrook et al., 2014; Kasser & Kanner, 2004). This is very different from what was the norm in the past, at least among the masses. One can argue that historically, the basis of life consisted primarily of relationships that were established and maintained through community, family, and religion (Cova, 1997). Arguably, the role of each of these institutions and, consequently, the importance of relationships, have declined appreciably. Many communities, for instance, have morphed into collections of fortified houses between which social interaction has long since ceased to occur (Baumeister, 1997; Pipher, 1996). With incessant time demands on its members and the virtual dissolution of the marriage bond as an article of permanence, the family has in many ways, become an anachronism in itself. Bailie states "the family, as an institution, is in such disarray that sitcoms have to redefine it each fall in order to appear relevant" (2002, p. 4). Finally, the weakening of the role of religion in individuals' lives is well documented (Altemeyer, 2004). Consequently, the lives of individuals are no longer as entwined with relationships with others as they once were (Cova, 1996).

The lessening of the prevalence and importance of relationships have had a profound effect on individuals' selves, or their identities. Historically, individuals' identities were established and played out within the framework of relationships with others (Burns, 2010). Consequently, with the declining quality and quantity of relationships, the role played by relationships in the development and maintenance of individuals' identities has likewise diminished. With the decline in the role of relationships, there becomes a need for individuals to rely upon a different base for their selves, or their identities. Many argue that, instead of relationships, individuals' selves have become something to be achieved or constructed by an individual (Kaiser, Chandler, & Hammidi, 2001; Paterson, 2006). Indeed, Slater (1997) suggests that today, identity can be achieved only through one's individual choices. This alternative basis of the self typically involves one's achievement or one's possessions.

Basing one's self on achievement tends to be a precarious undertaking. Achievement often is transient and is difficult to maintain. If achievement is based on physical accomplishments, for instance, what happens as one ages? The uncertainty of achievement and the stress of trying to maintain a level of achievement makes achievement a less-than-satisfactory alternative to relationships onto which to base one's self. Instead, in consumer cultures, one's possessions typically becomes the preferred basis of one's self. As a basis of the self, possessions lend individuals a higher degree of control over their selves since possessions can often be relatively easily acquired. Furthermore, basing one's self on possessions provides individuals with the additional benefit of being relatively easy be change, permitting individuals a level of flexibility in defining their selves that is not available through other means. The ability for individuals' selves to be developed and maintained through actions taken in the marketplace has, in turn, increased the role and the importance of the marketplace.

Consequently, a key quality of consumer culture is materialism, a quality that pervades the lives of most individuals (Belk, 2015; Larsen, Sirgy, & Wright, 1999). "Materialists place possessions and their acquisition at the center of their lives" (Richins & Dawson, 1992, p. 304). Although materialism is not new, its pervasiveness is. Given that most physical needs of individuals in consumer cultures are met, it seems contradictory that possessions should gain such a level of importance within these cultures. This level of importance, however, originates in the different role that possessions play in consumer cultures – within consumer cultures, the primary driving force of purchases is not to satisfy physical needs. Instead, the primary role of possessions is its role in establishing and communicating individuals' identities or their selves (Ferreira & Scaraboto, 2016; Thompson & Loveland, 2015). "Knowingly or unknowingly, intentionally or unintentionally, we regard possessions as ourselves… That we are what we have is perhaps the most basic and powerful fact of consumer behavior" (Belk, 1988, p. 139). Within consumer cultures, some suggest that individuals' selves are formed primarily through presentation made possible through products acquired and displayed (Zukin & Maguire, 2004). Ferguson suggests that

…all consumption becomes conceivable as the desire for, as well as the desire of, the self. ... We then seek, in consuming such objects (products), to incorporate an idealized self, to make the self more real, and to end the inner despair of not having a self (Ferguson, 1992, p. 27, 28).

For many, everyday life in a consumer culture has been transformed into an exercise of personal construction (Burns, 2006; Zukin & Maguire, 2004). Within this environment, products become the measuring rod upon which relative success is measured (Richins & Dawson, 1992). Consequently, products are not consumed primarily to satisfy consumers' physical needs; instead, they act primarily as tools to use in the process of self-construction, and only secondarily as a means to satisfy physical needs (Fitzmaurice & Comegys, 2006). The role played by many products, therefore, is as building blocks consumers can use to construct their desired selves (Cooper, McLaughlin, & Keating, 2005; LaPoint & Hambrick-Dixon, 2004; Woodward, 2005). The importance of consumption activities has increased to such an extent that some suggest that the self today is formed totally through consumption activities (e.g. Brownlie et al., 1999).

Central to the construction of one's self is establishing a point of difference from others (Snyder & Fromkin, 1980; Tian, Bearden, & Hunter, 2001) or, in other words, constructing a self that is unique and, in some way, superior to that possessed by others (Schaefers, 2014). Hence, the acquisition and display of products becomes the basis for interpersonal competition (Paterson, 2006; Robbins, 2000). The realization that possessions are used by individuals in a competitive fashion is not new. Indeed, Fromm

(1976) recognized that possessions can be acquired and displayed as a means to display superiority over others. Possessions become the weapons for engaging, competing with, and, at times, attempting to defeat others' selves (Burns & Warren, 2009). Burns and Warren (2008) developed the term, consumer warfare, to describe this behavior. The inherent competitive nature of consumption is well recognized (Jardine, 2004; Pooler, 2003; Schor, 2004).

The competitive nature of consumption is not a new idea. Indeed, Veblen's (1897) conspicuous consumption is, in fact, a form of competitive consumption. The reality of the competitive nature of consumption today becomes particularly apparent when advertising is observed – the acquisition of products are often depicted as means by which superiority over others can be expressed (e.g., ads for cosmetics, automobiles, electronics). The widespread reality of competitive consumption has even infiltrated societies previously characterized by cooperation (Pack, 2012). Relatively little empirical research has examined this phenomenon. Research on desire, however, provides additional insight.

DESIRE

Girard's (1979) theory of desire highlights the competitive nature of interpersonal interaction including competition manifest in the marketplace, and provides a theoretical basis for this behavior (Burns, 2010). As referenced above, within consumer cultures, "there is a spreading consensus that much, if not all, consumption has been quite wrongly characterized as involving processes of need fulfillment, utility maximization, and reasoned choice" (Belk, Ger, & Askegaard, 2003, p. 326). Instead, arguably most purchases today are made in response to desire, not need (Burns, 2010). "Needs are anticipated, controlled... and gratified through logical instrumental processes. Desires, on the other hand, are overpowering; something we give in to ... and totally dominate our thoughts, feelings, and actions" (Belk, Ger, & Askegaard, 2003, p. 99). Unlike needs that are usually associated with particular types of products capable of satisfying the specific need, desire is not necessarily associated with particular types of products – the targets of desire are not definitive (Miller, 2004; Vaughan, 2002). Instead, desire is based in involves imagination involving the symbolic value that is ascribed to products (Fleming, 2004) and, hence, can be attached and directed toward virtually any item (Corrigan, 1997). As Skerrett states "we desire before we know what we want" (2003, p. 793). Consequently, desire cannot be satisfied with the acquisition of any specific product and, hence, is largely unsatisfiable or insatiable (Miller, 2004; Twitchell, 1999). Desire is depicted as the primary driver of the acquisition of products in consumer cultures (Burns & Warren, 2008).

Contrary to how it is typically portrayed, desire is fundamentally externally based (Girard, 1979). Girard highlights this mimetic nature of desire through observing the behavior of small children. The desires of a small child are often aroused and directed by the presence of perceived desires of another small child. A toy, for instance, even though it may previously have been rejected by a child, becomes desirable in the child's eyes simply when another child is perceived as desiring the toy (typically determined by observing the other child playing with the toy). Adult desires appear to gain direction similarly (Girard, 1997b; Kaplan, 2016). When another is seen as desiring a particular product (typically determined by observing the other's acquisition/possession of the product), one's desire is aroused toward the product. Desire, therefore, receives direction and becomes oriented toward a specific product simply because it is perceived as being desired by another (Stirling, 2004). Consequently, individuals 'learn' their desires from others (Stirling, 2004). It is important to note that it is not the product itself that is being desired, but the symbolism that is ascribed to the product that is developed, enhanced, and/or directed by observing someone else seemingly enjoying the product. Consequently, Wallace and Smith (1994) refer to mimetic desire as a "basic human drive." Similarly, Grande (2015) believes mimetic desire is the drive having the largest effect on the actions of individuals and society today. Realizing the broad-reaching effects mimetic desire can potentially produce, Livingston (1992) suggests that a failure to understand the mimetic nature of desire is a fundamental blind spot of many researchers in the social sciences.

Consequently, desire is the direct outcome of the competitive nature of individuals and, given the role played by products in self-construction in consumer cultures, is played out primarily in the marketplace. Competitive consumption consists of desire for acquiring the images associated with products in the marketplace, with the objective of improving one's self relative to others (Burns & Warren, 2009).

Referent Others

Referent others, a classic concept in marketing, are individuals or groups who provide a frame of reference from which an individual makes evaluations (Schulz, 2015). Referent others are individuals or groups with which one compares themselves to assess their relative personal state. Within the viewpoint of mimetic desire, referent others are the targets of individuals' desires or their rivals. Rivals can take various forms, including neighbors, colleagues, groups, famous celebrities, or images created through marketing activities (Burns, 2010). Although each of these groups of individuals frequently serve as rivals and, consequently, each are frequently included in marketing communications, given their close proximity, individuals with whom one directly interacts, such as one's neighbors, tend to play a central role. Referent others serve as the targets with which individuals compare themselves. The results of this comparison, in turn, drives many consumption choices (Escalas & Bettman, 2005; Tanner et al., 2008).

The choice of one's rivals is often made unconsciously and involves referent others whose very essence is viewed to be the most threatening – often the individuals who are perceived to have the highest level of similarity to oneself (Elliot, 1997; Girard, 1997a). Within this context, desire seeks to increase one's standing relative to one's rivals, often accompanied by feelings of envy toward the rival (Wharff, 2007). The product choices of the rival are viewed to be associated with the essence of the rival which, in turn, come to be viewed as embodying the rival's very being (Fleming, 2004). Given the mimetic nature of desire, one's desire is always aroused by the perceived desire of another; we desire what another desires (Girard, 1979).

Desire, therefore, is "interdividual" in nature (Golsan, 2002) – desire does not arise from within an individual, but arises from the perceived desires of one's rivals. "Rather than simply arising spontaneously, either through an act of subjective will or due to the inherent attraction of a particular object, desires are evoked by the conduct and attitudes of others towards objects" (Daniels, 2009, p. 91). When a rival makes a purchase or is perceived as having interest in a particular product, the result is desire. Desire, in turn, prompts a defensive response, usually consisting of purchase(s) of products in an attempt to ether copy, or preferably, surpass the rival (Wharff, 2007). In other words, arguably, desire becomes the primary driving force behind most consumer activity in the marketplace. Instead of focusing on products primarily as means to satisfy physical needs, the primary purpose of products is to act as means by which desire can be addressed, albeit only temporarily. One's defensive response to the perceived actions of a rival (consisting of the acquisition of additional possessions(s)), in turn, becomes viewed as an offensive response by the rival (the purchase will likely adversely affect the relative self of another), prompting a defensive response by the rival (consisting of the purchase of additional possession(s)), beginning a never-ending escalation of activity in the marketplace.

APPLICATION: THE JONESES

The primary focus of this paper is to illustrate mimetic desire through a recent film. The film, The Jones (2009), is a social commentary on the consumer society, clearly showing the manifestation of mimetic desire in an upper-middle class neighborhood in suburban Atlanta. The essence of the movie is a "family," which is not a family in the true sense of the word, but is actually a group of salespeople whose sole purpose is to sell products among their neighbors. What makes the movie an example of marketer's use of mimesis is the mode by which the characters "sell." The family members do not sell products in what may be viewed to be the usual sales process, but instead, they sell through facilitating mimetic desire by becoming a rival to their neighbors – by establishing the standard to be emulated.

The "family" is comprised of four unrelated individuals; husband Steve Jones (David Duchovny), wife Kate Jones (Demi Moore), daughter Jenn Jones (Amber Heard), and son Mick Jones (Benjamin Hollingsworth). (These are the names of characters in their "family," with the appropriate name of "Jones" from the common phrase "Keeping Up with the Joneses)." Kate is the leader of the "family" who perform the role of stealth marketers, individuals whose lives consist of product placement. The family integrates itself into the neighborhood with the objective of establishing trends based on the products they are selling.

Several neighbors (target customers) are included in the movie, the primary ones being Larry Symonds (Gary Cole) and Summer Symonds (Glenne Headly). The neighbors in the neighborhood are typical upper-middle class households pursuing successful professional careers with the corresponding incomes. Living in houses that some might derogatorily regard as "McMansions," acquiring and possessing products play significant roles in the lives of the residents in the neighborhood. As would be suggested in the theories of Rene Girard, the role of products as depicted in the movie is primarily external – although individuals are depicted as obtaining pleasure from products, the source of the pleasure comes from how the product affects one's level of perceived attainment relative to others. To further illuminate the use of mimetic desire, a few specific scenes from the movie (selected from many) will be briefly reviewed.

The movie begins by establishing that the activities of the Joneses are not unusual or extraordinary, but are actually the norm in consumer culture. In one of the first scenes in the movie, where neighbors Larry and Summer first meet the newly arrived Jones family, the greeting is product-based, with Summer giving a gift consisting of samples from the Robustion cosmetic line she is selling. This welcoming scene establishes that the relationships existing between people in the neighborhood are most frequently product-based – a theme which frequently presents itself in the movie.

In a conversation with KC (Laura Hutton), the family's boss, where she is encouraging Steve to sell more products to the neighbors, she states; "You are not selling things anymore. To succeed here, you can't just sell things. You are here to sell a lifestyle, an attitude. If people want you, they will want what you've got." KC clearly recognizes the role of mimetic nature of desire. Desire does not result from the product itself, but other's desire for the product.

From the start of the movie, neighbor Larry is obviously suffering problems with his relationship with his wife and with his job. He continues, however, to strive for materialistic solutions – trying to acquire the successful essence of his acquaintances, particularly Steve. Regarding his relationship with his wife, Steve tells Larry that, the key to keep involved with his wife and to "keep things fresh" is to give her "a steady stream of gifts," such as an extremely expensive set of earrings he is "giving" to his wife as a "Tuesday gift." The way presented to Larry to improve his relationship with his wife was through the marketplace. Through the party organized by Steve and Summer that occurred shortly thereafter, the relationship between Steve and Kate "his wife" was continually played up to build desire in others. The relationship is depicted as being highly dependent on products – the purchase of particular products will lead to improved relationships with one's spouse.

At the party, Steve uses an imagined quest up Mount Everest to showcase the products that supposedly kept him warm with the pictures displayed on his new audio-visual equipment (with references to his video service provider). The route to the success and happiness depicted by Steve ultimately is pictured as the acquisition of the correct products. Simultaneously, his "son" Mick similarly engages his "friends" by displaying his video system located elsewhere in the house. The success of Mick's activities is displayed by a classmate of Mick (Naomi Madsen (Christine Evangelista)) who states, "you have this whole cult following at school ... everyone is drinking your Kool-Aid." He was successful in establishing himself as the "rival" to his colleagues – someone whose very essence is to be copied by others.

While at the party, Mick says to Naomi "Do you know why all those people are in my house, so that my so-called family can show off all their s***." Naomi agrees with this statement, clearly acknowledging that the display of one's possessions is the reason people have parties in their neighborhood. Parties are used as a tool to try to establish one's superiority over others. Although Steve and Summer's party was explicitly organized to sell products, the essence of the party did not differ from the parties held by anyone else in the neighborhood.

The success of the party is indicated later that night where Summer expresses to Larry her desire for the Joneses' possessions and focuses on need to make more money to be able to acquire them. She subsequently rejects her husband's advances since not to do so is viewed to adversely affect her selling abilities.

(It should be noted that the "family" of marketers were not immune from the materialistic attitudes held by the neighbors. Kate, for instance, is continually focused on selling more, including working on her day off, to make more money. Indeed, the rationale for being a part of the "family" is to make significant amounts of money so that they can participate in the consumer culture as well).

The scene with Larry buying a new Audi convertible is the clearest display of the effects of mimetic desire. Larry's mimetic desire toward Steve's Audi convertible prompts Larry to buy a similar Audi convertible (which he cannot afford) to copy Steve, but he purchases it in red which he views to be a superior color. Larry also begins to give his wife a steady stream of gifts (as he believes that Steve is doing with Kate) that he also cannot afford. Consequently, Larry is happy and becomes "a new person." Larry's happiness does not last, however. He sees Steve getting a new Audi R8, which is a significant step up from his previous Audi. When Larry sees the new car, he is speechless and his countenance immediately falls. Larry, who was at the top of his world with his previous purchases, suddenly crashes down when he sees that his possessions are no longer competitive with Steve's. Steve comments "I just ruined his (Larry's) day." How was Larry's day ruined? His possessions and his life did not change, but how he viewed his life relative to Steve's did.

Later, at a party at Larry and Summer's place (which was organized not just to display their possessions, but also as a means for Summer to sell more Robustion cosmetics), Steve tries to convince Larry that he has a good life, saying "You two have a great life. You don't know about my life. You have everything." Larry's focus, however, remains on Steve, or more specifically, how his possessions compare with Steve's possessions, including talking about his larger TV. Larry is engaged in this conversation while realizing that he cannot pay his bills and he is going to lose his house to foreclosure. Even with his world caving in around him. Larry remains fixated on competing with Steve. In his mind, he has no other alternative. To admit that he cannot compete is not simply a financial realization, but a realization that as an individual, he no longer has a competitive self. He is empty. With this realization that his "life" is over, Larry then takes his own life.

The ending of the movie tries to bring a message of the futility of a life focused on mimetic desire. Steve abandons his life as a stealth marketer. Kate, after the prompting of Steve, does likewise. However, in the ending scene showing them traveling to Arizona to meet Steve's father, they drive off in an expensive Audi SUV. This scene is similar to the message reflected in "Hotel California" (which is a picture of consumer culture) "You can check-out any time you like, but you can never leave" and that we are "We are all just prisoners here, of our own device." We can go to Arizona, but will things actually change or will Steve and Kate just ultimately find new occupations to engage in the consumer culture?

SOLUTIONS AND RECOMMENDATIONS

Economic theory and much of consumer behavior and marketing thought generally assumes that most desires of individuals are consciously determined based on personal "felt needs" or as the result of a purposeful thoughtful process (Pham & Higgins, 2005). In other words, individuals' desires are viewed to be fostered and directed through a personal process (affected by the various external influences that are addressed in most consumer behavior textbooks). This paper, however, suggests the opposite – that individuals' desires are determined primarily in the marketplace by the marketplace. Indeed, "since we all imitate models, mimetic rivalry is a nearly ubiquitous feature of human relations" (Stirling, 2004, p. 18). Desire appears not to be determined internally, but is determined "obliquely in the gaze of others" (Orlean, 1988, p. 102). Consequently, desire is viewed to be "interdividual" and hence, does not possess focal points outside of the marketplace and the presence of others (rivals), and it is not directed toward any particular product or outcome. Desire is indefinite, it is fluidic, and it can never come to a point of resolution. Several conclusions can be drawn.

First, in a consumer culture, the marketing of particular products seems to have relatively little importance in the study of consumer behavior. If desire can be reduced to issues of interpersonal competition and imitation (Orlean, 1988) and if desire is "other-centered," not "object centered" (Schweiker, 1994), the focus of desire on a particular product will be almost coincidental. Indeed, "in a quite real sense, every commodity becomes identical, the necessary but inconsequential carrier of ultimate value" (Ferguson, 1992, p. 174).

Second, the value ascribed to most products is not the result of the intrinsic qualities of the product, nor its ability to directly supply comfort and bliss to individuals. Instead, the value ascribed to a product is more likely equal to its mimetic value, which is derived from its desire value and its uniqueness value. Although this realization is not new (e.g., Marx & Engels, 1992 [1848]), much consumer research addressing price overlooks this reality. A product's desire value is a measure of the degree that the product is desired by others; the more that a product is desired, the higher the value which will be assigned to it regardless of any intrinsic appeal that the product may or may not possess.

Third, for most, consumer activity is an integral and necessary part of everyday life.

Fourth, explanations are provided for several seeming paradoxes. Increases in affluence, for instance, has not led to the leisure society predicted in the past. Furthermore, the essence of mimetic desire accounts for the fact that the greatly increased standards of living which consumer culture has delivered have not been able to raise individuals' happiness levels. If individuals obtained utility from the intrinsic qualities of products, one would expect that increases in the quality and quantity of products acquired should lead to corresponding increases in happiness. This has not been observed in Western society (e.g., Binswanger, 2006; Lane, 1998; Myers, 2000). Indeed, some (e.g., Kasser & Ryan, 1996, 1993) have observed a negative relationship between happiness and income (the ability to buy more products). If most products, however, are not purchased for their intrinsic value, but for their mimetic value, the results are logical. Mimetic desire can never be satisfied. Acquiring products for mimetic reasons will only lead to further mimetic desire.

FUTURE RESEARCH DIRECTIONS

The ever-advancing consumer culture fueled by mimetic desire does not seem to possess an end. Although ever-increasing consumption seems to be a relatively benign way for individuals to compete, as seen in The Joneses, there are losers. Even when the losers do not lose their lives like Larry, the emotional costs can still be great. Although fostering mimetic desire has proven to be a successful marketing strategy, the effects on individuals have not been appropriately examined. Future research should focus on mimetic desire. Mimetic desire does not need to be attached to material products, but material products tend to be a relatively nonthreatening outlet. Girard (2001), however, suggests a transcendent alternative. The contentions of Girard should be examined in greater depth.

CONCLUSION

In conclusion, the primary role of the marketplace today is not merely to satisfy individuals' survival needs, nor is it merely to provide luxuries for individuals to enjoy. The marketplace then, must be understood as a central societal institution, and consumer activities must be interpreted through this framework. The movie, The Joneses, very clearly depicts the reality of mimetic desire and its outcomes. Although the situation depicted is fictional, the value in the movie is its proximity to real life. For decades, marketers have made free products available to individuals they view to be able to serve as rivals for others. Although marketers in the past did not use the terms rival, or mimetic desire, mimetic desire serves as the basis for many terms that formed that basis of their practices, such as reference groups and others (rivals) or conspicuous consumption (mimetic desire). The practice of paying famous and/or influential individuals to promote products is consistent with this orientation.

In summary, the mimetic desire, as clearly depicted in the movie, The Joneses, likely underlies most of the choices made in the marketplace. Although marketers are very aware of this reality, most individuals are not, raising a number of possible ethical issues for future analyses.

REFERENCES

Altemeyer, B. (2004). Perspectives: The decline of organized religion in Western civilization. *The International Journal for the Psychology of Religion, 14*(2), 77–89. doi:10.120715327582ijpr1402_1

Bailie, G. (2002). *Violence unveiled: Humanity at the crossroads.* New York, NY: Crossroad.

Baumeister, R. F. (1997). The self and society: Changes, problems, and opportunities. In R. D. Ashmore & L. Jussim (Eds.), *Self and identity* (pp. 191–217). New York, NY: Oxford University Press.

Belk, R. W. (1988). Possessions and the extended self. *The Journal of Consumer Research, 15*(2), 139–168. doi:10.1086/209154

Belk, R. W. (2015). Frontiers of culture and psychology. In S. Ng & A. Y. Lee (Eds.), *Handbook of culture and consumer behavior* (pp. 290–323). New York, NY: Oxford University Press.

Belk, R. W., Ger, G., & Askegaard, S. (2003). The fire of desire: A multisited inquiry into consumer passion. *The Journal of Consumer Research, 30*(3), 326–351. doi:10.1086/378613

Binswanger, M. (2006). Why does income growth fail to make us happier? Searching for the treadmills behind the paradox of happiness. *Journal of Socio-Economics, 35*(2), 366–381. doi:10.1016/j.socec.2005.11.040

Brownlie, D., Saren, M., Wensley, R., & Whittington, R. (1999). Marketing disequilibrium: On redress and restoration. In D. Brownlie, M. Saren, R. Wensley, & R. Whittington (Eds.), *Rethinking marketing: Toward critical marketing accounting* (pp. 1–22). Thousand Oaks, CA: Sage Publications. doi:10.4135/9781446280058.n2

Burns, D. J. (2006). Self-construction through consumption activities: An analysis and review of alternatives. In P. C. Vitz & S. M. Felch (Eds.), *The self: Beyond the postmodern crisis* (pp. 149–167). Wilmington, DE: Intercollegiate Studies Institute.

Burns, D. J. (2010). Mimeticism and the basis of value: Toward a theory of fashion marketing. *Journal of Global Fashion Marketing, 1*(1), 40–50. doi:10.1080/20932685.2010.10593056

Burns, D. J., & Warren, H. B. (2008). Consumer warfare: Implications for marketing strategy. *The Journal of Business Strategy, 29*(6), 44–52. doi:10.1108/02756660810917237

Burns, D. J., & Warren, H. B. (2009). Are marketers nothing more than arms dealers? *Journal of Business Management and Change, 4*(1), 9–26.

Cooper, S., McLoughlin, D., & Keating, A. (2005). Individual and neo-tribal consumption: Tales from the Simpsons of Springfield. *Journal of Consumer Behaviour, 4*(5), 330–344. doi:10.1002/cb.17

Corrigan, P. (1997). *The sovereignty of consumption: An introduction.* Thousand Oaks, CA: Sage.

Cova, B. (1996). What postmodernism means to marketing managers. *European Management Journal, 14*(5), 494–499. doi:10.1016/0263-2373(96)00043-6

Cova, B. (1997). Community and consumption: Towards a definition of the 'linking value' of products or services. *European Journal of Marketing, 3*(3/4), 297–316. doi:10.1108/03090569710162380

Daniels, J. (2008). Wanting nothing: Imitation and production in the economy of desire. *New Blackfriars, 90*(1025), 90–107. doi:10.1111/j.1741-2005.2008.00237.x

Easterbrook, M. J., Wright, M. L., Dittmar, H., & Banerjee, R. (2014). Consumer culture ideals, extrinsic motivations, and well-being in children. *European Journal of Social Psychology, 44*(4), 349–359. doi:10.1002/ejsp.2020

Elliott, R. (1997). Existential consumption and irrational desire. *European Journal of Marketing, 31*(3/4), 285–296. doi:10.1108/03090569710162371

Escalas, J. E., & Bettman, J. R. (2005). Self-construal, reference groups and brand meaning. *The Journal of Consumer Research, 32*(3), 378–389. doi:10.1086/497549

Ferguson, H. (1992). *Religious transformation in Western society: The end of happiness*. New York: Routledge.

Ferreira, M. C., & Scaraboto, D. (2016). 'My plastic dreams:' Towards an extended understanding of materiality and the shaping of consumer identities. *Journal of Business Research, 69*(1), 191–207. doi:10.1016/j.jbusres.2015.07.032

Fitzmaurice, J., & Comegys, C. (2006). Materialism and social construction. *Journal of Marketing Theory and Practice, 14*(4), 287–299. doi:10.2753/MTP1069-6679140403

Fleming, C. (2004). *Rene Girard: Violence and mimesis*. Malden, MA: Polity Press.

Fromm, E. (1976). *To have or to be?* New York, NY: Harper & Row.

Girard, R. (1979). *Violence and the sacred* (P. Gregory, Trans.). Baltimore, MD: Johns Hopkins University.

Girard, R. (1997a). From mimetic desire to the monstrous double. In T. Murray (Ed.), *Mimesis, masochism and mime: The politics of theatricality in contemporary French thought* (pp. 87–111). Ann Arbor, MI: University of Michigan Press.

Girard, R. (1997b). *Resurrection from the underground: Feodor Dostoevsky* (J. G. Williams, Trans.). New York, NY: Crossroad.

Girard, R. (2001). *I see Satan fall like lightning* (J. G. Williams, Trans.). Maryknoll, NY: Orbis Books.

Golsan, R. J. (2002). *Rene Girard and myth*. New York, NY: Routledge.

Grande, P. B. (2015). Desire in the Great Gatsby. *Anthropoetics, 21*(1), 2–18.

Jardine, M. (2004). *The making and unmaking of technological society: How Christianity can save modernity from itself*. Grand Rapids, MI: Brazos Press.

Kaiser, S. B., Chandler, J., & Hammidi, T. (2001). Minding appearances in female academic culture. In A. Guy, E. Green, & M. Banim (Eds.), *Through the wardrobe: Women's relationships with their clothes* (pp. 117–136). New York, NY: Berg. doi:10.2752/9781847888921/THRWARD0012

Kaplan, G. (2016). *René Girard, Unlikely apologist: Mimetic theory and fundamental theology*. Notre Dame, IN: University of Notre Dame Press.

Kasser, T., & Kanner, A. D. (2004). Where is the psychology of consumer culture? In T. Kasser & A. D. Kanner (Eds.), *Psychology and consumer culture: The struggle for a good life in a materialistic world* (pp. 3–7). Washington, DC: American Psychological Association. doi:10.1037/10658-001

Kasser, T., & Ryan, R. M. (1993). A dark side of the American dream: Correlates of financial success as a central life aspiration. *Journal of Personality and Social Psychology*, *65*(2), 410–422. doi:10.1037/0022-3514.65.2.410 PMID:8366427

Kasser, T., & Ryan, R. M. (1996). Further examining the American dream: Differential correlates of intrinsic and extrinsic goals. *Personality and Social Psychology Bulletin*, *22*(3), 280–287. doi:10.1177/0146167296223006

Lane, R. E. (1998). The road not taken: Friendship, consumerism and happiness. In D. A. Crocker & T. Linden (Eds.), *Ethics in consumption: The good life, justice and global stewardship* (pp. 218–248). Lantham, MD: Rowman & Littlefield.

Lapoint, V. D., & Hambrick-Dixon, P. J. (2004). Consumerism's influence on black youth: The case of dress-related challenges. In T. Kasser & A. D. Kanner (Eds.), *Psychology and consumer culture: The struggle for a good life in a materialistic world* (pp. 233–250). Washington, DC: American Psychological Association. doi:10.1037/10658-013

Larsen, V., Sirgy, M. J., & Wright, N. D. (1999). Materialism: The construct, measures, antecedents and consequences. *Academy of Marketing Studies Journal*, *3*, 78–110.

Leete, L., & Schor, J. B. (1994). Assessing the time-squeeze hypothesis: Hours worked in the United States, 1969-1989. *Industrial Relations*, *33*(1), 25–43. doi:10.1111/j.1468-232X.1994.tb00325.x

Livingston, P. (1992). *Models of desire: Rene Girard and the psychology of mimesis*. Baltimore, MD: Johns Hopkins University Press.

Marx, K., & Engels, F. (1992). *The communist manifesto*. New York, NY: Bantam Books. (Original work published 1848)

Miller, V. (2004). *Consuming religion: Christian faith and practice in a consumer culture*. New York, NY: Continuum.

Myers, D. G. (2000). *The American paradox: Spiritual hunger in an age of plenty*. New Haven, CT: Yale University Press.

Orlean, A. (1988). Money and mimetic speculation. In P. Dumouchel (Ed.), *Violence and truth: On the work of Rene Girard* (AnspaughM. A., Trans.; pp. 1–112). Stanford, CA: Stanford University Press.

Pack, S. (2012). Keeping up with the Begays: Observations of competitive consumption in contemporary Navajo society. *Native Studies Review*, *21*(1), 83–101.

Paterson, M. (2006). *Consumption and everyday life*. New York, NY: Routledge.

Pham, M. T., & Higgins, E. T. (2005). Promotion and prevention in consumer decision making: The state of the art and theoretical propositions. In S. Ratneshwar & D. G. Mick (Eds.), *Inside consumption: Consumer motives, goals and desires* (pp. 8–43). New York, NY: Routledge.

Pipher, M. (1996). *The shelter of each other: Rebuilding our families*. New York, NY: Ballantine.

Pooler, J. (2003). *Why we shop: Emotional rewards and retail strategies*. Westport, CT: Praeger.

Richins, M. L., & Dawson, S. (1992). Consumer values orientation for materialism and its measurement: Scale development and validation. *The Journal of Consumer Research, 19*(3), 303–316. doi:10.1086/209304

Robbins, P. R. (2000). *Aggression and violence: An interdisciplinary approach*. Jefferson, NC: McFarland & Company.

Schaefers, T. (2007). Standing out from the crowd: Niche product choice as a form of conspicuous consumption. *European Journal of Marketing, 48*(9/10), 1805–1827. doi:10.1108/EJM-03-2013-0121

Schor, J. B. (1994). Decline of leisure time in America. *Vital Speeches of the Day, 60*(24), 748–752.

Schor, J. B. (1998). *The overspent American: Upscaling, downshifting, and the new consumer*. New York, NY: Basic Books.

Schor, J. B. (2004). The problem of overconsumption: Why economists don't get it. In D. Doherty & A. Etzioni (Eds.), *Voluntary simplicity: Responding to the consumer culture* (pp. 65–82). Lanham, MD: Rowman & Littlefield.

Schulz, H. M. (2015). Reference group influence in consumer role rehearsal narratives. *Qualitative Market Research, 18*(2), 210–229. doi:10.1108/QMR-02-2012-0009

Schweiker, W. (1994). Religion and the philosophers of mimesis. In M. I. Wallace & T. H. Smith (Eds.), *Curing violence* (pp. 25–44). Sonoma, CA: Polebridge Press.

Skerrett, K. R. (2003). Desire and anathema: Mimetic rivalry in defense of plenitude. *Journal of the American Academy of Religion, 71*(4), 793–809. doi:10.1093/jaarel/lfg099

Slater, D. (1997). *Consumer culture and modernity*. Cambridge, UK: Polity Press.

Snyder, C. R., & Fromkin, H. L. (1980). *Uniqueness: The human pursuit of difference*. New York, NY: Plenum Press. doi:10.1007/978-1-4684-3659-4

Stirling, M. C. (2004). Violent religion: Rene Girard's theory of culture. In J. H. Ellenus (Ed.), *The destructive power of religion: Violence in Judaism, Christianity, and Islam* (pp. 11–50). Westport, CT: Praeger.

Tanner, R. J., Ferraro, R., Chartrand, T. L., Bettman, J. R., & Van Baaren, R. (2008). Of chameleons and consumption: The impact of mimicry on choice and preferences. *The Journal of Consumer Research, 34*(6), 754–766. doi:10.1086/522322

Thompson, S. A., & Loveland, J. M. (2015). Integrating identity and consumption: An identity investment theory. *Journal of Marketing Theory and Practice, 23*(3), 235–253. doi:10.1080/10696679.2015.1032471

Tian, K. T., Bearden, W. O., & Hunter, G. L. (2001). Consumers' need for uniqueness: Scale development and validation. *The Journal of Consumer Research, 28*(1), 50–66. doi:10.1086/321947

Twitchell, J. B. (1999). *Lead us into temptation: The triumph of American materialism*. New York, NY: Columbia University Press.

Vaughan, B. (2002). The punitive consequences of consumer culture. *Punishment & Society*, *4*(2), 195–211. doi:10.1177/14624740222228545

Veblen, T. B. (1897). *The theory of the leisure class*. New York, NY: Macmillan.

Wallace, M. I., & Smith, T. H. (1994). Religion as cure or religion as structure of violence. In M. I. Wallace & T. H. Smith (Eds.), *Curing violence* (pp. xvii–xx). Sonoma, CA: Polebridge Press.

Wharff, J. (2007). Bernard of Clairvaux and René Girard on desire and envy. *Cistercian Studies Quarterly*, *42*(2), 183–207.

Woodward, S. (2005). Looking good: Feeling right – Aesthetics of the self. In S. Küchler & D. Miller (Eds.), *Clothing as material culture* (pp. 21–39). Oxford, UK: Berg. doi:10.2752/9780857854056/CLMATCULT0005

Yount, D. (1997). *Spiritual simplicity: Simplify your life and enrich your soul*. New York, NY: Simon & Schuster.

Zukin, S., & Maguire, J. S. (2004). Consumers and consumption. *Annual Review of Sociology*, *30*(1), 173–197. doi:10.1146/annurev.soc.30.012703.110553

ADDITIONAL READING

Adams, R. (2000). Loving mimesis and Girard's 'scapegoat of the text:' A creative reassessment of mimetic desire. In W. Swartely (Ed.), *Violence renounced: René Girard, Biblical studies, and peacemaking* (pp. 260–269). Telford, PA: Pandora Press.

Burns, D. J., Hutchins, J., & Mathisen, R. (2017). When rivals purchase: This means war! Or does it? *Journal of Business and Behavioral Sciences*, *29*, 122–139.

Girard, R. (1997). *The Girard reader*. New York, NY: Crossroad.

Grande, P. B. (2015). Desire in The Great Gatsby. *Anthropoetics*, *21*(1), 2–18.

Iacoboni, M. (2008). Imitation, empathy, and mirror neurons. *Annual Review of Psychology*, *60*(1), 653–670. doi:10.1146/annurev.psych.60.110707.163604 PMID:18793090

Lawtoo, N. (2017). The plasticity of mimesis. *Modern Language Notes*, *132*(5), 1201–1224.

Palaver, W. (2013). *René Girard's mimetic theory*. Ann Arbor, MI: Michigan State University Press.

Schwager, R. (2005). *Banished from Eden: Original sin and evolutionary theory in the drama of salvation* (J. G. Williams, Trans.). Herefordshire, UK: Gracewing Publishing/Inigo.

Steinmair-Pösel, P. (2007). Original sin, grace, and positive mimesis. *Contagion: Journal of Violence, Mimesis, and Culture*, (14), 1-12.

KEY TERMS AND DEFINITIONS

Competitive Consumption: The use of product acquisition as a way to express superiority over others.

Consumer Culture: A culture characterized by a focus on the marketplace as the central societal institution.

Identity: One's assessment of who they are – their self.

Materialism: The belief that physical possessions are central to life and the source of happiness.

Mimetic Desire: Desire that is copied from the perceived desires of others.

Referent Others: Individuals and groups who serve as models for one's choices.

Value: A measure of the relative worth of an item.

Section 2

The Effects of Consumer Culture on Individuals, Families, and Society

Chapter 5
"Money Worlds" and Wellbeing:
An Empirical Test of Tatzel's Model of Consumption

Leisa Reinecke Flynn
University of Southern Mississippi, USA

Ronald Earl Goldsmith
Florida State University, USA

Michael Brusco
Florida State University, USA

ABSTRACT

Tatzel proposed a theory of money worlds and wellbeing comprised of four prototypical consumer patterns based on whether consumers are high/low on materialism and simultaneously tight or loose with money. Tatzel proposes that the four prototypes (value-seekers, non-spenders, big-spenders, and experiencers) differ strikingly along many values, attitudes, and behaviors. This study uses data from 1,016 U.S. student consumers to test empirically the typology and differences. A cluster analysis confirmed that a four-cluster solution best represented the data, supporting Tatzel's model. Subsequent ANOVAs showed that two of the four groups differed predictably in the hypothesized directions. Significant differences between big-spenders and non-spenders appeared in levels of price sensitivity, status consumption, generosity, brand engagement, worry about debt, and spending. The other two groups, value-seekers and experiencers, fell between them. The findings partially confirm Tatzel's theory and suggest that "money worlds" are one way of conceptualizing consumer culture.

INTRODUCTION

In 2002 and 2003, Miriam Tatzel published a pair of papers that lay out a matrix for classifying consumers by their levels of materialism and their orientation towards spending money. Tatzel (2002, p. 105) found a contradiction in the literature in that "people who are loose with money are happier than people who are tight with money; that materialists are loose with money; and that on-materialists are happier

DOI: 10.4018/978-1-5225-6120-0.ch005

than materialists." She designed her theoretical classification system to resolve that contradiction by delineating four different "ideal types" of consumers, thereby explaining materialistic behavior in the marketplace. As of March 28, 2018, her two articles have been cited more than 300 times as reported by Google Scholar, indicating some interest in her proposals.

A number of researchers have used Tatzel's ideas to examine the role of materialism in such areas as the importance of brand names in purchase decisions (Flynn, Goldsmith, & Pollitte, 2016; Liao & Wang, 2009; Ostrovskaya & Sarabia-Sánchez, 2013; Podoshen & Andrzejewski, 2012) and the relationship between well-being and materialism (Handa & Khare, 2013). These questions appear to be important aspects of any view of consumer culture; namely, how do predilections toward spending and desire for material goods interact to shape broad patterns of consumer behavior? In the end, however attractive a theory may appear, its ultimate value is dependent on its conceptual soundness; unfortunately, validity tests are few and far between. Only three studies report actual operationalizations and tests of Tatzel's theoretical model (Pham, Yap, & Dowling, 2012; Tatzel, 2014; Troisi, Christopher, & Marek, 2006). None of these studies, however, have attempted to empirically confirm the four hypothesized consumer archetypes.

The present study builds on the three existing operationalizations, using a more rigorous methodology, in an attempt to provide a more definitive confirmation of Tatzel's Materialism, Money Orientation matrix. The study uses established scales, cluster analysis, and a large sample of U.S. college students to see if the model, as predicted, differentiates types of consumers who vary in their materialistic and spending orientations. Consequently, the first objective of the study is to attempt to reproduce empirically the matrix proposed by Tatzel (2002), rather than just forming groups *a priori* as in earlier studies. This evidence could provide important additional support for the theoretical distinctions Tatzel proposes. The second objective is to compare the four groups of consumers comprising the matrix, using a set of criteria different from earlier studies, in order to determine if the four categories of consumers differ in the theoretically predicted ways. This evidence should further support the meaningfulness of the distinctions among the groups, thus providing a broader basis for better-targeted marketing efforts by emphasizing the distinctive marketplace behaviors of each group.

MATERIALISM AND MONEY DISPOSITIONS

Tatzel's Theory: "Money Worlds"

Tatzel proposes the concepts of materialism and attitudes towards money as the two key concepts defining consumer culture. Using a 2 X 2 matrix (see Table 1), Tatzel (2002) classifies consumers as high in materialism and tight with money (*Value-Seekers*), high in materialism and loose with money (*Big-Spenders*), low in materialism and tight with money (*Non-Spenders*), and low in materialism and loose with money (*Experiencers*). This paper proceeds by first examining materialism and money orientations in the literature, and then by describing Tatzel's model in more detail. Prior uses of the model are discussed, and predictions are made about how each of the four proposed consumer types might differ when investigated using six new dependent variables, unaddressed by the previous studies: price sensitivity, status consumption, generosity, brand engagement in self-concept, debt worry, and self-reported spending.

Table 1. Tatzel's matrix: Consumer Styles based on materialism and money disposition

High Materialism	*Value-Seeker*	*Big-Spender*
Public meaning of things "Thingify" experiences Self-monitoring Dissatisfied, want more	Bargain Hunter Hold possessions Enjoy price comparison shopping Cool involvement "Save-to-spend"	Exhibitionist Replace possessions Price-quality schema Trend conscious Debt prone
Low Materialism	***Non-Spender***	***Experiencer***
Private meaning of things Non-material values	Saver Ascetic Lifestyle Price averse Quality less important	Generous Spend for recreation, self-development and services

Based on Tatzel (2002, p. 115)

Materialism

Materialism, which is "the importance a consumer attaches to worldly possessions" (Belk, 1985, p. 291), is an individual difference variable. Research shows that high materialism might account for numerous consumer traits, including: increased spending (Flynn & Goldsmith, 2015), increased shopping (Fitzmaurice & Comegys, 2006), overuse of credit (Richins, 2011), social anxiety (Schroeder & Dugal, 1995), self-monitoring (Chatterjee & Hunt, 1996), and self-ambivalence (Frost, Kyrios, McCarthy, & Matthews, 2007). Materialism also has a prominent place in academic literature outside of psychology and business. For example, sociologists view materialism as an explanation for lack of wellness in groups. A recent example finds that Malaysian students are less satisfied with life when they are lonely and materialistic (Ang, Mansor, & Tan, 2014). In this example, it was shown that subjects' social needs increased their need for material goods, but the goods did not increase life satisfaction. Materialism is also a topic in religion where it is usually defined as a negative characteristic seen to represent over-concern with the things of the world rather than with spiritual concerns. Other disciplines also criticize materialism (Belk, 1985; Tatzel, 2002). The bottom line, explained well in a recent meta-analysis on materialism, is that, firstly, those scoring higher in materialistic tendencies are more externally oriented and experience reduced levels of well-being, and that, secondly, materialism is best operationalized as a broad tendency rather than a simpler focus on money (Dittmar, Bond, Hurst, & Kasser, 2014). The tendency of materialists to look outside themselves for happiness does not seem to bring contentment. Instead, those scoring high in materialism strive to constantly expand their collections of possessions when the existing objects no longer deliver happiness.

Money Dispositions

Researchers have not studied how people feel about spending money nearly as much as they have studied materialism itself. Money dispositions is a narrower concept. In marketing, the central articles come from Lastovicka, Bettencourt, Hughner, and Kuntze (1999) and from Rick, Cryder, and Loewenstein (2008). Lastovicka *et al.* (1999) study frugality, which they define (p. 88) as "a consumer lifestyle trait characterized by the degree to which consumers are both restrained in acquiring and in resourcefully using economic goods and services to achieve longer-term goals." They develop a scale to measure the construct and they show that frugality correlates positively with value consciousness and price consciousness and negatively with compulsive buying and materialism. The Lastovicka *et al.* (1999) scale and the Rick *et al.* (2008) Spendthrift-Tightwad Scale (ST-TW) differ mostly in their specificity. The frugality scale measures the tendency toward a thrifty lifestyle, and the ST-TW scale measures only feelings about spending money. Frugality also correlates positively with antipathy towards shopping and with market mavenism (Bove, Nagpal, & Dorsett, 2009). A more recent application of the frugality scale shows it negatively correlated with brand engagement in self-concept and positively related to consumer independence (Goldsmith, Flynn, & Clark, 2014). Restraint in buying and in disposition manifests as a reluctance to spend money and leads to less of a connection with branded goods and to more interest in spending wisely.

Tatzel's (2002) concern is primarily with the effects of materialism and money orientation on mental health/well-being. By necessity, most marketing related research is from the point of view of a business that is concerned not with mental health but with predicting what consumers will do. Still, constructs that describe consumer behavior, such as frugality are also viewable from a mental health stance. Miserliness, an expression of extreme frugality, is negatively related to sadness. At the same time, sadder people, moderated by self-focus, spend more for the same goods as other people (Cryder, Lerner, Gross, & Dahl, 2008). Miserliness also has a genetic component and is an individual difference variable (Hur, Jeong, Schermer, & Rushton, 2011).

THE MATRIX: FOUR CONSUMER TYPES

Value-Seekers

The *Value-Seeker* category consists of consumers who see price as a negative and are frugal with money, but who at the same time are materialistic by nature (Tatzel, 2002). These people work to amass physical possessions and spend as little as they can while doing it. They might become hoarders in the most extreme and unhealthy scenarios (Frost *et al.*, 2007), but in more typical situations they shop for bargains, might be collectors, and tend to hold on to what they have.

A prominent variety of consumer behavior can be found in consumers who look for a good deal on what they buy. It is probably fair to say that this tendency is the most common, day-by-day type of consumer behavior. Certainly, ads for sales and cents-off abound. See for example, the success of the Walmart Corporation, which trades on low prices on an extremely wide variety of consumer goods. In the moderate ranges, this consumer behavior is perfectly normal. In Tatzel's (2002, 2014) world, higher materialism and tightness with money motivate these consumers. Constructs that researchers have developed to describe *Value-Seekers* include deal proneness, which recent research shows is passed on from parents to children (Schindler, Lala, & Corcoran, 2014) and price sensitivity, which is studied in economics and finance as well as in consumer behavior where it is seen as an individual difference variable (*cf.*, Aroean & Michaelidou, 2014; Flynn, Goldsmith, & Kim, 2000). Tatzel shows that price mavenism is a characteristic of the *Value-Seeker* group (Tatzel, 2014).

Big-Spenders

Tatzel's (2002, 2014) *Big-Spender* category is the high materialism, free spending quadrant. These people see price as an indicator of quality, spend for show, and generally use money to feed their materialistic urges. At least part of the activity of *Big-Spenders* is to connote status. In their eyes, paying a lot for a product or service adds to its value (Tatzel, 2014). As opposed to the *Value-Seeker*, Tatzel predicts, and then confirms, that *Big-Spenders* are more likely to be debt prone (Tatzel, 2014). Normal *Big-Spender* behavior can include status consumption, reliance on price as an indicator of quality, and other well-studied consumer attributes (Bearden & Haws, 2012; Flynn, Goldsmith, & Kim, 2013; Goldsmith *et al.*, 2014). Membership in this category does not necessarily connote problematic or clinical consumer behavior, but it could trend into the maladaptive in its extremes when consumers spend beyond their means. Pham *et al.* (2012) find *Big-Spenders* likely to be compulsive spenders, and Tatzel (2014) shows that *Big-Spenders* often have financial difficulties and report low well-being. Moreover, Kasser (2002) summarizes a stream of research indicating that materialism is counter to sound mental health.

Non-Spenders

Non-Spenders cluster in the low materialism, frugal quadrant. Tatzel predicts that these consumers save more, are price-averse, and live a simpler lifestyle compared to others. Again, this type of consumer appears in the literature. Albinsson, Wolf, and Kopf (2010) explore how *Non-Spenders* have a strong presence in former East Germany, where there exists a predominant frugality ethic. In other research, shopping antipathy and market mavenism are positively related to frugality (Bove *et al.*, 2009), and frugal consumer behavior cycles with the economy (Ryan, 2012). Moreover, although it seems logical that *Non-Spenders* would also be socially conscious and practice sustainable consumption, there is evidence both against that assumption (Pepper, Jackson, & Uzzell, 2009), probably because of the increased cost for many green products, and for it (Walther & Sandlin, 2013), likely due to reduced usage.

Experiencers

Experiencers fall into the category defined by low materialism and big-spending. Instead of possessions, however, they tend to spend on experiences. While all three of the other categories describe types of consumers, the consumer behavior literature leaves the impression that the Experiencer type is more problematic. Tatzel (2002) describes these consumers as willing to spend big on vacations and on fine restaurants, and also as generous with giving money to others. Simply put, they are happy to spend money, but are not interested in possessions *per se*. One way to look at the *Experiencers* is to think of them as being at the top of Maslow's hierarchy. One might think of *Experiencers* as spending for meaning, to express themselves or to learn. According to Terrero (2007), the self-actualized have risen above more pedestrian needs and gone on to work on maximizing their potential in less economic ways. This is also a tenet of the work of Kasser and Ahuvia (2002). Another way to see *Experiencers* is that perhaps they are very other-oriented, and therefore, that spending on others makes them happiest. This category is unlikely to be useful for predicting different types of consumer behavior. Belk (1985) posits a lack of generosity as a quasi-factor of materialistic tendencies, so one could argue that generosity characterizes those low in materialistic tendencies. Logically too, while expensive vacations and meals are not possessions, they can be symbolic of having attained a luxurious and/or privileged lifestyle and can thus be a way to help consumers show status (Üstüner & Holt, 2014).

Tatzel (2002) argues that these consumers do not gather physical possessions, and thus are not materialistic, but they do spend heavily on fine dining and travel. Eating at expensive restaurants and going to exotic destinations are forms of luxury consumption that Kilsheimer (1993) found to be related to materialistic behaviors. While it is reasonable to expect that consumers who are low in materialism are more generous, it is hard to argue that they are loose with money (not frugal). It is possible that some people, perhaps uncommon, ascetic consumers, might have money that they are very generously giving to charity while living a modest lifestyle; here one might think of Warren Buffett, but even the billionaire, Bill Gates, who is now known for his generosity, lives in a 66,000-square foot house (Wikipedia, 2018). This paper argues that it is difficult to find people truly low in materialism who are not frugal. These constructs are almost the opposite of each other. Thus, the study predicts that it will be difficult to distinguish a pure Experiencer type.

Previous Tests of the Theory

Three published reports test Tatzel's model. Troisi *et al.* (2006) use a sample of 266 U.S. adults and college students (63% female). They operationalize Tatzel's taxonomy with Richins's 18-item materialism scale and 11 items from two different money conservation scales. They use regression analysis to test the impact of materialism and money conservation and their interaction on four dependent variables: impulse buying, attitude toward debt, openness to experience, and sensation seeking. They find, among other things, that the low materialism, non-frugal *Experiencers* score the highest on openness to experience. They find more differences between the *Big-Spender*s and the *Non-Spenders* than between the *Value-Seeker*s and *Experiencers*. Troisi *et al.* (2006) also find that the Non-Spender group has the most negative attitude towards incurring debt. They show that the frugal groups, *Value-Seeker*s and *Non-Spenders*, have more negative attitudes towards debt and towards impulse spending. Troisi *et al.* (2006) also find *Experiencers* to be the highest of the four groups in openness to experience and in sensation seeking. Overall, the results presented by Troisi *et al.* (2006) show that materialism and money conservation have more of an additive than an interactive effect on the outcome variables. However, low reliability in the money conservation scale colors the results. Moreover, to directly partition their sample into the ideal types defined by Tatzel's (2002, 2003) model, they arbitrarily select the top and bottom thirds of the distributions to represent the four types.

Using a sample of 118 Australian students (62% female), Pham *et al.* (2012) build on Troisi *et al.* (2014) and use Tatzel's (2002) theory to examine compulsive spending with an emphasis on financial management practices. Pham *et al.*'s (2012) method includes Richins's short-form (2004) Material Values Scale and measures money-disposition modified from Parotta and Johnson's (1998) Financial Attitudes Scale. They show that adding a lack of frugality to materialism in a regression analysis increases the severity of compulsive spending. This finding implies that Tatzel's *Big-Spender* group is the most likely to be compulsive spenders. They also find that poor financial management skills, when paired with high materialism scores, lead to more incidences of clinical compulsive buying. This finding implies that the *Big-Spender* category is most susceptible to problems with over-spending. Results also show that consumers with high materialism and good financial management practices are not at increased risk for spending problems. Correspondingly, the previous research shows that *Value-Seeker*s should not be compulsive spenders (Pham *et al.*, 2012). In the end, the study by Pham et al. (2012) is a less literal adaptation of Tatzel's model because they use regression and do not attempt to delineate the four consumer types.

Finally, Tatzel (2014) herself shows how her theorized groups fit with a broad range of outcome variables using data from two samples of more than 600 adult college students, about two-thirds female. These two studies represent the most direct and detailed test of her taxonomy. Her findings show that the consumer groups differ in their irrational credit card use, price mavenism, price/quality reliance, attitude toward debt, impulse buying, windfall spending, intrinsic versus extrinsic motivation, subjective well-being, and happiness. She uses two methods to analyze the data. To perform the first analyses, she operationalizes the groups this way: "*Value-Seeker*s are defined as those who score in the top third in materialism and the top third in frugality; *Big-Spender*s score in the top third in materialism and the bottom third in frugality, and so on for *Non-Spenders* (low materialism and high frugality) and *Experiencers* (low materialism and low frugality)," (p. 83). The first analyses are separate 3 X 3 ANOVAs to test group differences for five consumer outcome variables: irrational credit card use, price mavenism, belief in the price-quality schema, attitudes toward debt, and impulse buying. These results show that while the *Big-Spender*s and *Non-Spenders* differ in expected ways, the *Value-Seeker*s and *Experiencers* show very close scores on most variables tested. Price mavenism is the only outcome on which the *Value-Seeker*s stand out from the *Experiencers*. Tatzel's method, however, continues to partition the data *a priori* and arbitrarily in order to form the groups for subsequent comparison. What is lacking is a more objective analysis that seeks to find the four groups by employing statistical analysis, namely clustering, rather than arbitrarily dividing the sample based on the theory.

What remains is a less than complete picture of how all four categories of consumers are different. Prior studies appear to provide only weak evidence that the four groups can be distinguished by constructs other than the two (Materialism and attitudes toward money and spending). While the *Big-Spender*s and *Non-Spenders* consistently show divergent behavioral paths, one could classify them on materialism or frugality alone likely with the same results. The other two classifications are less distinct. There is evidence that *Value-Seeker*s are price mavens and that *Experiencers* have stronger openness to experience, but other than those differences, the two off diagonal categories tend to blend. The design of the present study is to help confirm the existence of all four segments by using cluster analysis to uncover grouping patterns in the data. Subsequently, provided that groups can be distinguished by the cluster analysis, the groups will be compared across six outcome variables that prior studies did not employ, thereby extending the scope of the theory.

OUTCOME VARIABLES

If indeed, consumers fall into one of the four categories hypothesized by Tatzel (2002, 2014), then one would expect to see positively and negatively related consumer behavior characteristics for each cluster. Thus, this paper proposes outcome variables and their relationships for the consumers in each of the four quadrants. These outcomes were chosen in order to support and extend previous work and for their value in understanding these aspects of consumer culture. Hypotheses predict the expected relationships between Tatzel's categories and six different consumer behavior constructs.

Price Sensitivity

Consumers high on price sensitivity tend to make price the most important factor in purchase decisions (González-Benito, Martos-Partal, & Fustinoni-Venturini, 2014; Martínez & Montaner, 2008). Higher price sensitivity is also associated with heavy use and high purchase volume (Kim & Rossi, 1994). Consumers who buy, and one would expect use, a lot of a specific product category tend to be more price sensitive (Kim & Rossi, 1994). Potentially, large families, who may need to budget wisely to provide for many household members, would shop for price. This supposition argues for higher price sensitivity as a characteristic of the *Value-Seeker* quadrant. Tatzel (2014) shows *Value-Seeker*s to be price mavens, experts on prices in the marketplace. Frugality and price sensitivity are constructs that go hand in hand. Lastovicka *et al.* (1999, p. 90) report a .45 ($p < .05$) correlation between frugality and price consciousness. Therefore, the high frugality of *Non-Spenders* makes them good candidates for being price sensitive. Also, Eastman and Iyer (2012) and Goldsmith, Flynn, and Kim (2010) find price sensitivity to be negatively correlated with consuming for status, clothing involvement, and innovativeness, while status consumption and materialism are positively correlated (Flynn & Goldsmith, 2015). These correlations suggest that *Big-Spenders*, in contrast, are almost certain to be relatively price insensitive, owing to their attitudes toward spending.

- **Hypothesis One:** Price sensitivity is expected to be a characteristic of *Value-Seeker*s and *Non-Spenders*, but uncharacteristic of *Big-Spenders*.

Status Consumption

Status consumption is defined as "the motivational process by which individuals strive to improve their social standing through the conspicuous consumption of consumer products" (Eastman, Goldsmith, & Flynn, 1999, p 41). This definition implies that, in the eyes of status consumers, products have a value beyond their functional properties. Materialism connotes the same thing, meaning consuming for status and materialism go hand in hand (Belk, 1985; Chan & Prendergast, 2008; Wang & Wallendorf, 2006). Tatzel (2002) calls the consumers in the *Big-Spender* category "Exhibitionists," implying that they like to show off what they have. Consuming for status is a very similar idea.

The strength of the relationship between status consumption and materialism leads us to believe that any consumer showing high materialism will also show high tendency to consume for status. However, in the Tatzel matrix, although both have higher materialism, *Value-Seeker*s may be less likely to exhibit conspicuous consumption than do *Big-Spender*s. Status consumption relates negatively with value consciousness (Geiger-Oneto, Gelb, Walker, & Hess, 2013). Thus:

- **Hypothesis Two:** There exists a unique relationship between status consumption and ideal types such that status consumption will be a characteristic of the *Big-Spender*s category only.

Generosity

A characteristic of the *Experiencers*, consumers with low materialism and low frugality, according to Tatzel, is likely to be generosity. Belk (1985) considers "non-generosity" to be a trait of materialists whom he predicts are negatively predisposed towards charity. Mathur (2013) tests Belk's contention and finds that materialism does not preclude generosity, but has a more complicated relationship with giving. Web and Wong (2014) find no relationship between materialism and charitable giving in Singapore. From the opposite perspective, Gambrel and Cafaro (2010) see simplicity, similar to frugality, as going hand in hand with generosity. This position argues against *Experiencers* being generous. In the end, there is no consensus on how materialism and giving as a surrogate for generosity relate to each other. The materialism literature and Tatzel's model predict that:

- **Hypothesis Three:** Owing to their low materialism, *Non-Spenders* and *Experiencers* are more likely than other groups to be generous.

Brand Engagement With Self-Concept

Consumers use brands as symbols of their internal views of themselves (Fournier, 1998; Sprott, Czellar, & Spangenberg, 2009). This tendency argues that, for some consumers, branded goods have a greater meaning than simple utility. Essentially, the symbolic value of the brand to the consumer and to others can add value for consumers. Sprott *et al.* (2009), arguing that consumers vary in the extent to which they use brands to represent or enhance their self-concepts, developed a construct, Brand Engagement in Self-Concept (BESC), to measure consumers' individual differences. Sprott *et al.* (2009) define BESC as, "an individual difference representing consumers' propensity to include important brands as part of how they view themselves," (p. 92). BESC is positively related to materialism and negatively related to frugality (Goldsmith *et al.*, 2014; Flynn *et al.*, 2013).

Tatzel's (2002) categories can help to interpret the findings regarding BESC and to predict that the quadrants with high materialism, *i.e.*, *Value-Seeker*s and *Big-Spender*s, will both also show high BESC. However, this thinking is at odds with the basic premise of the four-category consumer matrix. Considering both money attitudes and materialism, one should be able to identify individuals who are uniquely different from those who are high or low in one or the other of the constructs. Tatzel (2002, 2014) makes this point indirectly by describing the characteristics of each of the four groups. Despite the more general findings that exist concerning BESC and materialism, and instead using Tatzel's original descriptions (2002), the next hypothesis states that *Big-Spender*s are the only group high in BESC. Essentially, frugality is expected to temper materialism in *Value-Seeker*s, thereby preventing shows of status; whereas *Big-Spender*s' tendency toward conspicuous consumption makes them the best candidates for higher BESC.

- **Hypothesis Four:** *Big-Spender*s will be high in BESC while the other three categories will be low in BESC.

Attitudes Towards Using Credit

Materialism goes hand-in-hand with spending money, and frugality is its opposite. It is not as easy to explain, however, how each group feels about money. For example, Garðarsdóttir and Dittmar (2012) show that materialists are both likely to spend more and are more likely to be worried about the potential outcomes of their heavy spending behavior. On the other hand, Richins (2011) shows only a marginal relationship between concern about overusing credit and materialism. Watson (1998) found that both higher debt and positive attitudes toward debt are associated with high materialism. Another study compares materialism and management of credit card balances and finds high materialism reduces the ability to manage credit card debt efficiently (Limbu, Huhmann, & Xu, 2012).

In general, consumers high in materialism are expected to have more debt than other consumers and to feel better about incurring debt as it helps them achieve their accumulation of possessions. The next hypothesis predicts that this greater affinity for debt will lead to a greater likelihood of problems with debt, and therefore greater worry about debt. Mapping these suppositions onto Tatzel's (2002) matrix suggests that only the *Big-Spenders* are likely to have difficulty with overuse of credit. The other high materialism group, the *Value-Seekers*, are predicted to be bargain shoppers and people who "save to spend" (Tatzel, 2014, p. 115) and who are therefore not as likely to have debt problems. Thus,

- **Hypothesis Five:** *Big-Spenders* will be high in credit overuse concern, while the other three categories will be low in credit overuse concern.

Low Spending

How much various consumers are likely to spend in the marketplace is of great interest to observers of consumer culture. Consumers who are low on materialism and tight with money are the classic frugal consumers. In the marketplace, these consumers simply shop and spend less across most categories. People who actively dislike shopping are more frugal than those who like shopping (Bove *et al.*, 2009). Frugal people are less likely to be compulsive shoppers (Lastovicka *et al.*, 1999) and have less personal debt (Nepomuceno & Laroche, 2015). These consumers live an abstemious lifestyle, and some are oriented to sustainable living (Albinsson *et al.*, 2010; Gambrel & Cafaro, 2010; Rose, Smith, & Segrist, 2010). Goldsmith *et al.* (2014) show that frugality is associated with lower materialism, lower status consciousness, lower brand involvement, and higher independence from the opinions of other consumers when it comes to consumer decision making.

Value-Seekers, with high materialism and high frugality, present a dilemma when predicting whether they will be low spenders. Tatzel (2002, p. 115) predicts that they will be bargain hunters and that they will "enjoy price comparison shopping." A predicted tendency towards more shopping leads the expectation that they will not be low spenders. *Value-Seekers* probably spend less than *Big-Spenders*, however, more shopping will also lead them to more spending (Bove *et al.*, 2009). Therefore:

- **Hypothesis Six:** *Non-Spenders* will be the only group who reflect a low spending orientation.

METHOD

Data Collection and Participants

Undergraduate business students at three universities in the Southeast US provided data. Since the purpose of the present study was to test the theory of Money Worlds and extend its scope, rather than to provide generalizable point and interval estimates to any specific population, the sample is acceptable. Additionally, college students were considered suitable subjects because the results permit direct comparison with thee prior empirical studies, which also used student subjects. After the three pertinent institutional review boards approved the questionnaire, it was subsequently loaded into the online survey system, Qualtrics, for administration. Students were recruited by class announcements or participation in student testing centers. E-mail invitations containing a link to the questionnaire were sent to participants. Subject compensation took the form of extra credit points.

Qualtrics yielded 1,129 cases, but 31 of these were blank, leaving 1,098 cases. This sample is larger than those in the prior studies (n = 266, 118, and 600, respectively) and thus provides sufficient statistical power to detect the hypothesized effects. The questionnaire contained three items scattered among the other scales worded "If you read this item, do not respond to it," to detect blind checking or random responding (Osborne & Blanchard, 2011). This process removed 82 survey participants who did respond to at least one of these items. An effective sample size of 1,016 remained, although selective missing data for age and gender reduced some individual analyses.

The sample consisted of 585 (58%) women and 430 (42%) men with 1 missing value for gender. Ages ranged from 18 years to 63 years, with a mean of 21 and median of 20, with 18 missing values. Age was highly skewed, with 95% of the sample between the ages of 18 and 24 (skewness = 6.0). Six hundred eighty-five (67%) of the sample was white, 157 (16%), was African American, 142 (14%) was Hispanic, with "other" accounting for 32 (3%).

Table 2. Scale items and factor loadings

Scale	Items
Materialism (Richins 2004)	I admire people who own expensive homes, cars, and clothes.
	The things I own say a lot about how well I'm doing in life.
	I like to own things that impress people.
	I try to keep my life simple, as far as possessions are concerned.
	Buying things gives me a lot of pleasure.
	I like a lot of luxury in my life.
	My life would be better if I owned certain things I don't have.
	I'd be happier if I could afford to buy more things.
	It sometimes bothers me quite a bit that I can't afford to buy all the things I'd like.
Frugality (Lastovicka *et al.*, 1999)	I believe in being careful in how I spend my money.
	I discipline myself to get the most from my money.
	If you take good care of your possessions, you will definitely save money in the long run.
	Making better use of my resources makes me feel good.
	There are many things that are normally thrown away that are still quite useful.
	There are things I resist buying today so I can save for tomorrow.
Price Sensitivity (Goldsmith, Flynn, & Kim, 2010)	I don't mind paying more to try out a product.
	I don't mind spending a lot of money to buy a new product.
	I am less willing to buy a product if I think that it will be high in price.
	I know that a product is likely to be more expensive than older ones, but that doesn't matter to me.
	A really great product is worth paying a lot of money for.

continued on following page

Table 2. Continued

Scale	Items
	In general, the price or cost of buying things is important to me.
Status Consumption (Eastman, Goldsmith, & Flynn, 1999)	A product is more valuable to me if it has some snob appeal.
	I am interested in new products with status.
	I would buy a product just because it has status.
	I would pay more for a product if it had status.
	The status of a product is irrelevant to me.
Generosity (Belk, 1985)	I enjoy having guests stay in my home.
	I enjoy sharing what I have.
	I don't like to lend things, even to good friends.
	It makes sense to buy a lawnmower with a neighbor and share it.
	I don't mind giving rides to those who don't have a car.
	I don't like to have anyone in my home when I am not there.
	I enjoy donating to charities.
Brand Engagement in Self-Concept (Sprott, Czellar, & Spangenberg, 2009)	I have a special bond with the brands that I like.
	I consider my favorite brands to be a part of myself.
	I often feel a personal connection between my brands and me.
	Part of me is defined by important brands in my life.
	I feel as if I have a close personal connection with the brands I most prefer.
	I can identify with important brands in my life.
	There are links between the brands that I prefer and how I view myself.
	My favorite brands are an important indication of who I am.
Debt Worry (Richins, 2011)	I worry about how I will pay off my credit card debt
	I am discouraged about the amount of money I own on my credit card bills
	I think a lot about my debts
	I am uncomfortable with the amount of debt I am in
	I worry about repaying my loans
Spending	In an average month, how much money would you estimate you spend online or in stores for things other than groceries?

Questionnaire and Measures

Previously published multi-item scales operationalized the constructs. Each scale used a five-point Agree/Disagree response format. Just as with Tatzel (2014), both the Richins (2004) three-factor, nine-item measure of materialism, and the (Lastovicka *et al.*, 1999) Frugality Scale to measure money dispositions appeared in the survey. The source and number of items in each scale appear in Table 2. The online questionnaire program was set to randomize the order in which each scale was presented to each participant. Programming also included random presentation of the individual items forming each scale. In addition to guaranteeing anonymity and confidentiality, this survey technique, using random scale and item presentation order, is recommended to control common method variance arising from using a similar method to operationalize variables (Chang *et al.*, 2010).

DATA ANALYSES AND RESULTS

Initial Data Analysis

Summation and coding of each scale assured that the total scale scores for each construct were in the positive direction, where higher scores represented higher levels for each construct. That is, higher scores indicate higher levels of price sensitivity, status consumption, generosity, brand engagement, debt worry, and spending. Descriptive statistics for the scales appear in Table 3, and correlations among the variables are shown in Table 4. Of the 21 correlations between the scaled variables, 14 were statistically significant ($p < .05$) and 7 were near .00. Many of these significant correlations are consistent with prior results, discussed above; hence, the presence of one-third of the possible outcomes at or near .00 suggests that common method variance did not artificially inflate the findings.

Cluster Analysis

Cluster analysis was applied to investigate whether empirical evidence supports Tatzel's classification of materialists and spending orientations into four groups. More specifically, K-means clustering was used to organize consumers into meaningful groups (or clusters) based on their average scores on both the materialism and the frugality scales. Although K-means clustering is not, properly speaking, a confirmatory data analysis procedure, in this case it was the best available method to assess whether Tatzel's four groups of consumers are inherently discoverable in the data. Moreover, it is not uncommon to see cluster analysis used in attempts to evaluate a previously established taxonomy. For example, Miller and Roth (1994) developed a three-cluster taxonomy of manufacturing strategies that was subsequently

Table 3. Descriptive statistics

Variable	n	Range	Mean	SD	Skewness	Kurtosis	Alpha
Materialism	1016	9-45	29.4	5.8	-0.187	0.204	0.81
Frugality	1016	7 – 35	28.5	3.4	-0.685	2.600	0.75
Price Sensitivity	1016	8-29	19.0	3.3	-0.134	0.260	0.69
Status Consumption	1016	5-25	14.1	3.8	-0.288	-0.404	0.82
Generosity	1016	11 – 35	23.9	3.8	-0.235	0.465	0.65
Brand Engagement	1016	8 – 40	24.4	6.6	-0.227	-0.260	0.92
Debt Worry	1016	5 – 25	12.7	5.0	0.240	-0.584	0.87
Spending	1014	1 – 9	4.4	2.5	0.545	-0.798	
Age	1000	18 - 63	21.1	3.9	6.000	44.00	

Table 4. Correlations between study variables

Variable	Mat	Frug	Price	Status	Gen	BESC	Debt	Spend	Age
Materialism	--								
Frugality	-.16**	--							
Price	-.26**	.31**	--						
Status	.51**	-.17**	-.30**	--					
Generosity	-.10**	0.05	-0.03	-0.06	--				
BESC	.39**	-.23**	-.23**	.37**	0	--			
Debt Worry	.11**	0	.06*	-0.01	0.02	.07*	--		
Spending	.23**	-.24**	-.28**	.20**	-0.03	.18**	-0.04	--	
Age	-.21**	0.01	0.04	-.15**	-0.05	-.07*	.12**	0.03	--
Gender	.07*	0.02	-.09**	.07*	-0.03	0.02	0.04	-0.04	0

Note: N = 1016 except for missing value for spending, age, and gender (where 0 = female and 1 = male).
** $p < .01$ * $p < .05$

re-examined using cluster analysis in other manufacturing (Frohlich & Dixon, 2001; Sum *et al.*, 2004) and service (Menor *et al.*, 2001) contexts. It is important to emphasize that a four-cluster solution was not imposed on the data. Instead, K-means clustering was applied for a range of different numbers of clusters, and statistical information was used to choose the best number of groups.

The overall fit of the theoretical model to the data was addressed by running 10,000 restarts of K-means clustering for each number of clusters (K) on the interval between 2 and 7. A large number of restarts of the algorithm from different random starting solutions mitigates the possibility of a poor local optimum from just a single restart. This has been shown to be extremely effective in simulation studies focusing on the recovery of cluster structure (Steinley & Brusco, 2007).

Once the best solution across 10,000 restarts was obtained for each value of K on the interval $2 \leq K \leq 7$, the selection of the number of clusters was made based on a Pseudo-R^2 index, which measures the proportion of variation in the clustering variables that is explained by the clustering process. More specifically, the total sum-of-squared variation in the data is decomposed into a between-cluster sum of squares (*i.e.*, variation explained by the clusters) and a within-cluster sum of squares (*i.e.*, unexplained variation within the clusters), where the Pseudo-R^2 index is the ratio of the between-cluster sum of squares to the total sum-of-squares. Although the Pseudo-R^2 index monotonically increases over the range of K, there was a relatively large increase when going from three to four clusters, but a rather small increase when going from four to five clusters. Accordingly, support for a K = 4-cluster solution is afforded by the index. For this reason, subsequent analyses focus on the four-cluster solution.

Interpreting the Clustering Solution

A summary of the four-cluster solution appears in Table 5. The largest cluster (n = 319) consisted of consumers who scored low on materialism and low on frugality. These consumers correspond well to Tatzel's description of *Experiencers* who spend for recreation, self-development, and services. The nature of the student sample might inflate the number of these consumers. The second largest cluster (n = 263) scored high on materialism and high on frugality. These appear to be Tatzel's *Value-Seekers*.

Table 5. Cluster Solution

Cluster Number	Mean Materialism	Mean Frugality
Cluster 1: n = 319 (*Value-Seekers*)		
Low materialism and low frugality	3.16	3.76
Cluster 2: n = 263 (*Experiencers*)		
High materialism and high frugality	3.48	4.51
Cluster 3: n = 223 (Non-Spenders)		
Low materialism and high frugality	2.41	4.28
Cluster 4: n = 211 (*Big-Spenders*)		
High materialism and low frugality	4.08	3.78
Mean for full sample	3.27	4.07
S.D. for full sample	0.64	0.49

The third largest cluster (n = 223) scored low on materialism but high on frugality. These are Tatzel's price-averse *Non-Spenders*. Finally, the smallest cluster (n = 211) scored high on materialism and low on frugality. These Tatzel *Big-Spenders* are loose with money and enjoy spending. They likely are the Super Consumers described by Flynn and Goldsmith (2015). In summary, the best solution derived from the cluster analyses is a four-group solution that compares favorably with Tatzel's theoretical model.

The Demographics of the Clusters

Because the participants were college undergraduates, comparing the four consumer groups in terms of the demographic variables (age, gender, race, and income) showed few significant differences. For instance, there was no statistically significant ($p < .05$) relationship between either gender and cluster membership or race and cluster membership. Likewise, comparing the self-reported income of the four clusters by means of a Kruskal-Wallis test also yielded a non-significant result. Finally, a one-way ANOVA, using cluster membership as the categorical independent variable and age as the metric dependent variable, did yield a statistically significant difference ($F_{(3, 996)} = 10.5, p < .001$). The mean age (22.3 years) of the "price-averse *Non-Spenders*" cluster was higher than that of the other three groups because that group contained the largest proportion of study participants age 25 and over.

Cluster Membership and Outcome Variables (Hypothesis Tests)

A one-way ANOVA was used to test for the predicted relationships between cluster membership and the outcome variables. The overall F tests were all statistically significant (3/1012 df, $p < .05$). Results of *post hoc* pairwise comparisons appear in Table 6 and Figure 1. A relatively clear pattern of differences emerges. With regard to the first outcome variable, price sensitivity, the results partially support H1: Price sensitivity is expected to be a characteristic of *Value-Seekers* and *Non-Spenders*, but uncharacteristic of *Big-Spenders*. In this case, the *Experiencers* also appear to be price sensitive. Regarding H2, "There exists a unique relationship between status consumption and ideal types such that status consumption will be a characteristic of the *Big-Spenders* category only," the *Big-Spenders* met expectations and scored higher

Table 6. Means of the outcome variables

Outcome	*Value-Seekers*	*Experiencers*	*Non-Spenders*	*Big-Spenders*	Eta²
	(n = 319)	(n = 263)	(n = 223)	(n = 211)	
Price Sensitivity	3.13[a]	3.25[b]	3.38[c]	2.93[d]	0.082
Status Consumption	2.78[a]	2.90[a]	2.29[b]	3.37[c]	0.216
Generosity	3.43[a]	3.47[a]	3.47[a]	3.29[b]	0.016
Brand Engagement	3.00[a]	3.07[a]	2.65[b]	3.50[c]	0.114
Debt Worry	2.49[a]	2.55[a]	2.44[a]	2.69[b]	0.008
Spending	4.61[a]	4.21[a]	3.48[b]	5.31[c]	0.063

Note: means with the same superscripts are not significantly different at $p < .05$ by a Bonferroni *post hoc* test.
Value-Seekers = low materialistic and low frugality
Experiencers = high materialism and high frugality
Non-Spenders= low materialism and high frugality
Big-Spenders = high materialism and low frugality

than the other consumer groups. For comparison, the *Non-Spenders* score the lowest, with *Value-Seekers* and *Experiencers* in between, showing that H2 is supported. As hypothesized in H3, the *Non-Spenders* and *Experiencers* score the highest on generosity. In this sample, the *Value-Seekers* are not far behind, but the *Big-Spenders* look much less generous than other consumers. Thus, while H3 is supported, the low internal consistency (.65) of this scale argues for additional testing of this construct using a more reliable operationalization to provide more rigorous tests. Hypothesis 4 predicted that *Big-Spenders* would be more brand engaged than other consumers, and data bears this out. *Big-Spenders* score much higher on this measure than the other groups, with *Non-Spenders* scoring the lowest. Hypothesis 5 proposed that *Big Spenders* would be more worried about their debts than the other groups would, and the data support H5 as well. All the other consumers are much less worried about debt than the *Big-Spenders*, with the *Non-Spenders* scoring the lowest on this scale. Finally, H6 proposed that the *Non-Spenders*, virtually by definition, would be the sole group with a low spending orientation, and this is shown in the data. Though *Big-Spenders* spend more, *Value-Seekers* and *Experiencers*, true to Tatzel's theory, are not averse to spending, if it gains them the outcomes they seek.

In the present analysis, clusters 1 and 2, which correspond to Tatzel's *Experiencers* and *Value-Seekers*, are less distinct. Both groups fall in the middle, between *Non-Spenders* and *Big-Spenders*, on price sensitivity, status consumption, BESC, attitude toward credit, and spending. Their scores are not significantly different from *Non-Spenders* on generosity or on debt worry. At the same time, the *Experiencers* and *Value-Seekers* score significantly differently from the *Big-Spenders* on all six of the outcome variables. In short, while a four-group solution fits the data, the first two groups, *Value-Seekers* and *Experiencers*, are alike on most of the outcome measures in this study.

Regression Results

In a final analysis, the researchers used hierarchical linear regression to see if the data yield results similar to that reported by Pham *et al.* (2012), Tatzel (2014), and Troisi *et al.* (2006). Thus, each outcome variable was regressed on materialism and frugality scores plus their interaction after mean centering. Detailed results appear in the Appendix (Table 7). To summarize the results, for no outcome variables

Figure 1. Means plots for outcome variables

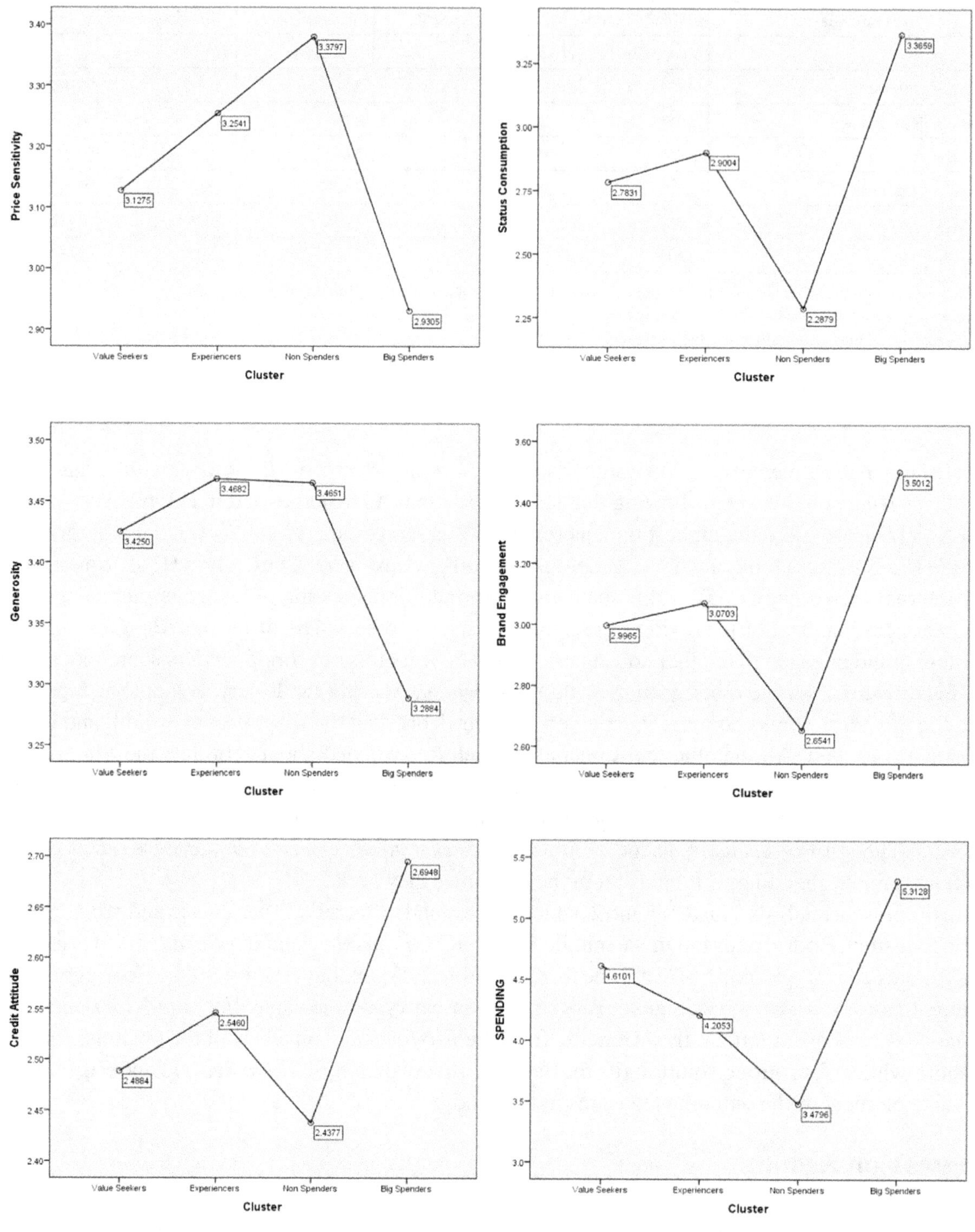

was the interaction statistically significant (*cf.*, Troisi *et al.*, 2006). Materialism related significantly to every outcome variable, while frugality was significant only for two: price sensitivity and spending. In a third step in the analysis (not shown) gender and age did not change these results, even when gender and age had their own independent relationships with the outcome variables.

DISCUSSION

This study has two objectives. The first, to test empirically the theoretical matrix proposed by Tatzel in 2002, to see if four groups actually appear as predicted. In doing so, it is the first test that uses cluster analysis to see if the predicted groups form. The goal is to tease apart materialistic and frugal tendencies to better explain primarily materialistic behavior, and also, possibly, to understand the seeming contradiction that both materialists and stingy people are less happy. The second objective compares the four categories using six outcome variables, some replicative and some new, to test the predictive value of the original model, thus providing new insights into this perspective on consumer culture.

While cluster analysis shows the existence of the four hypothesized quadrants, it is still not a perfect solution. Clusters 1 and 2, the *Experiencers* and the *Value-Seekers*, are not strongly distinct along the materialism dimension. While their materialism rankings mean that each group falls in the appropriate quadrants, the means are relatively closer than predicted by the theoretical model. The model predicts the *Experiencers* should have materialism scores similar to the *Non-Spenders*, and that the *Value-Seekers* should have materialism scores similar to the *Big-Spenders*. Instead, both the *Experiencers* and the *Value-Seekers* fall somewhere in between the other two clusters. This result is not too surprising considering that the concept developed by Tatzel (2002) is somewhat radical and at odds with the received view that is essentially dichotomous: materialistic or not and frugal or not. Tatzel notes that the *Value-Seekers* exist in a "state of conflict" (Tatzel, 2002, p. 116). Still, if the two positive/negative groups have different consumer behavior profiles, the model can be of value, and studies by Tatzel (2014) and Troisi *et al.* (2006), as well as the current study, do find evidence that these two middle groups differ in marketplace behavior from the other two groups.

This less than perfect finding could come from a number of issues. First, the measure of materialism is not a perfect measure. It has been shown to be marginally reliable (Goldsmith, Flynn & Clark, 2014; Richins and Dawson, 1992). Second, it is possible that Tatzel's theory itself somewhat misrepresents reality. The theory is stated in a very linear fashion but perhaps reality is not that simple. There could be a third factor that influences *Experiencers* and/or *Value-Seekers* beyond materialism and frugality. In, other words, perhaps the measure and model were not rich enough. It is also possibly the case that our sample was not diverse enough.

The researchers tested each of the four clusters against validated measures of five individual difference variables and one measure of spending. The results show that the *Non-Spender* and *Big-Spender* clusters have statistically different scores on all six of the outcome measures. These two clusters are different in the predicted directions on price sensitivity, status consumption, generosity, BESC, concern for credit use, and spending on items other than groceries. While this is good news, it does not really give any more information than just using either the materialism or the frugality measure alone. Both are essentially the mirror opposites of each other and these results only support that notion.

The two off diagonal clusters, the theoretically materialistic and frugal *Value-Seeker*s and the low materialism, non-frugal *Experiencers*, do not yield as close a fit with the model's predictions and fail to show much distinction from each other. The *Experiencers* and the *Value-Seeker*s do not statistically differ from each other on any of the six outcome variables. Tatzel (2002) predicts that the *Experiencers* should be more generous than the other quadrants. In the results, the only cluster that differs on that construct are the highly materialistic *Big-Spender*s, who are substantially less generous than the other three, confirming Belk's (1985) original conceptualization of materialists as non-generous. The two off diagonal clusters are also statistically the same as the *Non-Spenders* in terms of their concern for debt. Only the *Big-Spender*s are statistically higher in their concern about credit use. The *Big-Spender*s' high materialism and low frugality scores likely make them more vulnerable to overuse and thus worry about their credit situation.

The *Experiencers* and *Value-Seeker*s do show differences from the other two clusters on some outcome variables. *Value-Seeker*s and *Experiencers* are different from both *Non-Spenders* and *Big-Spender*s on the price sensitivity, status consumption, BESC and the spending measures. Therefore, clusters one and two stand apart from clusters three and four, but not from each other. Because neither group scores particularly high or low on materialism, they probably form separate clusters because of their differences on the F-scale.

What remains is a less than clear picture. While cluster analysis shows four distinct groups, the patterns of the outcome variables show what looks to be more like three groups. While the means of the outcome variables for clusters one and two all differ in the correct direction, not one of the differences is statistically significant. Given the large size of the sample, the test should be relatively robust. Perhaps a more age diverse sample might yield clearer results.

More than half of the sample of college students fall into clusters one and two, *Experiencers* and *Value-Seeker*s. The two clusters have somewhat mid-range materialism scores, and together make up the middle of the distribution of materialism scores. They might reflect more typical consumers than those at the top and bottom extremes of the materialism and frugality scales. They also show mid-range scores on each of the six outcome variables, with non-significant shadings of differences. At the same time, these two clusters are different from the other two on price sensitivity, status consumption, BESC, and spending. They are more price sensitive than the *Big-Spender*s, less likely to consume for status than the *Big-Spender*s, less brand engaged, and lower spenders. Additionally, the members of the sample who fall into the *Value-Seeker* quadrant do not respond exactly along the lines Tatzel (2002) predicts. Her theory has this group as price sensitive materialists. In the present sample, they were not statistically more price sensitive than the *Experiencers*, but rather fall between the *Big-Spender*s and *Non-Spenders*.

The results for the *Experiencers* category are a little different from what the model predicts. The cluster is quasi non-materialistic and not frugal. None of the outcome variables for the *Experiencers* is any different from those for the *Value-Seeker*s. Tatzel describes the *Experiencers* to be particularly generous as they are free with money and not materialistic. In the present study, the *Experiencers* are more generous than the *Big-Spender*s, but not statistically different from either of the other two groups. Tatzel also says that *Experiencers* might be debt prone due to their free spending. Again, the *Experiencers* are no different from the *Value-Seeker*s or *Non-Spenders* with regard to credit concern and different only from the *Big-Spender*s who have the most worries about their credit.

In terms of the outcome variables, the *Big-Spender*s, highest in materialism and lowest in frugality, are the most different. The scores on all six of the outcome measures put them into leagues of their own, as the least price sensitive, most likely to consume for status, least generous, most brand engaged, highest in worry about credit, and the biggest spenders. These findings hold clues about diminished happiness for materialists. People who give more to charity report being happier (Rosato, 2012), and people with more debt are less happy (Chancellor & Lyubomirsky, 2011).

On the other end of the spectrum are the *Non-Spenders*, who are frugal non-materialists. Some research argues that the most frugal people are less happy (McClure, 1984). In the present sample, the *Non-Spenders* report less frugality than the *Experiencers* report, but also have the lowest mean score on debt concern (though not significantly different from *Experiencers* and *Value-Seeker*s). The *Non-Spenders* are also even with *Experiencers* and *Value-Seeker*s on generosity, which is associated with happiness (Rosato, 2012). The *Non-Spenders* stand alone as the cluster that is most price sensitive, the least likely to consume for status, the least brand engaged, and the least reported actual spending.

The results are mostly consistent with those of the three previous tests of the model (Tatzel, 2014; Pham *et al.*, 2012; Troisi *et al.*, 2006). The earlier studies manage to distinguish between the two off diagonal groups only in openness to experience (for *Experiencers*) and price mavenism (for *Value-Seeker*s). The present study did not find that same distinction using a validated measure of price sensitivity. It appears as if the close materialism scores for these two groups make it difficult to find strong outcome differences between them. The lack of distinctiveness is even present when the study places subjects *a priori* into groups excluding those scoring in the middle of the scales (Tatzel, 2014; Troisi *et al.*, 2006). Perhaps a different measurement scale for materialism would help tease out effects. On the other hand, perhaps these two groups of consumers are very similar on these dimensions so that the differences are minor and of little consequence to the groups' actual marketplace behavior.

The practical significance of these findings lies in their reinforcement of earlier tests and their statistical support for the existence of four consumer archetypes. The blurriness of the two biggest groups, *Experiencers* and *Value-Seeker*s, is also worthwhile in that it encourages researchers to question the underlying theory. As long as researchers are putting subjects into *a priori* groups, they are stacking the deck in favor of supporting the theory. Our use of cluster analysis allows the data to show us, impartially, what is actually being revealed.

FUTURE RESEARCH DIRECTIONS

The study of luxury consumption purchases is a strong trend in academic and applied marketing research. The Money Worlds model could play a valuable part in segmenting the market for such goods. This paper extends the foundation of characteristics for each quadrant of the model. Future work should focus on extending our understanding of how consumers react, not only to luxury appeals, but also to bargain and deal appeals. As an example, it would be interesting to see how the *Value-Seeker*s would respond to a measure of deal-proneness or how the *Experiencers* shop for vacation packages.

CONCLUSION

The student sample and the absence of experimentation are limitations of this study. As the theory is presented, it does not specify any specific population of interest. Applying the theory in order to guarantee generalizable results to any specific population requires studies using samples from that population. That was not the goal of this study, which was theory-testing in orientation. Because we used a sample similar to those used in the previous tests, our results are comparable to theirs and generally support the theory. Had we found different results, they could have been interpreted as a strong challenge to the validity of the theory. Future studies using samples from different populations are required in order to replicate the findings of the existing studies and extend generalizability; and only the findings from experimental studies would evidence causal relationships.

One shortcoming in the study lies in the poor psychometric properties of the Generosity scale. Not only did it have the lowest internal consistency, factor analysis showed that it was not unidimensional. These defects might account for the inability of the scale to distinguish three of the groups from each other, although the *Big-Spender* group did score significantly lower than the other three groups as hypothesized.

The biggest difference between the present study and the previous ones were that it did not use *a priori* methods to assign consumers to the groups. It also did not leave out the middle groups on both frugality and materialism. In a separate analysis (not shown) if the cluster analysis does form two groups of *Value-Seeker*s and *Experiencers* using only the top and bottom thirds of the materialism and frugality scales, some differences do become statistically significant. Thus, the two groups likely exist, but as much smaller segments than when the whole ranges of scores are considered. As "ideal types," the *Value-Seeker*s and *Experiencers* likely do represent small groups of consumers at the extreme ends of the continua, that is, high on both materialism and frugality or low on both. Thus, Tatzel's fundamental insight is correct and the issue remains as to how large these groups of consumers really are. Moreover, other consumer behavior or personality variables might differently relate to the four clusters. For instance, non-conformity or self-monitoring, innovativeness or opinion leadership might distinguish between the *Value-Seeker*s and *Experiencers*. Even more consumption related and domain specific measures like fashion innovativeness or green consumption might be distinctive outcomes.

As always, more study is needed to learn the value and importance of the model. In general, consumer behavior is more complex than can be explained by one individual difference variables and Tatzel's model is valuable in that it uses two variables to enable examination of shades of differences in groups of consumers.

REFERENCES

Albinsson, P. A., Wolf, M., & Kopf, D. A. (2010). Anti-consumption in East Germany: Consumer resistance to hyperconsumption. *Journal of Consumer Behaviour*, *9*(6), 412–425. doi:10.1002/cb.333

Ang, C.-S., Mansor, A., & Tan, K.-A. (2014). Pangs of loneliness breed material lifestyle but do not power up life satisfaction of young people: The moderating effect of gender. *Social Indicators Research*, *117*(2), 353–365. doi:10.100711205-013-0349-0

Aroean, L., & Michaelidou, N. (2014). Are innovative consumers emotional and prestigiously sensitive to price? *Journal of Marketing Management, 30*(3/4), 245–267. doi:10.1080/0267257X.2013.811094

Bearden, W., & Haws, K. (2012). How low spending control harms consumers. *Journal of the Academy of Marketing Science, 40*(1), 181–193. doi:10.100711747-011-0282-1

Belk, R. W. (1985). Materialism: Trait aspects of living in the material world. *The Journal of Consumer Research, 12*(3), 265–280. doi:10.1086/208515

Bove, L. L., Nagpal, A., & Dorsett, A. S. (2009). Exploring the determinants of the frugal shopper. *Journal of Retailing and Consumer Services, 16*(4), 291–297. doi:10.1016/j.jretconser.2009.02.004

Chan, K., & Prendergast, G. P. (2008). Social comparison, imitation of celebrity models and materialism among Chinese youth. *International Journal of Advertising, 27*(5), 799–826. doi:10.2501/S026504870808030X

Chancellor, J., & Lyubomirsky, S. (2011). Happiness and thrift: When (spending) less is (hedonically) more. *Journal of Consumer Psychology, 21*(2), 131–138. doi:10.1016/j.jcps.2011.02.004

Chang, S. J., van Witteloostuijn, A., & Eden, L. (2010). From the editors: common method variance in international business research. Journal of International Business Studies, 41(2), 178-184.

Chatterjee, A., & Hunt, J. M. (1996). Self-monitoring as a personality correlate of materialism: An investigation of related cognitive. *Psychological Reports, 79*(2), 523–528. doi:10.2466/pr0.1996.79.2.523

Cryder, C. E., Lerner, J. S., Gross, J. J., & Dahl, R. E. (2008). Misery is not miserly: Sad and self-focused individuals spend more. *Psychological Science, 19*(6), 525–530. doi:10.1111/j.1467-9280.2008.02118.x PMID:18578840

Dittmar, H., Bond, R., Hurst, M., & Kasser, T. (2014). The relationship between materialism and personal well-being: A meta-analysis. *Journal of Personality and Social Psychology, 107*(5), 879–924. doi:10.1037/a0037409 PMID:25347131

Eastman, J. K., Goldsmith, R. E., & Flynn, L. R. (1999). Status consumption in consumer behavior: Scale development and validation. *Journal of Marketing Theory and Practice, 7*(3), 41–51. doi:10.1080/10696679.1999.11501839

Eastman, J. K., & Iyer, R. (2012). The relationship between cognitive age and status consumption: An exploratory look. *The Marketing Management Journal, 22*(1), 80–96.

Fitzmaurice, J., & Comegys, C. (2006). Materialism and social consumption. *Journal of Marketing Theory and Practice, 14*(4), 287–299. doi:10.2753/MTP1069-6679140403

Flynn, L. R., & Goldsmith, R. E. (2015). Introducing the super consumer. *Journal of Consumer Behaviour, 15*(3), 201–207. doi:10.1002/cb.1535

Flynn, L. R., Goldsmith, R. E., & Kim, W.-M. (2000). A cross-cultural validation of three new marketing scales for fashion research: Involvement, opinion seeking, and knowledge. *Journal of Fashion Marketing and Management, 4*(2), 110–120. doi:10.1108/eb022583

Flynn, L. R., Goldsmith, R. E., & Kim, W.-M. (2013). A cross-cultural study of materialism and brand engagement. *Journal of Multi-Disciplinary Studies*, *5*(3), 49–69.

Flynn, L. R., Goldsmith, R. E., & Pollitte, W. (2016). Materialism, status consumption, and market involved consumers. *Psychology and Marketing*, *33*(9), 761–776. doi:10.1002/mar.20915

Fournier, S. (1998). Consumers and their brands: Developing relationship theory in consumer research. *The Journal of Consumer Research*, *24*(4), 343–373. doi:10.1086/209515

Frohlich, M. T., & Dixon, J. R. (2001). A taxonomy of manufacturing strategies revisited. *Journal of Operations Management*, *19*(5), 541–558. doi:10.1016/S0272-6963(01)00063-8

Frost, R. O., Kyrios, M., McCarthy, K. D., & Matthews, Y. (2007). Self-ambivalence and attachment to possessions. *Journal of Cognitive Psychotherapy*, *21*(3), 232–242. doi:10.1891/088983907781494582

Gambrel, J. C., & Cafaro, P. (2010). The virtue of simplicity. *Journal of Agricultural & Environmental Ethics*, *23*(1/2), 85–108. doi:10.100710806-009-9187-0

Garðarsdóttir, R. B., & Dittmar, H. (2012). The relationship of materialism to debt and financial well-being: The case of Iceland's perceived prosperity. *Journal of Economic Psychology*, *33*(3), 471–481. doi:10.1016/j.joep.2011.12.008

Geiger-Oneto, S., Gelb, B. D., Walker, D., & Hess, J. D. (2013). 'Buying status' by choosing or rejecting luxury brands and their counterfeits. *Journal of the Academy of Marketing Science*, *41*(3), 357–372. doi:10.100711747-012-0314-5

Goldsmith, R. E., Flynn, L. R., & Clark, R. A. (2014). The etiology of the frugal consumer. *Journal of Retailing and Consumer Services*, *21*(2), 175–184. doi:10.1016/j.jretconser.2013.11.005

Goldsmith, R. E., Flynn, L. R., & Kim, D. (2010). Status consumption and price sensitivity. *Journal of Marketing Theory and Practice*, *18*(4), 323–338. doi:10.2753/MTP1069-6679180402

González-Benito, Ó., Martos-Partal, M., & Fustinoni-Venturini, M. (2014). Retailers' price positioning and the motivational profiling of store-brand shoppers: The case of Spain. *Psychology and Marketing*, *31*(2), 115–125. doi:10.1002/mar.20680

Handa, M., & Khare, A. (2013). Gender as a moderator of the relationship between materialism and fashion clothing involvement among Indian youth. *International Journal of Consumer Studies*, *37*(1), 112–120. doi:10.1111/j.1470-6431.2011.01057.x

Hur, Y.-M., Jeong, H.-U., Schermer, J. A., & Rushton, J. P. (2011). Miserliness is heritable. *Personality and Individual Differences*, *51*(8), 1052–1055. doi:10.1016/j.paid.2011.08.005

Kasser, T. (2002). *The high price of materialism*. Cambridge, MA: The MIT Press.

Kasser, T., & Ahuvia, A. (2002). Materialistic values and well-being in business students. *European Journal of Social Psychology*, *32*(1), 137–146. doi:10.1002/ejsp.85

Kilsheimer, J. C. (1993). *Status consumption: The development and implications of a scale measuring the motivation to consume for status* (PhD Dissertation). Florida State University.

Kim, B.-D., & Rossi, P. E. (1994). Purchase frequency, sample selection, and price sensitivity: The heavy-user bias. *Marketing Letters*, *5*(1), 57–67. doi:10.1007/BF00993958

Lastovicka, J. L., Bettencourt, L. A., Hughner, R. S., & Kuntze, R. J. (1999). Lifestyle of the tight and frugal: Theory and measurement. *The Journal of Consumer Research*, *26*(1), 85–98. doi:10.1086/209552

Liao, J., & Wang, L. (2009). Face as a mediator of the relationship between material value and brand consciousness. *Psychology and Marketing*, *26*(11), 987–1001. doi:10.1002/mar.20309

Limbu, Y. B., Huhmann, B. A., & Xu, B. (2012). Are college students at greater risk of credit card abuse? Age, gender, materialism and parental influence on consumer response to credit cards. *Journal of Financial Services Marketing*, *17*(2), 148–162. doi:10.1057/fsm.2012.9

Martínez, E., & Montaner, T. (2008). Characterization of Spanish store brand consumers. *International Journal of Retail & Distribution Management*, *36*(4), 477–493. doi:10.1108/09590550810873947

Mathur, A. (2013). Materialism and charitable giving: Can they co-exist? *Journal of Consumer Behaviour*, *12*(3), 149–158. doi:10.1002/cb.1404

McClure, R. F. (1984). The relationship between money attitudes and overall pathology. *Psychology: A Quarterly Journal of Human Behavior*, *21*(1), 4–6.

Menor, L. J., Roth, A. V., & Mason, C. H. (2001). Agility in retail banking: A numerical taxonomy of strategic service groups. *Manufacturing & Service Operations Management: M & SOM*, *3*(4), 273–292. doi:10.1287/msom.3.4.273.9969

Miller, J. G., & Roth, A. V. (1994). A taxonomy of manufacturing strategies. *Management Science*, *40*(3), 285–304. doi:10.1287/mnsc.40.3.285

Nepomuceno, M. V., & Laroche, M. (2015). The impact of materialism and anti-consumption lifestyles on personal debt and account balances. *Journal of Business Research*, *68*(3), 654–664. doi:10.1016/j.jbusres.2014.08.006

Osborne, J. W., & Blanchard, M. R. (2011). Random responding from participants is a threat to the validity of social science research results. *Frontiers in Psychology*, *1*, 1–7. doi:10.3389/fpsyg.2010.00220 PMID:21833275

Ostrovskaya, L., & Sarabia-Sánchez, F. (2013). Effect of materialism on the use of the brand name in purchasing decisions from a cross-cultural perspective. *Esic Market Economic and Business Journal*, *44*(1), 91–115. doi:10.7200/esicm.144.0441.3i

Parotta, J. L., & Johnson, P. J. (1998). The impact of financial attitudes and knowledge on financial management and satisfaction of recently married individuals. *Financial Counseling and Planning*, *9*(2), 59–75.

Pepper, M., Jackson, T., & Uzzell, D. (2009). An examination of the values that motivate socially conscious and frugal consumer behaviours. *International Journal of Consumer Studies*, *33*(2), 126–136. doi:10.1111/j.1470-6431.2009.00753.x

Pham, T. H., Yap, K., & Dowling, N. A. (2012). The impact of financial management practices and financial attitudes on the relationship between materialism and compulsive buying. *Journal of Economic Psychology*, *33*(3), 461–470. doi:10.1016/j.joep.2011.12.007

Podoshen, J. S., & Andrzejewski, S. A. (2012). An examination of the relationships between materialism, conspicuous consumption, impulse buying, and brand loyalty. *Journal of Marketing Theory and Practice*, *20*(3), 319–334. doi:10.2753/MTP1069-6679200306

Richins, M. L. (2004). The Material Values Scale: Measurement properties and development of a short form. *The Journal of Consumer Research*, *31*(1), 209–219. doi:10.1086/383436

Richins, M. L. (2011). Materialism, transformation expectations, and spending: Implications for credit use. *Journal of Public Policy & Marketing*, *30*(2), 141–156. doi:10.1509/jppm.30.2.141

Richins, M. L., & Dawson, S. (1992). A consumer values orientation for materialism and its measurement: Scale development and validation. *The Journal of Consumer Research*, *19*(3), 303–316. doi:10.1086/209304

Rick, S. I., Cryder, C. E., & Loewenstein, G. (2008). Tightwads and spendthrifts. *The Journal of Consumer Research*, *34*(6), 767–782. doi:10.1086/523285

Rosato, D. (2012, January). Get happy in 2012. *Money,* 14-15.

Rose, P., Smith, S. T., & Segrist, D. J. (2010). Too cheap to chug: Frugality as a buffer against college-student drinking. *Journal of Consumer Behaviour*, *9*(3), 228–238. doi:10.1002/cb.314

Ryan, T. (2012). What is the new normal? *Retailwire*. Retrieved May 15, 2018, from http://www.retailwire.com/discussion/16192/what-is-the-new-normal

Schindler, R. M., Lala, V., & Corcoran, C. (2014). Intergenerational influence in consumer deal proneness. *Psychology and Marketing*, *31*(5), 307–320. doi:10.1002/mar.20696

Schroeder, J. E., & Dugal, S. (1995). Psychological correlates of the materialism construct. *Journal of Social Behavior and Personality*, *10*(1), 243–253.

Sprott, D., Czellar, S., & Spangenberg, E. (2009). The importance of a general measure of brand engagement on market behavior: Development and validation of a scale. *JMR, Journal of Marketing Research*, *46*(1), 92–104. doi:10.1509/jmkr.46.1.92

Steinley, D., & Brusco, M. J. (2007). Initializing K-means batch clustering: A critical analysis of several techniques. *Journal of Classification*, *24*(1), 99–121. doi:10.100700357-007-0003-0

Sum, C.-C., Kow, L. S.-J., & Chen, C.-S. (2004). A taxonomy of operations strategies of high performing small and medium enterprises in Singapore. *International Journal of Operations & Production Management*, *24*(3), 321–345. doi:10.1108/01443570410519051

Tatzel, M. (2002). 'Money worlds' and well-being: An integration of money dispositions, materialism and price-related behavior. *Journal of Economic Psychology*, *23*(1), 103–126. doi:10.1016/S0167-4870(01)00069-1

Tatzel, M. (2003). The art of buying: Coming to terms with money and materialism. *Journal of Happiness Studies*, *4*(4), 405–435. doi:10.1023/B:JOHS.0000005770.92248.77

Tatzel, M. (2014). Value-seekers, big-spenders, non-spenders, and experiencers: Consumption, personality, and well-being. In M. Tatzel (Ed.), Consumption and well-being in the material world (pp. 75-108). Dordrecht, The Netherlands: Springer.

Terrero, R. (2007). Ultra-luxe Travel Trends. *Travel Agent*, *329*(11), 8.

Troisi, J. D., Christopher, A. N., & Marek, P. (2006). Materialism and money spending disposition as predictors of economic and personality variables. *North American Journal of Psychology*, *8*(3), 421–436.

Üstüner, T., & Holt, D. B. (2014). Toward a theory of status consumption in less industrialized countries. *The Journal of Consumer Research*, *37*(1), S248–S267.

Walther, C. S., & Sandlin, J. A. (2013). Green capital and social reproduction within families practicing voluntary simplicity in the US. *International Journal of Consumer Studies*, *37*(1), 36–45. doi:10.1111/j.1470-6431.2011.01050.x

Wang, J., & Wallendorf, M. (2006). Materialism, status signaling, and product satisfaction. *Journal of the Academy of Marketing Science*, *34*(4), 494–505. doi:10.1177/0092070306289291

Watson, J. J. (1998). Materialism and debt: A study of current attitudes and behaviors. *Advances in Consumer Research. Association for Consumer Research (U. S.)*, *25*(1), 203–207.

Webb, D., & Wong, J. (2014). Exploring antecedents of charitable giving and their impact on subjective well-being in Singapore. *Social Indicators Research*, *117*(1), 65–87. doi:10.100711205-013-0331-x

Wikipedia. (2018). *Bill Gates's House*. Retrieved from https://en.wikipedia.org/wiki/Bill_Gates%27s_house

KEY TERMS AND DEFINITIONS

Brand Engagement in Self-Concept: A consumer trait describing how important brands and brand images are to how consumers view their own identities; the symbolic value of the brand.

Cluster Analysis: A statistical procedure that sorts data into groups based on the similarities among the variables.

Generosity: Often regarded as a social virtue and referring to the giving of time, money, or possessions to others with no expectation of reciprocity.

Price Sensitivity: A consumer trait describing how strongly consumers react to high or low prices and to price changes.

Tatzel: Miriam Tatzel is a psychologist who developed the theory of "money worlds" describing subtle differences in spending patterns that define four unique groups of consumers.

Typology: A classification of individuals into mutually exclusive groups.

Wellbeing: The various aspects of life related to quality of life, which can range from positive to negative.

APPENDIX

Table 7. Hierarchical regression analyses predicting outcome variables

Price Sensitivity	B	β	R^2	$R^2_{Adj.}$	ΔR^2
Step 1					
Materialism	-0.122	-.216*			
Frugality	0.266	.278*	0.142	0.141	
Step 2					
Materialism	-0.121	-.215*			
Frugality	0.267	.279*			
Interaction	-0.002	-0.015	0.143	0.140	0.000
Status Consumption	**B**	**β**	R^2	$R^2_{Adj.}$	ΔR^2
Step 1					
Materialism	0.325	.492*			
Frugality	-0.105	-0.094	0.265	0.264	
Step 2					
Materialism	0.326	.493*			
Frugality	-0.103	-0.092			
Interaction	-0.003	-0.019	0.266	0.263	0.000
Generosity	**B**	**β**	R^2	$R^2_{Adj.}$	ΔR^2
Step 1					
Materialism	-0.063	-.095*			
Frugality	0.040	0.035	0.011	0.011	
Step 2					
Materialism	-0.065	-.098*			
Frugality	0.034	0.030			
Interaction	0.009	0.055	0.014	0.003	
Brand Engagement	**B**	**β**	R^2	$R^2_{Adj.}$	ΔR^2
Step 1					
Materialism	0.443	.387*			
Frugality	-0.049	-0.025	0.153	0.152	
Step 2					
Materialism	0.443	.387*			
Frugality	-0.049	-0.025			
Interaction	-0.001	-0.002	0.153	0.151	0.000

continued on following page

Table 7. Continued

Credit Card Worry	B	β	R^2	$R^2_{Adj.}$	ΔR^2
Step 1					
Materialism	0.098	.113*			
Frugality	0.030	0.021	0.012	0.010	
Step 2					
Materialism	0.098	.112*			
Frugality	0.029	0.020			
Interaction	0.002	0.011	0.013	0.010	0.000
Spending	**B**	**β**	R^2	$R^2_{Adj.}$	ΔR^2
Step 1					
Materialism	0.083	.194*			
Frugality	-0.153	-.206*	0.094	0.092	
Step 2					
Materialism	0.084	.195*			
Frugality	-0.151	-.204*			
Interaction	-0.001	-0.013	0.094	0.091	0.000

Chapter 6
Youth Consumer Practices and Social Alienation

John Graham Wilson
Assumption University of Thailand, Thailand

ABSTRACT

This chapter argues that traditional institutions (education and the family) have lost their influence, and consequently, among youth, there is a marked presence of deficiencies in their lives. As the main focus of society, mass-consumerism is implicated as a wide-ranging source of manipulation involving the consumption behavior of the young. How much independence-seeking subcultural groups can claim independence from the prevailing wider culture is explored. Many diverse sociological persuasions are examined in the search for workable explanations to account for the phenomenon of youth alienation in the Western world.

INTRODUCTION

Elusive and evasive, yet often blatant and malign, youth alienation seems to crop up inside every classroom, under every family roof, and wandering loose and aimless in shopping malls and precincts in every town. It is a source of much bewilderment amongst parents and educators. Indefinite yet familiar, the aberrant behaviour of youth evades precise sociological descriptions; but, in its worst violent manifestations, goes as far as to provoke moral panic (McRobbie & Thornton, 1995).

Within an attempted explanation, excessive consumerism is much criticised as a contagious, divisive, socially transmitted disease disrupting society, damaging relations inside the family and community (De Graaf et al., 2005; Schor, 2008). In the case of youth alienation, the young are the current descendants of this curious phenomenon throughout Western culture. So, how does youth alienation connect with widespread consumerism?

This paper try trying to pin down the concept of youth alienation as it occurs in localisable spaces and accumulates over specific stages, whereby a media-dominated consumer culture recruits young people into an individualistic, private, consumer-led lifestyle that simultaneously eschews association with other people in a society that was once supported by 20th century community values, thus depleting the

DOI: 10.4018/978-1-5225-6120-0.ch006

general sensation of belonging to a human association of individuals, as part of a once-cohesive society with coherent aims and community values shared by all. It will be argued that traditional institutions (education and the family) have been emarginated, and have lost their influence in terms of helping to establish a secure and durable sense of identity for youth. In particular, this occurs where there is a presence of significant deficiencies in individuals' lives. This is often expressed in terms of powerlessness, meaninglessness, normlessness and estrangement within the family, at school and amongst peers. Today, there is far less consideration than there was for providing affection, protection, concern and support for the young—they are often forced to look to themselves. But, as a special focus, how mass-consumerism is implicated as a wide-ranging source of manipulation and control will be considered. Has youth alienation occurred unprompted? Is it a spontaneous phenomenon? Defying explanation, as some kind of causeless condition in the midst of bewilderingly accelerated social change? Does it have any relation to the ongoing parallels of overwork, greed and narcissism in the wider economy? It will be argued that it does have causes and these can be detected in the wider world.

Consideration will also be given to how much independence-seeking subcultural collectives – the peer group – amidst often inarticulate forms of rebellion, can genuinely claim independence from the prevailing wider culture. What kind of impact has marketing research made upon youth as consumers of fashion and fads? How has youth culture been specifically targeted by researchers, and marketing strategists who seek to harvest the expanding youth market?

A SENSE OF NOT BELONGING

Powerlessness, Meaninglessness, Normlessness, and Estrangement Within Family, School, and Peers

It is well known that the weakening of institutional control leaves today's populations far freer to enjoy leisure time, seek out a variety of entertainments, and, for youth, cultivate lifestyles that seem to counter the values of the surrounding adult culture (Giddens, 1991). Recently, the emergence of commercially influenced youth cultures, makes analysis of the peer group especially salient regarding the life of young people. Social changes that have occurred in the last fifty years, have remodelled relations of influence, from stable institutions such as the family and school, to an increasingly intrusive, one-way domination through ubiquitous media communication. There are ever-increasing mass media marketing methods for influencing the young. Do their rebellious tendencies of youth avoid undue influence, or are they easily managed – perhaps even cloned – to reproduce consumption-driven outlooks and behaviour?

Schultz and Rubel (2011) note that there is insufficient qualitative research on adolescent alienation and, in particular, not much in print that represents the astute detections of the young people themselves. Their voices need to be heard and their experiences better understood. The inseparability of discourses, institutions and cultural practices need to be understood as well as a more holistic understanding of youth, perhaps explained in terms of Foucault's subjugated knowledges (Foucault, 1980) and grounded in an intimate knowledge of local peer-group discourse fields, the subject's own experiences and a more particularised understanding (Hartman, 2000).

According to Erikson and Erikson (1998), youth is the period when ideals and identities are formed, where the transition from youth to adulthood is still precarious, with much adaptation and backtracking along the way. Emargination (mostly from family and school) that often characterises contemporary adolescent alienation and the role that a ubiquitous consumer society, with its widespread corporate practices and values, plays in the absence of old moral certainties is the focus of this paper. Alienation is a term often used without a clear definition but it is evident when an individual experiences "the big four:" *powerlessness, meaninglessness, normlessness and estrangement* (see Brown *et al.*, 2003) principally within another "big three"; the tripartite relationship of *family, school and peers*.

The psychological sciences still consider adolescence to be a stage to be passed through where a fragile cognitive and emotional development takes place amidst episodes of emotional squalls and non-cooperation (Besley, 2009; Erikson & Erikson, 1998). As a result, attention is given, often in psychoanalytic form, to the focus on individual adolescent problems concerning a minority who do not live up to expected norms. Many writers regard such problems to be individually based, but others think society itself may be the major contributor. Many contend the resultant alienation is inadvertently blamed on the victim instead of revealing how social change could be attributed to explain disaffection, especially where self and identity has become such a problem on a larger scale (Baudrillard & Petit, 1998; Baumeister, 1987; Besley, 2009; Featherstone, 2007; Geertz, 1973; Giddens, 1991).

Rebelliousness, as a core indicator for alienation, reveals an insistence on separation, a reaction against powerlessness, often occurring in adolescence to reveal a quasi-organised force such as sabotage behaviours in the classroom and uncooperative attitudes at home. But subversion of elders' power could just be a veiled attempt to defeat their existing authority, frequently imbued with defenceless, hypocritical self-justifications of their own. In a similar vein, localised dissidence could take on the appearance of a social critique rather than simple on-the-fly opposition, and yet, though sometimes skilfully articulate, rarely presents a coherent or developed plan, let alone the mark of an incipient counter-ideology (Brady, 2017). Frequent oppositional strategies are employed at school to disrupt classroom procedures (Klein & Sawchuk, 2000).

Brady (2017) maintains that subversiveness contains an essential questioning dimension whereby disillusioned adolescents can demonstrate their antagonism towards an authority that has lost its veneer, and that some of these behaviours are an unconscious effort to provoke an improved system of responses. Adult conventions are seen to be promoted primarily for their own convenience, involving a superficial conformity not good enough to satisfy young critical minds (Brady, 2017). But, at present, 'subversion' may be too strong a word when consumerist ideology permeates a collective so thoroughly as an influence on active consumption behaviour. For several decades, marketers have become aware that the teenage market is an increasingly profitable sector and all kinds of strategies have evolved to capture the teen market and apply new forms of conventionality (see especially, Klein & Sawchuk, 2000).[1]

To what extent are adolescents aware of their place within the social world? A personal sense of agency, if applied inside contexts free of surveillance and control, encourages the notion that adolescents are actors who interpret the social world they live in and determine, in each micro-situation, their own particular responses. When feeling marginalized or undervalued, there can be an intuitive reaction against institutionalized power provoking spontaneous reactions aiming at a retrieval of freedom, plus a reclaimed, individualized sense of identity without necessarily occurring as conceptually polished, or even verbalised (as an example of 'thetic awareness'). At the same time, there is an expectation that identity will be at least partially constructed through consumer practices in which buyers will engage, often observed through eye-catching appearances and fashion accessories (Blackman & Kempson, 2016; Neubauer & Hurrelmann, 1995). Moreover,

Mainstream commercial discourse constructs identities that are not only compatible with capitalist relations of production but also enable the re-production of such relations of power and imagery in social and cultural life (Wearing, 2003, p. 4).

To what extent is any *authentic* individualism being realised, however?

School Violence, Shootings, Exclusion From Peer Group

Some of the worst cases of youth estrangement involve inexplicable outbursts of violence, as in school shooting incidents. Frymer (2009) analyses media coverage of the 1999 Columbine shootings, revealing an alien youth that no longer remotely shares the values of previous generations. Analysis of the Columbine story reveals an extensive assemblage of wild threats and coercions, emanating from the very lifeworlds of formerly inoffensive white U.S. youth. These lifeworlds become more comprehensible in terms of a specific distancing from families, parents and schools; in fact, all major institutions within the prevailing culture of U.S. life (Collins & Yeskel, 2011; Frymer, 2009). Such behaviour is a part of the list of four: *estrangement*.

One theory proposes that the feeling of exclusion by mainstream society leads young people to reject the societal norms that generally inhibit aggressive reactions thereby releasing impulsive and instinctual tendencies to fight back against specific antagonists (and not just against other people in general) (see Twenge, Baumeister, Tice, & Stucke, 2001; Reijntjes *et al.*, 2010). This highlights the amoral implications of the third determinant: *normlessness*. For revenge is an activity that can be recognised as fairly normative, but what is surprising is the extremity of the actions undertaken as a soon demonstrably clear instance of narcissistic injury. (The shooters had been extensively belittled and abused by their peers.)

In the following paragraphs the idea of a marketed rebellion, expressing "peacocky" antipathy, and encouraging narcissism, amidst an increasing amount of peer dependence where status is created amongst ones local associates; one that seeks to provide substitute meanings and values during adult-free deviant leisure time; where, amidst a dearth of active roles in the prevailing society, school, as a once-promoted enterprise of promoting equality, fails to stem dissatisfaction running between aspiration and personal goals will be considered. Where, as a substitute, marketing strategies employ devious "Trojan horse" methods of promoting "cool capitalism" via advertising that seeks conversion from within, employing the "chic of the forbidden" amidst a widespread perennial penchant for shallow living.

Narcissism and Narcissistic Rage

Narcissism overspills into fury when the peer group (the only lingering social group that can effectively bestow approval) withdraws its endorsement of a young person's value. Narcissistic rage is a reaction to narcissistic injury, which is a powerful threat to a narcissist's self-worth. Narcissistic injury (or narcissistic scar) was a phrase first used by Sigmund Freud (1914). The term, as used by later theorists, resides on a continuum from instances of aloofness and the expression of mild irritation or annoyance, to serious outbursts aimed at others, including violent attacks (consider the phenomenon of road-rage).

Narcissistic rage reactions are not always recognised according to the standardised DSM descriptions and may, therefore, escape detection by psychologists. It has also been suggested that narcissists have two distinct types of rancour: the first layer can be thought of as a persistent anger (specifically towards someone else), with another layer being a wrath aimed at oneself due to semi-unconscious acts of self-condemnation (Malmquist, 2007).

Schools are increasingly highlighted as centres of violence. The amok man (a Malaysian word) is oblivious to his surroundings and 'runs amok' on a rampage of indiscriminate destruction, lashing out and killing whoever he might meet. Amok behavior is mostly triggered by an idea that has humiliated the proponent, whose life has been shattered by an intolerable insult witnessed in public by the local society in which he/she lives. The amok runner hopes to reverse the insult and rehabilitate his/her name by acts of destruction (Kellner, 2015). Similarly, school shooters having run amok later complain about having been bullied and harassed by dominant alpha males in school themselves, in turn, reacting with pathological intensity (Kellner, 2015).

The popular press often treat these events as media spectacles and whip up further moral panic through 'packaging and promotion' to lengthen the attention of media spectators for a profitable period. Few of these periodicals endeavour to find the root causes for such behaviours, but

We believe that the escalation of rape, weapon rampages, and teenage alienation in white, middle-class enclaves, especially school sites, is directly attributable to the growing rejection by students of the materialistic and dehumanizing culture that bore them (Smith et al., 2003, p. 35).

The Role of Deviant Leisure

According to Eriksonian sociological theory, during the transition from childhood to adulthood, adolescents are expected to leave behind the sanctuary of freedom and pleasures that accompany childhood and conventionally move into a comprehension and adoption of the rights, responsibilities, values, and opportunities that accompany adulthood (Erikson, 1994) Subversion is an important part of the adolescent maturation process because it renegotiates the boundaries of relationships and cedes the centre of gravity onto a subsequent generation (Brady, 2017). But it may be that this transition, has more often been disenabled by a manifold process of gradual alienation, and maladaptive coping mechanisms, whereby the young person will look for substitute diversionary activities that satisfy immediate and more pressing desires. Music, concert-going, appearance fashion, mind-altering substances, may offer hedonistic and fun-loving aspects of being "cool."

But it is not only amongst peers that current youth discovers rancour. Another noticeable and extreme expression of adolescent reactions against the power of others takes place in deviant leisure activities that flirt with loose behaviour, danger and illegality (consistent with the aforesaid notion of *normlessness*). The meaning of deviancy, amongst commentators, however, seems rather flexible, ranging from insignificant unconventionality to breaking the law (Glover, 2003; Gordon & Caltabiano, 1996; Mahoney & Stattin, 2000; Rojek, 1999; Trainor *et al.*, 2010; Wearing, 2003).

Agency, if applied in the context of youth, suggests that adolescents are social actors who interpret social situations and actively determine, in each setting, their own responses to these situations. Resistance is a struggle against institutionalized power and it is only possible under conditions of relative freedom (Glover, 2003, p. 310). Deviancy may occur in settings as banal as deliberately breaking the speed limit, jay-walking, engaging in acts of trespass, bending or sending up axioms and mores of collective life through conversation, comedy and dramatic entertainment (Rojek, 1999, p. 162).

How can this be described as leisure? The very notion of leisure entails relaxation of institutional control, or work norms, with obligations to conform. In a location where one is free to be oneself, freedom of expression and experimentation with dicey ideas and contrary values comes to the fore with like-minded experimenters associating in the same age group (Constantinople, 1969). Contrastive outlooks and behaviours can take on the appearance of antisocial behaviour, putatively, simply by comparison with the adult hegemony (Glover, 2003). Many goings-on embody the idea of deviance when experimentation flirts with chancy and unlawful activities, the very appeal of these activities being raucous, extravagant, sensational and enticing (Rojek, 1999). Obviously, such leisure activities have values in contradistinction to institutional practices. But, being in relatively low-surveillance contexts, where people are relaxed and speak open-mindedly, they are ideal for the dissemination of antisocial values and further opportunities for deviance (Glover, 2003).

Young people seek out activities where they may expend energy, try out imaginative alternatives, satisfy yearnings and realise longings. Without sufficiently stimulating opportunities, they will look for self-confirmation and exhilaration via risk-taking behaviours in public places with people of their own age; experimenting with absenteeism from school, drugs and alcohol, promiscuity and delinquency. By contrast with the family and school, a heavy dependence on peers has been found to be one of the strongest predictors of problem behaviour in adolescence and young adulthood but contradistinction may occur there too (Butters, 2010; Latendresse *et al.*, 2008; Pulkkinen, 1996). Significantly, these young people are lacking in quality face-time, support, encouragement and directional advice in the home – the parents are just too busily occupied elsewhere. And the school no longer offers credible advice on how to live. Consequently, competition within the peer group and the struggle for self-definition becomes strongly associated with consumer practices.

Theorists such as Schor (2014) and Bronfenbrenner (1986) explain that youth problems have their origins in the new patterns of work behaviour where adults are pressured to do more in less time for smaller wages, this, in turn, has an effect on Bronfenbrenner's exosystem: a social setting in which the adolescent does not have an active role and must passively accept the new economic order as a non-optional given. This new neo-liberal economic system, with ever-increasing wage disparities (and the emergence of a semi-invisibilised top-layer executive class with highly inflated incomes) exacerbates a causal chain of depletion of contact within family life, running alongside affluenza (the desire for ever more consumption) within a recently augmented system of social inequality. Parents want more goods and need to spend more time at work to get them. Bronfenbrenner (1986) mentions 25% of US families have, at some time, lived below the poverty line.

It is arguable that an extra measure of teenage alienation has its roots in widespread adult enthusiasm for increased consumption, plus a decline in the purchasing power of wages, longer working hours, and the looming spectre of debt. For many of the young, they understand there is little place for them apart from ramping up debt for higher education or lining up for the dull low-paying 'McJobs' in the service sector. Life with far less parent collaboration and support seems dismal and the future looks bleak (Besley, 2009). "The adoption of a resistant identity and deviant behaviour allows adolescents to access forms of power" (Wearing, 2003, p. 4).

The Role of the Teenage Market

Western consumer studies indicate that adolescent consumption practices are increasingly marketed, packaged and purchased as forms of leisure activities that lean towards deviance and challenging the status quo, incorporating resistance to the hegemonic adult culture (Wearing & McGehee, 2013). Over time, seeking of singularity for themselves can become pre-packaged as marketed and conspicuous deviance within rebellious practices and behaviour such as impromptu raves, wearing wild T-shirts with obscene slogans.

McGuigan (2009) similarly argues that cool capitalism takes disaffection and feeds it back into capitalism itself through consumption processes, absorbing and thereby neutralising rebellion, whilst weakening any latent opposition to the present system of consumerist values (McGuigan, 2009). Thus, what starts as being hip and individualistic becomes recycled merchandise by the same commercial system that the young individualists were originally trying to transcend; peacocky antipathy is not enough. These marketing practices are becoming increasingly sophisticated; punk faces on garment advertisements, teenage facial-snarls on soft-drink commercials, major record labels hiring street crews of black American youth to broadcast hip-hop albums in their own zones of habitation and further publicise through guerrilla-style postering activities (Heath & Potter, 2005; Klein & Sawchuk, 2000; McGuigan, 2009; Sandlin & Callahan, 2009). Once oppositional characters reappear cloned on advertisements where cheeky slogans constantly invite youth to be daring and different.

The stealing of subcultural style by the mainstream is an intended process whereby corporates seek to replenish and enrich their mass products, making them appear more authentic, relevant and exciting. (Blackman & Kempson, 2016, p 9).

Exploitation of the underprivileged and a posited hip originality confute.

Moreover, most adolescent deviant leisure occurs ad hoc, is casual, without external restraint, without specific organisation and has no long-term ambitions beyond the transitory pleasures of self-expression and the moment. At the same time, camaraderie, or differentiation, and status can be expressed through consumer products that have sometimes been carefully chosen to accommodate for anti-consumerist outlooks, as in the case of punk fashions.

The Role of Declining Family Interaction

While young people experience disaffiliation from the three once-interactive faces of family, school and peer group, they are, at the same time, encouraged to be active members of a society in terms of an ongoing consumption lifestyle with the fostering of their own emerging distinctive social prominence thereby.

In my view, consumerism is about an attitude and an ideology, a particular way of relating to consumer goods in which they take on central importance in the construction of culture, identity and social life. Consumer society I define as a situation in which the vast majority of people have a consumerist attitude or are living consumerist lifestyles (Schor in Holt, 2005, p. 5).

So, consumerism, inside the wider wage-earning adult culture, has become the meaning of the good life and has supplanted religion, work, and politics as a means to achieve satisfaction in life. Conspicuous consumption, furthermore, establishes social status, fixing prestige and the display of one's personal worth in the minds of self and others (Gabriel & Lang, 2015). Consumerism now takes on the appearance of a self-enhancing moral doctrine, such that low-wage earners, and their offspring, cannot compete and thereby take on the appearance of ethical failures.[2]

For Schor, the unbridled expansion of consumerism is a seriously divisive social problem because, increasingly, the need to increase work time, to pay for more consumer products, makes it difficult to deliver free family time for employees with commitments to childcare. Without adequate free time, bonding, the maintenance of close, interpersonal relationships within the family, erodes. For Schor, this means entire communities eventually suffer, albeit slowly and not so perceivably. So, a decline in family relations exacerbates the condition of alienated youth, through or the fourth characteristic – *estrangement* – and that consumerism, with its incumbent demands for decreased family interaction, is much to blame for this (Schor, 1999).

Particularly in American society, there has been a decline in face-to-face intimate interaction inside families and, similarly, much less interaction through wider socialising in the community. In the large metropolitan areas, prejudices related to class-consciousness and a general fear of others (crime) contributes to another diminishing of interaction outside work and consumption (see Rokach *et al.*, 2001). Much of child-rearing has been taken over by a child-focussed media intent on recruiting new consumers where the wellbeing of young people has been sacrificed for maximising corporate profits. Overconsumption in private life has become a substitute for an alternative use of free time focussed on community welfare (Schor, 2000).

Schor argues that more savings, more leisure time, and more public consumption in the form of improved social services would raise the general standard of wellbeing, as is largely represented in Scandinavian countries where taxes are higher but public provision is made to assist the family. She points out that individual Americans are often more interested in supplying a great wardrobe or buying a SUV – *private* consumption – rather than investing time in a happy marriage, intervals with the children, and a meaningful job. Significantly, the young are recruited early in this project via media exposure. There are now market specialists in advertising, aiming at adolescents, fostering the inculcation of consumer habits, decreased models of self-esteem as a result of behaving otherwise, and a competitive outlook towards others concerning acquisition (Schor, 2014).

Problems get worse when the previous fabric of social cohesion begins to unravel (see Bronfenbrenner, 1994). Typically, both parents are working and have less time for home life in the time-starved households where work stress provokes irritation at home plus marital conflict. As Schor points out, US adults are locked into a work/spend cycle where family time is scarce and increased hyper-consumption means people continuously buy things they don't really need. But, corporations, supported by tax laws, want their employees to be at work for longer periods, cutting leisure time and holidays. At the time of writing, the US has had a nearly 60% increase in production since the 80s. Meanwhile, the multinationals are laying off workers and exporting jobs overseas for cheaper labour. According to Schor, a third of Americans do not use all their vacation allowance, whilst another third feel continuously overworked (Schor, 2008). The children exit for fast food and socialise outside the family within their own peer groups in mostly socially enclosed neighbourhoods.

Mobility enforces separation from significant others and generally occurs as a result of a parent's job transfer, financial problems, or marital problems. Hence, increased relocating threatens many U.S. adolescents when they try admittance into new peer groups. For many adolescents, parental mobility leaves them feeling powerless and isolated as they travel from school to school in search of continual peer acceptance (Calabrese, 1989). Adolescents now exhibit a high level of isolation from significant others, increasing the experience of lonesomeness for college-age youth and worsened by learned helplessness—more instances of the fourth criterion: *estrangement* (Goswick & Jones, 1982; Ponzetti, 1990).

Defining Alienation as Threats to Belonging

Alienation, in social psychology, is a phenomenon that is not easy to determine within distinct notional borders. Beliefs concerning adolescent alienation may be popularly associated with pockets of maudlin discontent, classroom opposition, signs of parental neglect; emarginated youth that lacks a voice, by some described as a politically disadvantaged subclass (Harber, 2008; Wearing & McGehee 2013).

Alienation may be a popular term for denoting everything that is marginalised or discontented within a wider culture, connoting complainers, malcontents, rebels and mischief-makers; people who have in some sense failed to integrate into a society—and so the blameworthiness rests with them. But other sociologists will say that alienation is a condition affecting all marginalised collectives, imposed upon by contemporary liberal capitalism, and that it is a social malady exacerbated by under-employment, dissatisfaction with the jobs that exist, all being indications that capitalism is not working as it should. Others still, may define alienation as a temporary condition: one that is easily dismissed once appropriate integration has been achieved (Giroux quoted in Besley, 2009; Mau, 1992; Seeman, 1959; Williamson & Cullingford, 1997).

Twining (1980), and Barakat (1969) have separately shown that alienation is a cumulative and stage-driven process that subtly evolves in conditions of powerlessness, estrangement and depersonalisation where the individual feels unsupported and superfluous in a society that has little regard for their singular needs. Alienated youth are principally a negatively asserted condition emphasising separation by affirming what one is not. The alienated youth is far better at denying than affirming—where 'separate from' has the makings of a sensation of self.

Hence, in many instances it may be more a matter of what one is not than what one is. Creating distinction through conspicuous appearances can represent opposition simply through the use of flagrant contrast. But that contrast does not inspire specific alternatives concerning affirmations or a stated ideology. It may be that the floating nature of fashion signifiers is such that negation and ambiguity becomes a convenient part of their instinctive modus operandi. The opposition displayed is available for interpretation inside and outside a fabricated appearance, but it need not be either discursive or dialectical. Signifiers require no specific contentions or avowals in speech.

Adolescent alienation is further defined as a condition that emerges in a limited number of sequential stages related to ideological and economic conditions within contemporary Western society and that adolescent alienation is thereby principally definable in terms of an individual's *lack* of satisfactory relations within the family, school, and peer associations. So, youth alienation is not simply an individual personality trait, but a situation-relevant variable also dependent on cognitive awareness, nascent powers of understanding concerning one's immediate environment, and emotional maturity (Dean & Kanazawa, 1989). The pessimism, disparagement and cynicism often displayed by the young also emerges from the process undergoing stages evolving from the aforementioned state of powerlessness, normlessness, and so on, but followed by dissatisfaction with the dominant value concerns of the society surrounding them. Consumer culture, in its place, has much influence on the development of this kind of alienation.

Barakat (1969) has described social alienation as a process undergoing stages beginning with feelings of powerlessness and depersonalisation caused by overcontrol within a social order that makes implicit demands for conformity within its structure—then aggravated by undercontrol in one's personal surroundings where relations between self and world collapse into a normless discontinuity: there is a dissociation between personal goals and the available means for their attainment. Individual appreciation of this condition is followed by dissatisfaction with the dominant concerns of the wider neighbourhood—plus the larger society itself—in particular, its ideals, activities and objectives. This, in turn, may be followed by retreating negatively into shallow living, isolation (sometimes even suicide), or, positively through engaged opposition and increasingly militant behaviour (Barakat, 1969).

As a further component in this depiction, Twining's (1980) three-phase concept of alienation in is similarly sequential but is more grounded in ideas focussing on economic structures and the work environment of society, all emanating from the economic infrastructure of society which determines all other relationships within society—including the relationships of human beings to themselves (Marx, 1964; Twining, 1980). Twining's analysis can easily be integrated into the adolescent's experience of school. In Twining's first phase, there is a historical context in which individuals are embedded in a capitalist system of production which maintains rigidity in the workplace and confines continuously subordinated workers in a process based on authority from above and economic efficiency (running since the 19th century industrial revolution). What is produced by the worker confronts him as an alien object unconnected with his personal needs. The fate of the commodity is not meaningfully connected with the producer and so disappears down the line of production; there is no reason to produce apart from a wage at the end of it. The means of production, moreover, dictate the function of the worker, while the role of management focuses on efficiency and profit. Individual workers experience a loss of control in the situation, feel a separateness between themselves and their actions at work. This felt separateness may be construed as a feeling of detachment from the daily activity (without the motivational purpose of extrinsic gain) in which the worker becomes an extension of the machine. Interestingly, many lower-middle-class managers also do not feel to be their real selves have feelings of sterility, impoverishment and emptiness and disconfirmed expectations due to draconian interference from higher up the chain of command (Korman *et al.*, 1981). Young people are aware of this situation, as described by their parents, and expect a similar fate awaiting them. Interestingly, there may be many parallels between detachment from the daily activity at work and an adolescent's experience of school.

Twining's second phase involves a perceived loss of control and meaning within situationally specific relations which leads to a condition of social isolation and, ultimately, self-estrangement. In this phase, as with Barakat, there is a growing isolation of self away from others, stretching beyond the initially alienating work situation, which then pushes even further towards a self-estrangement via the impossibility of recognising any meaningful self while occupied with the daily grind. It is at this final point that the participants lose their identity as meaningful contributors to the interaction process (Twining, 1980).

Twining's third phase consists of interpreting and reacting to a situation which has by now been thoroughly negatively evaluated. A large proportion of the workforce will resign themselves to the situation, involving tensions inside subordination, competitiveness, monotony and drudgery, exploitation and economic instability and yet remain at work to maintain a necessary economic base which permits other, more rewarding social relations outside (see Barbash, 1972). Twining states:

Alienation can now be defined as an interactional, or relational, consequence of a negative encounter of some duration which involves the degree of felt separateness from fundamental social situations in which self is being defined (Twining, 1980, p. 422).

Although Twining refers mostly to adult labour relations, it is not difficult to spot similar events occurring in youth collectives. The general population regards such situations as natural and inevitable, seeking life satisfactions at home, inside the distractions of consumerism and the family (Twining, 1980). Reification of this process, for the young, is accomplished by early socialisation and schooling plus the workforce remaining underinformed about alternatives.

Twining (1980) insists the response of total alienation may be classified as a contemporary mental disorder finding its place amidst depression, anxiety and social withdrawal. Loneliness, as a form of social alienation, is an interpersonal deficit that exists as a result of insufficient or unsatisfying personal relationships, much less than a person desires, and is highly correlated with depression and the feeling of helplessness in their condition (Ponzetti, 1990). Similarly, among college students, lonely individuals report feelings of emptiness, hopelessness, restlessness, alienation, anxiety, and being unloved (Hays & DiMatteo, 1987; Perlman & Peplau, 1981).

From the foregoing, perceptions of exclusion and weak ties with institutions impose a severe threat to fundamental human needs of belonging, and a meaningful existence involving self-esteem and self-control can be seen. When these needs are severely thwarted, feelings of frustration and anger emerge and provoke aggressive reactions directed at anybody who seems to represent the forces of exclusion, as can be seen with aggression in schools (see also Berkowitz, 1989).

Reijntjes *et al.* (2010), asked respondents to rate statements such as "Hardly anyone I know is interested in how I really feel inside." This described alienated youth as feeling powerless in the face of social forces and rules which they cannot control or modify. The Reijntjes sample also indirectly cited the previous axiom of meaninglessness in terms of a lack of a sense of purpose and direction in one's life, especially concerning a significant use for what they are doing now for the future (e.g. studying). Once more, normlessness was named in terms of individuals being voided of an ethical outlook towards the society that has already emarginated them as insignificant individuals awaiting worthless outcomes for a nebulous future; and, finally, estrangement, where individuals believed they had nothing in common with others and would rather spend their time alone (see also Brown *et al.,* 2003).

As a complement to Barakat's stage-driven concept, and Twining's social process, many adolescents experience meaninglessness at school and a corresponding lack in terms of what they produce in terms of direction and purpose in life.[3] They also feel unable to influence what is happening to them and, as common, feel powerless to alter things on the production line between school and work: they are caught in a role limbo where they are neither children nor adults (Brown & Merritt, 2002; Erikson, 1994).

So, in a society where many adolescents are painfully aware of themselves as beings of lack, fulfilment is sought away from the prevailing culture which neither supplies esteem through purposeful activities at school nor convincing support from inside the family. A footloose, situationless, street-outsider condition ensues—one where one looks to leisure practices as the arena where narcissistic esteem-building techniques concerning dress and appearance are displayed—a compensatory prioritising of one's own good looks, putative accomplishments on the dance floor, self-affirmation achieved through extrovert manners, displays of minor proficiency and prowess; where the peer group applauds and celebrates amidst a host of mutual self-affirmations thereby. The peer group may be acting as the last-chance call for a de-alienated lifestyle.

Peer group friendships allow self-disclosure, reciprocity, compromise, and mutual support in relationships in a culture where self-identity is continuously problematized (Moore & Boldero, 1991). At the same time, there is still a high correlation between peer group interaction and consumption styles, suggesting peer group relations have a special effect on purchasing. Shim (1996) found that peer group activity greatly influenced fashion consciousness, concerning the range of products consumed, induced brand consciousness, brand loyalty concerning the expressive component regarding novelty (Shim, 1996). As will be seen, marketers have been quick to catch on to the influence of this kind of peer activity—and target accordingly. Not only this, but marketers are delighted with their success when squalls of impulsive buying occurs. If you sell to one, you sell to everyone in their class (Klein & Sawchuk, 2000).

The Role of the Peer Group and Consumer Practices

Despite frantic claims for a singular individualism, the subcultural subject becomes a product of the social environment they inhabit—the peer group (Blackman, 2016). Youth identities and personalities are thereby re-defined within a local social terrain of subcultural action and practice and formed within the marketplace of consumer practices where style and identity are inextricably mixed (Besley, 2009). This, however, may be alternatively suggested as a temporary developmental process where the young person eventually settles on a stable identity, when a stable self-esteem is the outcome of successful terminations of each Eriksonian developmental crisis—self-esteem being based upon the degree of success with which each peak has been surmounted (Constantinople, 1969; Erikson 1994).

Later writers will disagree. Woodman and Bennett (2015) offer the idea that the experience of youth is simply a set of ephemerally acquired subcultural practices. Other theorists maintain socially imposed class distinctions are still the most powerful influences to operate as a means of identity formation (Hollands in Rojek, 1999). At the same time, without referring to media influences, the youths themselves often insist on an elevated and independent subcultural status by distinguishing themselves on top of denigrated others (Hodkinson, 2015; Illouz, 2009). Youths involved in deviant productions such as zines, were given an improved zine star status. In other words, youth subcultures have their own class-conscious distinction-making practices and frequently jockey for position with each other inside ongoing virtual hierarchies (Blackman & Kempson, 2016).

Searches for an alternative identity may also cut across social class, gender, ethnicity, and geo-territorial boundaries so that adolescents living in distant communities, where ostensibly there are no political affinities, or contrastively manifest antagonism (say, Los Angeles vs. Tel Aviv) but may sport the same hairstyles and listen to similar music, even interiorising much of the verbal content. Therefore, in the case of adopted fashion signifiers, there is no homogeneity concerning an associative ideological meaning—and hence they are, once again, truly floating. What may be subsumed in one similar culture may be eschewed by another.

In such a varied social terrain, youth experience and action creates heterotopias of difference that seek to distinguish themselves and generate cultures of against in terms of the wider society, but without references to theories of alienation (*cf.* Foucault, 1980; 1984). Much of this, as aforesaid, is displayed in ostentatious configurations of speech, dress, broadcast music, discourteous language and cloned expressions taken from celebrity discourse, occurring without a thetic reflexivity concerning the socio-political environment and a detachment founded in ideology (Galbo, 1988; Illouz, 2009; Schultz & Rubel, 2011).

Among youth, the adoption of distinctive styles of dress acts as a kind of persistent semiotic code-declaiming independence from wider social norms through the display of signifiers such as hair-styles or distinctive adornments; style in the use of assemblages; bricolage, pastiche, blends, hybridization; where, although a particular stylistic theme may be temporarily adopted, there is frequently some particular element of difference devised by the youth as an attempt to assert their own individuality within that group (Besley, 2009). These practices may seek to circumvent the aforementioned state of powerlessness and overcontrol, aggravated by media purloining (see Trojan horses below). Dissident attitudinal poses; unclear, tacit, allusive references; are often cloned from youth celebrities, often in speech, conveniently summed up as attitude—a kind of quasi-ideological distancing from conventionality—but one that never states its case during the attempt to knit together a succinct personality; itself still acting as an almost-original (but still makeshift) form of identity. Indeed, momentary expressions of sincerity can even be drawn from remarks attesting anti-insidership (Force, 2009) or a cynical spoofing of rival consumer practices (Klein & Sawchuk, 2000).

Giddens (1991) believes that consumption practices within the pluralized world of post-traditional society offer wider possibilities for individual autonomy but, at the same time, provoke anxiety concerning self-identity and to whom one should turn to for guidance. Sartorial adornment is accepted as the first and most blatant means for aligning oneself with a frequent subcultural gathering, consistent with an implied disaffiliation from the wider culture and any local rival factions. But where a proliferation of subcultures offer so many alternatives, and the conspicuous consumption of goods becomes a suggestive substitute for a reflective ideology-based development of the self, adolescents will be confused as to which actions establish a genuinely distinctive choice; all this provoking even more unconventional choices that go against the grain such as unmarketable punk jewellery (safety-pins, razors) and attempts to shock by displaying the point-blank ugliness of obscene remarks on T-shirts.

In a youth culture where personal identity is threatened by being inconspicuous and embedded in a mass culture of unexceptional wage-earners, the project of deviancy, the clawing back of some empowerment, and who one turns to may turn out to be oneself. Where there is an attempt to recover some measure of distinction and control, the individual may retreat into narcissistic preoccupations once more involving personal appearance where one may look upon oneself as exceptional (Giddens, 1991). This kind of narcissism provides a magnification of the self-expressed in terms of escalating wants, demands, individual rights; pressing towards self-evaluations that help to substitute for the depersonalising effects of look-alike mass appearances; working against the feeling of being objectified, categorised and emarginated by a surrounding culture which constantly lauds celebrity, ignores the ordinary, and demands a lot more than it provides in terms of the appreciation of average people (Schulz & Rubel, 2011).

Forms of adolescent deviance, involving resistance as expressed through narcissism, are regularised by marketing practices appealing to the young person, during their leisure time, in the form of challenging, thrilling, and precarious activities whilst providing a means to cultivate improved conceptions of personal power, wealth and prestige, via conspicuous consumption and how the individual would like to be seen thereby.

Popular music lyrics and film, directed at the young, while offering alternatives in dress and behaviour, often foster unrealistic expectations, escapism, and misleading depictions of the successful life with famous personalities available as attractive mentors. The entertainment industry, substantially geared toward same-age groups, offers developing adolescents considerable freedom to experiment with unconventional role-models, philandering lifestyles, smart-talker speech, a frivolous party subculture; anti-social values, and norms well outside the influence of family and school, augmenting the peer group's showy prominence in a lifeworld, at the expense of the temperance and sobriety needed for genuine and lasting accomplishments. It is mostly all show.[4]

At the same time, shallow and cynical alternatives, offered in self and identity, are a tit-for-tat spinoff that counteracts unlikely media fictions (soaps), soon intuited by adolescent subcultures as facile and controvertible (Blackman & Kempson, 2016; Rokach *et al.*, 2001). The rise of narcissism in young people – suspiciously recalling Freud's idea of a reaction formation – against galling anonymity, as preoccupation with dress and body-image, accompanies bragging, a craving for admiration and specialness, often without evidence of success in any supporting field of endeavour (Besley, 2009; Lasch, 1991). Narcissism may cover a range of alarming but conveniently self-confirming behaviours:

... in which people are pathologically self-preoccupied; unable to relate to others as equals; approaching others not as ends in themselves but as means to selfish ends and where people resort to self-soothing behaviours including substance abuse, deliberate self-harm, (including self-sabotage and the contamination of relationships), meaningless and promiscuous sex; thereby becoming self-defeatingly insular yet virtually self-reliant (Holmes, 2001, p. 36).

It can be argued that these dispositions are a consequence – and a reaction formation – aimed at the aforesaid feelings of powerlessness, meaninglessness, normlessness and estrangement; the defining states of alienation axiomatised in the introduction. This is paralleled by fashion consumption from an advertising culture that coquettishly encourages a display of the self, plus the display of one's attractive possessions, as the standard by which an individual is judged as worthy; again reinforced by marketers aiming at the teenage sector by offering procrustean solutions to their pre-conscious beliefs concerning ignominy. Moreover, that youth alienation is a process that occurs incrementally in definite stages and can be understood in terms of a progressive cline (as in Twining and Barakat, also above); culminating in the demonstration, that narcissism is an unconscious reaction against the poverty of the prevailing neoliberal ideology; where, disinterested in the past and the future, to live for the moment and to live instinctively for yourself, provides an ephemeral sensation of wellbeing.

It is argued that targeting youth with specific products such as: skateboarding paraphernalia, lurid comics, alcopops, hair gel, tattoos, computer gaming technologies, how to magazine articles on pubescent sex, demonic cosmetic presentations, violent video games, have all been commodified and contribute to the growth of the narcissistic self through commodified leisure aimed at the youth experience inside shopping malls, gaming centres, cinema complexes, race tracks, sports arenas and coffee shops (Gordon *et al.* 1996; Mahoney & Stattin, 2000; Wearing & McGehee, 2013).

Many youth identities have thus been constructed amidst market-based regimes, such as punk fashion, vampire clothing, biker products; ostensibly to challenge the social order and give an impression of freedom from societal norms, but, in actuality, feeding off the once-original signifiers and a ubiquitous organisation of mass consumption within modern capitalism, as in the case of teenage box-office movies and a corporatised music industry. TV is soaked in advertisements, where companies have paid for a product to appear, aimed at the young, which have been classified and composed by skilled researchers looking into age, ethnicity, gender, social class and location; in turn, encouraging an empathic emotional branding, capturing the teen and tween wallet by seeing the world through kids' eyes, perpetually aiming to inculcate a transplanted brand loyalty. The highest spending categories for exploitation are currently: unhealthy foods: sweets, chewing gum, snacks and beverages; supplemented side-by-side with TV programmes full of violence, alcohol, drugs and guns' body-image and gender stereotypes (Illouz, 2009; Schor, 2014).

Researchers now also creep into everyday interactions to understand small group development at a micro-level where recorded subcultural discourses can inform an emerging biographical picture, as first-hand experience of the social world of the potential targets for marketing, so they can pre-structure and anticipate the agency of consumers through this discourse analysis of budding consumers communicating with each other in the peer group setting (Blackman & Kempson, 2016; Klein & Sawchuk, 2000).[5]

Narcissism and Beings of Lack

Teenage narcissism belongs to a version of Barakat's engaged opposition and as a response to universal feelings of lack. As previously mentioned, narcissism may also be viewed as a reaction formation but, it principally concerns the general feeling of lack. Freudian reaction formation, which may be mostly unconscious, occurs when a person seeks to cover up something unacceptable to themselves by adopting a contradictory stance in order to convince others that the opposite is true and, in this particular case, to reduce anxiety from the only partially revealed conviction that one is insignificant and powerless (see also Erwin, 2002); the semi-aware yet inarticulate consciousness – that one has little to offer as a significant member of society; i.e. that one's life is pervaded by lack of privilege, a lack of success, not enough excitement, and, from others – from society itself – not enough regard; such that, that nobody esteems one, one gets little affection, and, in a youth culture that forever lauds celebrity happenings in sports and music, one suffers from a distinct scarcity of accomplishments (Freud, 1992; Illouz, 2009). Today, this can be accompanied by pathological symptoms such as acute depression, depersonalization, detachment of mind from the body, absence of any hobbies or interests, disinclination to speak out or communicate, and eventual indifference to one's fate (Brown & Merritt, 2002).

The Role of Education, The School and Later Employment

Mahoney and Stattin (2000) found that highly structured leisure activities involving skills building have a low correspondence with anti-social behaviour, whereas, for low structured leisure, had high associations with deviance and crime.[6] The latter also related to poor parent-child relationships with little trust involved and low support given. These adolescents often stayed out late, had poor academic records and had been in trouble with the police. Thorlindsson and Bernburg (2006) confirmed much of this and found that sport activities were the most effective in reducing alcohol and drug consumption where participants were shielded from anti-establishment viewpoints and deviant subcultural values, norms, and behaviors. Whereas a non-participative *ad lib* party subculture increased them.

Concerning the big four mentioned earlier, the influence of school is constantly waning in terms of previous promises as "the great equalise" – a term from John Dewey. A cursory glance at school websites shows them boldly proclaiming thriving communities of academic excellence where highly motivated staff offer pastoral care for innovative, passionate, self-reliant pupils excelling in academic commitment, dress and demeanour. These deceptive exercises in impression management cannot afford to allude to the high levels of current disengagement, where such exists, as discussed by the many authors listed in this chapter. No institution wants to boast a minority of its members were probed late at night by the police, or suspected of substance abuse when questioned (Elsbach & Sutton, 1992; Schlenker, 1980; Tedeschi, 2013).

However, the integrative function of education – school as a preparation for society – is currently a manifest failure and very divisive in terms of its accessibility. Fees for the best colleges, where elites assemble and circulate, are exorbitant and prohibitive such that, lower down, students nowadays acquire a life-long debt for a college education. The grading system establishes a code of judgement which separates the scholastically successful from those of a practical bent where exclusions and rewards endorse a system based on competition and class-division; where the economically disadvantaged increasingly cannot compete. In their *Economic Apartheid in America*, Collins and Yeskel (2011) provide startling statistical information concerning these differences.

For the young, things have not always been like this. Bowles and Gintis (1976) emphasised the recognition of individual differences, and concentrated on personality development involving the whole child, the particular needs of learners, intrinsic motivation relating to persistent life situations, bridging the gap between home and school, teaching children as individuals and not simply as the passive recipients of academic subjects. The latter, they wrote, is neither democratic nor egalitarian. The authors make the startling assertion that, under corporate capitalism, the objectives of liberal educational reform are contradictory.

Moreover, by integrating new generations into an already established social order, schools are constrained to justify and reproduce inequality rather than ameliorate it (Bowles & Gintis, 1976). So, according to such authors, the US education system, as a tool of social policy, has rarely promoted social equality or a full human development. Today, the widening gap between rich and poor has become chronically exacerbated, whilst programmes for social welfare are being decimated. These views have been elaborated upon and supported by other writers (see Collins & Yeskel, 2011; Mcall, 1990).

Amongst older youths, Case (2008) found that older, alienated college students had problems integrating into a higher education community, both socially and academically. She described their estrangement as tallied with aversions to the utilising system of disempowering assessment practices (Case, 2008). Emdin (2010) maintains these students have now regarded themselves as outside, and seen to be so; urban students are regarded as uninterested in school, difficult to teach, and unable to do well in challenging academic subjects (Emdin, 2007). Emdin (2007) maintains students feel alienated from formal education and they often respond with a contrary reaction by deeply affiliating themselves with hip-hop culture; that is, seeking affiliation in peer groups outside the prevailing culture. These contrasting paradigms takes the form of a contempt for schools and an embracing of the hip-hop exterior that masks a longing for full participation in what is going on in the classroom. Students spend hours studying an antithetical discourse within hip-hop lyrics, the lifestyles of the artists and their media-managed personas (Emdin, 2007).

As a result of these observations, one might suggest that there are yawning contrasts between hip-hop culture, urban youth identity, and government-sponsored education; perhaps related to the banging, for hours on lunchroom tables, creating complex rhythms, perfecting raps, in small peer groups, plus gravity-defying break-dancing consistent with other hip-hop practices. These connections, specific to hip-hop culture, are the direct result of the student's unconscious belief that hip-hop is an essential branch of a reclaimed identity, as both consumers and producers of rap music; whilst, by implication, distancing themselves from the academic classroom and the values of an all-powerful, authoritative hegemony. As already discussed, the marketing of deviance (and here rap music, in particular) becomes adroitly deconstructed and repackaged through commodification. But there are still, at the same time, hip-hop fusions occurring amongst other spatially disparate subcultural communities that have avoided commercial distribution (it's being sold).

The approaching work environments are not much better. Previous 20th century working-class culture encouraged group identities, political allegiances, shared mutual experiences inside a common habitus that drew working people together. Today's young people show a hard-edged instrumentalist attitude towards labour, and see their jobs as transitory and isolating. They avoid socialising at work, preferring to get out as quick as possible after a shift is over. Work is something to be done and forgotten (more meaninglessness and estrangement). Work identities, such as they might exist, have very little significance when everyone there just hates the place (Winlow & Hall, 2009).

So, once again, the sole surviving arena of affective cohesion is the peer group. Calabrese mentions peer group relations as replacing the inadequate measure of affection felt at home, especially amongst similarly situated others (Calabrese, 1989). However, Winlow and Hall (2009) doubt whether extra-familial bonding provides true friendship. Surviving amidst the competitive pressures of pointless, alienating and exploitative work, can friendships survive? A North of England study found that the transitory nature of precarious employment was an impediment to nurturing and prolonging friendships,

as the culture of advanced capitalism increasingly forces instrumentalism to the very core of self-identity, truly empathetic, altruistic and durable forms of togetherness are becoming increasingly rare amongst those deeply and actively incorporated into consumer culture (Winlow & Hall, 2009, p. 105).

Unlike previous generations who found grounded association offered by families and school, "Now the same types of youth group often reveal growing divisions, fragmentation, alienation and isolation" (Winlow & Hall, 2009, p. 108). Socialising outside, as with clubbing and alcohol use, people avoid talking about work. "We don't want to hear about depressing stuff cos it's going to spoil the night" (Winlow & Hall, 2009, p. 107). When the battle for prosperity and distinction enters an exclusively consumer-based phase, youth finds it prudent to act unencumbered by enduring affective and social bonds. Attachments, and the obligations that inevitably arrive with them, are unwanted complications as individuals reorganise their lives to fit in with fewer hours for leisure and the competitive thrust of showy consumer society. Fun is the priority. While reciprocity remains important in intimate human relations, the need to maximize material benefit for the self seems inescapable (Beck & Beck-Gernsheim, 1995; Winlow & Hall, 2009). Youth leisure-time seems to revolve around the short-time benefits of clubbing. The young become instrumental solos inside a bleak dystopian world of atomization (Winlow & Hall, 2009). Work environments and peer group activities do not cohere, especially where the peer group is mostly ad lib and ephemeral.

Various studies show that, in their deeper need for association and bonding, adolescents are not so independent as they would like to be. Competition, difference and differentiation are active among the young when they associate with peers in local groups at school or shopping malls, where taste acts as markers of social status in a leisure-based collective. The possession of consumer products modulate impression management, where a youth can display and score points for seeming up-to-date, attractive and exceptional. Thus, spiky hair gel on boys can give an Amazonian, warlike appearance of alpha proportions—and attract girls.[7]

Media bombardment and the early recruitment of young people into consumerist values ensures later compliance to overconsumption and initiates competitiveness as a socially divisive practice. Famously, North American culture accentuates individual achievement, a tacit antagonism, and easily detached relations (Rokach *et al.*, 2001), whilst capitalist values are transmitted as far back as early childhood within the family, stressing highly materialistic values (Schor, 2014). Furthermore, personal relationships become esteemed and managed in a commodity-like way, strategized with an eye on advantages and returns. This is demonstrated by competitive social hierarchies in the high school society of *Mean Girls* (2004) where influential opinion leaders dictate what is fashionable, stylish or chic—especially when such leaders have parents of higher social standing. Years ago, Fromm (1956) contended human beings are naturally aggressive, greedy and self-interested, making way for a competitive society where rivalry is an expected norm (Fromm, 1956; McDonald & Wearing, 2013).

Many U.S. children are now overweight and can fly into narcissistic rages if denied immoderate intake (McDonald, 2013; Schor, 2014). So, popularity amongst peers, social wellbeing and individual standing, for the young, are commensurate with publicly observable consumption habits. At school, rivalry is encouraged, exacerbated by emotions of jealousy and rancour, along with corrosive feelings of shame and low self-esteem when these media-implanted cravings are not satisfied (another step towards powerlessness). It can be shown that these dispositions are also correlated with school violence erupting in the by now famous mass shootings where resentment was the key factor.

The commercialisation of teen culture has, these days, outsourced specialised marketers who approach youth workers, school coaches, Girl Scouts and teachers. They make sound recordings of peer-to-peer subcultural discourse which find their way into captions and headings on the front pages of teen appeal magazines like *Seventeen*. Focus groups test a product, then adjust brand positioning through stealth advertising, indirectly targeting age-based portions of the population where brand messages pose as public service communications. Moreover, there are now only-for-profit public schools run by large companies that seek to recruit management of consumers at an early stage (Molnar, 1996). The sponsor's advertisements appear on every desk, in every nook, including the bathrooms.

Currently, the main attribute teenagers are attracted by is cool. Cool possessions rapidly establish prestige and induce further competitive relationships with others within the inception of a conspicuous status-consumption (Schor points out this happens as early as six years old.) So, social distinction is now compounded at an early age and acts as the foundation of many later competing relations between friends and acquaintances in adult life (Goldberg *et al.*, 2003; Schor, 2014). Fashion and taste, amongst the young, establishes indirect modes of social discrimination through the claiming of subcultural capital, the accomplishment of credibility and renown within a local group of youngster (Bourdieu, 1984). Inevitably, one-parent or low-income families cannot compete.

The Chic of the Forbidden

The power and influence exerted by contemporary marketing practices on still underdeveloped minds can now be appreciated. Significant criticism concerning marketing practices focuses on the idea that consumerism exists within a structure of domination, where there is an inevitable recursive interplay between consumer resistance and marketing agents. Blackman (2004) notes that the young may still engage in forms of associated consumption behaviour due to the attendant appeal of illicit intake. Saturated with the language of intoxication, drug-use parallels are injected into the minds of potential consumers by the media to encourage alternative forms of counterhegemonic satisfaction. Blackman maintains drugs are now part of the mainstream economy (e.g. Enjoy cocaine T-shirts) and contemporary advertisements tap into drug usage as a means of similar gratification using inside knowledge to associate their product as cool, as in perfumes like Opium, to offer the decoding of other possible messages included in heroin chic—coded metaphors that encourage trajectories of thought transferable to attractive branding. Thus, shrewd marketing has once more tapped into deviance and the forbidden as a means of selling to the young and effectively bypassing any counterhegemonic reaction to the ubiquity of advertising by using conversion from within.

In the chic of the forbidden, marketing has once more tapped into the interplay of youthful deviance with the exotic and prohibited, as a means of selling to the young—and effectively pre-empting any emerging political consciousness via conversion from within, where this within remains impetuously non-thetic. The success of strategic marketing still depends on cultivating illaudable aspects of humanity: instinct, selfishness, narcissism.

These close and personal methods attempt to intimate marketing practices more intensely into the lives of young consumers by accessing the kind of trust existing alongside adjacent confidential relationships with peers, feeding on subculturally-specific discourse fields involving the hipness of substance use and other highly charged, intense experiences. Practically any leisure activity practised by the young, with its attendant discourse fields, can be spied upon by current research methods, the pirated cool ideas and phraseology fed back into marketing strategies aimed at those self-same potential customers.

So brand value is now calculated according to the place it occupies in the world of its consumers. It runs on the ability the brand has to create trust, affect and conviction amidst people's shared meanings—a social construction of truth, utility and beauty—plus their ability to foster and command the content of wider discourse fields (Arvidsson, 2005). In such a model of society, teenagers become a walking set of advertisements for brand stretching and parallel marketing. Teenagerhood now involves an unconscious insemination of entrepreneurial processes and a supportive consumer ideology.

The inevitable recursive interplay between consumer resistance and marketing agents involves a Ping-Pong game of astuteness, with the young, who might easily expose the Trojan horses grafted from their everyday speech. Clearly, such debunking cannot be accomplished without some informed measure of detachment and reflexivity. Such an achievement would necessarily involve the development of a more sophisticated thetic consciousness concerning their own position in society.

Teenage alienation is a confrontation with absence—a lack of sense of belonging, feeling cut off in many directions, mainly from the tripartite relation of family, school and peers. It is the inability to connect meaningfully with other people, a feeling of aloneness, a feeling that no one is like them, and that they are not what others want them to be (Brown *et al.*, 2003). This pervasiveness of alienation, in particular that highlighting loneliness, nowadays runs throughout all age groups and becomes a frequent presenting issue on US telephone hot lines, college counselling clinics, and within youth psychological services (Jones *et al.*, 1990). Loneliness is discovered to be inversely related to dealings involving self-esteem (Jones *et al.*, 1981) and, especially in the US, has been strongly associated with anxiety, depression, interpersonal hostility and substance abuse (Hansson *et al.*, 1986).

Rebellion, as the stepping outside of social standards, rejecting the norms advanced by those in authority, empowers some by defining themselves through what they are not (also Force, 2009). Short-term fashions, such as Punk, refract more than reject consumerism, despite an oft-attributed resistance to it.

Thus, from the previous dicussion, it can be seen that, as catering for beings of lack, consumer capitalism does not assist the young in stabilising their own identity, but instead fosters a shallow status-affirming private consumption, encouraging distancing practices including narcissism, and a concomitant stage-driven alienation, whereby facile subcultural practices erode social cohesion, further expressed by alienation from others (towards an alienation from the self) where, finally, a lack of belonging distinguishes disembedding, a condition of psychological stress and loneliness often associated with substance abuse and mental disorders. Is the only solution consumer resistance? Or to attempt a reintegration back into the work/spend cycle?

CONCLUSION

By now, it should be fairly obvious that the principle sources of adolescent alienation lie in local conditions regarding family, school and peer group, in addition to the wider, seemingly less conspicuous, conditions of an over-occupied society that provides little recognition of youth, nor a welcoming space for youth in which to be. In a society where parents are pressed for time at work and handling their children, where competitive social relations at school and diminishing future prospects of employment far outweigh the chances of egalitarian cooperation; where young people are judged by performance measures in school at the cost of a more Dewey-like, generous-hearted and encouraging environment that accepts all members in a society; where it is tactically convenient and advantageous for marginalised groups to distant themselves and form more amicable relations during their own smaller-group leisure time. Where all this is not possible, through the third vital area of association—the peer group—a total alienation sets in; one that can germinate pathological behaviour that hits the headlines to provoke moral panics and proliferate bewilderment further afield.

Even though young people find themselves struggling with proto-typical identities that cut across gender, social class backgrounds, ethnicity, and national boundaries, contrastive status-claiming behaviour at every turn with "in" groups and "out" groups is found. Thus the seeds of consubstantial social divisiveness are sown and class distinctions re-emerge, at every turn, even amidst the most convention-defying deviant behaviour. Exclusion from such groups is often determined by strict codes of acceptability concerning what looks cool, with competition for what looks and sounds impressive. The distinction and class divisions seem to appear almost spontaneously in youth collectives, which often ostentatiously claim they are free from any convention, and that much of youth culture contains exactly those same mechanisms of social division that can be perpetuated in later life. Thus, unlike the youth-led resistances and anti-capitalist counterculture advocated by John Lennon, today's gatherings are too much of a medley of still-to-be-formed alliances. During the massive *en fusions* of the 60s, when large assemblies of youth united to protest against the Vietnam War, coalescence dissipated as its members grew older and the war concluded (Besley, 2009).

REFERENCES

Arvidsson, A. (2005). Brands: A critical perspective. *Journal of Consumer Culture*, *5*(2), 235–258. doi:10.1177/1469540505053093

Barakat, H. (1969). Alienation: A process of encounter between utopia and reality. *The British Journal of Sociology*, *20*(1), 1–10. doi:10.2307/588995 PMID:5771898

Baudrillard, J., & Petit, P. (1998). *Paroxysm: Interviews with Philippe Petit*. London, UK: Verso.

Baumeister, R. F. (1987). How the self became a problem: A psychological review of historical research. *Journal of Personality and Social Psychology*, *52*(1), 163–176. doi:10.1037/0022-3514.52.1.163

Beck, U., & Beck-Gernsheim, E. (1996). Individualization and 'precarious freedoms': Perspectives and controversies of a subject-oriented sociology. In P. Heelas, S. Lash, & P. Morris (Eds.), *Detraditionalization: critical reflections on authority and identity* (pp. 23–48). Cambridge, MA: Blackwell.

Berkowitz, L. (1989). Frustration-aggression hypothesis: Examination and reformulation. *Psychological Bulletin, 106*(1), 59–73. doi:10.1037/0033-2909.106.1.59 PMID:2667009

Besley, T. A. (2009). Governmentality of Youth: Beyond Cultural Studies. *Contemporary Readings in Law & Social Justice, 1*(2), 36–83.

Blackman, S. (2004). *Chilling out: The cultural politics of substance consumption, youth and drug policy*. London, UK: McGraw-Hill.

Blackman, S., & Kempson, M. (Eds.). (2016). *The subcultural imagination: Theory, research and reflexivity in contemporary youth culture (youth, young adulthood and society)*. Abington, UK: Routledge.

Bourdieu, P. (1984). *Distinction: A social critique of the judgement of taste*. London, UK: Routledge.

Bowles, S., & Gintis, H. (1976). *Schooling in capitalist America*. New York: Basic Books.

Brady, M. T. (2017). Subversiveness in adolescence. *Contemporary Psychoanalysis, 53*(3), 346–361. doi:10.1080/00107530.2017.1355693

Bronfenbrenner, U. (1986). Alienation and the four worlds of childhood. *Phi Delta Kappan, 67*(6), 430–436.

Bronfenbrenner, U. (1994). Ecological models of human development. In *International encyclopedia of education* (2nd ed.; Vol. 3). Oxford, UK: Elsevier.

Brown, B., & Merritt, R. (2002). *No easy answers: The truth behind death at Columbine*. New York, NY: Lantern Books.

Brown, M. R., Higgins, K., Pierce, T., Hong, E., & Thoma, C. (2003). Secondary students' perceptions of school life with regard to alienation: The effects of disability, gender and race. *Learning Disability Quarterly, 26*(4), 227–238. doi:10.2307/1593636

Butters, C. (2010). *An examination of arousal in experienced skydivers*. Fullerton, CA: California State University.

Calabrese, R. L. (1989). The effects of mobility on adolescent alienation. *High School Journal, 73*(1), 41–46.

Case, J. M. (2008). Alienation and engagement: Development of an alternative theoretical framework for understanding student learning. *Higher Education, 55*(3), 321–332. doi:10.100710734-007-9057-5

Collins, C., & Yeskel, F. (2011). *Economic apartheid in America: A primer on economic inequality & insecurity*. New York, NY: The New Press.

Constantinople, A. (1969). An Eriksonian measure of personality development in college students. *Developmental Psychology, 1*(4), 357–372. doi:10.1037/h0027706

De Graaf, J., Wann, D., & Naylor, T. H. (2005). *Affluenza: The all-consuming epidemic*. San Francisco, CA: Berrett-Koehler Publishers.

Dean, T., & Kanazawa, K. (1989). A model for reasoning about persistence and causation. *Computational Intelligence*, *5*(2), 142–150. doi:10.1111/j.1467-8640.1989.tb00324.x

Elsbach, K. D., & Sutton, R. I. (1992). Acquiring organizational legitimacy through illegitimate actions: A marriage of institutional and impression management theories. *Academy of Management Journal*, *35*(4), 699–738.

Emdin, C. (2007). Exploring the contexts of urban science classrooms. Part 2: The emergence of rituals in the learning of science. *Cultural Studies of Science Education*, *2*(2), 351–392. doi:10.100711422-007-9057-x

Emdin, C. (2010). Affiliation and alienation: Hip-hop, rap, and urban science education. *Journal of Curriculum Studies*, *42*(1), 1–25. doi:10.1080/00220270903161118

Erikson, E. H. (1994). *Identity: Youth and crisis*. New York, NY: WW Norton & Company.

Erikson, E. H., & Erikson, J. M. (1998). *The life cycle completed (extended version)*. New York, NY: WW Norton & Company.

Erwin, E. (Ed.). (2002). *The Freud encyclopedia: Theory, therapy, and culture*. New York, NY: Taylor & Francis.

Featherstone, M. (2007). *Consumer culture and postmodernism*. London, UK: Sage.

Force, W. R. (2009). Consumption styles and the fluid complexity of punk authenticity. *Symbolic Interaction*, *32*(4), 289–309. doi:10.1525i.2009.32.4.289

Foucault, M. (1980). *Power/knowledge: Selected interviews and other writings, 1972-1977*. New York, NY: Pantheon.

Foucault, M. (1984). *The Foucault reader*. New York, NY: Pantheon.

Freud, A. (1992). *The ego and the mechanisms of defence*. New York, NY: Karnac Books.

Freud, S. (1914). On narcissism: An introduction. In *The standard edition of the complete psychological works of Sigmund Freud* (J. Strachey, Trans.; vol. 14, pp. 67–102). London, UK: Hogarth Press.

Fromm, E. (1956). *The art of loving: An enquiry into the nature of love*. New York, NY: Harper.

Frymer, B. (2009). The media spectacle of Columbine: Alienated youth as an object of fear. *The American Behavioral Scientist*, *52*(10), 1387–1404. doi:10.1177/0002764209332554

Gabriel, Y., & Lang, T. (2015). *The unmanageable consumer*. London, UK: Sage.

Galbo, J. J. (1988). An exploration of the effects of the relationships of adolescents and adults on learning in secondary schools. *High School Journal*, *71*(2), 97–102.

Geertz, C. (1973). Thick description: Toward and interpretive theory of culture, the interpretation of culture. In C. Geertz (Ed.), *The interpretation of cultures: selected essays* (pp. 3–30). New York: Basic Books.

Giddens, A. (1991). *Modernity and self-identity*. Cambridge, UK: Polity Press.

Glover, T. D. (2003). Regulating the rave scene: Exploring the policy alternatives of government. *Leisure Sciences*, *25*(4), 307–325. doi:10.1080/714044493

Gordon, W. R., & Caltabiano, M. L. (1996). Urban-rural differences in adolescent self-esteem, leisure boredom, and sensation-seeking as predictors of leisure-time usage and satisfaction. *Adolescence*, *31*(124), 883–901. PMID:8970661

Goswick, R. A., & Jones, W. H. (1982). Components of loneliness during adolescence. *Journal of Youth and Adolescence*, *11*(5), 373–383. doi:10.1007/BF01540375 PMID:24310911

Hansson, R. O., Jones, W. H., Carpenter, B. N., & Remondet, I. (1986). Loneliness and adjustment to old age. *International Journal of Aging & Human Development*, *24*(1), 41–53. doi:10.2190/82XB-5L9T-JWKE-U6T8 PMID:3557646

Harber, C. (2008). Perpetrating disaffection: Schooling as an international problem. *Educational Studies*, *34*(5), 457–467. doi:10.1080/03055690802288445

Hartman, A. (2000). In search of subjugated knowledge. *Feminism, Community, and Communication, 11*(4), 19-23.

Hays, R. D., & DiMatteo, M. R. (1987). A short-form measure of loneliness. *Journal of Personality Assessment*, *51*(1), 69–81. doi:10.120715327752jpa5101_6 PMID:3572711

Heath, J., & Potter, A. (2005). *Nation of rebels: Why counterculture became consumer culture*. New York, NY: HarperCollins.

Hodkinson, A. (2015). *Key issues in special educational needs and inclusion*. London, UK: Sage.

Holman, B., & Ziedenberg, J. (2006). *The dangers of detention: The impact of incarcerating youth in detention and other secure facilities*. Washington, DC: Justice Policy Institute.

Holmes, J. (2001). *The search for the secure base: Attachment theory and psychotherapy*. New York, NY: Routledge.

Holt, D. B. (2005). An interview with Juliet Schor. *Journal of Consumer Culture*, *5*(1), 5–21. doi:10.1177/1469540505049847

Illouz, E. (2009). Emotions, imagination and consumption: A new research agenda. *Journal of Consumer Culture*, *9*(3), 377–413. doi:10.1177/1469540509342053

Jones, W. H., Freeman, J. R., & Goswick, R. A. (1981). The persistence of loneliness: Self and other determinants. *Journal of Personality*, *49*(1), 27–48. doi:10.1111/j.1467-6494.1981.tb00844.x

Jones, W. H., Rose, J., & Russell, D. (1990). Loneliness and social anxiety. In H. Leitenberg (Ed.), *Handbook of Social and Evaluation Anxiety* (pp. 247–266). New York, NY: Plenum. doi:10.1007/978-1-4899-2504-6_9

Kellner, D. (2015). *Guys and guns amok: Domestic terrorism and school shootings from the Oklahoma City bombing to the Virginia Tech massacre*. Abington, UK: Routledge.

Klein, N., & Sawchuk, K. (2000). No logo: Taking aim at the brand bullies. *Canadian Journal of Communication, 25*(4), 576–578.

Korman, A. K., Wittig-Berman, U., & Lang, D. (1981). Career success and personal failure: Alienation in professionals and managers. *Academy of Management Journal, 24*(2), 342–360.

Lasch, C. (1991). *The culture of narcissism: American life in an age of diminishing expectations*. New York, NY: WW Norton & Company.

Latendresse, S. J., Rose, R. J., Viken, R. J., Pulkkinen, L., Kaprio, J., & Dick, D. M. (2008). Parenting mechanisms in links between parents' and adolescents' alcohol use behaviors. *Alcoholism, Clinical and Experimental Research, 32*(2), 322–330. doi:10.1111/j.1530-0277.2007.00583.x PMID:18162066

Lerach, W. S. (2002). Plundering America: How American investors got taken for trillions by corporate insiders – The rise of the new corporate kleptocracy. *Stanford Journal of Law, Business & Finance, 8*(1), 69–126.

Mahoney, J. L., & Stattin, H. (2000). Leisure activities and adolescent antisocial behavior: The role of structure and social context. *Journal of Adolescence, 23*(2), 113–127. doi:10.1006/jado.2000.0302 PMID:10831137

Malmquist, C. P. (2007). *Homicide: A psychiatric perspective*. Washington, DC: American Psychiatric Publications.

Marx, K. (1964). *The Economic and Philosophic Manuscripts of 1844* (D. Struik, Ed.). New York, NY: International Publishers.

Mau, R. Y. (1992). The validity and devolution of a concept: Student alienation. *Adolescence, 27*(107), 731–741. PMID:1414583

McAll, C. (1990). Structural seclusion: Making structural inequality possible. In C. McAll (Ed.), *Class, ethnicity, and social inequality* (pp. 203–215). Montreal, Canada: McGill-Queen's Press.

McDonald, M., & Wearing, S. (2013). *Social psychology and theories of consumer culture: A political economy perspective*. East Sussex, UK: Routledge.

McGuigan, J. (2009). *Cool capitalism*. London, UK: Pluto Press.

McRobbie, A., & Thornton, S. L. (1995). Rethinking 'moral panic' for multi-mediated social worlds. *The British Journal of Sociology, 46*(4), 559–574. doi:10.2307/591571

Molnar, A. (1996). *Giving kids the business: The commercialization of America's schools*. Dunmore, PA: Westview Press.

Moore, S., & Boldero, J. (1991). Psychosocial development and friendship functions in adolescence. *Sex Roles*, *25*(9-10), 521–536. doi:10.1007/BF00290061

Neubauer, G., & Hurrelmann, K. (Eds.). (1995). *Individualization in childhood and adolescence*. Berlin: Walter de Gruyter. doi:10.1515/9783110811001

Office of Juvenile Justice and Delinquency Prevention. (2008). *Introduction to the survey of youth in residential placement*. Washington, DC: Author.

Perlman, D., & Peplau, L. A. (1981). Toward a social psychology of loneliness. In S. W. Duck & R. Gilmour (Eds.), *Personal relationships in disorder* (pp. 31–56). London, UK: Academic Press.

Ponzetti, J. J. Jr. (1990). Loneliness among college students. *Family Relations*, *39*(3), 336–340. doi:10.2307/584881

Pulkkinen, L. (1996). Impulse control in children. *Journal of Forensic Psychiatry*, *7*(2), 228–233. doi:10.1080/09585189608415008

Reijntjes, A., Thomaes, S., Bushman, B. J., Boelen, P. A., de Castro, B. O., & Telch, M. J. (2010). The outcast-lash-out effect in youth: Alienation increases aggression following peer rejection. *Psychological Science*, *21*(10), 1394–1398. doi:10.1177/0956797610381509 PMID:20739674

Rojek, C. (1999). *Leisure and culture*. Berlin: Springer.

Rokach, A., Orzeck, T., Cripps, J., Lackovic-Grgin, Ķ., & Penezic, Z. (2001). The effects of culture on the meaning of loneliness. *Social Indicators Research*, *53*(1), 17–31. doi:10.1023/A:1007183101458

Sandlin, J., & Callahan, J. (2009). Deviance, dissonance, and détournement: Culture jammers' use of emotion in consumer resistance. *Journal of Consumer Culture*, *9*(1), 79–115. doi:10.1177/1469540508099703

Schlenker, B. R. (1980). *Impression management*. Pacific Grove, CA: Brooks/Cole Publishing Company.

Schor, J. (2000). The New Politics of Consumption. In J. Cohen & J. Rogers (Eds.), *Do Americans shop too much?* (pp. 3–35). Boston, MA: Beacon Press.

Schor, J. (2008). *The overworked American: The unexpected decline of leisure*. New York, NY: Basic Books.

Schor, J. B. (1999). *The overspent American: Why we want what we don't need*. New York, NY: HarperPerennial.

Schor, J. B. (2014). *Born to buy: the commercialized child and the new consumer cult*. New York, NY: Simon and Schuster.

Schulz, L., & Rubel, D. (2011). A phenomenology of alienation in high school: The experiences of five male non-completers. *Professional School Counseling*, *14*(5), 286–298. doi:10.5330/PSC.n.2011-14.286

Seeman, M. (1959). On the meaning of alienation. *American Sociological Review*, *24*(6), 783–791. doi:10.2307/2088565

Shim, S. (1996). Adolescent consumer decision-making styles: The consumer socialization perspective. *Psychology and Marketing*, *13*(6), 547–569. doi:10.1002/(SICI)1520-6793(199609)13:6<547::AID-MAR2>3.0.CO;2-8

Smith, P. K., Ananiadou, K., & Cowie, H. (2003). Interventions to reduce school bullying. *Canadian Journal of Psychiatry*, *48*(9), 591–599. doi:10.1177/070674370304800905 PMID:14631879

Tedeschi, J. T. (Ed.). (2013). *Impression management theory and social psychological research*. New York, NY: Academic Press.

Thorlindsson, T., & Bernburg, J. G. (2006). Peer groups and substance use: Examining the direct and interactive effect of leisure activity. *Adolescence*, *41*(162), 321–339. PMID:16981620

Trainor, S., Delfabbro, P., Anderson, S., & Winefield, A. (2010). Leisure activities and adolescent psychological well-being. *Journal of Adolescence*, *33*(1), 173–186. doi:10.1016/j.adolescence.2009.03.013 PMID:19406463

Twenge, J. M., Baumeister, R. F., Tice, D. M., & Stucke, T. S. (2001). If you can't join them, beat them: Effects of social exclusion on aggressive behavior. *Journal of Personality and Social Psychology*, *81*(6), 1058–1069. doi:10.1037/0022-3514.81.6.1058 PMID:11761307

Twining, J. E. (1980). Alienation as a social process. *The Sociological Quarterly*, *21*(3), 417–428. doi:10.1111/j.1533-8525.1980.tb00622.x

Wearing, S., & McGehee, N. G. (2013). Volunteer tourism: A review. *Tourism Management*, *38*(October), 120–130. doi:10.1016/j.tourman.2013.03.002

Wearing, S. L. (2003). *Volunteer tourism: Experiences that make a difference*. New York, NY: Taylor & Francis.

Williamson, I., & Cullingford, C. (1997). The uses and misuses of 'alienation'in the social sciences and education. *British Journal of Educational Studies*, *45*(3), 263–275. doi:10.1111/1467-8527.00051

Woodman, D., & Bennett, A. (2015). Cultures, transitions, and generations: The case for a new youth studies. In D. Woodman & A. Bennett (Eds.), *Youth cultures, transitions, and generations* (pp. 1–15). London, UK: Palgrave Macmillan UK. doi:10.1057/9781137377234_1

ADDITIONAL READING

Archibald, W. P. (2009). Marx, globalization and alienation: Received and underappreciated wisdoms. *Critical Sociology*, *35*(2), 151–174. doi:10.1177/0896920508099190

Barber, B. (2007). *Consumed: How capitalism corrupts children, infantilizes adults and swallows citizens whole*. New York, NY: Norton & Co.

Beck, U. (1992). *Risk society: Towards a new modernity*. London, UK: Sage.

Cherrier, H. (2009). Anti-consumption discourses and consumer-resistant identities. *Journal of Business Research*, *62*(2), 181–190. doi:10.1016/j.jbusres.2008.01.025

Davidson, S. (2012). Consider the fact that I am considerate. In A. Sparman, B. Sandin, & S. Sjoberg (Eds.), *Situating child consumption: Rethinking values and notions of children, childhood and consumption* (pp. 97–114). Lund, Sweden: Nordic Academic Press.

Dewey, J. (2004). *Democracy and education*. North Chelmsford, MA: Courier Corporation.

Giddens, A. (2003). An interview with Anthony Giddens. *Journal of Consumer Culture*, *3*(3), 387–399. doi:10.1177/14695405030033013

Goldberg, M., Gorn, G., Peracchio, L., & Bamossy, G. (2003). Materialism among youth. *Journal of Consumer Behaviour*, *13*(3), 278–288.

Lerach, W. S. (2002). Plundering America: How American investors got taken for trillions by corporate insiders – The rise of the new corporate kleptocracy. *Stanford Journal of Law. Business & Finance.*, *8*(1), 69–126.

Martin, A. J., & Dowson, M. (2009). Interpersonal relationships, motivation, engagement, and achievement: Yields for theory, current issues, and educational practice. *Review of Educational Research*, *79*(1), 327–365. doi:10.3102/0034654308325583

Marx, K. (2005). *Early writings*. London, UK: Penguin.

Moor, E. (2003). Branded spaces: The scope of 'new marketing.'. *Journal of Consumer Culture*, *3*(1), 39–60. doi:10.1177/1469540503003001929

Putnam, R. D. (2001). *Bowling alone: The collapse and revival of American community*. New York, NY: Simon and Schuster.

Rice, P. F. (1996). The adolescent: Development, relationships and culture. *Adolescence*, *31*(121), 250.

Sartre, J. P. (1984). *Being and nothingness* (H. E. Barnes, Trans.). New York: NY Washington Square Press.

Tucker-Ladd, P. R. (1990). Alienated adolescents: How can schools help? *The Clearing House: A Journal of Educational Strategies, Issues and Ideas*, *64*(2), 112–114. doi:10.1080/00098655.1990.9955823

ENDNOTES

1 The use of the term "adolescent" is used very widely, denoting mostly Western youth of later school age up to their first employment.

2 The marketplace providing glamour and excitement whilst the state provides shabby, run-down services; all compensated by consumer choices. See also Gabriel and Lang (2015).

3 The responsibility is being shifted onto them: "A genealogy of the entrepreneurial self reveals that it is the relationship, promoted by neoliberalism, that one establishes to oneself through forms of personal investment (for example, user charges, student loans) and insurance that becomes the central ethical component of a new individualized and privatized consumer welfare economy." (Besley, 2009, p. 47).

4 Teenage students would often boast they could behave as they wished and return home in the early hours with impunity.

5 Addictive and anti-social Grand Theft Auto IV broke industry records with sales of around 3.6 million units on its first day of release and grossed more than $500 million in revenue in the first week, from an estimated 6 million units sold worldwide.

6 The US criminal justice system exerts a heavy disciplinary power, currently incarcerating more youth than any other country in the world (Besley, 2009). On any given day more than 126,000 youth are serving time in jails and prisons based on rates from the year 2007 (Office of Juvenile Justice and Deliquency Precention, 2008). Approximately 500,000 – half a million – youth are brought to detention centres in a given year (Holman & Ziedenburg, 2006; Besley, 2009).

7 In the society of the spectacle, 'People responded to others as if their actions were being recorded and simultaneously transmitted to an unseen audience.' (Lasch, 1991, p. 239).

Chapter 7
Adolescent Self-Consciousness and the *En Fusion*

John Graham Wilson
Assumption University of Thailand, Thailand

ABSTRACT

This chapter aims to bypass the problem of categorizations for the young, offer an explanation of the en fusion as a quasi-organizational force in relation to youth association, and consider what kind of self-consciousness may be said to have developed amongst adolescents and whether any reflexive self-consciousness can act as a quasi-political force running against media manipulation.

INTRODUCTION

In a previous chapter, it was seen that contemporary youth culture is divided by uncertainties and ambiguities concerning appearance and selfhood, individual distinctiveness, and the search for an identity independent of the adult majority and worthy of the respect of others, especially peers. The indeterminacies of collective and class affiliation reveal an archipelago of dissimilar collectives, forever merging, transforming and disappearing, forever the prey of marketing strategies that seek to capture and disempower oppositional attitudes via marketing research and Trojan horse styles of advertising, converting dissent into consumer practices stimulating revenue for an outside economic oligarchy.

The kind of self-consciousness may be said to have developed amongst the young; reciprocally, in and out of the peer group, in contrast to the inadequate and procrustean depictions currently reflected throughout the mass media. It will be asked whether any reflexive self-consciousness, on the part of youth, can act as a quasi-political force running against media manipulation in the commercial world that is solely concerned with profits. Where youth collectives fail to coagulate into distinct notional groups, alternatives to taxonomy will be sought via a consideration of the *en fusion*, a French term stemming from Sartre's later philosophy concerning levels of human association. This is effected through the contrastive notion of seriality – a lone, socially disconnected condition – as compared to fusing groups involved in reciprocity and shared goals via perceived exigencies.

DOI: 10.4018/978-1-5225-6120-0.ch007

BACKGROUND

A working definition of any sociological phenomenon should satisfy both rigor and adequate coverage but this chapter notes that alienation rarely fits into any clear-cut categories as defined by a unifying set of attributes.

In print, academics frequently argue about what constitutes group membership (Kruks, 1992). Some theorists move away from the notion of set-theoretic subcultural identities, preferring to describe adolescents as permanently in transition where youth culture is but a fleeting set of options where young people transit through a succession of influences. But this has been contradicted by Bennett (2005) who insists class divisions are very much operative and there are still structurally embedded inequalities that supervene (Bennett, 2005; Shildrick & MacDonald, 2006). Moreover, theorists like Wearing *et al.* (2013) maintain that youth represents a quasi-political force wielding the power to contradict and threaten hegemonies.

How is one to create systems of classification amongst youth collectives according to, say, age group, gender, social, class, location, dress, behaviour and attitudes? Is this best accommodated by the fuzzy thinking in current sociology as vague differences between a subculture, a clubculture and a lifestyle? (see Winter & Kron, 2009). And how do such distinctions fuse or separate? What precise descriptors would satisfy critical readers from different theoretical persuasions? (Hollands, 2002). Attitudes – especially those bound up with the quaternity concerning states of alienation, are what notionally aggregate amidst variety, but these often report subjective outlooks, and have no objective status in the world—especially in relation to assertions concerning what they think they are not.[1]

A variety of commentators, appreciating that collectives have few discernible boundaries, and no strict criteria for inclusion or exclusion, have tried to narrow the referents as in the case of Winter and Kron's (2009) considerations regarding ambiguity; in our case, about whether an individual is classed as "in"or "out" of a particular peer group (Nahon, 2011; Santamarina & Chameau, 1987; Winter & Kron, 2009). Defining oneself by what one is not would be problematic for any set-theoretic system of classification; and yet perhaps, in part, explainable by Sartre's concept of alterity—the ever-present sense of negation as a vacuum pointing to our sense of aloneness—absence as an impressively negative presence within social relations.[2]

Hollands (2002) reports that even amidst the hybrid forms of youth identity currently in the north of England, night-time economies mostly managed by corporate concerns, show important distinctions based on spatial divisions and socially segmented consumption that could be classified as independent of selectivity and subjective choices. These youth groups are quick to discriminate and classify amongst each other as in the case of students, "townies," "scallies," "Kevs," and "charvers." For Hollands, traditional styles of masculinity and territoriality prevail. But then, for Thornton (1995), sub-cultural capital is simply mediated through displays of taste based around concepts surrounding authenticity and inauthenticity, hipness, as contrasted with the mainstream, or the subcultural underground versus mass media and commodification. (Hollands, 2010; Thornton, 1995). However, a major theme, throughout, is that consumption-related behaviour is a principal means by which social standing is accomplished as an ongoing process. And the protean nature of youth collectives often renders concepts too vague, and hence not sociologically useful. There is a need to constantly postulate (or invent) boundary demarcations—and then promptly dismantle them.

As a possible solution, we will discuss one theoretical means of categorising collectives via universal, yet abstract, principles of association, as a general theory of practical ensembles, with a view to clarifying whether youth culture should be regarded as a powerless, random and disassociated force, or as unified and markedly political potency when displaying similar kinds of opposition towards the newly prevailing consumerist culture. With this in mind, we have kept the range of the term "adolescent" very flexible and have used it as an umbrella term for a generously wide spectrum.

Do adolescents belong to temporary localised gatherings, or extended fusions? Is there any kind of ideological consensus that might bind them? One may question to what degree the new types of adolescent identities are coherent in terms of individual and group activities, both as nominal entities then as virtually self-conscious collectives, and to what extent adolescents, when influenced by media-driven consumerism, can be regarded as reciprocally communicating individuals within a widespread association free of intrusive media-meddling. Unlike classification according to the vagaries of musical tastes and clothes fashions, demarcation through universally regulatory principles of association will be attempted.

This perspective is derived from Sartre's *Critique of Dialectical Reason* (2004) in which he attempts to refine descriptions of collectives in terms of groups, organisations, institutions and the *en fusion* (a coming together), the last being a special type of gathering where beliefs are mutualised, coming from a cline running between dispersed anonymity and avowed-upon association. It makes an enormous difference whether youth collectives exist without much reciprocal communication (yet still around each other); as passive ensembles, widespread or contiguous; or whether they have a self-conscious understanding of their own situation with common understandings and aims that go beyond isolated acts of distinction-making in terms of dress and behaviour (Mahoney *et al.*, 2000; Sommer *et al.*, 2001; Wearing, *et al.*, 2013). Some authors contend adolescents act as a quasi-political force in society (e.g Wearing *et al.* 2013; Umemura & Šerek, 2016). But the latter is unlikely due to an impoverished means of a universal and reciprocal association; both in terms of contiguity, plus the lack of reciprocal, reflexive awareness unlikely to be endure in constantly dispersing gatherings. It is doubtful whether such collectives, in practising deviant consumption and behaviour, can be described as political since the meaning of political organisation commonly involves organised behaviour within distinct and durable groups that have specifiable beliefs, goals and norms of association.

Sartre's Critique of Dialectical Reason (CDR) was seminal in that it offered a new means by which to understand human association over a wide range of blurred collectives ranging from unaffiliated casual assemblies to permanent institutions. His account of isolation versus affiliation is a particularly convincing one for all kinds of human association, though made complex by his language and French standards of textual organisation (Catalano, 1986; Sartre, 2004). Sartre's analysis largely revolves around socialist inclinations (Kruks, 1995). But, when applied, his account makes considerable sense *without* adopting a Marxist viewpoint. It can easily pertain to any political outlook in contemporary society including a much larger range of collectives than he has covered.

The Lone Existence: Seriality

Sartre begins with a description of the lone individual living a city life amidst a host of other lone individuals. Such a serialised existence is characterised by passivity, alienation, alterity and multiplicity (Catalano, 1986; Sartre, 2004). In this case, examples of serialised existences would include young people who infrequently attend schools or colleges, classmates who never talk to each other; young fast-food workers who have little time to chat, teenagers who spend too much time alone in their bedrooms, or loosely wandering around in shopping malls.[3]

Interestingly, the serialised state, as offered by Sartre as a form of alienation, is still best conceived as an aspect of collective behaviour insofar as it requires negation and the concept of contiguous others to be 'alienated from'. So, like for us, it is significant for Sartre that the composition of remote ensembles is defined as much by what they are not as by what they are (2004). But the lone teenager, lamenting his/her friendless existence and watching TV alone in his/her bedroom is still exposed to a media aimed at the young and may privately pursue fashion in clothes. The individual is, by this token, a member of a passive ensemble—indirectly connected through television. Conceptually, aloneness is not an absolute aloneness but merely belongs to the aloneness of the serialised collective of all teenagers who mope in their bedrooms. In Sartre's terms, the practice of staying alone is not only one realising him/herself as distinct from others, but also a practice of the other as much as she is one of those others to herself (cf. Catalano, 1986). On this level, the teenager is "as the other" alone in their bedroom, but the significance is always elsewhere, out there in the series. There is little thetic awareness of the experienced condition. This depiction can be understood better when considering reciprocity and shared experiences amongst adolescents as the target of marketing practices. Hence, common forms of isolation exist not just as a neutral non-contiguous ensemble—it is rather a particular type of negative reciprocity. The lone teenager in one's bedroom interiorises the isolation as singular but is negatively bonded by the others of similar type. It will, therefore, be very significant if young people do not develop much thetic comprehension of the marketing strategies that surround and interpenetrate their local peer groups. Where a punk-style consumer cynicism creeps in, an attempt to extend the scope of product-positive affective bonds between young consumers and brands becomes effectively sabotaged.

Sartre uses the term "collective" (*le collectif*) to describe ensembles that are constituted by the structure of an external field of the manmade organisation of matter—technology—which acts upon individuals and their future choices. Under this rubric, the human world of infrastructure, utilities and consumer products are conceived as an arrangement constructed by previous freedoms to regulate the freedom of others. Our examples of unassociated others can include adolescent TV viewers, readers of teen magazines, a lone youth in a park drinking cider; those whose constitution as an ensemble is formed by the material facts of physical separation from each other—as an indirect assembly, frequently subject to broadcasting technology and the use of one-way communication in print and broadcasting. Significantly, it is the technology that determines to what extent this collective is free to associate—or not (Sartre, 2004). The obligation of alterity (otherness) is imposed upon TV watchers as an impotent relation of non-reciprocity existing between each observer when separately watching diverse advertisements for Pepsi, peanut butter, chocolate bars and hot fashion deals – they are communicated to, but not between, they are simultaneously present to the broadcast, but not to each other.

Where inequitable hegemonic forms of power have commandeered the one-way, top-down communication system in advertising and the omnipresent media, which define and situate youth in a false depiction of their aims, only local reciprocities may still obtain to convey resistance to this prevalence (Poyntz, 2006). As said above, other aspects of seriality may be voluntary as in the case of adolescents ignoring each other on a dance floor or, in Sartre's example, of people in a bus queue who have no connections with each other apart from their separate intentions to get to a destination (Sartre, 2004).

So, adolescents, as the recipients of media and marketing techniques, can be seen as those who experience an overwhelmingly one-way means of communication. As an essentially passive ensemble; they have little choice but to undergo a constant bombardment of their leisure time, encouraged to do things like glam it up with makeover ideas or get flirty in awesome party hairstyles; but not to contemporaneously criticise such practices together. The celebrated mass-media culture is one in which dissent, or any critical activity ("Yuk, that looks gross") is persistently obviated by the one-way technologies of broadcasting.

The difference between passive collectives and groups is considerable. Unlike passive assemblies, groups are highly active and mediated by reciprocal interaction. It is in the group that teenagers associate to compare their acquisitions and indulge in the aforesaid status-claiming behaviour. Sartre employs the term "group" to denote persons who come together in a purposive and organised manner. Unlike the common loose use of the word, he defines groups by their also recognising exigencies which press them to rescind certain individualistic freedoms and act as a whole, based on the reciprocal perception of common needs, in our case, perhaps to determine what is "in" and what is "out" as a current fashion, or to jointly confirm a particular dance-style as "cool." To this extent pledges might be agreed on to confirm group membership, such as 'pink on Wednesdays' as practiced by the Plastics in *Mean Girls* (2004) or regular booze-soaked evenings with Renton trapped amidst the Edinburgh drug scene in *Trainspotting* (1996). In groups, individuals see themselves in each other (Sartre, 2004) as in the case of music fans who meet specifically to celebrate, learn and practice a particular style of dance. Each member celebrates the dance style as an attainment, and joins together in cooperation, fulfilling an undisclosed need for common association. In order for the group to succeed (say, as a performance organised locally) members must pledge themselves to regular attendance and participation. Principles like this will apply to many collectives of this type including clubs, basketball teams, football teams, bands, gangs, and cliques sometimes widening out and formalising—morphing from a sporadic group into an organisation with membership rules, joining ceremonies, premises, officials and their own publicity.

Despite often seeming so distinct and tangible, groups are nevertheless ephemeral in the long run, forever in transition (*en cours*) and may dissolve, evaporate, or institutionalise into circular seriality where everybody is actively implicated in the group's eventual demise, as in the case of an out-of-date fan club (Sartre, 2004). Significantly, for Sartre, there can be no we-subject in group relations – a single entity functioning as an ego-like embodiment of a corporate will (i.e. no true punk; no absolute Sloan). Since goals may change, and pledges can be revoked, most members remain free to abandon a morphing group at any time by their own independent volition; the group's composition is therefore forever uncertain, unspoken, couched and implicit, as in the case of occasional clubbing or going to a rave.

Totalisation

Individuals may, or may not, conceive of their own situation through what Sartre calls totalisation. By this term, Sartre means the constantly developing degree to which individuals can effectively conceive of and define themselves as living within a particularised social milieu, with specific relations to society as a whole (2004). Totalisation will involve a conscious recognition of one's state of affairs, as personally lived, but also as an event that happens to everybody reifying through broadening increments of thetic awareness. It will involve, at least, a partially informed knowledge of economics, employment conditions, rights and duties (or the lack of them) and the interplay of wider social forces. Thus, a totalising individual will thetically understand why she is feeling powerless and how she has become estranged.

Within a totalisation of the alienation quaternity, situations become schematised and comprehensible. An inclusive totalisation must include comprehension of the social milieu in which an adolescent group forms, involving topical considerations such as social class, disposable income, the local economy, local employment conditions, and an appreciation of their own consumer behaviour; by which it is being cajoled and channelled by effective advertising, into pre-planned, corporatized consumer lifestyles—yet without any genuine consent. In other words, totalisation would be the beginnings of a political consciousness that appreciates the dynamics of power relations in the wider world, in which the individual is placed, and how one is constantly affected thereby. Thus, for example, teenagers may, or may not, totalise themselves as affluent, middle-class, or marginalised, with an articulate comprehension of why one seems to be engaged in meaningless tasks, or *becomes* estranged amidst unconnected lonely others (CDR:366-73; Catalano, 1986).

Unsurprisingly, adolescents who do not totalise their situation will be the victim of what appears to be forever unconnected circumstances.

The *En Fusion*

Having described a lack of affiliation, one can still say when adolescents agree to meet at a site of consumption for the purpose of entertainments or deviant leisure, they can become, no matter how temporarily, an *en fusion*. That is, they evidence emerging group-like behaviour by finding what they have in common and launching into it, there and then. But once the *en fusion* coalesces into some degree of permanence (follow-up meetings), they can start to launch principles of association (e.g., no drugs or alcohol at our gatherings), timed get-togethers (e.g. adolescent parties organised on Facebook where hundreds of young people converge at a particular site), recognise emergent leaders, embark on decision-making procedures concerning the music to be played, debate perceived needs such as parking, or bathroom facilities, where the *en fusion* may further reify itself increasingly in a group-like arrangement, culminating with the pledge to continue – but, then again, such associations may turn out simply *ad hoc* and easily dissolve back into seriality.

Remarks about an absence of political association may be periodically subject to doubt. During the 60s, collectives involving college-aged young people were overtly political, widespread and very well-organised; staging demonstrations and sit-ins, and occupying buildings, college campuses and highways. More recently, encounters such as Occupy and Nuit Debout involved a high percentage of young participants. Over the decades, quasi-political discourse has been planted in music-led collectives (rock, rasta, rap).

One must therefore be careful when using the terms collectives, *en fusion,* and group. Unlike organisations (political parties, institutions) there will be an ongoing absence of discrete classifications and stability. The opacity of this conception will have import for this chapter's conclusion.

Broadcasting and the Media: *Détournement*

Working on the principles of loose association, broadcasting aimed at youth through the media capitalises on the apparent disunity in gatherings when they are corralled, inveigled and persuaded via the technology of broadcasting. The technology of broadcasting ensures distance and impotence on the part of the listener who, unlike contiguous gatherings, cannot provide any feedback.

Mainstream media constitutes a hegemonic apparatus that organizes and exercises power, as an apparatus for distributing information throughout Western culture (Masterman, 1997, 1993). In our case of the Trojan horses, mainstream broadcasting attempts an exteriorisation of the interiority of the audience. Here Klein's "colonisation of the mind" can be understood where marketing strategists attempt to redefine a subcultural genre in the services of selling. But it is a disfigured and foreign simulation, as evidenced by too many smiles, pre-planned knowing glances and hammy acting that adolescents are quick to spot as counterfeit (Klein & Sawchuk, 2000). Characters in a transmission (serials, soaps, advertising) can never be simply themselves for they always speak as participators in a previously structured transmission designed to replicate current stereotypes. In order to act effectively in the service of a corporatized transmission, everyone involved in the broadcasting freely chooses to be someone than him/herself so each employee acts as the other, who is now other than himself (Catalano, 1986; Sartre, 2004). Sartre regards the broadcasting voice as vertiginous, that is to be a broadcaster is to be other than oneself and to increase fictions through a multiplicity of indiscernibles; a non-human voice with a non-identity. This does not imply that the affirmations of the broadcaster are necessarily false, but it does imply that their sincerity cannot be authentically individualised. And, within the broadcast, there is a double alterity: the presenters and actors speak as other than themselves whilst the audience members experience themselves as put upon concerning the verisimilitude of the message (Catalano 1986; Sartre, 2004). Here, it may be pointed out that this kind of impotence is adverse to the bonding and positive reciprocity characteristic of associating collectives. No genuine reciprocity can be founded on a bogus representation. Inside this cuckoo's nest of simulation, the marketers proffer yet more modified versions of their own researched conception of the adolescent consumer—with a view to making sales. And advertising is on the whole successful in attracting new consumers.

Such productions aim at the dissemination of a false totality—a totality that tacitly insists on the formal appearance of a synthetic unity and, as widely disseminated, acts as a powerful counter-force against our previous definitions of totalisation, by lone individuals, experiencing powerlessness, meaninglessness and estrangement in their alienated state (Sartre, 2004). This means that what viewers used to identify as truth and sincerity has become diaphanous. In order to survive the crisis of youth, young people, these days, will need to invent different standards of verification concerning productions relevant to their own situation. Truth is therefore now being cramped and confined amidst small circles (local peer groups) of trusting intersubjectivities where bottom-up interpretations can be circulated and young audiences may resist the polished flow of edited hoopla (Masterman, 1983).

Where the media has a ubiquitous presence, local youth can easily be swamped by the snappy counterfeit versions of their privately constructed social reality, and so they develop a demeanour of wary suspicion, the general mistrust often noted by teachers in classrooms, and their own intuitive techniques of deflecting polluted information. So, from this critical standpoint, advertising broadcasts cannot, and will not, act to bring young people together as a force of consensually unified action; rather, they address each individual in the privacy of an isolation created and sustained by the fabrications perpetuated by broadcasting technology. Corporate controlled broadcasting sustains an illusion of a false and incomplete totality within which an audience-inspired totalisation is constantly deflected, Sartre insists, precisely in order that society may be impeded in forming authentically motivated groups that might threaten their power (see also Catalano, 1986). The abstract individual, as a target of the media, has long been a ready-made notion, "a schema forged both in experience and through the schematisations of the mass media" (Sartre, 2004, p. 273), thus anticipating other writers like Jameson (1991) who maintains that the market as a concept has little to do with freedom of choice due to the all-pervasive influence of capitalism (Jameson, 1991).

In such cases, teenagers are not able to see themselves in each other if the model selves they have been exposed to are a) inauthentic fictions and b) marketed by invisiblised groups that have no discernible provenance as organisations acting in good faith. For the sponsored broadcasts by advertisers (where programme content and the three-minute adverts are practically indistinguishable) are but digital chimera and, despite the posturings of charismatic chumminess, cannot establish credibility within wider collectives.

In order to fight back, opposition to a deceptive, one-way communication system, irony, sarcasm, and caustic wit can be used locally amongst those in the know. A specific technique, known as *détournement* is, in effect, a form of copy-cat irony where the source of the meaning of an original representation is subverted and rerouted to create a new kind of antithetical meaning that serves a new, often revelatory, intention. Familiar depictions are turned upside down and re-presented. When you mimic somebody, in a humorous reproduction of what they have said, this is a détournement. It works on the original to create a humorous effect – which can also excoriate the original and reduce credibility. There is always an element of dominance-seeking antagonism between producer and receiver; in our mass media case, of aggressive pseudo-representations manufactured to beguile the young. But it is a two-edged sword. The new meaning can serve the exploiter, or the exploited, according to which faction is creating, or responding to, the message. The marketers must therefore always be 'one step ahead' of spectator accommodation to their plans.

Détournement is a method of recovering a sense of control and avoiding an imposed feeling of *powerlessness*. With détournement, outside advertisers have detoured a common scene as a means of selling sneakers. The original consists of the well-known slogan, "Just do it." The détournement consists of the reconfigured inked-in retort: "Child labour? Just do it." [4] Another detours commercial beauty ideals by ironizing emaciated models, using zombie chic as from beyond the grave, where improvised inked-in skulls are used to declaim that the beauty industry actively encourages eating disorders (Klein & Sawchuk, 2000).[5]

Advertisements often play on fears. In the movie, *Mean Girls* (2004), appearances are marketed as "pink on Wednesdays," tank-tops and miniskirts, where cruelties are cleverly broadcast to put others down who do not measure up. Anyone watching The Plastics will observe their consumption of fashion articles in order to keep up and become dominant within that peer group. (Regina: "Get in loser. We're going shopping.") (*Mean Girls*; 2004). Competition between the mean girls is strong: there is backstabbing and slander in virtually every scene. Attractiveness is the key to power and position in North Shore High. Desired, envied and loathed, the girls flaunt their sexuality and constantly seek confirmation of their status as Plastics.[6]

As noted above, researchers successfully penetrate youth consciousness by examining the language of spied-upon discourse fields – the fields where comments and observations made by young people are skimmed-off for later readjustment and dissemination. This is accomplished with a view to hijacking and rerouting youth's early, yet-to-be-formed values, and to discourage any emergent anti-consumerist outlooks through still malleable, uninformed predilections. Captured belief will endlessly fund mass production. Pseudo-representations attempt the detouring of private, local subjectivities into generalised styles of consumption behaviour, but are often pre-empted, unmasked and lampooned by their ironic targets who have a reservoir of resentment building up against manipulative attempts to garner their shopping behaviour.

Hence, seemingly, these pseudo-representations are not entirely credible, for the more-alert among us. But, such media fictions can still be cloned into someone's interiority, inside one-way communication and the passive culture of spectatorship; especially when the target collectives remain dispersed, disorganised and ill-informed concerning the intentions running behind such ubiquitous media productions.

Social Networking and Teenage Communities

One may raise the issue that one-way communication has become far less prevalent since the advent of social media where young people can interact independently of monopolies and exchange thetic views on any topic. But Reich (2010) asks whether social networking sites create a sense of community with the necessary solidarity of established groups. Bearing in mind that the users do not meet in physical space (so they cannot readily be said to hang out), Reich points out that such collectives have boundaries withal concerning membership and normative behaviour (perhaps echoing Sartre's discussion of pledge-like affiliation and Bennet's concept of class consciousness), a sense of personal investment involving emotional benefits resembling those in face-to-face gatherings (seeing oneself in the other), plus common value systems, norms, rules, and the sense of identity, commitment, and association that also characterize various physical communities and other communities of interest Reich, 2010).

One may say that some, but not all, of Sartre's defining characteristics for group behaviour have been satisfied. Moreover, powerlessness and estrangement are somewhat on the wane as net-surfing adolescents legitimise each other's perspectives and bond together on networks. Nevertheless, these collectives are forever loosely constituted and they are open to an alternative critical description of networked individualism where alterity re-emerges via dissociative practices such as reduced participation (lurking), breaking of the rules concerning respectful behaviour, lack of commitment to any tacit norms and values, or simply disappearing from the network at any time. Reich completes her article by insisting that, amidst adolescent social networking, although participants show habit-forming enthusiasm for going online, individualism still reigns in such communities where site members have never attested to a common sense of identity (again like seeing oneself in the other), or specified purposes (exigencies), and where spiteful jabs, rumours and misunderstandings circulate, some members getting banned, and there is frequent emotional dissonance contrasting with periodic flares of adorational intimacy (Moore & Boldero, 1991; Reich, 2010). A distinct sense of community continuously falters.

So, these online communities look fragmentary when alterity reigns through intermittent 'disassembling assemblies'. Wearing's (2003) thought that youth antagonism advocates emergent political activity becomes unsustainable. For one needs to ask what strengthens any emergent political activity? The main constituent is organisation.

Countercultures?

The idea of a counterculture is frequently offered as an antidote to the consumer-dominated world that surrounds us, but is largely ineffective, and, according to some, has helped to create exactly the consumer society radicals want to destroy (Heath & Potter, 2005).

As mentioned above, the difficulty with finding coherence in oppositional behaviour from Western teenagers is weakened by its disorganised constitution which lacks coherent verbal expression or programmes for disseminating organised opinion. It has none of the characteristics of, say, organised labour or consumer activist groups working in other collectives. Distance and fragmentation confirm further aspects of alienation (estrangement and powerlessness) where participants are still unwilling to ascribe themselves as belonging to a distinct collective with common aims, whilst others may be involved in an almost politicised activism (Gabriel & Lang, 2015; Winlow & Hall, 2009).

Western teenagers are rarely cohesively organised into groups with the characteristics of political association as specified by Sartre (see especially Collins & Yeskel, 2011). They lack a unified voice or provide any substantial spokespersons that can claim to represent a political faction. There is, hence, little sense of a we-subject; little evidence of a *mitsein* beyond that of the usual pleasure-seeking collectives. Larger assemblies, where performers venture into political commentary, foster some kind of us-ness but, like a concert audience, the us-ness evaporates as soon as one goes through the exit doors—or switches off the screen.

It is soon obvious that such signifiers only broadcast loosely connotative meanings; that is, they may allude to ideological notions (e.g. within political and social commentary found in, say, African-American rap music) variously associated with coherent opposition and dissent, emanating from subcultural sources, and, oppositionally, diverge from the norms of the prevailing wider culture in which they are embedded; but they rarely encapsulate schematic propositional meanings with a qualified sense and reference, truly representative of some joint opinion. Though the words in rap songs may coagulate opinion to an extent, in certain corners, this can be, once again, simply seeming little more than loosely associated grumblings, earning only a nominal presence in the media (Collins & Yeskel, 2011).

Again, there are few explicitly socio-political references beyond the simplified one-off anodyne expressions found on t-shirts (Just do it, Be legendary.) and the throw-away expressions from randomly selected media citations (Live your life. Be happy.) Moreover, the signs used by Western teenagers have mostly been borrowed from other networks of association, so diverse in their fuzzy logic that they will rarely gel into any coherent notional whole. The discourse fields from which they obtain are far too wide, indiscriminate, and often glibly contradictory. Therefore, in addition to lacking the qualities necessary to produce organised dissent, there is no cohesive or lucid expression, other than to proclaim the perennial we are against. But who is the "we" and what is "the against?" As anything approaching a putative ideational or directional strategy, the current oppositional strategies of collectivised youth, as a generality, remain the still unfocussed mumblings of "rebels without a cause."[7] Or are they? Against all this, someone may argue that the prevailing wider culture is similarly diffuse and indefinite in its composition. Furthermore, that youth culture does not need a sense of coherent opposition in order to make its presence felt. In fact, it may be better that a youth culture refrains from the kind of organisation insisted on by Sartre in order that it may not be pinned down and contained.

In a similarly sober vein, Wearing states:

Needless to say such quietism benefits capitalist social relations in that even strong youth resistance, when it does occur, can never break up the social fabric via revolutionary movement because youth are largely submerged in familial and territorial networks as well as the dominant relations of socio-cultural regulation that commonly define them as non-voters and without a say in their own futures. (Wearing, 2003, p. 4).

Thetic Consciousness

So, once again there is no *thetic* consciousness implied within a fashion statement such as. I wear torn jeans because I identify with poverty and the downtrodden. That is, there is no coherent philosophy or implied interlocking systems of belief existing within common discourse fields managing ideas of socio-political import. Like 50s beatnik counterparts, the torn-jeans wearer cannot coherently explain why torn jeans are worn. Rather, adoption of fashion styles belongs to the generalised expression of cool where this floating signifier does not specify a political outlook but may (temporarily, attitudinally) allude to one.

For some, however, a measure of curiosity and some cognitive processing may incite ideological reflection concerning the larger social setting in which a particular distancing takes place, especially if embedded in a non-optional situation of subordination, competitiveness, monotony and drudgery, exploitation and economic instability (Barbash, 1972).

Torn jeans may signify a rejection of values found amongst smart professionals but they do not, in themselves, imply an adoption of the values found amidst, say, the torn clothes of the labouring classes (cf. Baudrillard, 2017). As an aspect of cool, pre-torn jeans can be purveyed as a brand-led entity piggy-backing on the whims of teen shoppers. Notions of cool can be planted, like the Trojan horse, within the structure of one-way communication where freedom styles itself as an inevitable recursive interplay between consumer resistance and marketing agents (Penaloza & Price, 1993).

CONCLUSION

Youth alienation is not an unprompted, spontaneous phenomenon without causes outside the individual subjectivity; but alienation is effected mostly within individual subjectivities, primarily on a serial basis. Furthermore, youth alienation occurs in temporally specific stages. Some aspects of youth alienation can be explained in terms of *lack* – something that is all-pervasively not there – especially in relation to affection, acceptance, support and regard. Moreover, outshoots of reactive rebellion, deviance and risk-taking can be subverted and commandeered by marketing methods, then fed back to youth through 'Trojan horse' practices in advertising. It has been noted that techniques of marketing research have reached highly sophisticated levels of penetration into peer-group consciousness, beyond the cognitive awareness of most young consumers, and that youth culture has been specifically targeted where individuals may be confounded within skilfully imposed mystification, via manipulating concepts of cool.

Today, dissent is still happening in small pockets with the youth *en fusion*. But, the numbers are smaller than, say, the 60s and the exigencies lack clarity and widespread coherence. Unlike the 60s, a general capacity to imagine, propose and beget qualitative social change, obfuscated within inordinately media-managed youth audiences, has been greatly blurred and accommodated by commercial interests (Cohen, 2016).

It has been asserted that the transcendence of the foregoing may only be accomplished by the development of a reflexive, thetic consciousness that totalises the individual situation looking at economic and social reality from the individual situational standpoint; that current neoliberal ideology is tacitly hostile towards any discourse field that might weaken their dominion, where contemporary estimations of human wellbeing are still mostly assessed in terms of private personal fortune, ignoring community welfare, as a preparation for future shallow, materialistic lifestyles. The question is, of course, whether such a thetic consciousness may develop and spread to unify dissent.

REFERENCES

Barbash, J. (1972). *The tensions of work*. Madison, WI: Industrial Relations Research Institute.

Baudrillard, J. (2017). *The consumer society* (C. Turner, Trans.). London, UK: Sage.

Bennett, A. (2005). In defence of neo-tribes: A response to Blackman and Hesmondhalgh. *Journal of Youth Studies*, *9*(2), 255–259. doi:10.1080/13676260500149402

Catalano, J. S. (1986). A commentary on Jean-Paul Sartre's critique of dialectical reason: Vol. 1. *Theory of practical ensembles*. Chicago, IL: University of Chicago Press.

Cohen, P. (2016). From here to modernity. In S. Blackman & M. Kempson (Eds.), *The subcultural imagination: Theory, research and reflexivity in contemporary youth cultures* (pp. 19–32). New York, NY: Routledge.

Collins, C., & Yeskel, F. (2011). *Economic apartheid in America: A primer on economic inequality & insecurity*. New York, NY: The New Press.

Gabriel, Y., & Lang, T. (2015). *The unmanageable consumer*. London, UK: Sage.

Heath, J., & Potter, A. (2005). *Nation of rebels: Why counterculture became consumer culture*. New York, NY: HarperCollins.

Hollands, R. (2002). Divisions in the dark: Youth cultures, transitions and segmented consumption spaces in the night-time economy. *Journal of Youth Studies*, *5*(2), 153–171. doi:10.1080/13676260220134421

Jameson, F. (1991). *Postmodernism, or, the cultural logic of late capitalism*. Durham, NC: Duke University Press.

Klein, N., & Sawchuk, J. K. (2000). No Logo: Taking aim at the brand bullies. *Canadian Journal of Communication*, *25*(4), 576–578.

Kruks, S. (1992). Gender and subjectivity: Simone de Beauvoir and contemporary feminism. *Signs (Chicago, Ill.)*, *18*(1), 89–110. doi:10.1086/494780

Mahoney, J. L., & Stattin, H. (2000). Leisure activities and adolescent antisocial behavior: The role of structure and social context. *Journal of Adolescence*, *23*(2), 113–127. doi:10.1006/jado.2000.0302 PMID:10831137

Mandiberg, M. (Ed.). (2012). *The social media reader*. New York, NY: NYU Press.

Masterman, L. (1983). Media education in the 1980s. *Journal of Educational Television*, *9*(1), 7–20. doi:10.1080/0260741830090102

Masterman, L. (1993). The media education revolution. *Canadian Journal of Educational Communication*, *22*(1), 5–14.

Masterman, L. (1997). A rationale for media education. In R. W. Kubey (Ed.), *Media literacy in the information age* (pp. 15–68). New Brunswick, NJ: Transaction Publishers.

Mau, R. (1992). The validity and devolution of a concept: Student alienation. *Adolescence*, *27*(107), 731–741. PMID:1414583

Mean Girls. (2004). Paramount Pictures.

Moore, S., & Boldero, J. (1991). Psychosocial development and friendship functions in adolescence. *Sex Roles*, *25*(9), 521–536. doi:10.1007/BF00290061

Nahon, K. (2011). Network theoryl Fuzziness of inclusion/exclusion in networks. *International Journal of Communication*, *5*, 756–772.

Penaloza, L., & Price, L. (1993). Consumer resistance: A conceptual overview. In L. McAlister & M. L. Rothschild (Eds.), *Advances in consumer research* (pp. 123–128). Provo, UT: Association for Consumer Research.

Poyntz, S. R. (2006). Independent media, youth agency, and the promise of media education. *Canadian Journal of Education/Revue canadienne de l'éducation, 29*(1), 154-175.

Reich, S. M. (2010). Adolescents' sense of community on myspace and facebook: A mixed-methods approach. *Journal of Community Psychology*, *38*(6), 688–705. doi:10.1002/jcop.20389

Santamarina, J. C., & Chameau, J. L. (1987). Membership functions II: Trends in fuzziness and implications. *International Journal of Approximate Reasoning*, *1*(3), 303–317. doi:10.1016/S0888-613X(87)80004-X

Sartre, J. P. (2004). *Critique of dialectical reason: Theory of practical ensembles* (Vol. 1). New York, NY: Verso.

Shildrick, T., & MacDonald, R. (2006). In defence of subculture: Young people, leisure and social divisions. *Journal of Youth Studies*, *9*(2), 125–140. doi:10.1080/13676260600635599

Sommer, K. L., Williams, K. D., Ciarocco, N. J., & Baumeister, R. F. (2001). When silence speaks louder than words: Explorations into the intrapsychic and interpersonal consequences of social ostracism. *Basic and Applied Social Psychology*, *23*(4), 225–243. doi:10.1207/S15324834BASP2304_1

Thornton, S. (1995). *Club cultures*. Cambridge, UK: Polity.

Trainspotting. (1996). Miramax.

Twining, J. E. (1980). Alienation as a social process. *The Sociological Quarterly*, *21*(3), 417–428. doi:10.1111/j.1533-8525.1980.tb00622.x

Umemura, T., & Šerek, J. (2016). Different Developmental Pathways from Parental Warmth to Adolescents' Trust in Peers and Politicians: Mediating Roles of Adolescent–Parent Attachment and Belief in a Just World. *Social Justice Research*, *29*(2), 186–205. doi:10.100711211-016-0258-x

Wearing, S. L. (2003). *Volunteer tourism: Experiences that make a difference*. New Yiork, NY: Taylor & Francis.

Wearing, S. L., McDonald, M., & Wearing, M. (2013). Consumer culture, the mobilisation of the narcissistic self and adolescent deviant leisure. *Leisure Studies*, *32*(4), 367–381. doi:10.1080/02614367.2012.668557

Winlow, S., & Hall, S. (2009). Living for the weekend: Youth identities in northeast England. *Ethnography, 10*(1), 91–113. doi:10.1177/1466138108099588

Winter, L., & Kron, T. (2009). Fuzzy thinking in sociology. In R. Seising (Ed.), *Views on fuzzy sets and systems from different perspectives* (pp. 301–320). Berlin, Germany: Springer. doi:10.1007/978-3-540-93802-6_14

ADDITIONAL READING

Bourdieu, P. (1999). *The weight of the world: Social suffering in contemporary society*. Stanford, CA: Polity Press.

Boyd, D. (2014). *It's complicated: The social lives of networked teens*. New Haven, CT: Yale University Press.

Young, J. (2009). Moral panic: Its origins in resistance, ressentiment and the translation of fantasy into reality. *British Journal of Criminology, 49*(1), 4–16. doi:10.1093/bjc/azn074

ENDNOTES

1 There are no grammatical predicates to bind with a non-existent subject phrase.

2 Sartre insists our intuition of absence or nothingness make up real presences in the world. See Sartre, J. P. (1966). Being and Nothingness. 1943. Trans. Hazel E. Barnes). New York: Washington Square.

3 An extreme example of this is *Hikkomori* where Japanese teenagers refuse to come out of their bedrooms for months at a time.

4 https://www.deviantart.com/art/Nike-child-145928937

5 In another good example an advert declaims: 'If this car was a lady, it would get its bottom pinched.' The spray-can détournement ran, 'If this lady was a car, she would run you down.' An airline advert ran 'Breakfast in London, lunch in New York.' The added sprayed détournement ran: 'Luggage in New Delhi.'

6 Gretchen: Well, I mean you wouldn't buy a skirt without asking your friends first if it looks good on you. Cady: I wouldn't? Gretchen: Right. Oh, and it's the same with guys. Like, you may think you like someone, but you could be wrong. http://www.imdb.com/title/tt0377092/quotes, downloaded 24th December 2017.

7 See *Rebel Without a Cause* (1955). Retrieved November 2nd, 2017 from: http://www.imdb.com/title/tt0048545/

Chapter 8
Waste and Efficiency in a Consumer Economy

Steven McMullen
Hope College, USA

ABSTRACT

Some complaints about consumerism rest on the perceived wastefulness of economic practices, for example, (1) the observation that individuals and firms discard large quantities of valuable goods, (2) the mass production of low-quality consumer goods, (3) research and product development serve the desires of the wealthy, (4) rapid product cycles and obsolescence encourage a constant stream of new purchases, and (5) consumption practices undervalue environmental and ecological goods. This chapter argues that a practice is "wasteful" if it is systemic, avoidable, and results in a lower-than-possible wellbeing. Each of the observed "wasteful" elements of the consumer economy can be explained by economic and marketing practices, though only a subset are avoidable and diminish consumer wellbeing, and are therefore truly excessive. This chapter concludes by examining some proposed solutions to economic wastefulness, as well as some alternative visions of economic progress that can more powerfully distinguish between justified and wasteful practices.

INTRODUCTION

In many urban areas, both when it is legal and when it is not, you can find individuals gaining a large portion of their consumable goods from the refuse available around their city. Once the occupation only of those in extreme poverty, "dumpster diving" or practicing "freeganism" has grown as an underground phenomenon among those wishing to protest the excesses of the modern consumer economy. As an anti-consumerist protest this practice is notably coherent: it is only possible to live well consuming out of dumpsters if there are significant quantities of discarded goods available in the system. By pulling their food out of dumpsters, these activists are refusing to contribute to the demand for consumer goods (Ferrell, 2006; Shantz, 2005). More importantly, this practice draws attention to the sometimes staggering volume of wasted goods that are discarded each day in a large city. Statistics about food waste and landfill contents reinforce this point and highlight a paradox about our economic system – it may often be the case that the "efficient" practice is to discard a large quantity of useful goods.

DOI: 10.4018/978-1-5225-6120-0.ch008

Overall, our economic system is efficient in a number of important ways. We get far more value out of each unit of energy, we do a much better job using and preserving manufacturing materials, and recycling continues to improve. Given the strengths of a competitive market system, this kind of growing efficiency makes sense. What requires explanation is the cluster of complaints about the wastefulness of our consumer economy that warrant examination. There are a number of features of modern market economies that often strike participants as excessive or misaligned in some fashion. Consider the following list:

1. Each day, vast quantities of food and other valuable goods are discarded, often before being sold.
2. Our culture seems awash in redundant, inexpensive, consumer goods in the midst of economic insecurity.
3. Research and product development are focused on goods that cater to a small, wealthy portion of the population.
4. Products turnover rapidly and become obsolete, fashions change, and so the rate of new consumption is accelerated.
5. Overconsumption of goods and energy causes a wide variety of environmental and ecological problems.

Each of these complaints targets the particular mix of goods and services produced in the economy. In economic terms, each of these complaints focus on the allocation of resources – a wasteful allocation occurs if we are using scarce time, talent, and materials to produce something that does not maximize well-being. Further, if the complaints are warranted, they indicate that we could collectively be better served by devoting our considerable productive capacity to a different bundle of goods and services. For example, we could produce less food if we wasted less, and we might receive some benefit from improved infrastructure and fewer resources devoted to the fleeting enjoyment of inexpensive consumer goods.

BACKGROUND

It is worth noting, from the outset, that none of these phenomena are entirely new or unique to consumer capitalism. People were finding treasures in the trash, producing cheap junk, selling luxuries to the rich, and following fickle fashions long before anyone could point to a consumer economy. Moreover, the term "waste" has a number of different uses. This implies that the problem of consumer waste requires careful definition. For these complaints to qualify as a critique of our economic system, two criteria must be met. First, it must be the case that our current economic practices encourage these types of waste to a point of excess. The fact that individual human error will always result in some food waste is not enough. Second, to count as waste, a practice should, in some sense, be worth changing. If all available solutions are more costly than the problem, then the critique fails. Stated differently, it should be the case that there is some other feasible allocation of resources that would improve human well-being. These criteria will hereafter be referred to as requirements that waste be *systemic* and *avoidable*. Alternatively, "waste" (or wasteful) will, in this chapter, be used to refer to systemic and avoidable practices in our consumer economy that diminish our ability to make people better off.

The remainder of this paper will argue that each of these complaints about waste have their root in current economic practices, and are thus systemic, but that only some of them are avoidable, and then point to the need for an alternative standard of progress to address the critique. In particular, a simple utilitarian liberalism that equates progress with the meeting of human desires is not robust enough to critique this culture of waste. Instead, this critique requires that we develop a standard of consumer rationality that is stable enough to distinguish between real consumer well-being and the manipulation of tastes through marketing. With this standard, we can point policy toward a system that results in true welfare-enhancing consumption and limits the excesses of a wasteful economy.

Wealth and Waste

There are three substantial economic changes that have come to define industrial economies in the 20th century that are also essential for understanding consumer waste. First, one of the most important phenomena of modern history is the increase in standards of living and productivity among some parts of the world's population. A large amount of energy has gone into academic explanations for this dramatic change.[1] For individuals living in the midst of this newfound wealth, the world is a substantially different place than it was in the recent past. Consider that less than two percent of the population in wealthy countries can easily produce enough food for the other 98%. Factories that, in the past, employed large numbers of workers productively are now producing more output with far fewer workers. This productivity is the source of our wealth: we are rich, in large part, because we are able to produce so many more goods and services per person. At the heart of this is a strong underlying trend of greater efficiency. In general, our use of resources in production, and often in consumption, is far more efficient today than it has been in the past: we get far more goods and services of value from each kilowatt of electricity and acre of land, and are, on average, much more wealthy.

Second, in recent years there has been a steady expansion of the labor force, as women steadily exchange household production activities for jobs in the formal sector. While barriers and inequality remain, opportunities have changed dramatically for women in the economy. More recently in the U.S., this expansion seems to have plateaued while male labor force participation has declined, but the decline in home production seems permanent. It is now often more lucrative for a woman to work in the formal sector than to spend that time caring for children and producing goods in the home.

Third, over the long term, there has been a steady increase in the number of years devoted to education. The amount of education that is required for professional occupations, in particular, has steadily increased. Moreover, on average, the labor market has continued to reward higher levels of education with higher wages. These demographic changes have resulted in a significantly expanded labor force and more productive population than was the case in previous generations. Most notably, for this argument, the expansion of education has coincided with greater specialization and greater labor market opportunities than were often available a century prior.

These three economic and demographic observations can explain some of the consumer waste that is challenged by activists. Tristan Stuart estimates that as much as 50% of food produced is wasted (Stuart, 2009). Can this level of waste be anything other than gross inefficiency? While it is possible that we could profitably find ways to throw away less food, there is a good reason to believe that such a change would not be worth the cost. In particular, as food is produced in greater quantities at a lower cost, it becomes less profitable to make efficient use of the stock of food produced. In times of shortage or famine, food is zealously preserved and utilized. In the midst of the abundance that is now normal for the wealthy, however, it is often more profitable for a restaurant or grocery store to throw out slightly damaged food rather than find some use for it. Wealthy customers learn to demand the highest quality produce, therefore, limiting the possibility of a secondary market for the collection of goods that stores and restaurants cannot sell. Importantly, if you take into account the value of the time it would take to collect, sort, and find uses for the cast-off goods, it may well be cheaper to throw these goods away than to use the food stock more efficiently. In short, labor is costly, food is inexpensive, and so firms have a strong incentive to save labor-time, even if it means discarding food. This labor-cost explanation for food waste, then, means that discarded food is a systemic, but not avoidable, problem.

Moreover, it is not just food waste that can be attributed to our newfound wealth. Cultural practices that survived generations are quickly cast aside in the face of cheaper alternatives. Very few households today make or even repair clothes, in large part because clothing, relative to current incomes, is far cheaper than it was 100 years ago. Table 1 shows, relative to total expenditures, how both food and clothing have become much less expensive over the last century. Part of this dynamic, moreover, is attributable to the fact that with women entering the labor force in greater numbers, fewer households have an adult at home with the inclination to repair clothes or preserve food, practices which defined household labor only two generations ago. While these traditional household practices are preserved in some households as crafts or hobbies, it is not economically worthwhile to invest time in these tasks when the comparable market goods are so cheap and labor market opportunities are expanding.

The cultural change described here can be painted even more broadly. Education and work have pushed individuals and firms toward greater specialization; a move that is reinforced by lower relative prices for basic goods and services. Specialization, moreover, has undermined the set of skills and practices that would have resulted in less food waste, less discarded clothing, and less consumption. Homes have become sites of consumption, not production, and firms have made an analogous change, outsourcing those services that might have previously been done in-house.

This practice of discarding valuable goods might be economically desirable, if it has a basis in real increases in productivity and wealth. If eliminating these practices from the economy required a decrease in living standards across the board, few would call that progress, barring the achievement of some other goal. Even traditional notions of the virtue of frugality might need updating for an age in which material goods are not scarce in the same way that they were in the past, and so it is no longer worth forgoing some other good in order to preserve them.

Some of the concerns about waste in a consumer economy can be attributed to the raw demographic facts of economic development and inequality. Cultural habits regarding consumption change predictably in response to wealth, opportunity, and technology. In some sense, then, the dumpster-divers who protest the disposal of large amounts of edible food are fighting against tangible progress – even the lowest wage workers earn too much money to justify paying them to make better use of picked-over

Table 1. U.S. household expenditure shares

	1901	2002
Food	43%	13%
Clothing	14%	4%
Housing	23%	33%

Source: (Bureau of labor Statistics, 2006)

produce. Similarly, the decline in household production of clothes and food can be directly attributed to better job market opportunities and cheaper retail alternatives. Whereas sewing and canning were signs of frugality 100 years ago, today, they would be signs of either dire poverty or wealth-enabled leisure.

Inequality

While the trends discussed so far have been largely positive, there have been other large-scale changes that are less clearly positive. Even as household incomes have increased over the last century, inequality has increased dramatically. By most measures, inequality of income and consumption was high at the start of the 20th century in the United States, dropped in the post-war era, and has risen steadily since the early 1970's.[2] While income inequality changes more dramatically than consumption inequality (Krueger & Perri, 2006), this inequality has two relevant implications. First, even if the value of time is accounted for, it is not clear that discarding food is defensible for the wealthy when others are still poor enough to lack basic sustenance. Second, income inequality can have a dramatic impact on the mix of consumer goods and services produced. Each of these complications will be considered in turn.

The combination of wealth and poverty, in close proximity, is a substantial ethical concern in a consumer economy. Under some circumstances, moreover, this will undermine the limited defense of consumer waste presented here. In the case of food, if the wasted food could be transferred to those in need, and if that transfer would be less costly than the provision of food through other means, then clearly discarding the food would constitute a misallocation of resources and would be wasteful. Under most circumstances, however, such a transfer is not inexpensive. Perishable goods, in particular, cannot be transported and stored for those in need without substantial cost. The resulting logic is similar to the argument presented earlier. The low cost of food makes preserving the food, even for those in need, a waste of time and energy. While providing food for those in need is clearly a laudable and primary goal, in many cases, it would be cheaper to purchase and provide that food through normal distribution networks, rather than by reusing discarded food. The fact that food is discarded in large quantities, therefore, probably says little about indifference to poverty and says a lot about the productivity of the food production system.

Moving beyond food production, however, the second impact of economic inequality could be more important. Wider income gaps lead to wider gaps in living standards and thus, a larger gap between the types of goods demanded by the rich and those demanded by the poor. Furthermore, the expansion of incomes at the top means that there are more profits to be had meeting the needs and desires of those in the top income groups. It is possible, therefore, that the mix of goods created in a highly unequal consumer economy is weighted heavily toward a small segment of the population, even if larger welfare gains are possible through production aimed at the less well-off.

While global inequality has been diminishing in recent years, these inequality-related consumption effects are even more pronounced at the global level. The consumer goods that get the most research and development dollars, and that are produced in scale, are those that assume an infrastructure and set of needs of those in rich societies. This leaves vital needs of the income-poor regions of the world with far fewer investment dollars and fewer options. As long as medicine, cars, computers, and phones are produced by for-profit corporations in a market economy, this kind of inequality in wealth will correspond to an inequality in targeted innovation. If this kind of critique is not obviously wasteful, it is only because the kind of waste described here is not visible in the same way that discarded food is. Instead, this critique rests on the argument that massive resources are being invested to produce things that are good, but not as good as could be produced with a different set of priorities. This is a problem of investment, particularly in the form of product development, that is not aligned with maximizing human well-being. This is clearly a systemic problem, and one that is possibly avoidable, but it is only one of a collection of similar complaints worth examining.

A Profitable Chaos

The wasteful consumer culture under examination is not only the result of broad economic and demographic facts. It is also the result of a particular set of business practices that capitalize on human psychology. There are great profits to be had in the constant churn of products, technologies, fashions, and trends. This is most vividly seen in consumer technologies, where the rate of technological progress has enabled a constant stream of improvements. Consumers and firms alike are faced with a rate of technological progress that has accelerated the pace of obsolescence. Firms are faced with the need to manage the life cycle of their products, struggling to keep pace with the rate of change spurred by competition (Agarwal & Gort, 2002; Kumar & Krob, 2005).

Because of the network externalities associated with many emerging technologies (Katz & Shapiro, 1985, 1994), there is an incentive for both firms and consumers to "keep up" with the ever-changing standards in the marketplace. As a host of complementary products change, compatibility becomes important, and the value of goods depends on the degree to which they fit into the network of new products that other consumers and firms are using. For this reason, "opting out" of the product cycle is often not a realistic option. This constant rate of change in technologies is the direct result of the rates of productivity and population growth that drive innovation and economic progress. If product turnover is the result of fast improvement, can it be wasteful?

While many technological improvements do result in new products, the rate of turnover is often accelerated by practices that are profitable for firms but do not improve the well-being of consumers. For example, firms can capitalize on the constant product turnover by marketing "cutting-edge" products with marginal improvements over their competition, profiting from the cultural value of having the latest technology or fashion. Alternatively, firms can produce goods that increase turnover by engineering a lifespan into the product, as with mobile phones that do not have replaceable batteries. Situated within the constant product churn, these engineering choices do not cause protest from consumers, but the alternative engineering choices, in which products are built to be useable for longer periods of time, could dramatically improve consumer well-being, and could result in lower overall resource-use.

This process of product turnover can be even more problematic in the cases where consumers value goods primarily insomuch as they compare favorably to the goods sported by their peers. Ludwig and Myers (1979) explain how consumers, according to the "relative depravation principle," tend to compare with an aspirational group of peers when evaluating their own standard of living. Moreover, there is a significant body of evidence that consumers build their identity by associating with the products and brands that they consume (Burns, 2010, 2002; Newholm & Hopkinson, 2009; Taylor, 2007). Both through conformity and the appropriation of brand associations, people signal social status, their group identity, and to the extent possible, some individuality through the bundle of conspicuous consumption goods that they purchase. In areas like clothing fashions, it is common for the signaled value of a clothing item to depreciate faster than the physical object itself, making it necessary for the consumer to purchase new items in order to maintain their identity.

If many people are engaged in aspirational conspicuous consumption, they end up finding themselves in competition with each other in a kind of consumption arms race. In this "consumer warfare" (Burns & Warren, 2009), consumers end up imposing a "consumption externality" on other consumers every time they purchase new expensive goods. Frank (2005) argues that there is good evidence that these externalities cause significant welfare loss. He points to the evidence that consumption by the very rich impacts the consumption norms among those less wealthy. The recent increase in income inequality can exacerbate this kind of positional consumption, driving more households into bankruptcy as they compete with ever richer peers.

Marketers, in turn, have capitalized on this kind of consumer competition, knowing that they can define new patterns of "normal" consumption by encouraging aspirational comparisons or marketing individuality (Heath & Potter, 2004). Despite the questionable moral status of such efforts (Sher, 2011), marketers are conscious of these identity-forming elements of advertisements and make use of them. The result is a created dissatisfaction tied directly to the consumption patterns of consumers, a dissatisfaction for which the only advertised solution is additional purchases.

While it may not be simple to imagine ways in which these kinds of systemic over-consumption could be avoided, the rapid product turnover and competitive consumption described here goes to the heart of what is often disparaged as "consumerism." As with the problem of new product development aimed at the wealthy, the waste described here is one of resources devoted to goods that are discarded prematurely, replaced quickly, or which serve only a fleeting comparative desire. A reduction in consumption churn, or a change which increased product durability, could result in increased well-being across firms and consumers. Notably, though, such a change would have to be systemic, since individuals are not well-situated to opt out of the competitive cycle on their own.

Biased Marketing

If marketers are able to truly manufacture desires in consumers, or even merely sway them in the favor of the types of goods that are marketed, then there will be a larger systematic bias in the types of goods that are produced. For example, Heath and Potter (2004) argue that modern economies over-produce "medium sized dried goods" that individual households can easily consume. If one examines the types of goods and services that are subject to advertising it is obvious that not all types of goods are given equal time. Heath and Potter focus on the distinction between public and private goods, arguing that large goods that require the contributions of many consumers, such as infrastructure, parks, and public institutions, get too little attention. The cultural emphasis on private property, they argue, undermines the opportunities for collective purchases, thus leading to a "private opulence amid public squalor" (Gibson, 2011).

This bias, however, also has another dimension. Marketing efforts are subject to significant economies of scale. Modern innovations in targeted marketing notwithstanding, the technology of mass media make it more efficient to market to large numbers of people at the same time. As a result, marketing of this type is most profitable for those companies selling mass-market products. This type of product also has particular characteristics: (i) they must be products with mass appeal, so that there will be sufficient demand, (ii) the products themselves must have a production technology that exhibits economies of scale, so that mass-production is efficient, and (iii) the products must contribute to a particular brand image that is worth investing in. While these three characteristics are not true of many of the goods we could choose to purchase, they all describe the majority of the goods that are advertised and purchased in modern consumer cultures.

It is worth considering the type of economy that is encouraged by this bias. In the realm of food, industrial agriculture is favored over smaller-scale food production, not just because of the cost savings, but also because of the complementarity with advertising. This is one of the structural reasons why farmed animals are worse off today, in a richer consumer economy, than they were 100 years ago (McMullen, 2015, 2016). Similarly, local retailers that can build a local reputation but cannot afford to market to a larger audience will have a hard time competing with larger retailers that can build a national reputation. These nation-wide brands are even more valuable as the population becomes more mobile, and as people are less likely to build connections with local, small-scale brands.

The effectiveness of private, for-profit, mass-market advertising is directly causally linked to the formation of a particular kind of consumer economy – one that places far more resources into private goods rather than public goods, mass produced goods rather than small scale goods and services, and national brands rather than local ones. Note that this explanation requires no conscious strategy on the part of firms or marketers. Even the most ethical and introspective advertisers will find their services in most demand from the large companies that mass-produce consumer goods. These are the types of companies that have the most to gain from advertising.

If this kind of systemic bias is wasteful, it is because the kinds of goods that we might be able to profitably produce and consume are limited by this focus on mass-production and mass-marketing. The system is structured to produce disposable consumer goods in a manner that is clearly systemic and avoidable. Alternative economic structures emphasize alternative allocations of productive resources, and a quick comparison across modern economies reveals dramatic differences in the types of public goods provided, even if there is a kind of pull toward the consumer outcomes described here.

Efficiency and Progress

The above arguments, taken together, provide a mixed critique of our modern market system. On the one hand, some of the apparent "waste" in the economy seems to be a function of genuine progress. As people get richer, things that were once valuable become trivial. On a large scale, this results in the disposal of food, clothing and durable goods that others could use. Using the conventional economic conception of efficiency -- maximizing beneficial exchanges – this kind of waste is actually "efficient." If more valuable resources would have to be expended to allocate these goods to those who could use them, disposal is clearly the best option.

It may be the presence of inequality that makes this culture of disposal problematic. In some markets, second-hand retailers do an efficient job of re-allocating these goods to those who can be made better off. In other cases, food retailers and manufacturers donate a significant amount of food to the poor. While these efforts are significant, there remains the juxtaposition, in the U.S., of hunger in the midst of waste. The hunger that remains, however, is not the result of there being insufficient food to feed everyone. Instead, this hunger is a symptom of being, voluntarily or involuntarily, excluded from process of wealth creation that has led to the abundance of goods.

Other kinds of wastefulness described here are more clearly a critique of the system. The pursuit of positional goods, and the encouragement of this consumer arms race by marketers, clearly leaves people collectively worse off than they could be. Even using the conventional economic definition of efficiency, this represents a clear case of a negative externality. Moreover, given the scale of the problem, this externality problem clearly calls for large scale collective solutions. Frank (2005) has proposed a progressive consumption tax, which would give incentives to save, invest, and scale back consumer competition. Given the potential for people to use a wide variety of goods as status signals, from cars and clothes to houses and schools, it would be difficult to target such a tax at blatantly conspicuous consumption. For this and other reasons, a broadly targeted consumption tax could be the best policy.

Heath and Potter (2004) and Gibson (2011) also suggest limiting the advertising industry through limiting subsidies or tax deductions for marketing activities. It could even be possible to create a kind of progressive marketing tax, discouraging the kind of mass-marketing described here while still encouraging the promotion of smaller enterprises. While these kinds of limits would have some effect on the amount of money spent on advertising, they might not significantly diminish the total amount of advertisements observed by most people.[3] Moreover, some limits on marketing that are already established could be expanded. For example, the ban on television advertisements for tobacco products recognizes the particular public health risks of tobacco consumption. Similar restrictions could be designed using existing ethical standards in the marketing literature (Sher, 2011).

Much more broadly, once we recognize the possibility that marketing can change a person's preferences, the conventional definition of efficiency becomes far less useful. Since economists measure welfare based on the satisfaction of preferences, it is unclear whether the pre-marketing or post-marketing preferences are the standard to use for consumer welfare. In short, the principle of consumer sovereignty – that people's free choices reveal which goods and services will best increase their well-being – is clearly suspect, but difficult to replace. David George (2004) draws on a long line of research[4] about preference formation to offer one framework for examining the implications of "endogenous preferences." He argues that "second-order" preferences, or those preferences one has upon reflection over time, can be used as a standard to judge the short-term preferences often manipulated by marketing. A standard of this sort motivates George's and Heath and Potter's criticisms of the excesses of consumerism within a broadly liberal framework.

If we accept, moreover, that the marketing of goods and services tends to bias preferences toward a certain set of goods and services, and if we use some pre-marketing or "second-order" preferences as a standard for welfare, then the direction for progress is clear. We can intuit that people would be better off if there were greater investment in the type of goods that are not mass-produced consumer goods: public goods, local services, and intangible social goods. While these types of goods can be subsidized or provided through public policy, there are no clear criteria for establishing an efficient level of production if revealed preference and market mechanisms cannot be trusted. Nevertheless, knowing the direction of the biases can point public policy in a fruitful direction.

A rejection of simple consumer sovereignty, however, even in favor of a more nuanced utilitarian construct such as "reflective preferences," requires a commitment or consensus around an alternative vision of progress. It is fair to say, moreover, that any nuanced critique of the modern consumer economy should be based in an alternative normative standard by which to evaluate alternatives. If we agree that there is rampant waste in modern capitalism, we should be able to articulate the reason why free individual choices are not optimal. The kind of psychological critique offered here, or offered by some parts of behavioral economics (Akerlof & Shiller, 2015), is only one avenue through which these practices could be subjected to critique.

Environmental Sustainability

In order to fill out the discussion of consumer waste, it is worth considering at least one powerful alternative critique. One of the most common critiques is offered by those considering the environmental cost of modern consumption practices.[5] There has been a sustained accumulation of environmental and ecological concerns that are directly tied to the consumption levels that are common in wealthy economies (Garvey, 2008; Steinfeld et al., 2006). Moreover, there are good reasons to believe that our consumption of natural resources is excessive, systemic, and at least partially avoidable.

Most notably, even the attenuated approval of food disposal practices described here and the acceptance of broad aspects of the modern consumer economy require a kind of trust in the pricing of resources and environmental goods. If there are broad and significant negative external costs, imposed worldwide, as a result of consumption or production practices, or if we are systematically under-valuing the future resource needs of humanity, it is plausible that the prices of many goods are far too low. More specifically, these kinds of problems can impose a cost that is not visible to people at the point of purchase, thus encouraging wide over-consumption of goods that have a high environmental cost. As just one example, Simon (2013) documents the hidden costs of meat consumption in the United States, including subsidies, and the costs to health, the environment, and animal welfare. His conservative estimates indicate that the hidden costs amount to $414.8 billion each year in the U.S., a cost that dwarfs the sticker price on those food items. Even if his estimates are wildly inflated, the implication is clear – people consume far more meat than they would if they bore the full cost up front. The result is clearly wasteful: the artificially low prices produce systemic and avoidable overconsumption of goods with a high environmental cost.

Solutions to this kind of wastefulness are easy to find. Simon proposes a meat tax, which would reduce meat consumption and raise revenue that could be used to assuage some of the harm caused by our diets. Many have argued, in similar fashion, for a tax on carbon or pollution, or other activities that impose a broad cost on the population. The advantage of these kinds of proposals is that they offer solutions that preserve the ability of people to make individual consumption choices while building in some of the cost of the shared environmental burden. Most importantly, consumption and production patterns can change in response to the taxes which push the economy toward goods and services with less of an environmental cost.

A more fundamental environmental critique that moves somewhat beyond the purposes of this chapter, however, would raise large questions about the place of humans in the economy and environment, and the real possibility that progress should require fewer humans or humans that are less well off in order to preserve other species. If, for example, we considered not just the external cost on humans, but also the cost to non-human animals and ecosystems, the implied kinds of waste in the economy would be very different, and the implied change in economic practices could be dramatic.

FUTURE RESEARCH DIRECTIONS

While economic principles can explain and sometimes offer solutions for these problems, complaints about wastefulness usually point to a normative economic standard that defies the analysis of an amoral liberal academic discipline. This chapter discusses the work of scholars examining preference formation largely from within the dominant framework, but other approaches could be fruitful as well. The underlying vision of progress and efficiency used here was the economic standard of preference satisfaction. The popular "capabilities" approach (Nussbaum, 2001; Sen, 1999), or an approach based on some tradition of religion or ethics could provide an alternative way to distinguish between different types of goods, and alternative criteria for comparing possible states of the world. Whichever approach is used, there needs to be a more thorough examination of the possible forms that market economies could take. Without such an exploration, either defense or critique of the current system could be a wasted effort.

CONCLUSION

Overall, the modern market economy has produced extraordinary improvements in efficiency. Nevertheless, a general anxiety about our "wasteful" consumer economy can be examined fruitfully with some knowledge of economic systems, demographics, and business practices. Complaints considered here can be distilled into five areas of excess: (i) the disposal of useful goods, (ii) an over-emphasis on mass-produced consumer goods, (iii) production focused on the desires of the wealthy, (iv) rapid product turnover and obsolescence and (v) the overconsumption of goods that impose a broad environmental cost. In some cases, "waste" can be justified as a result of the rising levels of wealth, productivity, and improved opportunities. In other cases, waste is clearly a symptom of inequality and poverty that is too common. Finally, in some cases, the wastefulness can be a structural problem in the system, as with competitive consumption and marketing bias, or the systemic under-valuation of environmental goods.

Across this survey of concerns, there is a common critique of the kind of priorities that are implicitly embedded in the consumer economy. There is a real case to be made that the kind of liberal institutions that have come to dominate wealthy economies have encouraged excessive consumption of a certain kind of goods. This excess implies, moreover, that people would be broadly better off if institutions shifted decision-making toward a different mix of goods, reflecting a different kind of economic priorities: more durable goods, public goods, and goods with a smaller environmental cost.

ACKNOWLEDGMENT

This research was supported by the Lilly Endowment; Calvin College; and Hope College.

REFERENCES

Acemoglu, D., & Robinson, J. (2012). *Why nations fail: The origins of power, prosperity, and poverty.* New York, NY: Crown Business.

Agarwal, R., & Gort, M. (2002). Firm and product life cycles and firm survival. *The American Economic Review, 92*(2), 184–190. doi:10.1257/000282802320189221

Akerlof, G. A., & Shiller, R. J. (2015). *Phishing for phools: The economics of manipulation and deception.* Princeton, NJ: Princeton University Press. doi:10.1515/9781400873265

Blank, R. M., & Blinder, A. S. (1985). *Macroeconomics, income distribution, and poverty.* National Bureau of Economic Research working paper series, No. 1567. Retrieved May 15, 2018, from http://www.nber.org/papers/w1567

Bowles, S. (1998). Endogenous preferences: The cultural consequences of markets and other economic institutions. *Journal of Economic Literature, 36*(1), 75–111.

Bowles, S. (2008). Policies designed for self-interested citizens may undermine "the moral sentiments:" Evidence from economic experiments. *Science, 320*(5883), 1605–1609. doi:10.1126cience.1152110 PMID:18566278

Bowles, S. (2011). Is liberal society a parasite on tradition? *Philosophy & Public Affairs, 39*(1), 46–81. doi:10.1111/j.1088-4963.2011.01201.x

Burns, D. J. (2002). *Identity through consumption activities: A review and critical analysis.* Unpublished Manuscript, Xavier University.

Burns, D. J. (2010). Mimeticism and the basis of value: Toward a theory of fashion marketing. *Journal of Global Fashion Marketing, 1*(1), 40–50. doi:10.1080/20932685.2010.10593056

Burns, D. J., & Warren, H. B. (2009). Are marketers nothing more than arms dealers. *Journal of Business Management and Change, 4*(1), 9–26.

Clark, G. (2009). *A farewell to alms: A brief economic history of the world.* Princeton, NJ: Princeton University Press.

Daly, H. E., & Cobb, J. B. (1994). *For the common good: Redirecting the economy toward community, the environment, and a sustainable future (2nd ed.).* Boston, MA: Beacon Press.

Dauvergne, P. (2010). *The shadows of consumption: Consequences for the global environment.* Cambridge, MA: The MIT Press.

Diamond, J. M. (1999). *Guns, germs, and steel: The fates of human societies.* New York, NY: W. W. Norton & Company.

Ferrell, J. (2006). *Empire of scrounge: Inside the urban underground of dumpster diving, trash picking, and street scavenging.* New York, NY: NYU Press.

Fortin, N. M., & Lemieux, T. (1997). Institutional changes and rising wage inequality: Is there a linkage? *The Journal of Economic Perspectives, 11*(2), 75–96. doi:10.1257/jep.11.2.75

Frank, R. H. (2005). Positional externalities cause large and preventable welfare losses. *The American Economic Review, 95*(2), 137–141. doi:10.1257/000282805774670392

Garvey, J. (2008). *The ethics of climate change: Right and wrong in a warming world.* New York, NY: Bloomsbury Academic.

George, D. (2004). *Preference pollution: How markets create the desires we dislike.* Ann Arbor, MI: University of Michigan Press.

Gibson, A. (2011). Ideas and practices in the critique of consumerism. *Environmental Philosophy*, *8*(2), 171–188. doi:10.5840/envirophil20118219

Goldin, C. D., & Katz, L. F. (2008). *The race between education and technology*. Boston, MA: Harvard University Press.

Heath, J., & Potter, A. (2004). *The rebel sell: Why the culture can't be jammed*. New York, NY: HarperCollins.

Katz, M. L., & Shapiro, C. (1985). Network externalities, competition, and compatibility. *The American Economic Review*, *75*(3), 424–440.

Katz, M. L., & Shapiro, C. (1994). Systems competition and network effects. *The Journal of Economic Perspectives*, *8*(2), 93–115. doi:10.1257/jep.8.2.93

Krueger, D., & Perri, F. (2006). Does income inequality lead to consumption inequality? Evidence and theory. *The Review of Economic Studies*, *73*(1), 163–193. doi:10.1111/j.1467-937X.2006.00373.x

Kumar, S., & Krob, W. A. (2005). *Managing product life cycle in a supply chain context: A prescription based on empirical research*. New York, NY: Springer.

Leonard, A. (2011). *The story of stuff: The impact of overconsumption on the planet, our communities, and our health--and how we can make it petter (Reprint edition)*. New York, NY: Free Press.

Ludwig, T., & Myers, D. (1979). How Christians can cope with inflation. *The Christian Century, 96*, 609-613.

McCloskey, D. N. (2011). *Bourgeois dignity: Why economics can't explain the modern world*. Chicago, IL: University Of Chicago Press.

McMullen, S. (2015). Is capitalism to blame? Animal lives in the marketplace. *Journal of Animal Ethics*, *5*(2), 126–134. doi:10.5406/janimalethics.5.2.0126

McMullen, S. (2016). *Animals and the economy*. London, UK: Palgrave Macmillan. doi:10.1057/978-1-137-43474-6

Meadows, D. H. (1972). *Limits to growth*. New York, NY: Signet.

Meadows, D. H., Randers, J., & Meadows, D. L. (2004). *Limits to growth: The 30-year update* (3rd ed.). White River Junction, VT: Chelsea Green Publishing.

Newholm, T., & Hopkinson, G. C. (2009). I just tend to wear what I like: Contemporary consumption and the paradoxical construction of individuality. *Marketing Theory*, *9*(4), 439–462. doi:10.1177/1470593109346896

Nussbaum, M. C. (2001). *Women and human development: The capabilities approach*. Cambridge, UK: Cambridge University Press.

Piketty, T. (2014). *Capital in the twenty-first century*. Cambridge, MA: Belknap Press. doi:10.4159/9780674369542

Piketty, T., & Saez, E. (2006). The evolution of top incomes: A historical and international perspective. *The American Economic Review*, *96*(2), 200–205. doi:10.1257/000282806777212116

Sen, A. (1999). *Development as freedom*. New York, NY: Knopf.

Shantz, J. (2005). One person's garbage another person's treasure: Dumpster diving, freeganism, and anarchy. *VERB*, *3*(1), 9–19.

Sher, S. (2011). A framework for assessing immorally manipulative marketing tactics. *Journal of Business Ethics*, *102*(1), 97–118. doi:10.100710551-011-0802-4

Simon, D. R. (2013). *Meatonomics: How the rigged economics of meat and dairy make you consume too much--and how to eat better, live longer, and spend smarter*. Newburyport, MA: Conari Press.

Steinfeld, H., Gerber, P., Wassenaar, T., Castel, V., Rosales, M., & de Haan, C. (2006). *Livestock's long shadow*. Rome, Italy: Food and Agriculture Organization of the United Nations.

Stuart, T. (2009). *Waste: Uncovering the global food scandal*. New York, NY: W. W. Norton & Company.

Sunstein, C. R. (1991). Preferences and politics. *Philosophy & Public Affairs*, *20*(1), 3–34.

Sunstein, C. R. (1993). Endogenous preferences, environmental law. *The Journal of Legal Studies*, *22*(2), 217–254. doi:10.1086/468164

Sunstein, C. R. (1997). How law constructs preferences. *The Georgetown Law Journal*, *86*, 2637.

Taylor, C. (2007). Cultures of democracy and citizen efficacy. *Public Culture*, *19*(1), 117–150. doi:10.1215/08992363-2006-027

ADDITIONAL READING

Cavanaugh, W. T. (2008). *Being consumed: Economics and Christian desire*. Grand Rapids, MI: Wm. B. Eerdmans Publishing Company.

Tiemstra, J. P. (1992). Theories of regulation and the history of consumerism. *International Journal of Social Economics*, *19*(6), 3–27. doi:10.1108/03068299210012548

Viney, W. (2015). *Waste: A philosophy of things*. Bloomsbury Academic.

KEY TERMS AND DEFINITIONS

Consumer Economy: A kind of market or liberal economy in which the center of economic power resides with consumers. This can be contrasted with an industrial economy or an agricultural economy.

Efficiency: Getting the most benefit out of the resources and technology available to us. In economics, this is often more fully specified as "pareto efficiency," which characterizes the distribution, allocation, and use of resources and technology such that there is no way to make someone better off without hurting someone else.

Market(s): The institutions that allow decentralized production and exchange of goods and services in a liberal economy.

Marketing: The practice of advertising goods, services, or firms to potential customers.

Waste: Goods, services, or wealth that is attainable or exists, but is not used to its full benefit.

Wasteful Practices: Systemic and avoidable practices in the consumer economy that diminish our ability to make people better off.

Wealth: Any assets of value. In its broadest use, this term can encompass available services as well.

ENDNOTES

1 See, for example, McCloskey (2011), Acemoglu and Robinson (2012), Diamond (1999), and Clark (2009), to list a few recent titles that received considerable attention.

2 There has been an extensive documentation of these trends, and discussion of causes (Blank & Blinder, 1985; Fortin & Lemieux, 1997; Goldin & Katz, 2008; Krueger & Perri, 2006; Piketty, 2014; Piketty & Saez, 2006).

3 Actual advertising "volume" will depend on the ability of firms to creatively work around the legal definitions of marketing that would result, and also the elasticity of supply of advertising space.

4 Among the many scholars working through the implications of preference formation are Bowles (1998, 2008, 2011) and Sunstein (1991, 1993, 1997).

5 The classic, but somewhat dated and thus problematic, source for this critique is from Meadows, Meadows, and Randers (1972, 2004). Related arguments are common, however. Consider Cobb and Daly (1994), Dauvergne (2010), or Leonard (2011).

Section 3

Religious Aspects of Consumer Culture

Chapter 9
The Spirit of Capitalism vs. the Spirit of Consumerism: A Comparative Typology

Kent A. Van Til
Hope College, USA

ABSTRACT

Max Weber's protestant work ethic linked the Calvinist doctrine of election to the rise of capitalism. Weber saw the "worldly asceticism" among Calvinists as the motive for the hard work and savings that are required in capitalism. Though this theory has both detractors and critics, it remains dominant in both academic and popular writings. When this typology is extended to include consumerism, however, it fails, since the doctrine of election is not compatible with choice, which is the leading characteristic of consumerism. Arminian/free-will theology, on the other hand, has choice as its leading characteristic and practice. American evangelists asked their listeners to stand up and choose Christ at roughly the same time and in the same way that advertisers asked consumers to choose their products. Thus, a new typology is warranted which links the free-will theology of American evangelicalism to the choice that characterizes modern consumerism.

INTRODUCTION

Anyone who has spent five minutes or so reading in the sociology of religion or economics will recognize this title as a riff on Max Weber's classic—*The Protestant Ethic and the Spirit of Capitalism* (1930). The reference to Weber is intentional. Published in German in 1904 and in English in 1930, it has been the basis for extended debate about the nature of work, consumer behavior, and business values. This debate and discussion continues in religious and business literature to the present (Ghazawi & Smith, 2009; Miller, Woehr, & Hudspeth, 2001; Muller, 2006; Warr, 2008; Wuthnow, 1969). This article follows Weber's thesis, accepting it, with reservations, as a useful typology for describing the workings of capitalism. This article contends that the typology set up by Weber over a hundred years ago no longer fits 21st Century consumer culture. It thus proposes another type which better describes the current consumer marketplace. It will call that type free-will consumerism.

DOI: 10.4018/978-1-5225-6120-0.ch009

Weber's typology described a system or process—capitalism, and observed a prominent practice or practices that made the system function--diligent labor and savings. It then showed that these practices could be derived from the Calvinist doctrine of election. This Weberian type has been extended, analyzed and perhaps even overused (see Smith & Smith, 2011). As capitalism has sometimes been conflated or confused with consumerism, the Weber thesis has also been associated with consumerism. But the differences between capitalism and consumerism make that association problematic. A new typology specifically addressing consumerism as an independent type is in order. This new typology may provide a new means to understand labor and consumer behavior in the 21st Century. Whereas the first type is well known, treating consumerism as a distinct type is the unique contribution of this paper.

This article will follow a similar process as did Weber when describing capitalism as a type. Consumerism is a system that principally uses the practice of ***choice*** in shopping, even going so far as to "shop" for ones' personal identity. This practice of choosing an identity relates closely to the Arminian doctrine of free will, in which one must choose for Christ. The article will first sketch capitalism as typified by Weber, and then compare and contrast it to consumerism using the same pattern of—describing a system, noting its central practice, and aligning it to a corresponding theology.

WEBER AND CAPITALISM

In his famous *Inquiry into the Nature and Causes of the Wealth of Nations*, Adam Smith, (1776, 2012) recognized as the father of capitalist economics, proposed that the division of labor was the key to wealth creation. His story of the pin factory showed that the same number of laborers could produce many more of a product if they specialized in various aspects of work. The ability to produce more goods would result in greater profit and greater exchange, as each laborer exchanged his specialized goods for those of another. The "Invisible Hand" would guide each person to satisfy his desires while at the same time satisfying the desires of other customers or suppliers. This exchange process would build capital, and that capital could be re-invested *ad infinitum.* But to build capital required saving. Spending capital on personal luxuries or hoarding it as treasure would not contribute to a nations' growth. As noted later by Robert Heilbronner (1953), capitalism requires not only the creation of capital, but the constant circulation of capital. Hoarded capital would not create wealth in a nation, but capital in circulation would.

Roughly 125 years after the publication of *The Wealth of Nations,* Max Weber (1930) noted that capitalism had begun and prospered in lands that were primarily Protestant, such as England, northern Germany and the Netherlands. He too understood that successful capitalism required both specialized labor and capital accumulation for future ventures. He believed that among the Calvinists, he had found a people who would work diligently and save their capital, thus spurring forward capitalism. The Calvinists possessed what he called an ethic of "worldly asceticism." This asceticism was not of an "other-worldly" sort such as that of the monastics, in which the practitioner would detach himself from material goods altogether. Rather, a worldly ascetic would remain deeply involved in mundane and commercial matters. The worldly ascetic would use the capital gained from his labor to invest in additional worldly business.

Luther, the former monastic, used the idea of *Beruf*, or calling to distinguish this view of piety from that of medieval Catholicism (Weber, 1930). For Luther, the highest Christian ideal was no longer the monastic life, which he himself had practiced, but life in the present world, in which one could live out a divine calling. For Luther, any calling could be valid, divinely ordained, and worthwhile (Weber, 1930). Calvin followed Luther in this view of calling, and added to it an emphasis on God's election of individuals for service to God and neighbors within those callings. Thus, the Calvinist would work diligently in his calling, not squandering his wealth, but using it to serve God and others. Calvin says,

If we are only to pass through the earth, we ought undoubtedly to make such a use of its blessings as will assist rather than retard us in our journey. It is not without reason therefore, that Paul advises us to use the world as though we used it not, and to buy with the same disposition with which we sell. But that this is a difficult subject, and there is danger of falling into one of two opposite errors, let us endeavor to proceed on safe ground, that we may avoid both extremes (Calvin (1536/1960), Book III, 10, par.1).

Consumer behavior expert Arthur Berger (2005) explains, "The extremes Calvin cautioned about are extravagant excesses and intemperance on one side, and life-denying austerity and asceticism on the other" (p.5).

Weber (1930) believed that among the Calvinists, he had found a people who would labor vigorously in various occupations, but not lavish the fruits of their labor on themselves, since their goal was to fulfill a calling, rather than indulge themselves. The result of this diligent labor resulted in the build-up capital for re-investment, a key component of capitalism.

For Weber (1930), capitalism must not be confused with the desire for gain. That desire has been present in humanity since the beginning of time. Instead, capitalism is a modern system "identical with the pursuit of profit, and forever renewed profit, by means of continuous, rational, capitalistic enterprise" (Weber, 1930, p.17). Thus, the conqueror who pillaged his victims and used that lucre for his own self-indulgence is a different type altogether than the modern capitalist. The capitalist seeks profit in exchange in order that he might peacefully renew his profits through further investment, labor, and exchange.

In stark contrast to the pillaging conquistadores of Latin America were the Calvinistic Puritans of New England. They saw earning money and gaining capital as proof that God approved of one's calling, not as an end in itself (Weber, 1930). This proof was important to see, since for Calvinist there was no outward sign of salvation. Weber believed that this lack of an outward sign of salvation among Calvinists led to anxiety (Weber, 1930). So, although the Calvinist believed that God was working within him, he could perceive no outward sign of that divine work. Thus, he took it upon himself to show that God was in fact at work within him by fervent labor (Weber, 1930). This labor and God's blessing upon it served as the outward sign of salvation that was missing. The hard work of the Calvinist never made one worthy of salvation, but it did ward off any lingering doubts that one might not be among the elect (Weber, 1930).

Thus, in a somewhat ironic progression, the Calvinist, who placed complete belief in the unsearchable salvific act of God in election, was at the same time feverishly at work in the marketplace, proving to himself that God had in fact worked within him. In sum, the relationship between Calvinism and work, for Weber, is that profit derived from labor is a sign of the unseen: the visible work of man showing the invisible work of God. This thesis, often known as The Protestant Work Ethic, has proven most durable, and provoked debate that has yet to find an end (e.g. Green, 1959; Kitch, 1967; Lehman & Roth, 1993; Smith & Smith, 2011).

A Calvinist theologian could add a challenge to one aspect of Weber's thesis. It seems that Weber is correct in his basic observations: capitalism began and thrived in lands that were Protestant; those Protestant laborers worked diligently and saved their money, providing capital for investment. Weber makes a mistake, however, when he claims that their belief in unseen, divine election caused them to be so anxious about their salvation that they worked feverishly to convince themselves of it. Rather, divine election may well be what gave them the *confidence* to pursue profit-making business in a capitalist society.

Whereas it is true that Lutherans and Calvinists believe that God freely chooses (elects) those who are to be saved without any consideration of that person's own merits, the result among Calvinists is that they are assured of salvation, rather than anxious about it. Salvation, for the Calvinist, is a settled matter. Thus, if election is a source for the Calvinist's work ethic, it should be a source of confidence rather than a source of anxiety. The Calvinist feels free to go forward in his or her calling, confident that God approves of that calling. And one day, the Calvinist laborer may be treated to the divine blessing which states, "Well done, thou good and faithful servant, enter into my rest" (Matt. 25:21 KIV).

Of course, the Weber thesis has other questionable suppositions. Most importantly, one may question whether any theology at all stood behind the growth of capitalism in his selected countries. It may be that other non-religious influences better explain the rise of capitalism in Western Europe. As in most historical/social studies, cause and effect cannot be proven, and correlations are necessarily tenuous.

So, the Weber thesis is questionable, and its interpretations and applications varied. Nonetheless, what cannot be contested is that the Weber Thesis has carried considerable influence in foundational thinking in the literature on labor, consumer behavior, vocation, etc. Its wide-ranging influence is what motivated Smith and Smith (2001) to take up their examination. They say,

The PWE (Protestant Work Ethic) is, arguably, one of the best known of the work ethics. (…) Politicians and pundits refer to the PWE as the ethic 'that made our country great,' [A. May, 2010]. And later, The PWE also appears to be a core idea in various management disciplines…. (p.248).

In the next part of this paper the article will take up consumerism as a type. Many observe that consumerism has superseded capitalism as the dominant system in the late 20th and 21st centuries (Beaubot & Echeverria, 2011; Beaudoin, 2003; Berger, 2005; Bowlby, 2001; Burns & Fawcett, 2012; Doherty & Etzionni, 2003; James, 2011; Lastkovicka & Sirianni, 2012; Makant, 2010; Miller, 2004; Wachtel, 1983; Wuthnow, 1996). The article will contrast consumerism with capitalism using the same pattern that Weber does: instead of capitalism consumerism, instead of labor and savings—choice and identity creation, and instead of election—free will.

CONSUMERISM

It is critical to distinguish between capitalism and consumerism. Capitalism is the system of exchange that is unfettered by forces outside the market whereby people freely sell and purchase on the basis of price. Consumerism does indeed depend on the free market, but goes a great deal further, becoming a system of meaning as well as exchange. After reviewing Calvin and the Weber thesis, Arthur Asa Berger (2005) comments,

What this discussion of Calvin and Weber suggests is that there is, indeed, an important religious or sacred dimension to our consuming passions; and the same passions and fervor that animate religious belief in people are found in a desacralized—that is, secularized—form, shaping their behavior as consumers in contemporary societies Shopping, then, if we adopt a religious perspective on things, becomes a sacred act (p. 8).

Shopping is the process in which one chooses products or services. If it remains simply this, however, it is not yet a crucial aspect of "sacred consumerism." But as Berger goes on to note, "The act of buying is just the tip of the ice-berg" (2005, p. 46). He cites Ernest Dichter (2002), whom he describes as "one of the fathers of the study of consumer motivation."

Most people like to shop. When we ask them, however, why they bought a product, the answer implies a need. A much more important aspect of buying is that it gives a person a chance to be creative. In other words, every time we go out and ship for something, we are really trying to express our own creativeness in as easy a form as possible. (….) I think this factor is a very important one and should not be easily overlooked; every time we go out, we do so really to prove to ourselves that we have the power to express our innermost desires by the selection of a specific type of merchandise (p.170).

Choose. Choose me! So scream thousands of advertisements daily. Choose me and I will give you—smooth skin, a great driving experience, a great night's sleep, a well-toned body, etc. etc. Contrary to what may be popularly assumed, the chief characteristic of consumerism is not a high level of consumption, but a plethora of choices. Shopping, choosing, and purchasing express our desires; and these desires not only show that we want to have something, but that we want to become something. As Dichter (2002) elaborates, "The objects which surround us do not simply have utilitarian aspects; rather, they serve as a kind of mirror which reflects our own image. Objects which surround us permit us to discover more and more about ourselves" (p. 91).

The most crucial choice in the marketplace is the choice of one's identity. The self, in a consumer society, is one that we create. Every trip to the mall and each online product search asks us: Who are you? Who would you like to be? How will you be seen by others? Market choice is central to the construction of modern self-identity. (Beaudoin, 2003; Berger, 2005; Burns, 2014; Chernev, Hamilton, & Gal, 2011; Elliott & Kristsadarat, 1998; Newholm & Hopkinson, 2009). We choose to be part of certain online groups. We choose to be advocates for certain causes. We are golf, or tennis, or ski, or gardening or poker enthusiasts. We subscribe to magazines for these hobbies and spend time and money to support them. As sociologist Sharon Zukin (2005) puts it, "We are where we shop." "For many people, their sense of themselves—their social identity—is shaped in considerable measure by the kinds of stores they go to and the kinds of things they can afford" (p.84).

All of this is far distant from the identities our grandparents had. They were born as farmers or Catholics or tanners or millers, etc., in some cases taking the name of their trade as their identity. On the other hand, our children's identity may be even more loosely fitting than our own. Born in a suburb that could be anywhere in the U.S. or Canada, they grow up in similar houses and attend similar schools and churches as their contemporaries throughout the continent. They feel compelled to choose their identity at an early age, often when they go to the mall with their peers. They succumb to the ironic dilemma of being "different" together. They dress like their peers, and do the things that their peers do. But as this father can tell you, they are not content to be like all the other kids. One of my children decided that she was actually a far more interesting person than her typical white-girl looks and dress might suggest. Her solution: dreadlocks. She is no longer just another nice white girl, but stands out as one of only three on her campus with dreads.

She only did what psychologists and marketers have long recognized

A key to self-construction via consumption activity involves establishing a point of difference from others—to establish one's self as a distinct, independent entity It is not sufficient merely to 'keep up with the Joneses;' instead it is necessary to be different from the Joneses, or in other words, to possess an identity different from the Jones (cited in Burns, 2014).

This, the creation of an identity via consumption, is not an aspect of capitalism but it is a clear mark of consumerism. In early capitalism, the identity of the producers and the consumers were fixed by other means; conferred by family, church, town, guild or tribe. But as psychologist Paul Wachtel (1989) notes,

In the modern world we must make an identity for ourselves; we do not inherit one. We have outgrown the tradition that assigns one's way of life, one's station, and one's loyalties at birth And, for more and more of us, we outgrow too the particulars of our backgrounds. That we are from a particular place or class, or even the sons and daughters of particular mothers and fathers, does not determine who we are. In many ways, of course, this is liberating, but it makes an identity something we must achieve (p. 99).

The things we use to create our-selves are the products and services offered to us in the marketplace. Advertisers know this. Some of the tag-lines from ad campaigns directly address the fact that their product will create an identity for us. "Couldn't you see yourself in a .... If only your friends could see you now. You can always tell a XYZ woman," Etc. Celebrity endorsers are another common identity building tool They enable us to place our identity under the umbrella of a famous athlete or film star. For instance, You can "be like Mike." Your home furnishings can be designed by Martha. French sociologist Jean Baudrillard (1998) writes, "Modern man spends less and less of his life in production within work and more and more of it in the *production* and continual innovation of his own needs and well-being" (p. 80).

We use material things as symbols that stand for us and identify us. Those symbols are then either affirmed or denied by others. If they are affirmed, our identity is also confirmed. If they are denied, our identity is challenged. For example, if I purchase a classic car, I will want to attend club meetings and participate in parades for classic car lovers. But if I show up at the meeting and learn that I have messed up my classic car by using the wrong parts while restoring it, I will feel shame. I am then not really part of the classic car fanciers group. I am a pretender, a "wannabe."

So choose, and choose well. And then play the part. Others will confirm or deny whether you wear the symbols well. The hard thing about modern identity maintenance is that the symbols change. What once symbolized fine taste in food or art or fashion or autos or... may change next year. In fact, the producers of consumer goods intentionally change them, so that those who wish to maintain that identity will have to buy a new product in that niche. Berger (2005) states "In the post-modern lifestyle, identities are infinitely changeable and all require the consumption of products to generate the desired identity or image, and since constant identity change is now seen as normal, constant consumption is now required (p. 17). He concludes his study with the ironic observation that "The problem is that, in many cases, we become so wrapped up in our new and continually changing lifestyles that we lose our identities—any sense of who we really are" (p.125).

It is established then, that consumerism is far more than capitalism, though it could not exist without market exchange. Consumerism is ultimately a process by which we choose our identity. As Berger (2005) says, "Consumer culture is culture in which the personal consumption of goods and services becomes an all powerful force" (p.1).

This article has described a system--consumerism; and its primary activity or characteristic—choice. Next, the theological tradition in which that activity is also predominant—American Evangelicalism, and especially Revivalism will be examined.

FREE-WILL THEOLOGY

Needing to create our own identities is a relatively new problem, and its rise largely coincides with that of the Second Great Awakening of the early 19th Century. At the same time that Americans were urged to choose a particular product or service via advertising, they were also being urged to stand up and make a decision for Christ.

In contrast with the rigorous Calvinistic emphasis on election that Weber described, the camp meetings of the Second Great Awakening adjured those present to ***freely choose*** Christ. The attendees did not need to be catechized or educated; they only needed to accept the greatest product the world has ever known.

The emphasis on free will has been present in various forms throughout the history of the Church (e.g., John Chrysostom being an early representative, and Pelagius its most extreme example [Chewning, 2012]).[1] But in modern America the advocate who most greatly influenced society was the Dutch theologian, Jacobus Arminius. Arminius emphasized the need for humans to cooperate with the grace of God, arguing that prevenient grace from God enables people to make a choice in favor of, or against the offered salvation.

Among those who currently adopt the Arminian view are the Free-Will Baptists, taking their name from this important doctrine. The Wesleys were well recognized as Arminians. In the following Wesleyan hymn it can be observed that making a decision for Christ was not only part of his private doctrine, but became a part of church practice and worship in the Methodist tradition.[2]

The Gospel Feast. (Charles Wesley)

Come all ye souls by sin oppressed ye restless wanderers after rest;

Ye poor and maimed and halt and blind, in Christ a hearty welcome find.

My message as from God receive; ye all may come to Christ and live:

O let his love your hearts constrain, nor suffer him to die in vain.

See him set forth before your eyes, that precious bleeding sacrifice:

His offered benefits embrace, and freely now be saved by grace."

Compare these lyrics with those of the Calvinist hymn: '*Tis not that I did Choose Thee* (sung in a minor key).[3]

'Tis not that I did choose Thee, For Lord, that could not be;

This heart would still refuse Thee, Hadst Thou not chosen me.

Thou from the sin that stained me Hast cleansed and set me free;

Of old Thou hast ordained me, That I should live to Thee.

The Wesleyan tradition has long impacted North America, and nowhere has free-will theology been as predominant as it has in American Revivalism. In this tradition, one must openly "decide" for Jesus, preferably by standing or raising one's hand and then saying a prayer of repentance. This process is so indelibly written into the American Evangelical script that we can hardly imagine repentance and conversion being shown in any other way. "Making a decision for Christ" is what characterizes the free-will tradition. The Wesleyan emphasis on the need to choose was amplified in The Second Great Awakening by Charles Finney, its chief figure.

The later 19th Century revivalism of Dwight L. Moody continued to emphasize the need to ***choose*** in his preaching. The leading scholar of American revivalism writes, "The central and all-inclusive fact of Christian theology for Moody was that sinful men could all obtain eternal life simply by believing that Christ died for their sins. If men did not 'accept Christ', they would certainly spend eternity in hell" Moody believed that "We are free agents; God allows us to choose" (McLoughlin, 1959, pp. 247-48).

As religious historian Timothy Gloege (2015) also notes, "Like any good salesman, the content of Moody's preaching was instrumental, designed primarily to compel an audience to the moment of decision" (p.36). Gloege (2015) persuasively argues that there is a strong connection between the marketing practices of the time and revivalist preaching.

Many evangelical professionals considered business practices of all kinds to be uncontroversial reservoirs or spiritual insights. Their experience at work provided metaphors for understanding their faith and techniques for effectively practicing it. Evangelicals like Woodruff felt at home in the pages of Scott's book (Psychology of Advertising). Its advice on using emotional and sympathetic appeals, its five stages of human choosing, its taxonomies of decision makers, and its warnings that "individuals are different" and make their choices by 'diverse methods" confirmed their experiences in personal evangelism. But the exchange went both ways. Secular advertisers were happy to borrow insights into human psychology from religious professionals who spent years cajoling sinners to choose salvation. Both advertisers and evangelists were tackling the same problem of individual human choice, and both groups welcomed any art or science that gave them an advantage (Gloege, 2015, p.139).

The last in this series of Arminian evangelists, Billy Graham, flatly stated "I'm selling the greatest product in the world, why shouldn't it be promoted as well as soap" (McLoughlin, 1959, p. 513). The Graham campaign kept clear records of "decisions for Christ," and Graham's flagship magazine is called "Decision." His radio program, tellingly entitled "The Hour of Decision" first aired on Nov. 5, 1950.

There may be one other factor that pushed the emphasis in American theology away from election and toward free choice. In U.S. politics the *vote* was becoming the key sign of democracy--one man one vote, and later, one woman one vote. McLoughlin (1959) sees this as a contributing factor for the success of free-will theology of revivalist Charles Grandison Finney as well.

In American democracy, all the complex problems of freedom and power were reduced to voting for, or against, one of two candidates, Finney applied the political metaphor to religion: 'the world is divided into two great political parties; the difference between them is that one party choose Satan as the god of this world.... The other party chooses Jehovah for their governor.' Conversion was the decision to ***vote for Jehovah*** *and to support his administration (pp. 69-70).*

In these four giants of evangelical revivalism—Wesley, Finney, Moody and Graham, we find the culmination of Arminian free-will theology with its constant and clear call for a "Decision." Who are you? Whose side are you on? Which party do you vote for? Choose!

After his lengthy and thoroughgoing study of American Revivalism, McLoughlin (1959) provides this rather damning summary.

Even if revivalists could be credited for the fact that America today has proportionately more church members, more church wealth, and more church activity than any other nation in the world, it would not be an enviable achievement. For in spite of, or perhaps because of this quantitative religiosity, America has also acquired a reputation as the most materialistic and secularistic nation in the world (p. 529).

McLoughlin may have inadvertently put his finger on the connection between consumerism and religious "decisionism" here. His judgment about the relationship between religiosity and materialism is not coincidental. This is due to the fact that the chief characteristic of consumerism is also the chief characteristic of free-will revivalism; namely, choice that creates identity.

The similarity of market identity to religious self-identity is apparent. Both demand that the individual choose his or her own identity in a clearly scripted way; in one case by standing or raising the hand, in the other by shopping for a set of products and services. We are consumers of both faith and products, both of which create individual identity. Gloege (2015) confirms, saying, "This combination of consumer capitalism and evangelical religion… provided solutions to sticky ideological issues caused by the decline of autonomy at work and a new set of corresponding opportunities to create identities through the consumption of goods and services…." (p.139). Further,

Consumer culture thus encouraged a definition of what it meant to be authentically human that placed a particular emphasis on choice. (….) It was the freedom to choose whether by voting, marrying, or shopping, that differentiated civilized humanity from the beasts. The centrality of choice resonated most strongly with an evangelical disposition. Authentic faith was an individually chosen, personal relationship with God. And it was the act of choosing specifically that made one's faith authentic (Gloege, 2015, p. 141).

CONCLUSION

Returning to Weber's thesis then, we have seen a vast difference between the Protestant work ethic of capitalism, and the free-will identity choice of consumerism. Calvinists have rarely been accused, and never convicted of an excessive emphasis on free-will or choice. The Calvinist/capitalist dutifully marches from work, to savings, to capital accumulation, and sees his assurance of salvation within it. The free-will consumer waltzes in a different key and time signature. The free-will waltz is of three steps; choose your God, your candidate and your self-identity. You are free to do so in the marketplaces of religion, politics and products. Whereas Calvinist theology may connect to capitalism, it seems clear that it is free-will theology that connects to consumerism.

Again, what is presented here is a typology, not a claim of causality. It is not claimed that the choices demanded by revivalists caused Americans to also choose products, nor the reverse. But, the emphasis on theological choice and market choice did grow together in the same time period in the United States. Americans were being adjured to stand up and choose Christ at the same time that they were being asked to choose an identity in the marketplace and a political candidate at the polls.

FUTURE RESEARCH DIRECTIONS

This paper has shown that the connection between Calvinism and capitalism first delineated by Weber cannot also be used to typify the relation between Calvinism and consumerism. Consumerism is characterized by human choice, and Calvinism is characterized by divine election. Using Calvinist doctrine to illuminate consumerism is anachronistic, and does not recognize the great differences between capitalism and consumerism. The free-will theologies derived from Arminius however, emphasize choice as their characteristic practice. Free-will theology and consumerism are thus similar to each other, and represent a new typology that is apt for modern consumerism.

This article provides the opportunity to examine consumerism and free-will theology as a new and distinct type. In future research, this new typology for consumerism may yield further and even new reflections on labor, marketing and consumer behavior in the contemporary marketplace. Though the Protestant Work Ethic has stimulated vast amounts of research and comment, it is time to address the newer phenomenon of consumerism with a new theological correlate.

REFERENCES

Baudrillard, J. (1998). *The consumer society: Myths and structures*. Thousand Oaks, CA: Sage.

Beaubot, G., & Echeverria, E. (2011). The culture of consumerism: A Catholic and Personalist critique. *Journal of Markets & Morality*, *5*(2), 339–383.

Beaudoin, T. (2003). *Consuming faith: Integrating who we are with what we buy*. Lanham, MD: Rowan & Littlefield.

Berger, A. (2005). *Shop 'til you drop: Consumer behavior and American culture*. New York, NY: Rowman & Littlefield.

Bowlby, R. (2001). *Carried away: The invention of modern shopping*. New York, NY: Columbia University Press.

Burns, D. (2011). Consumption in consumer culture: The role of fear and internal longings. *Proceedings of the Colleagues in Jesuit Business Education Conference*.

Burns, D. (2014). *Identity through consumption activities: A review and critical analysis*. Unpublished paper.

Burns, D., & Fawcett, J. (2012). The role of brands in a consumer culture: Can strong brands serve as a substitute for a relationship with God? *Journal of Biblical Integration in Business, 15*(2), 28–42.

Calvin, J. (1960). Institutes of the Christian religion (J. T. McNeill, Ed.; F. L. Battles, Trans.). Philadelphia, PA: Westminster Press.

Chernev, A., Hamilton, R., & Gal, D. (2011). Competing for consumer identity: Limits to self-expression and the perils of lifestyle branding. *Journal of Marketing, 75*(3), 66–82. doi:10.1509/jmkg.75.3.66

Chewning, R. (2012). Augustine and Aquinas: Their theological progeny comes face to face with business as mission. *The Journal of Biblical Integration in Business, 15*(2), 64–83.

Dichter, E. (2002). *The strategy of desire*. New Brunswick, NJ: Transaction.

Doherty, D., & Etzioni, A. (2003). *Voluntary simplicity: Responding to consumer culture*. Lanham, MD: Rowan and Littlefield.

Elliott, R., & Wattanasuwan, K. (1998). Brands as symbolic resources for the construction of identity. *International Journal of Advertising, 17*(2), 131–144. doi:10.1080/02650487.1998.11104712

Ghazzawi, I., & Smith, Y. (2009). Crafting the whole employee: Job satisfaction, job commitment, and faith. *Business Review (Federal Reserve Bank of Philadelphia), 12*(2), 300–309.

Gloege, T. (2015). *Guaranteed pure: The Moody Bible Institute, business, and the making of modern Evangelicalism*. Chapel Hill, NC: University of North Carolina Press. doi:10.5149/northcarolina/9781469621012.001.0001

Green, R. (1959). *Protestantism and capitalism: The Weber thesis and its critics*. Boston, MA: D. C. Heath and Company.

Heilbronner, R. (1953). *The worldly philosophers*. New York, NY: Simon & Schuster.

James, R. (2011). *Shiny objects: Why we spend money we don't have in search of happiness we can't buy*. New York, NY: Harper One.

Kitch, M. J. (1967). *Capitalism and the Reformation*. London, UK: Longmans, Green & Co.

Lastovicka, J., & Sirianni, N. (2012). Truly, madly, deeply: Consumers in the throes of material possessive love. *The Journal of Consumer Research, 38*(2), 323–342. doi:10.1086/658338

Lehmann, H., & Roth, G. (1993). *Weber's Protestant ethic*. Cambridge, England: Cambridge University Press. doi:10.1017/CBO9781139052467

Makant, M. (2010). The pursuit of happiness: The virtue of consumption and the consumption of virtue. *Dialog: A Journal of Theology, 49*(4), 291-299.

McLoughlin, W. (1959). *Modern revivalism: Charles Grandison Finney to Billy Graham*. New York, NY: The Ronald Press Co.

Miller, M. J., Woehr, D. J., & Hudspeth, N. (2001). The meaning and measurement of work ethic: Construction and initial validation of a multidimensional inventory. *Journal of Vocational Behavior*, *60*(3), 451–489. doi:10.1006/jvbe.2001.1838

Miller, V. (2004). *Consuming religion: Christian faith and practice in a consumer culture*. New York, NY: Continuum.

Muller, H. (2006). Work and the conduct of life: Weber's legacy. *Max Weber Studies*, *6*(1), 119–145. doi:10.15543/MWS/2006/1/6

Newholm, T., & Hopkinson, G. (2009). I just tend to wear what I like: Contemporary consumption and the paradoxical construction of individuality. *Marketing Theory*, *9*(4), 439–462. doi:10.1177/1470593109346896

Smith, A. (2012). *An inquiry into the nature and causes of the wealth of nations*. London, UK: Wordsworth. (Original work published 1776)

Smith, V. O., & Smith, Y. S. (2013). Bias, history and the Protestant work ethic. *Journal of Management History*, *7*(3), 282–298.

Wachtel, P. (1983). *The poverty of affluence: A psychological portrait of the American way of life*. Philadelphia, PA: New Society Publishers.

Warr, P. (2008). Work values: Some demographic and cultural correlates. *Journal of Occupational and Organizational Psychology*, *81*(4), 751–775. doi:10.1348/096317907X263638

Weber, M. (1930). *The Protestant ethic and the spirit of capitalism. (T. Parsons, Ttrans.)*. London, England: Routledge.

Wuthnow, R. (1996). *Poor Richard's principle*. Princeton, NJ: Princeton University Press.

Zukin, S. (2005). *Point of purchase: How shopping changes American culture*. New York, NY: Routledge.

KEY TERMS AND DEFINITIONS

Asceticism: The religious practice of living simply and sparsely in this life in order to prepare for the life to come.

Calling: The idea that one's work is not merely toil that enables one to survive but a divine commission into a field of labor.

Calvinism: The system of doctrine derived from the 16th century reformer John Calvin that emphasized the absolute sovereignty of God in human affairs.

Capitalism: The economic system in which the market is free from outside interference. It requires efficient labor and capital reinvestment in order to yield profit.

Consumerism: A process in which individuals freely choose from a wide range of products and services that contribute to or create ones' identity.

Free-Will Theology: The doctrine that emphasizes the need for an individual to choose Christ.

Prevenient Grace: Arminian doctrine that sees the gracious work of God within all people before they receive Christ. It must find a response in the heart of believers by accepting Christ.

Typology: A technique for understanding the relationship between objects or ideas. For example, a collie is a type of dog, since it has all the characteristics of a dog. Similarities in characteristics can create a type; for example, Moses was a type for Christ in that he was a prophet and law-giver.

ENDNOTES

1 Robert Chewning sees the debate between the bondage of the will and the freedom of the will as occurring between neo-Augustinians and neo-Thomists. He applies this distinction to the subject of Business as Mission.

2 All hymn s from *HYMNS for the use of The Methodist Episcopal Church* New York: Carlton & Lanahan, 1849. Other related Methodist hymn texts include: *Now is the Accepted Time* by John Dobell, and *The Promises are Sure*. By Charles Wesley.

3 Published in 35 Reformed and Lutheran hymnals.

Chapter 10
Consumer Persona:
Segmentation Scheme Based on Buddhist Temperaments for Digital Marketing

Bu-nga Chaisuwan
National Institute of Development Administration, Thailand

Marissa Chantamas
Assumption University, Thailand

Kriengsin Prasongsukarn
Assumption University, Thailand

ABSTRACT

Religions have traditionally been used to explain the differences between peoples. However, this chapter aims to use religion, in this case Buddhism, to develop a segmentation scheme for international applications. It is aimed to improve the power of prediction of the segmentation schemes in terms of marketing mix stimuli response. The identification of the Buddhist temperaments would be useful in determining the response patterns observed in individuals. Application of this chapter includes developing segmentation for communications that are enabled by technology to tailor-make offers and messages to individuals depending upon their temperaments. Recommendations for future research includes using big data applications in order to determine individual temperaments as an alternative methodology for analyzing the consumer.

INTRODUCTION

From the assertion presented by Wolfe (1996), research has evolved in an effort to understand universality of moral intuitions. According to Brooks (2008), the self is a result of dynamic relationships honed through experiences. While people may have different religions, the core moral intuitions are the same. Religion is an integral part of daily life and consumption. As a consequence, this chapter aims to present an alternative perspective in using religious concepts in furthering the understanding of consumer behavior especially in the area of segmentation, which has many challenges for international applications.

DOI: 10.4018/978-1-5225-6120-0.ch010

Religion is one of the characteristics that identify the uniqueness of a culture linked to a national identity (Huntington, 1993). Traditional international segmentation schemes are based on the assumption that individuals in different countries differ due to their culture. As a result, culture influences implementation of the marketing mix in respective markets (Samiee & Jeong, 1994). Consequently, globalization has increased the need of understanding how culture affects consumer behavior (Patterson, Cowley, & Prasongsukarn, 2006). Steenkamp and Hofstede (2002) explained that current international segmentation can be classified as heuristics methods (Q or R-factor analysis and factor analysis) and model based international segmentation methods (epidemiological theory, model of innovation diffusion, and means-end chain theory). However, Steenkamp and Hofstede (2002) indicated that there are still segments in various countries that may not fit the schemes developed. This is due to problems in construct equivalence. Prasongsukarn (2009) argued that this limitation needs to be addressed because cultural orientation, attitudes, and behaviors stem from the same source. Thus, in order to better develop segmentation schemes applied to an international market setting, it is imperative to identify values that are common to a broad consumer base in a similar way to Maslow's Hierarchy of Needs (1954). Thus, this study aims to explore the fundamental element that drives creation of values that in turn influence consumer behavior. In addition, this chapter aims to propose an alternative segmentation scheme that is more suited to the digital marketing context, which is rapidly spreading across the globe.

BACKGROUND

Dahlsgaard, Peterson, and Seligman (2005) explained that to understand values, it is important to examine philosophical traditions of the major religions. The researchers did a study to compare Confucianism and Taoism (China), Buddhism and Hinduism (South, East, and Southeast Asia), and Judaism, Islam, and Christianity (the West). The study found that there were common positive values across all of the major religions.

These values have to be studied within the context of the entire value system. The better-known segmentation schemes used in marketing that are developed based on values are Values and Lifestyle (VALS) and List of Values (LOV). However, there are arguments for and against VALS and LOV in the international context. Steenkamp and Hofstede (2002) explained that segmentation has to deal with differences of people from different cultures. It is important to address this issue because segmentation aims to group people who have similar responses to marketing stimuli. As a result, it would be interesting to identify what factors drive motivational values that are fundamental and common to individuals across borders.

The attractiveness of segmentation using VALS and LOV is the depiction of individuals in colorful detail that can be used for marketing purposes (Kahle, Beatty, & Homer, 1986). Both segmentation schemes are based on Maslow's Hierarchy of Needs (1954). VALS was developed by Mitchell (1983) from Maslow's Hierarchy of Needs (1954) and the concept of social character (Riesman, Glazer, & Denney, 1950). LOV was developed based on Maslow's Hierarchy of Needs (1954) and values by Rokeach (1973). Both VALS and LOV identify an inner and outer orientation. As a result, values can be fulfilled through personal relationships, and personal factors, and personal achievement. Individuals differ in the development of these personal factors. Consequently, it is of interest how these personal factors affect the way values are fulfilled in the context of consumer behavior in marketing.

Kahle, Beatty, and Homer (1986) replicated the studies of VALS and LOV and found that the latter had better predictive power for consumer behavior. LOV has nine values—self-respect, security, warm relationships with others, sense of accomplishment, self-fulfillment, sense of belonging, being well respected, having fun and enjoyment in life, and excitement. However, one point of caution in using these segmentation schemes is the fact that the data collected in developing them have been done in the United States. Thus, its application to international markets needs to be considered carefully.

Culture has long been recognized as an important factor affecting consumer behavior across international markets (Aaker & Williams, 1998; Deshpande, Hoyer, & Donthu, 1986; Patterson, Cowley, & Prasongsukarn, 2006). Alden, Steenkamp and Batra (1999) posited that the rise of globalization has led to the creation of global consumer segments, who shared common consumption related symbols and meanings. This is a consequence of international marketing campaigns particularly in marketing communications aimed at creating global brands. However, despite this commonality of symbols and meanings individual consumers still differ in their behavior primarily due to their individual characteristics. The researchers propose a perspective that brands and religion do have a common goal, which is to gain followers (customers). This chapter hence, proposes the examination of concepts of religion that can be applied to segmentation, which is one of the basic building blocks of marketing.

Religion is among one of the four markers of civilization as described by Huntington (1993). It promotes homogeneity among those who are followers while highlighting the differences from non-followers. Often, religion is used in research either as a means to explain ethical concepts, which influence marketing (Hunt & Vitell, 2006; Hunt & Vitell, 1986; Schlegelmilch & Öberseder, 2010;), the marketing of religious organizations (El-Bassiouny, 2016; Mulyanegra, Tsarenko, & Mavondo, 2010; Wrenn, 2010), or as one study tried to link the process of religious indoctrination to the social marketing process (Van Esch, Van Esch, & Cowley, 2013). The research proposed by the authors suggested an interesting way of applying religious concepts to marketing. However, to date, the researchers have found no study that has applied the particular aspects of religious teachings to develop marketing constructs and corresponding scales. As a result, the major contribution of this chapter is applying the six Buddhist temperaments in the development of a segmentation scheme with international application.

Buddhism is a religion widely associated with Asia since its birth and spread covers much of the region (Dahlsgaard, Peterson, & Seligman, 2005). The ultimate goal of Buddhism is the attainment of nirvana, or bliss, which emanates from truly removing any attachment to self or desires (Bhatt, 2001; Dahlsgaard, Peterson, & Seligman, 2005; Dutt, 1983). In order to achieve this, Buddha taught the examination of the mind. Part of Buddha's teachings is dedicated to training the mind through the Eightfold Path, which are understanding, thinking, speech, action, livelihood, effort, mindfulness, and concentration. The Five Precepts reflect ideals of humanity, justice, and self-restraint from misdeeds (Dahlsgaard, Peterson, & Seligman, 2005). Buddha recognized early on that people are different and his teachings would have differing impact on each person. He described this concept in comparison with the lotus. He explained that humans are like lotus arising from the depths of mud, a condition which exemplifies a lack of knowledge. Some lotus buds never make it out of the mud; some are eaten by the fish and only a few make it to the surface and blossom beautifully. This has led Budhha to examine the characteristics of people leading to the development of the six temperaments categorization.

Six Buddhist Temperaments

There are six Buddhist temperaments as defined by Payutto (2000). The temperaments are explained as follows:

- Lustful Temperament (Materialism): These individuals tend to be attractive to novel things. They tend to be positive, seeing good in others and enjoy innovation. These individuals tend to like to "collect" things, friends, and admiration. They experience a constant craving for new experiences and wish to be recognized for being trendy and cool.
- Angry Temperament (Pride):These individuals are not positive to innovation. They tend to distance themselves from new things being more conservative and skeptical towards information in the media. These individuals would seek flaws and argue about whether something would work or not. In fact this group tend to be more analytical. However, they tend to judge quickly and act immediately in accordance to their conclusion.
- Deluded Temperament (Confused—no fixed stand point or opinion):These individuals tend to be confused or do not know how to react to any new information. As a result, they tend to refer to the opinion of others in order to form their own ideas. These individuals tend to have difficulty in making decisions, thus needing persuasion in order to come to a conclusion. They tend to be always having fantasies and going through scenarios but have a hard time pinning anything down into action.
- Faithful Temperament (Loyal/Conservative):These individuals tend to be domineering. They act in accordance to their beliefs and ideals. As a result, they tend to act as thought leaders through their personal belief that they can make the world a better place. These individuals are judgmental extremists. Due to their dedicated nature they would do anything to achieve their goal.
- Intelligent Temperament (Rational):These individuals are very pragmatic and realistic. They are intelligent individuals who dislike false claims. They are prone to seek for information to derive at the best solution for their needs. They tend to live in the moment letting go of the past and not fantasizing too much about the future.
- Speculative Temperament (Worrisome):These individuals are always worried. They tend to focus on the details without getting much done. They spend a lot of time thinking. They dislike risk taking. They change their minds often and find it hard to make any decision.

These six Buddhist temperaments can be said to be similar to the proto-psychological theory having its roots in Greek/Roman causal theory. The theory suggests that there are four types of personalities based on the underlying temperaments namely—sanguine (enthusiastic, active, and social) that corresponds to the lustful temperament, and choleric (short-tempered, fast or irritable) that corresponds to the angry temperament. However, the melancholic (analytical, wise and quiet) and phlegmatic (relaxed and peaceful) do not quite fit the remaining temperaments. But for the purpose of categorization, melancholic corresponds to intelligent and speculative types while phlegmatic represents the faithful and deluded temperaments. The definitions apparently do not fit very well but some of the characteristics can be used to assist in the categorization of individuals based on these temperaments.

MAIN FOCUS OF THE CHAPTER

Problems With Current Segmentation Schemes

Segmentation forms the basis for the development of marketing strategy (Wedel & Kamakura, 2002). Floh, Zauner, Koller, and Rusch (2014) explained that traditionally, segmentation includes culture, geographic and socioeconomic variables, personality, lifestyle, user status and user frequency. Ko et al., (2012) explained that it is indeed possible to create segmentation schemes for international market, based from global market strategy. The researchers identified eight segments from a study that covered four countries. Thus, the following section traces the development of segmentation and its subsequent limitations.

Smith (1956) first proposed the idea of segmentation. It was a necessary step that ensures marketers could implement repurchase, upsell, cross-sell strategies as well as promoting word of mouth. In addition, successful segmentation guarantees marketers that they could effectively address the needs of the consumers in order to improve their profitability (Andreasen, 1984; Smith, 1995; Maureen & Sally, 1998). However, over the years, segmentation studies have discovered problems in its implementation process (Kleinberg, Papadimitriou & Raghavan, 2004; Machauer & Morgner, 2001; Maureen & Sally, 1998; Reibstein, Day, & Wind, 2009; Smith, 1995; Suzanne, 2002; Yankelovich & Meer, 2006).

Some of the major issues in segmentation are presented as follows:

1. There is no clear guideline regarding the number of necessary factors needed to develop the segmentation scheme.
2. Once the segmentation is implemented different segments do not react differently to the elements of the marketing mix as hypothesized.
3. The segmentation developed does not suit the existing customer base. As a result, the recommendation is to use cluster analysis in analyzing the customers based on the segmentation variables defined (Kleinberg, Papadimitriou, & Raghavan, 2004; Nikolaus, Reisinger & Hoppe, 2009; Steenkamp & Hofstede, 2002).

Based on Kotler and Keller (2011) the following segmentation variables have been defined for the consumer market:

1. Geographic segmentation.
2. Demographics segmentation including age, gender, occupation, education, life cycle, and income.
3. Psychographic segmentation including social class, value, personality, and lifestyle.
4. Behavioral segmentation including knowledge, attitude, and users.

From previous researches, it can be summarized that successful segmentation need to follow the following five stages (Bailey, Baines, Wilson, & Clark, 2009; Duygu, 2011; Grönroos, 1998; Hoek, Gendall & Esslemont, 1996; Kleinberg, Papadimitriou, & Raghavan, 2004; Quinn, 2009; Rigby, Reichheld, & Schefter, 2002; Speed & Smith, 1992; Walsh, Hennig-Thurau, Wayne-Mitchell & Wiedmann, 2001).

1. Clearly defining the segmentation scheme whether it would be customer segmentation (only existing customers) or entire market segmenation. This decision would be dependent on the following factors:
   a. The organization's resources need to be considered because segmentation is costly and requires a major investment in terms of finances, human resources, and time.
   b. It is important to define the objectives clearly. Customer segmentation is usually done in the case of organizations that already have existing customers. Market/segmentation is usually much broader and is done for targeting purposes.
2. Clearly define the segmentation variables. It is recommended to use qualitative studies to clarify these variables (Dibb, 2001; Meadows & Dibb, 1988; Yankelovich & Meer, 2006).
3. Selecting the segmentation variables by considering the following factors:
   a. Availability of data –whether the marketer has access to information needed to develop the segmentation scheme. In case the data is not available, it is necessary to consider if proxy variables can be used in its place (Bailey, Baines, Wilson, & Clark, 2009; Kleinberg, Papadimitriou, & Raghavan, 2004; Patrick, 2006; Quinn, 2009).
   b. Consider whether the variables would yield a meaningful segmentation. This is defined as the clear difference in the attitude and behavior towards the various marketing mix (Novak, Leeuw, & MacEvoy, 1992; Rigby, Reichheld, & Schefter, 2002).
4. Once segmentation variables have been defined, they need to be verified regarding their power in explaining the differences between groups. It is recommended to use multistage segmentation by starting with a fundamental segmentation based on needs (Albert, 2003) and decision-making styles (Hoek, Gendall, & Esslemont, 1996; Walsh et al., 2001). Then other factors can be used as additional layers of segmentation.
5. Information has to be collected from the segments and analyzed to evaluate the discriminating power of the variables in order to further improve the segmentation scheme.

Part of the force driving this transformation in the consumer is the growth of technology, which allows them to reach more options and choices. The implication of this trend means that consumers are not going to fit typical segmentation schemes. As a consequence, a good segmentation scheme should be based on factors that are more stable yet play a role in affecting consumer behavior. Big data technology enables the analysis of information that encompasses beyond the typical demographics, to customer interactions, and social networking data (Elgendy & Elragal, 2014). This enables what is called micro-level segmentation that lends itself to the development of the customer persona. Hassan and Craft (2005) explained that currently marketers have started to recognize the importance of micro-level segmentation. Thus, this chapter proposes the use of temperaments in developing a consumer segmentation scheme applied in digital marketing, which is one of the means of micro-level segmentation.

Issues in Using Temperaments in Past Research

Cloninger (1994) explained that the differences in personality were accentuated by psychobiological systems that affect the way individuals perceive the environment around them. This can be classified as the temperament, which is the individual's perception-based habits. Cloninger (1994, 1987) explained that temperament influences perception and any associative learning that occurs. It is usually developed at an early age and remains relatively stable into adulthood. Thus, it can be explained that temperament is a neurobiological component that creates variation in personality.

Temperament can be further divided into four subsystems –behavioral inhibition, behavioral activation, behavioral dependence, and behavioral persistence. Cloninger (1991) explained that behavioral activation corresponds with novelty seeking behavior, in which a person actively seeks for unusual stimuli while avoiding adverse ones. Behavioral dependence is characterized by pessimism, shyness, fatigue, and anxiety. Individuals high in behavioral dependence are considered as having warm social characteristics; they are highly sympathetic and sensitive, who fears separation from others. Lastly, behavioral persistence corresponds with eagerness, ambition, determination, and poor adaptation to changes and inconsistencies. They are characterized as overachievers.

Cloninger (1987) studied temperament primarily to explain neurotic behavior. However, the concepts of temperament have been adapted to explain consumer behavior as well. As early as 1962, Westfall (1962) conducted a study using the Thurstone Temperament Schedule to assess temperament. In his definition, temperaments are traits that are relatively permanent to the individual notwithstanding his recent social experiences and media consumption. Westfall identified seven different characteristics. First, active describes people who like to take things quickly even without the need to. Vigorous refers to those who enjoy physical activities, working out or working with their hands. Impulsive are those who like to take chances and make decisions on the fly. Dominant corresponds to those who have a high level of initiative and like to be responsible; they are likely to start new projects and persuade others. Stable are those who can remain calm in a crisis and are less distracted, thus being able to maintain their concentration. Similar to Evans (1959) Westfall found weak evidence that the differences in personality had an impact on product choice (in both cases, cars). Other researchers (Kinnear & Taylor, 1976) have a different view. Similar constructs namely risk taking, pessimisive society, optimism, and active life, were used by Kinnear and Taylor (1976) to test beer drinkers. They found a significant difference between light and heavy beer drinkers.

In 1967, Cohen presented the idea that interpersonal orientation played a part in consumer behavior. Basing his framework from Horney (1937), individuals were classified into three categories namely compliant, aggressive, and detached (CAD). Those who were compliant tend to follow what others are saying, while aggressive people go against others. Detached people tend to move away from others. Cohen (1967) said that the probability that each orientation become dominant relied on the reinforcement along with accompanying attitude as well as the relevance of the orientation within the context of situation.

Shimp (1983) explained that CAD should not be used to predict product or brand consumption due to the failure of past researches (Cohen 1967; Woodside & Andress, 1975) and criticism from previous works (Noerager, 1979). However, in line with the work of Bagozzi (1980) and Ajzen and Fishbein (1980), such psychographic constructs should best be used to explain a general class of related behaviors. In this vein, Slama, Williams, and Tashchian (1988) used CAD to explain purchase involvement behavior. The authors found that purchase involvement behavior also correlated significantly with Rokeach values that form the basis of LOV.

This paper therefore, proposes temperament as an interesting concept because its application can be useful in the digital era were products, services and communications can be customized to suit individual preferences. Duncan and Moriarty (1998) explained that communications should be the cornerstone of marketing activities. The importance of communications as part of the promotional mix that has an impact on the rest of the marketing mix elements lies in the shift towards a relationship paradigm that is characterized by interactivity and connectivity (Vargo & Lusch, 2004). This trend is further facilitated by technological innovations in communications (Bhattacharya & Bolton, 2000). Technology enables personalization in the on-going conversation with the consumer that is also highly cost effective (Deighton & Barwise, 2000; Peppers & Rogers, 2004; Reinartz, Thomas, & Kumar, 2005). Personalization of communications has been supported by many studies as being an effective means for marketers to maintain a relationship with customers (Ansari & Mela, 2003; Burnham, Frele, & Mahajan, 2003; Leippe & Elkin, 1987; Petty & Cacioppo, 1979).

One segmentation scheme, which aims to increase relevance for marketing and communications purposes that has been gaining popularity among Fast Moving Consumer Goods (FMCG) companies is the use of personas. Persona is defined as representations of the ideal customers. This includes information in terms of demographics, online behavior, personal history, motivations and concerns. When describing customer personas, marketers generally refer to the customer journey that assists them to better understand the context of customer experience. Unilever defines customer persona, as the archetypal need state that enables the company to segment their customers. Previous research has demonstrated that the modification of the communications and creating an on-going conversation with the consumer has had a positive impact on the brand (Merisavo & Raulas, 2004). This chapter then emphasizes on the application of the temperaments to the type of message and offers with consideration the selection of appropriate channel for communications. By being able to make the communications more relevant to the consumer, it is reckoned to be more effective (Simonson, 2005).

SOLUTIONS AND RECOMMENDATIONS

Buddhist Temperament Scheme Development

Steenkamp and Hofstede (2002) cautioned that many of the international studies were exploratory in nature. However, the authors deem it a necessary first step in testing the validity of the construct being studied. The respondents consisted of international respondents selected from the volunteers of the project. The sample was selected using snowball technique in order to get people of the same nationality as the initial respondents (Malhotra & Birks, 2006). The initial respondents were recruited from students and faculty members from an international university in Thailand. The respondents represent countries in Asia, Africa, the Middle East, Europe, Africa, North America, and Latin America. This is considered comprehensive and rather representative of the population when compared to previous research that focused on using only student samples and conducted the study primarily in the US (Cohen, 1967; Kinnear & Taylor, 1976; Mitchell, 1983; Woodside & Andress, 1975). McCracken (1988) explained that eight respondents is sufficient in capturing the relevant themes for a phenomenon in conducting qualitative research. Based on this guideline, a total of 29 respondents were interviewed. Their profiles are summarized in the appendix (see table 4) .

The interview technique used was laddering technique as recommended by Pieters, Baumgartner and Allen (1995) to discover the aggregate values in this case LOV. Respondents were asked to talk about their daily routine and product use. They then were asked how their actions and preferences reflected their personality. Next, they were asked why they felt that way. This method enabled the researcher to construct the ladders to be used for further analysis.

Analysis was based on inductive categorization suggested by Spiggle (1994). In the first step, the interviews were coded to reflect the different type of values held by consumers. For the second step, the quotes under each label created in step one, were compared to assess similarities and differences. To control for the researcher bias in the analysis, two independent coders were employed to develop emergent themes, which were then compared to the notes developed by the researcher. In the third step, these themes were then referenced to CAD by Cohen. These schemes were selected due to their popularity in research and availability of items that can be used in the analysis. In addition, these scales provide useful reference for the development of items for future quantitative studies.

It is found that some of the six Buddhist temperaments overlapped with CAD constructs. For instance, consumers who were compliant appeared to have similar characteristics with those of the deluded temperament. They are reliant on information attained from others. Those who display aggressive personality traits also reported characteristics that were similar to those with anger temperament. They often challenged information they receive and were very opinionated. The detached personality type corresponded to a certain degree with the faithful temperament. From previous research, it is found that detached personality traits meant the individual would have limited interest in the matter at hand, thus, it can be interpreted that they do not actively seek novelty, instead they do things as usual to get things done. This is because they have other things that interest them and would prefer spending time doing so. They are described as more peaceful and calm in nature.

Individuals appeared to have varying degrees in exhibiting the six Buddhist temperaments. One of the temperaments tended to be dominant in determining the individual's perception, attitudes, and behavior. This is similar to the idea proposed by Sprotles and Kendall (1986) that consumer behavior is complex. In the development of their consumer styles inventory (CSI), eight dimensions were identified –perfectionism, brand consciousness, novelty-fashion consciousness, recreational shopping consciousness, price-value consciousness, impulsiveness-carelessness, confused by over choice, and brand-loyal-habitual. However, the limitation of CSI is generalizability because it has not been successfully replicated outside of the US (Walsh et al., 2001). The researchers conducted a study using CSI in Germany and ended up with six dimensions namely functional buyers, demanding comparative buyers, impulsive buyers, emotional buyers, brand oriented shopping conscious buyers, and fashion-conscious result-oriented buyers.

Like Walsh et al., (2001), the exploratory study conducted for this chapter yielded six segments. However, the definitions of these segments are different, and they bear more similarity to the original CSI proposed by Sprotles and Kendall (1986). The results in the exploratory study do not show a marked cultural difference between respondents although the weakness is the inability to attain a larger number of responses. In order to test the generalizability, further work has to be conducted to develop items that can be tested across different countries. The results of this exploratory study have been used to define each of the temperaments, which henceforth would be defined as consumer persona. The term persona is used to refer to the application of the temperaments in developing a comprehensive image of the segment in order to create relevance and deliver value effectively. The personas identified include materialism persona, pride persona, confused persona, loyal/conservative person, rational persona and worrisome persona. A brief definition of each persona is presented in the following section.

Those with materialism persona liked to show off materialistic possessions. They favored things and activities that tell of their status and loved beautifying themselves, their homes, and their other possessions including pets. They were attracted by messages and brands that projected an image of status and beauty. Brands that they chose had to be known to be luxurious and they loved flattery in the experience in purchasing brands. To them, this is an integral part of service.

Respondents with the pride persona tended to be quick to respond. They were rather confident in themselves and liked brands that were exclusive. They did not like mass luxury brands and preferred to be thought of as marketing mavens. This group tended to look for a lot of information due to their competitive nature. They believed they know a lot and wanted to share and influence others. They are disposed to make relatively quick decisions.

Confused persona individuals were major users of social media. They depended heavily on opinion leaders or net idols in making decisions. They followed the trend by jumping on the bandwagon and they loved to show to others what they have done, and what is hip and trendy on their social media. This group is easily swayed by the sentiments around them making purchases based on popularity. They are not loyal customers.

Loyal/Conservative persona individuals were those who were relatively loyal and stable in their brand choices. They made choices based on previous satisfied experiences rather than believing what others say. They considered some choices quite stable to the point of being automated thus, displaying brand loyalty and a compliance to routine. These respondents considered that it was not necessary to fuss on every detail. It is better for them to save energy and time to do things that interest them.

Rational persona individuals were highly rational consumers. Like those who have the angry temperament, they loved to seek information in making decisions but do not act hastily. The intelligent temperament individuals took their time in making the best decision for themselves. They did not care much about how others perceive them. Thus, they make purchases that are highly optimized in their opinion rather than what is popular.

Worrisome persona individuals were similar to the confused temperament in the sense that they think a lot and tended to be superficial in their search of information. However, this group worries a lot. They were characterized by uncertainty and need reinforcement in their decisions processes. In other words, they tended to make slower decisions, and prefer more human contact so that their questions and doubts can be addressed.

It is found that the individuals of differing personas tended to give importance to the nine LOV values—self -respect, security, warm relationships with others, sense of accomplishment, self-fulfillment, sense of belonging, being well-respected, fun and enjoyment in life, and excitement. This is because the values are goals that individuals may aspire to attain since they are founded on the fundamental needs explained by Maslow (1954). However, to test the differences between the individuals of different personas and the attainment of the LOV values, a future quantitative study needs to be conducted.

The development of the quantitative items would be discussed in a separate paper; however, additional analysis has to be done to confirm the qualitative findings. As a result, data from a major FMCG company was referenced to compare with findings from the qualitative study. The data in comparison came from the creation of customer journeys resulting in the development of the customer persona, which improves segmentation effectiveness. The persona is developed from keyword research (what consumers are searching in relation to the product) and social media analytics (including Facebook Insights). The consumer personas of two FMCG product categories have been selected for comparison. The first is the laundry category (women) and male fragrance (men). This is to ensure that the data cover both genders making it comparable to the initial qualitative study. From Table 1, it can be observed that the patterns of personas are similar based on their fundamental reactions to a broad purchase as posited by Bagozzi (1980) and Ajzen and Fishbein (1980).

Table 1. Persona comparison

	Persona Developed in this Study	Laundry Segmentation	Male Fragrance Segmentation
1.	Materialism;sensory, beauty, luxury	Sensory purchase: purchase on fragrance and luxury	Predator: all about pleasure
2.	Pride:confident, tries the best	Optimizing purchase: looks for new and improved ways for use	Natural talent: smart and confident
3.	Confused:needs to seek information for decision	Deal purchase: open to new brands in search of best deal	Enthusiastic novice: does not know what to do but goes ahead anyway
4.	Loyal/Conservative: stable and prefers the trusted and known	Routine purchase: avoid risk sticks to the tried and true brands	Marriage material: humble and respectful
5.	Rational: makes decision based on information and the benefits desired	Problem solution purchase: seeks solution to problems in use	Always friend: practical but not too appealing
6.	Worrisome: lacks certainty in the decision seeking the best option but still has concerns	Concerned buyer: has concerns in use such as environmental factors and seeking better options	Insecure novice: no clue what to do and needs advice

CONSUMER PERSONA SEGMENTATION SCHEME

The CAD temperament scheme has been shown to influence purchase involvement as proposed by Kassarjian (1981) and demonstrated by Slama et al. (1988). This is because purchase involvement differs by individual factors regardless of product or situation. This stand expands on the idea of CAD by introducing the six consumer personas as an alternative segmentation scheme. The benefit of this scheme is its ability to distinctively divide consumers based on their reaction to marketing mix elements which is important for successful segmentation (Novak, Leeuw, & MacEvoy, 1992; Rigby, Reichheld, & Schefter, 2002). One of the recommendations in the development of customer persona is to include information such as personal goals, challenges, behavior, and buzz words. As a result, Table 2 presents the quotes that best represent each of the personas, which can be observed in different countries, thus, demonstrating applicability of constructs in global context.

As explained earlier in the review of temperament studies, CAD was recommended to be applied to general class of behaviors (Ajzen & Fishbein, 1980; Bagozzi, 1980; Shimp, 1983). This is supported from the results that there is no real difference in terms of brand usage and preference among the consumers. This is in line with the study by Kennedy, Ehrenberg and Long (2000), who contended that segmentation scheme can be developed through the perception of consumers towards the promotion in the marketing mix. This application is made based on the importance of perception in determining the success of the promotional mix in affecting sales. In addition, this is supported by the advances in digital technology that lends itself well in creating tailor-made communications and offers that can stimulate immediate sales online or on mobile.

Based on the consumer persona and attainment of LOV values, the following communications strategies can be developed:

- **Materialism Persona:** Emphasis should be given to beauty and exclusiveness. The most important influencers are celebrities, who derive their fame from mass media. These consumers follow the news and series on mass media such as television and cable, or digital channels. They reference their styles on these celebrities. It doesn't take them long to make their decisions because

Table 2. Quotes reflecting consumer persona based on the Buddhist temperaments

Consumer Persona (Buddhist Temperament)	Persona Sample Profile	Sample Persona Behavior
Materialism (Lustful Temperament)	Female aged 45 Private Sector Employee Thailand	I follow the trend through mass media like watching series and star gossip. I only buy brand name bags that are being carried by the superstars. I search and check out what models they are. I do not want to be the same as others so I must make sure that I buy the trendiest thing available. I don't mind paying more. I don't have the time to go shopping at the physical store or flying to Hong Kong or Singapore to buy things so I buy online. I don't care if people ask me if it is fake. I know it is not. I choose to buy from vendors who are well rated on social media.
Pride (Angry Temperament)	Male aged 34 Business Owner Thailand	I like looking for information about my interests and business ideas. I find information from official sources, news, and talking to people or even attending seminars that provide business insights. I also am very observant when I travel so some of my ideas are derived from my trips abroad. Once I have enough information I make my decision and execute my ideas. I don't like to listen to people too much. They just talk and talk. Some of my ideas may fail but we all learn from our mistakes. Some will succeed so I think it works out fine.
Confused Deluded Temperament	Female aged 33 Faculty India	I take long hours shopping because I like to take my time finding what I want. My friends don't like shopping with me because they say I take so much time so I go with my sister. I will try dresses and shoes take photos and ask my friends what they think. I want to make sure I get what is good. I think time is immaterial in this sense. I enjoy doing this. Then I will post how I look when I wear my new dress or shoes or carry my new bag. I will check my ratings on Facebook or Instagram to see how well the post performed among my friends. I make sure I like every post of my friends so they will reciprocate liking mine. This is important for me to see that there are reactions to my posts.
Loyal/Conservative (Faithful Temperament)	Male aged 56 Faculty India	I choose the brands, restaurants, and activities based on what works for me and those close to me. I don't like to experiment too much because I don't think it is worth the time. For me the most important thing is trust. If I trust a person, a brand, or a service, I would remain loyal unless they disappoint me. If they do I would be very unforgiving because I think that if I invest my trust in them it should be reciprocated.
Rational (Intelligent Temperament)	Male aged 55 Business Owner Germany	I have a lot of experience in buying real estate because I have been working in many countries. When I decided to buy my new home, I looked at the company behind the property, the hospitality credentials, and the physical amenities before making my decision.
Worrisome (Speculative Temperament)	Male aged 51 Faculty US	I feel uncomfortable about my environment. I think that there is insufficient information for me to make decisions. There are so many people giving tidbits of information but I am not sure what to do. I feel that people are not really telling me the truth. But the problem is I don't know how to find out for sure. People say I complain a lot but I just want to talk and let others know what I think.

Table 3. Consumer persona communication strategies

Buddhist Temperament	Communications Channel	Content and Offer
Materialism Temperament	Mass Media Social Media	Emphasis on beauty, luxury, and exclusivity Use celebrities as presenters or opinion leaders Price is not an issue
Pride Temperament	Specialized Mass Media Social Media Expert Sources	Provide exclusive information Stimulate quick purchase by emphasizing they would be the first to have something
Confused Temperament	Mass Media Social Media Word of Mouth	Emphasis on gimmicks that fan their vanity and allows easy support for them to promote themselves in their social media
Loyal/Conservative Temperament	Personalized Communications Word of Mouth	Emphasis on CRM
Rational Temperament	Reputable Media Personalized Communications Word of Mouth	Provide information from multiple sources including reviews by reputable individuals. Combine with CRM and personalized offers In case of new products let them experience or try the product
Worrisome Temperament	Personal Communications	Using direct sales or sales representative would be helping in answering their worries Warranties to help alleviate their fears

they feel the need to be in trend. Thus, they need fixed time frames as to when they would get the product should they do a pre-order on line. For them, price is not an issue because getting the product and feeling exclusive achieves LOV values of sense of accomplishment, self-fulfillment, sense of belongingness, being well-respected, having fun and enjoyment in life, and excitement.

- **Pride Persona:** This provides exclusive information using the same strategy as innovators in the innovation diffusion model due to their need to be the first to have something. They are usually marketing mavens, who seek information and love to communicate these information to their friends (Feick & Price,1987). In a way, they are less compliant to others, but they are avid followers of trends, which they believe make up part of their personal character. They too make quick decisions, and promotions that drive immediate purchase are effective for this group. Their actions result in the accomplishment of LOV values including self-respect, warm relationships with others, and sense of accomplishment.
- **Confused Persona:** Emphasis on media is similar to the lustful temperament. However, for them, what is equally important is receiving approval from their social media networks. They are always consulting the recommendations and reviews by net idols, and when making purchase they ask their friends for advice. These people seek constant checking for approvals, and as a result the best strategy is to support the LOV values of self-respect and enjoyment in shopping.
- **Loyal/Conservative Persona:** Due to their more conservative nature, this group favors using brands with which they have a history and experience. For this group, the most important strategy is customer relationship management (CRM) that initiates customized personal communications. By knowing them and cultivating the trust, this group remain loyal customers. The LOV values fulfilled by their behaviors are security, warm relationships with others, and self-fulfillment.

- **Rational Persona:** These individuals are highly rational therefore they need access to varied information including sources from reputed mass media and personalized communication sent directly to them. They also rely from word of mouth usually from people close to them. The LOV values achieved are self-respect, warm relationships with others, sense of accomplishment, self-fulfillment, being well respected and enjoyment in life.
- **Worrisome Persona:** These individuals are highly anxious and apprehensive. The best way to communicate with them is to use personal communications by using direct marketing or sales people. This is because flexible communications that help them build up confidence in their purchase is necessary. In addition, warranties are important because it helps them to feel less risky in their purchases. The LOV values important to this group are self-respect, security, sense of accomplishment, self-fulfillment, and sense of belonging.

FUTURE RESEARCH DIRECTIONS

This study is an exploratory study revealing that individuals may be segmented based on temperaments. However, the methodology used for this study is qualitative, thus it is recommended that future research should be quantitative in order to further test the construct and its ability in categorizing individuals into distinct segments. With advances in technology, marketing insights through big data should be introduced as one of the methodologies for data collection in the effort to better define the segmentation scheme as suggested by Lavalle, Lesser, Shockley, Hopkins, and Kruschwitz (2011) and Sagiroglu and Duygu (2013).

In addition, it is suggested that future studies test the generalizability of the constructs by implementing the research in multiple countries as suggested by Walsh et al., (2001). It is the proposition of this chapter that the six consumer personas based on Buddhist temperaments should be applicable across cultures since it appears to be a fundamental factor in human personality. It has commonalities with scales such as CAD and CSI, which were developed for use in marketing based on the individual differences of the consumers. Although the evidence garnered in the exploratory study shows that there appears to be no marked difference between the responses of those from different countries, further quantitative studies are necessary to justify the applicability of this construct.

This particular chapter focuses on the promotional mix, which lends itself easily for modification in the digital space. Thus, it is of interest to study how the change in the other elements of the marketing mix specifically in digital marketing format affect the response to the individual's persona, and how it could create a positive impact on sales. In addition, the responses of those with different personas to messages and offers need to be explored further.

The final recommendation for future research is the analysis of the combination of personas and LOV with other variables for more complex layered segmentation. This chapter only focuses on temperaments and LOV that have been reviewed as related to previous researches (Slama et al., 1988). The applications in the multistage segmentation that applies more than two factors (So & Morrison, 2004) need to be explored further. So and Morrison (2004) proposed that behavioral and demographic segmentation should be two variable groups that can be added to create more meaningful segments.

CONCLUSION: APPLYING THE PERSONA TO MULTISTAGE SEGMENTATION

From previous reviews regarding segmentation, this study expands on the development of multistage segmentation as proposed by Albert (2003). The six consumer personas serve as a means to improve the multistage segmentation strategy similar to the decision-making styles explained by Hoek, Gendall, and Esslemont, (1996) and Walsh et al., (2001), which serves as the basis for further segmentation based on needs (Albert, 2003) defined as LOV in this study. The persona is an additional layer that can help to improve selecting the appropriate advertising or promotional content to the target. Its application is especially useful in the field of digital marketing where communications and offers can be personalized to fit the persona of the individual customer in order to maximize the benefit to the marketer.

Advances in big data technology through application of programs such as Google Analytics can assist marketers in determining basic demographic data. This basic data assists in creating the basic persona profile of the consumer. In addition, Facebook allows advertisers to determine the target to which they would like to serve their advertisements. Advertisers can choose from demographic characteristics, geographic location and interests. Moreover, a two-step segmentation scheme is currently being applied in Facebook through the use of Relevance Score, which is measured on a scale of 1 to 10. The scoring model measures the demographics of the target and the relevance of the message in terms of the interest of the consumer (determined from activities including words searched and posts liked or shared).

However, in addition to the Relevance Score, this chapter proposes identifying the individual's persona through the application of artificial intelligence (AI) with information gathered through Big Data to create a complete persona profile that includes psychographics, social factors and response behaviors to determine their character. Currently, Facebook allows advertisers to test different advertising formats against different targets in order to determine what works best. Adding the persona would reduce test-

Figure 1. Segmentation application

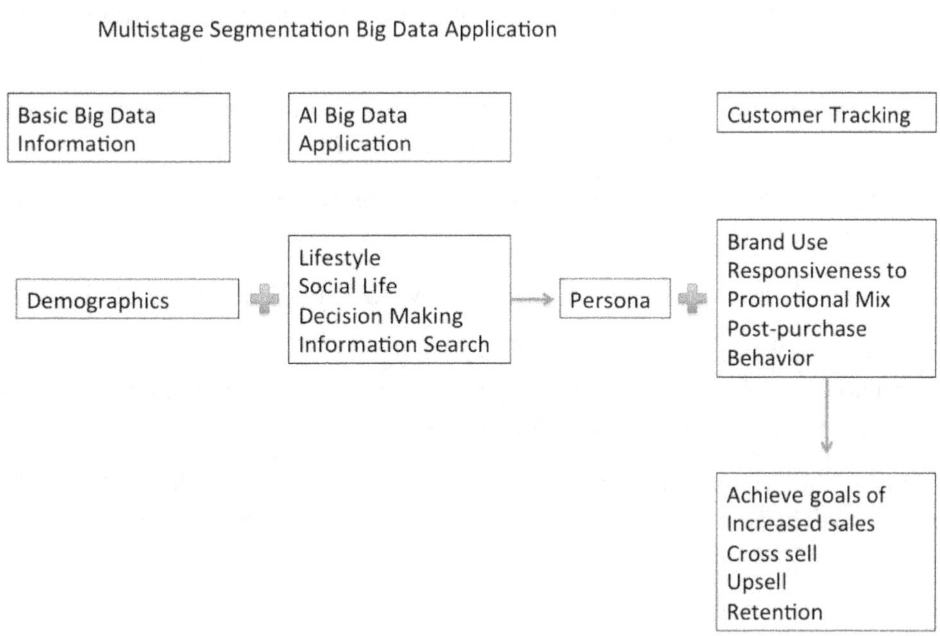

ing time and improve effectiveness of budget use for advertisers. The recommendation for creating the customer persona has to go beyond information but also encompasses the customer's goals and even their own words. As a consequence, applying the persona profile to improve targeting relevance should increase the effectiveness of the communications message and offers served to a particular consumer.

Based on the results of this study, it is found that religion is indeed a fertile ground in providing constructs that may be used for marketing applications. While Van Esch, Van Esch, and Cowley (2013) propose using the process of religious indoctrination to apply to social media marketing campaigns, this chapter capitalizes on the teachings of Buddha regarding the six temperaments in developing an international segmentation scheme. Future studies may study certain aspects of other religions for marketing applications. Islam is another major religion whose religious concepts can be applied for marketing purposes. For instance, Halal principles determine consumption in the Islamic world. It provides a fertile ground for the development of good governance guidelines that would certainly strike a chord with the socially and environmentally aware modern consumer.

REFERENCES

Aaker, J. L., & Williams, P. (1998). Empathy versus pride: The influence of emotional appeals across cultures. *The Journal of Consumer Research*, *25*(3), 241–261. doi:10.1086/209537

Ajzen, I., & Fishbein, M. (1980). *Understanding attitudes and predicting social behavior*. Ann Arbor, MI: Prentice Hall.

Albert, T. C. (2003). Need-based segmentation and customized communication strategies in a complex-commodity industry: A supply chain study. *Industrial Marketing Management*, *32*(4), 281–290. doi:10.1016/S0019-8501(02)00204-3

Alden, D. L., Steenkamp, J. B. E., & Batra, R. (1999). Brand positioning through advertising in Asia, North America, and Europe: The role of global consumer culture. *Journal of Marketing*, *63*(1), 75–87. doi:10.2307/1252002

Andreasen, A. R. (1984). Life status changes and changes in consumer preferences and satisfaction. *The Journal of Consumer Research*, *11*(3), 784–794. doi:10.1086/209014

Ansari, A., & Mela, C. F. (2003). E-customization. *JMR, Journal of Marketing Research*, *40*(2), 131–145. doi:10.1509/jmkr.40.2.131.19224

Bagozzi, R. P. (1980). *Causal models in marketing*. New York, NY: John Wiley & Sons.

Bailey, C., Baines, P. R., Wilson, H., & Clark, M. (2009). Segmentation and customer insight in contemporary services marketing practice: Why grouping customers is no longer enough. *Journal of Marketing Management*, *25*(3-4), 227–252. doi:10.1362/026725709X429737

Bhatt, S. R. (2001). The Buddhist doctrine of universal compassion and quality of life. In R. P. Singh & G. F. McLean (Eds.), The Buddhist world view (pp. 111-120). Faridabad, India: Om.

Bhattacharya, C. B., & Bolton, R. N. (2000). Relationship marketing in mass markets. In J. N. Sheth & A. Parvatiyar (Eds.), *Handbook of relationship marketing* (pp. 327–355). Thousand Oaks, CA: Sage Publications. doi:10.4135/9781452231310.n12

Brooks, D. (2008, May 13). The neural Buddhists. *The New York Times*, p.13.

Burnham, T. A., Frels, J. K., & Mahajan, V. (2003). Consumer switching costs: A typology, antecedents, and consequences. *Journal of the Academy of Marketing Science*, *31*(2), 109–126. doi:10.1177/0092070302250897

Cloninger, C. R. (1987). A systematic method for clinical description and classification of personality variants: A proposal. *Archives of General Psychiatry*, *44*(6), 573–588. doi:10.1001/archpsyc.1987.01800180093014 PMID:3579504

Cloninger, C. R. (1991). Brain networks underlying personality development. In B. J. Carroll & J. E. Barrett (Eds.), *Psychopathology and the brain* (pp. 183–208). New York, NY: Raven Press.

Cloninger, C. R. (1994). Temperament and personality. *Current Opinion in Neurobiology*, *4*(2), 266–273. doi:10.1016/0959-4388(94)90083-3 PMID:8038587

Cohen, J. B. (1967). An interpersonal orientation to the study of consumer behavior. *JMR, Journal of Marketing Research*, *4*(3), 270–278. doi:10.2307/3149459

Dahlsgaard, K., Peterson, C., & Seligman, M. E. (2005). Shared virtue: The convergence of valued human strengths across culture and history. *Review of General Psychology*, *9*(3), 203–213. doi:10.1037/1089-2680.9.3.203

Deighton, J., & Barwise, P. (2000). Digital marketing communication. Future media working waper, No. 00-801. London UK: London Business School.

Deshpande, R., Hoyer, W. D., & Donthu, N. (1986). The intensity of ethnic affiliation: A study of the sociology of Hispanic consumption. *The Journal of Consumer Research*, *13*(2), 214–220. doi:10.1086/209061

Dibb, S. (2001). New millennium, new segments: Moving towards the segment of one? *Journal of Strategic Marketing*, *9*(3), 193–213. doi:10.1080/713775742

Duncan, T., & Moriarty, S. E. (1998). A communication-based marketing model for managing relationships. *Journal of Marketing*, *62*(2), 1–13. doi:10.2307/1252157

Dutt, R. C. (1983). *Buddhism & Buddhist Civilisation in India*. Delhi, India: Seema.

Duygu, F. (2011). The use of decision making styles as a market segmentation variable: A study in Turkey. *The Journal of American Academy of Business, Cambridge*, *16*(2), 223–229.

El-Bassiouny, N. (2016). Where is "Islamic marketing" heading?: A commentary on Jafari and Sandikci's (2015) "Islamic" consumers, markets, and marketing. *Journal of Business Research*, *69*(2), 569–578. doi:10.1016/j.jbusres.2015.05.012

Elgendy, N., & Elragal, A. (2014). Big data analytics: a literature review paper. In *Industrial Conference on Data Mining* (pp. 214-227). Berlin, Germany: Springer. 10.1007/978-3-319-08976-8_16

Evans, F. B. (1959). Psychological and objective factors in the prediction of brand choice Ford versus Chevrolet. *The Journal of Business*, *32*(4), 340–369. doi:10.1086/294291

Feick, L. F., & Price, L. L. (1987). The market maven: A diffuser of marketplace information. *Journal of Marketing*, *51*(1), 83–97. doi:10.2307/1251146

Floh, A., Zauner, A., Koller, M., & Rusch, T. (2014). Customer segmentation using unobserved heterogeneity in the perceived-value–loyalty–intentions link. *Journal of Business Research*, *67*(5), 974–982. doi:10.1016/j.jbusres.2013.08.003

Grönroos, C. (1998). Marketing services: The case of a missing product. *Journal of Business and Industrial Marketing*, *13*(4/5), 322–338. doi:10.1108/08858629810226645

Hassan, S. S., & Craft, S. H. (2005). Linking global market segmentation decisions with strategic positioning options. *Journal of Consumer Marketing*, *22*(2), 81–89. doi:10.1108/07363760510589244

Hoek, J., Gendall, P., & Esslemont, D. (1996). Market segmentation: A search for the Holy Grail? *Journal of Marketing Practice: Applied Marketing Science*, *2*(1), 25–34. doi:10.1108/EUM0000000000005

Horney, K. (1937). *The neurotic personality of our time*. New York, NY: W.W. Norton & Company.

Hunt, S. D., & Vitell, S. (1986). A general theory of marketing ethics. *Journal of Macromarketing*, *6*(1), 5–16. doi:10.1177/027614678600600103

Hunt, S. D., & Vitell, S. J. (2006). The general theory of marketing ethics: A revision and three questions. *Journal of Macromarketing*, *26*(2), 143–153. doi:10.1177/0276146706290923

Huntington, S. P. (1993). The clash of civilizations? *Foreign Affairs*, *72*(3), 22–49. doi:10.2307/20045621

Kahle, L. R., Beatty, S. E., & Homer, P. (1986). Alternative measurement approaches to consumer values: The list of values (LOV) and values and life style (VALS). *The Journal of Consumer Research*, *13*(3), 405–409. doi:10.1086/209079

Kassarjian, H. H. (1981). Low involvement: A second look. In K. B. Monroe (Ed.), *ACR North American Advances in Consumer Research* (pp. 31–34). Ann Arbor, MI: Association for Consumer Research.

Kennedy, R., Ehrenberg, A., & Long, S. (2000). Competitive brand's user-profiles hardly differ. In *Market Research Society: Annual Conference Brighton England* (pp. 15 – 22). London, UK: Market Research Society.

Kinnear, T. C., & Taylor, J. R. (1976). Psychographics: Some additional findings. *JMR, Journal of Marketing Research*, *13*(4), 422–425. doi:10.2307/3151034

Kleinberg, J., Papadimitriou, C., & Raghavan, P. (2004). Segmentation problems. *Journal of the Association for Computing Machinery*, *51*(2), 263–280. doi:10.1145/972639.972644

Ko, E., Taylor, C. R., Sung, H., Lee, J., Wagner, U., Navarro, D. M. C., & Wang, F. (2012). Global marketing segmentation usefulness in the sportswear industry. *Journal of Business Research*, *65*(11), 1565–1575. doi:10.1016/j.jbusres.2011.02.041

Kotler, P., & Keller, K. (2011), Marketing management (14th ed.). London, UK: Pearson International Edition.

LaValle, S., Lesser, E., Shockley, R., Hopkins, M. S., & Kruschwitz, N. (2011). Big data, analytics and the path from insights to value. *MIT Sloan Management Review, 52*(2), 21.

Leippe, M. R., & Elkin, R. A. (1987). When motives clash: Issue involvement and response involvement as determinants of persuasion. *Journal of Personality and Social Psychology, 52*(2), 269–278. doi:10.1037/0022-3514.52.2.269

Machauer, A., & Morgner, S. (2001). Segmentation of bank customers by expected benefits and attitudes. *International Journal of Bank Marketing, 19*(1), 6–17. doi:10.1108/02652320110366472

Malhotra, N., & Birks, D. (2006). *Marketing research: An applied perspective*. Englewood Cliffs, NJ: Prentice Hall. doi:10.1108/S1548-6435(2006)2

Maslow, A. H. (1954). *Personality and motivation*. Harlow, UK: Longman.

Maureen, M., & Sally, D. (1998). Implementing market segmentation strategies in UK personal financial services: Problems and progress. *Service Industries Journal, 18*(2), 45–63. doi:10.1080/02642069800000018

McCracken, G. (1988). *The Long Interview*. London, UK: Sage. doi:10.4135/9781412986229

Meadows, M., & Dibb, S. (1988). Assessing the implementation of market segmentation in retail financial services. *International Journal of Service Quality Management, 9*(3), 266–279.

Merisavo, M., & Raulas, M. (2004). The impact of e-mail marketing on brand loyalty. *Journal of Product and Brand Management, 13*(7), 498–505. doi:10.1108/10610420410568435

Mitchell, A. (1983). *The VALS typology*. Basingstoke, UK: Macmillan Publishing.

Mulyanegara, R. C., Tsarenko, Y., & Mavondo, F. (2010). Church marketing: The effect of market orientation on perceived benefits and church participation. *Services Marketing Quarterly, 32*(1), 60–82. doi:10.1080/15332969.2011.533100

Nikolaus, F., Reisinger, H., & Hoppe, D. (2009). Remaining within-cluster heterogeneity: A mata-analysis of the "dark side" of clustering methods. *Journal of Marketing Management, 25*(3-4), 273–293. doi:10.1362/026725709X429755

Noerager, J. P. (1979). An assessment of CAD: A personality instrument developed specifically for marketing research. *JMR, Journal of Marketing Research, 16*(1), 53–59. doi:10.2307/3150874

Novak, T., Leeuw, J. D., & MacEvoy, B. (1992). Richness Curves for Evaluating Market Segmentation. *JMR, Journal of Marketing Research, 29*(2), 254–267. doi:10.2307/3172574

Patrick, D. (2006). Customer segmentation. *ABA Bankers News, 14*(9), 1.

Patterson, P. G., Cowley, E., & Prasongsukarn, K. (2006). Service failure recovery: The moderating impact of individual-level cultural value orientation on perceptions of justice. *International Journal of Research in Marketing, 23*(3), 263–277. doi:10.1016/j.ijresmar.2006.02.004

Payutto, P. A. (2000). *Dictionary of Buddhism*. Bangkok, Thailand: Suetawan.

Peppers, D., & Rogers, M. (2004). *Managing customer relationships: A strategic framework*. New York, NY: John Wiley & Sons.

Petty, R. E., & Cacioppo, J. T. (1979). Issue involvement can increase or decrease persuasion by enhancing message-relevant cognitive responses. *Journal of Personality and Social Psychology*, *37*(10), 1915–1926. doi:10.1037/0022-3514.37.10.1915

Pieters, R., Baumgartner, H., & Allen, D. (1995). A means-end chain approach to consumer goal structures. *International Journal of Research in Marketing*, *12*(3), 227–244. doi:10.1016/0167-8116(95)00023-U

Prasongsukarn, K. (2009). Validating the cultural value scale (CVSCALE): A case study of Thailand. *ABAC Journal*, *29*(2), 1–13.

Quinn, L. (2009). Market segmentation in managerial practice: A qualitative examination. *Journal of Marketing Management*, *25*(3-4), 253–272. doi:10.1362/026725709X429746

Reibstein, D. J., Day, G., & Wind, J. (2009). Guest editorial: Is marketing academia losing its way? *Journal of Marketing*, *73*(4), 1–3. doi:10.1509/jmkg.73.4.1

Reinartz, W., Thomas, J. S., & Kumar, V. (2005). Balancing acquisition and retention resources to maximize customer profitability. *Journal of Marketing*, *69*(1), 63–79. doi:10.1509/jmkg.69.1.63.55511

Riesman, D., Glazer, N., & Denney, R. (1950). *The lonely crowd: A study of the changing American character*. New Haven, CT: Yale.

Rigby, D. K., Reichheld, F. F., & Schefter, P. (2002). Avoid the four perils of CRM. *Harvard Business Review*, *80*(2), 101–109. PMID:11894676

Rokeach, M. (1973). *The nature of human values*. New York, NY: Free Press.

Sagiroglu, A., & Duygu, B. (2013). Big data: A review. Collaboration Technologies and Systems (CTS). *2013 International Conference on. IEEE.*

Samiee, S., & Jeong, I. (1994). Cross-cultural Research in Advertising: An Assessment of Methodologies. *Journal of the Academy of Marketing Science*, *22*(3), 205–217. doi:10.1177/0092070394223002

Schlegelmilch, B. B., & Öberseder, M. (2010). Half a century of marketing ethics: Shifting perspectives and emerging trends. *Journal of Business Ethics*, *93*(1), 1–19. doi:10.100710551-009-0182-1

Shimp, T. A. (1983). *A potpourri of consumer research methods. ACR North American Advances*. Ann Arbor, MI: Association for Consumer Research.

Simonson, I. (2005). Determinants of customers' responses to customized offers: Conceptual framework and research propositions. *Journal of Marketing*, *69*(1), 32–45. doi:10.1509/jmkg.69.1.32.55512

Slama, M. E., Williams, T. G., & Tashchian, A. (1988). *Compliant, aggressive and detached types differ in generalized purchasing involvement. In ACR North American Advances* (pp. 158–167). Ann Arbor, MI: Association for Consumer Research.

Smith, W. R. (1956). Product differentiation and market segmentation as alternative marketing strategies. *Journal of Marketing*, *21*(1), 3–8. doi:10.2307/1247695

Smith, W. R. (1995). Product differentiation and market segmentation as alternative marketing strategies. *Marketing Management, 4*(3), 63.

So, S. I., & Morrison, A. M. (2004). The repeat travel market for Taiwan: A multi-stage segmentation approach. *Asia Pacific Journal of Tourism Research, 9*(1), 71–87. doi:10.1080/1094166042000199585

Speed, R., & Smith, G. (1992). Retail financial services segmentation. *Service Industries Journal, 12*(3), 368–383. doi:10.1080/02642069200000045

Spiggle, S. (1994). Analysis and interpretation of qualitative data in consumer research. *The Journal of Consumer Research, 21*(3), 491–503. doi:10.1086/209413

Sprotles, G. B., & Kendall, E. L. (1986). A methodology for profiling consumers' decision-making styles. *The Journal of Consumer Affairs, 20*(2), 267–279. doi:10.1111/j.1745-6606.1986.tb00382.x

Steenkamp, J. B. E., & Hofstede, F. (2002). International market segmentation: Issues and perspectives. *International Journal of Research in Marketing, 19*(3), 185–213. doi:10.1016/S0167-8116(02)00076-9

Suzanne, S. (2002). The evolution of segmentation methods in financial services: Where next? *Journal of Financial Services Marketing, 7*(1), 67–74. doi:10.1057/palgrave.fsm.4770073

Van Esch, P., Van Esch, L., & Cowley, J. (2013). The dimensions of religion as underpinning constructs for mass media social marketing campaigns: An emerging concept. *International Journal of Marketing Studies, 5*(1), 96–106. doi:10.5539/ijms.v5n1p96

Vargo, S. L., & Lusch, R. F. (2004). Evolving to a new dominant logic for marketing. *Journal of Marketing, 68*(1), 1–17. doi:10.1509/jmkg.68.1.1.24036

Walsh, G., Hennig-Thurau, T., Wayne-Mitchell, V., & Wiedmann, K.-P. (2001). Consumers' decision-making style as a basis for market segmentation. *Journal of Targeting. Measurement and Analysis for Marketing, 10*(2), 117–131. doi:10.1057/palgrave.jt.5740039

Wedel, M., & Kamakura, W. (2002). Introduction to the special issue on market segmentation. *International Journal of Research in Marketing, 19*(3), 181–304. doi:10.1016/S0167-8116(02)00075-7

Westfall, R. (1962). Psychological factors in predicting product choice. *Journal of Marketing, 26*(2), 34–40. doi:10.2307/1248434

Wolfe, T. (1996). Sorry, but your soul just died. *Forbes ASAP*, 210-219.

Woodside, A. G., & Andress, R. (1975). CAD eight years later. *Journal of the Academy of Marketing Science, 3*(3-4), 309–313. doi:10.1007/BF02729291

Wrenn, B. (2010). Religious marketing is different. *Services Marketing Quarterly, 32*(1), 44–59. doi:10.1080/15332969.2011.533095

Yankelovich, D., & Meer, D. (2006). Rediscovering Market Segmentation. *Harvard Business Review, 84*(2), 122–131. PMID:16485810

ADDITIONAL READING

Baumgartner, H., & Steenkamp, J. B. E. (2001). Response styles in marketing research: A cross-national investigation. *JMR, Journal of Marketing Research*, *38*(2), 143–156. doi:10.1509/jmkr.38.2.143.18840

Bowles, S. (1998). Endogenous preferences: The cultural consequences of markets and other economic institutions. *Journal of Economic Literature*, *36*(1), 75–111.

Broderick, A. J., Greenley, G. E., & Mueller, R. D. (2007). The behavioural homogeneity evaluation framework: Multi-level evaluations of consumer involvement in international segmentation. *Journal of International Business Studies*, *38*(5), 746–763. doi:10.1057/palgrave.jibs.8400296

Eisenstadt, S. N. (1980). Cultural orientations, institutional entrepreneurs, and social change: Comparative analysis of traditional civilizations. *American Journal of Sociology*, *85*(4), 840–869. doi:10.1086/227091

Hofstede, F. T., Steenkamp, J. B. E., & Wedel, M. (1999). International market segmentation based on consumer-product relations. *JMR, Journal of Marketing Research*, *36*(1), 1–17. doi:10.2307/3151911

Steenkamp, J. B. E. (2001). The role of national culture in international marketing research. *International Marketing Review*, *18*(1), 30–44. doi:10.1108/02651330110381970

Thomas, S. M. (2000). Taking religious and cultural pluralism seriously: The global resurgence of religion and the transformation of international society. *Millennium*, *29*(3), 815–841. doi:10.1177/03058298000290030401

KEY TERMS AND DEFINITIONS

Buddhist Temperaments: The six perception-based habits influencing behavior, which Buddha used to classify individuals.

Confused Persona: People who exhibit this persona type tend to be in constant need of approval from others often depending on information from others in making decisions.

Consumer Persona: A means of profiling consumers based on their perceptions, habits, and responses to stimulus from external sources including people in their society and the media.

Loyal/Conservative Persona: People who exhibit this persona type tend to value tradition and rely on past experience in making their decisions as a means of reducing risks.

Materialism Persona: People who exhibit this persona type value beauty and luxury often modeling their values and actions based on well-known celebrities.

Pride Persona: People who exhibit this persona type tend to be narcissists who value flattery often making quick decisions to stay in trend to make sure others are always following them.

Rational Persona: People who exhibit this persona are not quick in making decisions often seeking out multiple sources of information and preferring personal communications.

Worrisome Persona: People who exhibit this persona are anxious and apprehensive needing reassurances preferably personal communications to help them make decisions.

APPENDIX

Table 4. Summary of respondents

Country	Age	Gender	Education	Employment
Thailand (10)	18 – 45	Male and Female	Bachelor's Degree and above	Student, Faculty, Government Employee, Private Sector Employee
China (5)	22 – 55	Male and Female	Bachelor's Degree and above	Student, Faculty, Business Owner
India (3)	28 – 56	Male	Master's Degree and above	Student and Faculty
Jordan (3)	25 – 57	Male	Bachelor's Degree and above	Student and Business Owner
France (4)	28 – 34	Male and Female	Bachelor's Degree and above	Faculty, Private Sector Employee, Business Owner
Germany (1)	55	Male	Bachelor's Degree and above	Business Owner
United States (1)	54	Male	Bachelor's Degree and above	Faculty
Costa Rica (2)	27	Male and Female	Bachelor's Degree and above	Faculty and Private Sector Employee

Chapter 11
Consumerism, Violence, and Dehumanization:
The Vicious Dynamic Circle

Carole J. Lambert
Azuza Pacific University, USA

ABSTRACT

This chapter proposes that some consumers risk becoming dehumanized by the current onslaught of marketing approaches. As these buyers are bombarded by advertisements from numerous media, they become shaped in ways that make them more vulnerable to the powers behind the marketing. This ultimately creates a vicious dynamic circle which must be exited if an authentic self is to emerge and survive in this dehumanizing, violent environment. This essay explores not only the reality of this "vicious dynamic circle," which often begins in childhood, but also some means of escaping from it: (1) recognition of the dehumanizing process occurring, (2) recollection of Western culture's two foundational metanarratives—Greco-Roman rationality and Judeo-Christian spirituality, (3) understanding what is needed to experience an authentic self, not one shaped by marketers' strategies, and (4) willingness to live according to self-chosen values culled from deep thinking about what is most authentic and precious in life.

INTRODUCTION

This chapter will explore the roots of consumerism and how it violates human dignity and agency, resulting in dehumanization. This ongoing process—consumerism, violence, and dehumanization—establishes a vicious dynamic circle out of which the wise and rational consumer must exit. Means for doing so are suggested below as well as ways to live life without obeying the injunction that one is obligated to consume products mindlessly.

DOI: 10.4018/978-1-5225-6120-0.ch011

An Explanation of Key Terms: Consumerism, Violence, and Dehumanization

In order to better understand the evolution of ideas resulting in consumerism's current influence over individuals and society, one must define the terms relevant to this vicious dynamic circle. Gregory R. Beabout and Eduardo J. Echeverria (2002) define **consumerism** as "a preoccupation with the consumption of goods and services" (p. 362). Consume signifies destroying or using up; thus potential **violence** may be a part of the destruction brought about by consumption, destruction of the objects being consumed, to be sure, but maybe also of those persons consuming these items. Marketers selling the objects to be consumed prey on consumers' weaknesses—their irrational, instinctual, and "appetitive" desires which influence them to yield to ploys in advertisements and other media. This results in **dehumanization**, which suggests a decreasing or depriving of human qualities or attributes because *all* that makes one human, especially relationships and rationality, is not being actualized during this seductive process. Dehumanization occurs when consumers become objectified, literally turned from human beings into objects useful to marketers and the corporations who employ them. Further, consumers may be blind to reality when marketers affirm that buying an item cultivates the purchaser's individuality; in reality, this consumer is being divested of individuality as he or she follows the unthinking crowd, thus becoming dehumanized. This **consumerism/violence/dehumanization** dynamic is at work in American society today, but it can be overcome, if readers *choose* to break out of this vicious dynamic circle.

Positive and Negative Aspects of Consumerism

One wonders why unveiling this process does not halt it. Two responses seem evident as answers to this query. First, some products are desired by consumers because they are both necessary and helpful to them. For example, Salk vaccine which prevents polio, synthesized after years of painstaking research, became an attractive product for parents to offer their children in lieu of the risk of the younger generation suffering the terrible consequences of acquiring this debilitating disease. All that makes one human, including compassionate care for children and rationality, affirms the positive benefit of a corporation producing this product, consumers buying it and having it administered to their children, and both producers and consumers averting the onset of a dreadful disease. In this instance, the potential predatory violence of corporate backed marketers is avoided and replaced by the innovative security and protection of children and adults who opt for vaccinations.

Second, however, is the situation when consumers somewhat mindlessly purchase products because of identification with a particular brand that affirms their self-constructed identities so that their external social status seems to be assured. Thus, the product may meet emotional, psychological, and social needs quite different from the physical protection the Salk vaccine offers in an environment where the outbreak of a devastating contagious disease may occur. For example, one may choose to drive a Lexus rather than a Honda Civic because of the aura created by the advertising of the Lexus and by the apparent social status of other Lexus drivers rather than because of the basic quality and affordability of a "work horse" automobile such as a Honda Civic. Auras are imaginative creations, more in the realm of fictional narratives than factual evidence verified by numerous experiments in a laboratory. One may choose an "aura" rather than a "fact," but one risks becoming less humanly rational in doing so and increasingly more objectified by the persons creating the auras who have the financial and artistic power to promote the illusion that the "aura" is indeed a "fact." This is a negative aspect of consumerism to which children become particularly vulnerable.

Children like and are seduced by colorful, enticing advertising. Jennifer Ann Hill (2011) notes, "At the heart of the struggle between childhood and consumerism child identity formation is at stake; the relentless bombardment of media messages that the self is predominantly defined by its capacity to consume begins at such an early age as to overtake many competing thought processes" (p. 348). Sometimes, parents patiently counter these illusions created by advertisers with rational explanations and evidence, but marketers often diminish the parents' attempts by "empowering" children to vanquish their parents' reservations about buying a certain well marketed product seemingly enjoyed by many other children and presented as a near necessity for all children to acquire. Such a three-way power struggle among marketer, child, and parent borders on violence because it invades the private space of the home as well as the sacred space of the parent and child relationship. As children become objectified by the money making marketers, so they become alienated from their compassionate, rational, financially aware, and perhaps also monetarily limited parents.

Consumerism Violating the Sacred Private and Communal Domains

Violence is etymologically rooted in the Latin word "violare" which means "to injure, dishonor, outrage, violate" (Lewis & Short, 1980, p. 1994). To violate suggests to break and enter someone's private or public domain, both of which are sacred to the individual or the community. A sexual violation such as rape results from unwanted force imposed on another to such an extent that one's most personal, private domain is invaded against one's will. A traffic violation means that one has transgressed the laws of the community which have been set in place in order to ensure the safety of all. The violence of consumerism falls on a spectrum involving these two domains of private and communal, for consumerism preys on consumers' weaknesses and violates their private and public spaces. The narrative "auras" of advertisers do not break any laws in a capitalistic society unless they promote products that are totally incapable of offering what they proclaim in their solicitations. However, many citizens in a democratic republic may acknowledge that telemarketers invading their home with advertising telephone messages are bordering on trespassing the private space of this domain, that flashy billboards on highways which mar the natural beauty of a landscape are violating communal domains, and that marketers urging children to persuade their parents to buy for them a cleverly advertised popular toy may be infringing on the sacred relationship between parent and child.

The term "sacred" seems foreign to a secular, postmodern world; yet it provides the possibility of the creation of a space outside of marketers' and corporate executives' reach. "Sacred" derives from the Latin adjective "sacer" which means "holy" (Lewis & Short, 1980). Its modern definition opposes it to "profane" and "secular" and suggests a sense of security from violation. One wonders if, in today's world, anything is "holy," but even secular Americans value the privacy of home and a certain "sacredness" of the family, for they have still been influenced by the Judeo-Christian tradition which has permeated Western culture, intertwined with strong Greco-Roman influences. This Judeo-Christian tradition provides a story for how one should live which may also be a counter to the advertisers' narratives attached to their products.

RECOLLECTION OF WESTERN CULTURE"S TWO FOUNDATIONAL METANARRATIVES

All people are born into cultures which influence them--perhaps an African tribe's such as that described in Chinua Achebe's *Things Fall Apart* (1988) or an American Southerner's such as the one portrayed by William Faulkner's *The Sound and the Fury* (1956). Globalization and its powerful communication networks have increased the knowledge about other cultures and encouraged their intermingling; thus minimally technologically sophisticated people may at any moment be able to tune into news and advertisements from around the world. It is unlikely that they would remain uninfluenced by these. Perhaps there is, then, a need to return to a simple Judeo-Christian narrative about culture that could be foundational to people of good will, whether religious or not; hence a reconsideration of the Bible's books of Genesis and Exodus follows.

In these books, one observes that God instituted culture. Adam's and Eve's tasks were to tend their Garden of Eden and to walk with God, enjoying their relationship with each other and Him. The reader of the first two chapters of Genesis senses a delightful harmony among humans, nature, and deity. However, this idyllic atmosphere was short-lived when seductive advertising by a talking serpent persuaded Eve to violate a clear commandment from God to avoid eating from the Tree of the Knowledge of Good and Evil (Gen. 3). Transgression of this boundary resulted, so the story goes, in banishment from the beautiful Garden, toil without the previous delight, pain during childbirth, death, and hope for Redemption from the evils incurred by this violation of a sacred decree, sacred because God, He Who decreed, is holy. Tragically, the relationship between humans and between them and God was deeply wounded, if not broken.

God then provides guidance for a postlapsarian culture via the Decalogue issued to His Chosen People, the Hebrews. The expectation of the prelapsarian culture that humans are, above all, to obey God remains as well as the desire to live in loving harmony with Him and each other. Further, recipients of His law are to establish no substitutes for God ("Thou shalt have no other god before me" [Ex. 20: 3, KJV]), including "any graven image" (Ex. 20: 4), and they shall not misuse God's name (Ex. 20: 7). In addition, modeling themselves on God's mode of creating, they are to *stop* laboring every seven days (Ex. 20: 8--11), a practice that would seem to discourage 100 percent productivity and 24/7 buying of products for consumption. Even more curious is a clear edict that children are to honor their parents (Ex. 20: 23), a statement that counters advertisers' goal of empowering children so that they will deconstruct and oppose their parents' objections to buying an item.

The cultural guidelines that God presents to his Chosen People continue: no killing, committing adultery, stealing, lying about neighbors, and overly desiring or coveting the neighbor's wife and possessions (Ex. 20: 13—17). Beabout and Echeverria (2002) posit that consumerism is, indeed, covetousness and that it leads to idolatry. Buying takes precedence over all else. The book of Exodus's basic guidelines still govern God's Chosen People, practicing Jews, as well as committed Christians, whose Lord and Savior, Jesus, was a Jew. European and American cultures have been significantly influenced by these admonitions. This foundational narrative, however, has been greatly diminished in its effect on postmodern societies which emphasize the abolishment of influential, controlling metanarratives, such as the one simplistically summarized above, to govern people today.

Modernism introduced a second impressive metanarrative as an Enlightenment alternative to the Biblical story. In the seventeenth century, René Descartes (2006) posited the "*cogito ergo sum*" ("I think therefore I am") as foundational to human beings. The concept of individual souls created by God is replaced with individual selves that are a "*tabula rasa*" (a clean slate) waiting to be written upon. Hence, the self must be constructed rationalistically.

Twentieth century existentialism, particularly as posited by Albert Camus and Jean Paul Sartre, built upon the Cartesian "*cogito*" and "*tabula rasa*" by emphasizing an individual's free will to choose his/her "essence." Existentialists posit that existence equates with essence which formerly was a Platonic concept suggesting a pure reality in the world of Ideas that becomes deformed and emerges as a tarnished image of its original when it is embodied. The individual's exertion of his or her will results in a choice that shapes his or her essence; an existence of choices thus constructs an earthly essence that one's will dynamically revises, decision by decision. This is a philosophical step that permits emotional, arbitrary decisions to be made, for Descartes's announcement that thinking or rationality (*Cogito*) equals the essence of a human being (*ergo sum*) is now only an optimistic backdrop to the center stage position of the will; it is inevitable that some choices will not be reasonable and may even appear totally irrational such as Meursault's shooting of the Arab in his way on a hot day on the Algerian beach in Camus's *L'Étranger* (1955). However, whatever the existentialist's choice, he or she must be ready and willing to accept full responsibility for it.

Hence, Camus's Meursault, the stranger in *L'Étranger*, must accept death from the guillotine after having shot this unnamed Arab. Following a story different from the Decalogue in the Bible, Meursault, although physically blinded by the sun and overheated by its glare, momentarily and arbitrarily *chooses* to shoot another human being and thus must take the responsibility of accepting the consequences of his choice, the death penalty. Camus shows his fatal action to be basically irrational, strongly shaped by physical discomfort. This narrative is far from the Biblical "Thou shalt not kill" and the Cartesian assumption that rationality is the essence of humanity.

Traces of the Biblical and existential stories for humanity remain in postmodern Western culture; most Westerners would agree that killing another seemingly defenseless human being on a Saturday afternoon on a beach is wrong; most would also admit that this action is unreasonable and, to use another key existentialist term, absurd. Both metanarratives, the Biblical and the Cartesian/existentialist, suggest that one becomes less than the ideal human when murder is committed and that the murderer's victim becomes objectified and dehumanized—a thing to be rid of. The individual, therefore, has the power via certain choices to dehumanize himself or herself when breaking one of the Ten Commandments and when choosing to act irrationally as well as the choice to dehumanize a victim. Does consumer behavior, definitely less extreme than outright murder, cause degrees of dehumanization in both human beings who consume and the marketers who entice them?

SHAPING AN AUTHENTIC HUMAN SELF:RECLAIMING PRIVATE AND PUBLIC SPACE

Many consumers feel that the power of advertising and marketing is so great that they have little freedom to fight back against this perceived tidal wave. Children are born into a culture with multiple communication modes that tempt them to act in certain ways. Perhaps only private communities like the Amish have the freedom to escape this technologically manipulative environment. Twenty-first century Westerners feel obligated to keep up with worldwide news and innovative products, including songs, films, sit-coms, reality performances, and other items that can be consumed physically, intellectually, and spiritually in order to be responsible citizens of the world. The story line of obligatory consumerism is perhaps the new metanarrative for the postmodern era which seemingly has discarded all other metanarratives. Sadly, yet humorously, Rodney Clapp (1998) mentions a personal experience of Lendol Calder when he participated in a Christian camp exercise along with many international college students: "A get-acquainted exercise involved dividing campers up by their nationalities and assigning them to come up with a song representing their culture that all could agree on and sing to the rest of the assembly" (p. 171). Most of the other groups took only ten or twenty minutes to prepare an often indigenous folk song to present to the entire assembly; however, the Americans present took an hour. Ultimately, they sang "Coca-Cola's 'I'd Like to Teach the World to Sing'" (Clapp, 1998). Consumerism is, in reality, an ongoing, pervasive mythos that permeates society and governs human beings' beliefs and actions regardless of their ages.

Consumers may be suffering dehumanization without even realizing that this is occurring because they are literally buying into a consumer culture's narrative which posits that "I shop; therefore I am" (Kavanaugh, 1991, p. 221). Indeed, as early as 1976, Erich Fromm (1976) notes, "I am=what I have and what I consume" (p. 27). One's self is signified by what one buys. The wide selection of products provides almost innumerable choices for this self-fashioning, and shaping the self with products promoted under a specific "brand" defines one's essence. Such a definition is essential, this narrative asserts, to one's humanity. This nearly omnipresent narrative inculcated into Westerners since childhood seems to leave little room for alternatives to this consumer lifestyle.

Sadly, marital relationships, family bonds, friendships, commitments to organizations and the polity, and intangible values that are not for sale become increasingly depreciated. This does violence to human beings conceived in God's image (*imago dei*), according to the Biblical narrative of the Judeo-Christian tradition, and to human beings defined as essentially rational creatures, according to the Cartesian narrative derived from Greco-Roman philosophical sources. Consumerism violates sacred and rational human space; can this space be reclaimed?

Conscious recognition of the need to create a consumer-free zone is the first step to liberation from following the dictates of the consumerism metanarrative. Westerners can construct such a space by drawing from the best concepts found in their two foundational narrative sources: indeed, the Judeo-Christian and Greco-Roman traditions that, in terms of ethics, can be amalgamated to some extent. For example, it is reasonable in a community to disallow murder, adultery, theft, and untruthful defamation of another's character. Without a polity that outlaws these actions, individuals would take justice into their own hands and thus perpetuate a cycle of violent revenge. The narrative of consumerism is, admittedly, powerful, but it is also relatively new and recent when compared to the two foundational narratives that still continue to resonate in the Western world. Most parents would prefer that their children be good citizens in their communities rather than expert consumers, no matter what the power players and their marketers advocate and enact. That preference is strong in itself and represents an exertion of the will that can be nurtured in order to guard this sacred space where spiritual, rational human beings are much more than purchasers of products.

The self that advertisers propose to consumers has replaced the self that emerges from the Judeo-Christian and Greco-Roman narratives. In 1981 Ronald Berman noted, "The institutions of family, religion, and education have grown noticeably weaker over each of the past three generations. The world itself seems to have grown more complex. In the absence of traditional authority [such as that suggested by Western culture's two key narratives], advertising has become a kind of social guide. It depicts in us all the myriad situations possible to a life of free choice. It provides ideas about style, morality, behavior" (p. 13).

Nevertheless, human beings can choose to be in charge of what they will buy (Salk vaccine, for example, rather than unnecessary objects or entertainments); *they need not be victims of consumerism*. They can avoid becoming victims of consumerism by guarding constantly a zone of choice, a boundary which they will not permit marketers and their supervisors to cross. Examples of persons who have refused dehumanization in extreme situations, where potential and actual violence reigned, can be found during the Holocaust when Primo Levi rationally held on to his belief that he was a human being, and not a dirty rag, and when Elie Wiesel maintained his belief in God and in himself as created in God's image even when he realized that God at Auschwitz, to his mind, had broken His Biblical covenant with the Jews.

Examples of Maintaining Private Space: Primo Levi and Elie Wiesel

Educated at the University of Turin in northern Italy as a chemist, Primo Levi had the opportunity to pass an oral examination in chemistry at Auschwitz-Birkenau in order to work in a laboratory where researchers tried to create synthetic rubber, an indoor assignment that would save his life when many others, like Wiesel, carried rocks under snowfall. On the walk back from Levi's passing this exam before a German officer elegantly groomed and dressed in his clean uniform, the concentration camp guard who accompanied Levi wiped his dirty, greasy hands on Levi's striped, threadbare prison shirt, seemingly turning the prisoner and his garment into a filthy rag. If Levi had physically reacted defensively to this insult, he would have been killed. His willed mental choice was to resolve not to accept in his own mind the denigration of his humanity to an object, a rag (Levi, 1996). Truly, the perpetrator of this act had dehumanized himself when forcefully using another human being in this way. Levi, however, maintained mentally a sacred, rational space where he could affirm his own humanity while carefully observing the dehumanization of his escort.

Elie Wiesel, an Auschwitz inmate at the same time as Primo Levi affirms that accepting the dehumanized dehumanizer's estimate of oneself causes that precious inner sacred space to be violated and then to collapse. A human being created in the image of God retains this spiritually imprinted image no matter what those around him say or do. In Wiesel's case, this includes even God. To his mind, at Auschwitz, God broke the sacred covenant He had established with His chosen people when Moses was their leader. Nevertheless, in his concentration camp setting, and for the rest of his life, Wiesel chose to continue honoring God, while frequently disputing with Him (Wiesel, 2006), and to never surrender his *imago dei* to anyone, no matter how he was treated. Primo Levi guarded his rationality and, hence, could analyze his guard as a character who dehumanized himself by his actions without dehumanizing his prisoner. Elie Wiesel could draw from his personal spirituality and his Jewish Hasidic tradition to worship and obey God despite arguing with Him; his tradition includes other arguers—Abraham, Moses, and Job, for example. Both Levi and Wiesel tapped into metanarratives rooted in Western tradition—Greco-Roman, Cartesian rationality for Levi and Hasidic Judaism for Wiesel. Both men guarded their inviolable inner sacred space and retained their human dignity in an atrociously dehumanizing environment.

Consumers, obviously and thankfully, are not in concentration camps, although the concentration of advertisements in their daily lives is forceful and almost ubiquitous. Clapp (1998) notes, "One observer estimates that the average American is exposed to 16,000 commercial messages, symbols and reminders every single day" (p. 170). These potential buyers, too, can use the rationality and spirituality still present in the two Western metanarratives which have been fragmented in this current postmodern era. Even the residual fragments of these key narratives can counter consumerism's almost omnipresent seductive sell. A diachronic look back at the past to persons who, like Levi and Wiesel, overcame exceedingly challenging situations in environments permeated with dehumanizing factors, can help to balance the synchronic focus on the present postmodern consumer society. A cultivation of the will, manifested in rational choices that enhance humanity and in spiritual decisions derived from understanding basic Judeo-Christian ethics, could do much to promote and maintain basic human dignity for all in the face of this consumerist onslaught.

Choosing to Live by Authentic Values Rather Than Marketers' Mythic Constructions

Colin Campbell (2010) notes, "If only individuals could restrict themselves to just buying only those things they really 'need', then consumers would not only be more content in themselves but they would have the time and resources to devote to more fulfilling and worthwhile activities" (p. 281). Advertisers may have created an international Tower of Babel where the Babel about services and products from around the world stifles the still, small voice governing ethical behavior. Advertisements which objectify men and women, which compete with each other for shock value and which purposefully entice young people to experience forbidden pleasures contribute to their viewers' dehumanization without them even realizing this because they may not be focused on God and His image within them, according to the Judeo-Christian narrative, or on what is most reasonable, good, and true for them, according to the Greco-Roman perspective.

Human beings are much more than buyers of products and services; buying is an important human function but not the only task at hand. Exchanging goods and services is necessary in a community for survival, but, once a level of survival is assured, other activities should take precedent, especially those enhancing loving relationships: cultivating family life, spirituality, friendship, education, and physical activities such as sports which promote health and cooperation as a team, not stardom awarded by million dollar contracts. Solid, authentic selves could then spend their time on activities worthier than shopping such as playing with children, visiting the elderly, studying and teaching, creating works of art—sculpting, painting, writing poetry and stories, not for profit but for joyful sharing with others – travelling, contributing responsibly to the *polis*, being a friend to those in need, and helping others to live fulfilling lives, too, to name only a few possibilities. This is a minimal list of the potentially truly self- and other-enhancing activities that could replace unnecessary buying, selling, and receiving in whatever form advertising for products and services. Rejecting rampant consumerism could contribute to the betterment of families and communities. Some consumer objects and services, such as dishwashers and home cleaners, do free up time, but, once again, the choice about how to use that free time has to be made. Marketers and their employers hope that, "[b]y reducing the amount of time required for daily tasks, more time is freed up for consumption" (Miller, 2003, p. 68). The consumer has the agency to choose the activities listed above rather than to go shopping at the mall.

Personal selves can be constructed through wholesome spiritual and rational choices rather than corporate executives' and marketers' decisions to brand and promote their products and services in order to sell an attractive image that breeds loyalty and dependency on an "aura" even more than on the item or activity itself and that makes a profit for the backers of the products and services. Personal selves are sustained by maintaining wholesome habits and by cultivating positive family and community traditions and relationships, not by profit motivated addictions; remembering and accepting one's own personal, familial, and ethnic history instead of continually shifting from one market-produced identity to another solidifies moral character. Even in a socially mobile society, one can hold on to one's ethnic heritage, one's family of origin's values, one's religious beliefs, and the remaining fragments of the Judeo-Christian and Greco-Roman narratives described above. The cultivation of a stable *real* self over a lifetime, in contrast to a superficial, easily altered identity manufactured not by oneself but by marketers, can enhance the personal freedom and sensitivity needed to detect the marketers' seductive ploys and to reject their unneeded products.

Contemporary philosophers have also testified to the current emptiness of the self. David F. Wells (1998) affirms, "A liberated self, it turns out, is no longer tethered to what used to be thought a virtue: [moral] consistency. . . . If consistency was once the hallmark of firm, rooted character, it is now the major impediment to the successful construction of the self. A flexible biography, a self that can adapt as needed to different environments, that can remake itself, refurbish itself, reinvent itself, reimagine itself and even remake its body, is the obvious psychological counterpart to our market-driven economy with its plethora of choices and required adaptation" (p. 95). He adds, "The very emptiness of the modern self sustains both our psychologists and our merchants" (Wells, 1998, p. 113). A strong, mature self, nurtured by loving relationships and able to lovingly give of itself to others, is the antidote to the dehumanization and consequent violence done to the self by the persons behind forceful consumerism.

Nurturing an Authentic, Solid Self

A solid self is, paradoxically, necessary for an authentic sacrifice of one's self for others. Self-sacrifice can occur in a moment, such as when saving the life of a drowning child, or over years, such as caring for a parent or spouse suffering from Alzheimer's Disease. The self in the first example responds instantaneously because habits of caring for others in danger have already been ingrained in one's character but probably not by corporate marketers. The self in the second example can sustain daily challenges of compassionately caring for the now demented family member who had lovingly cared for this self when this self, too, had been or had felt helpless and vulnerable. The strength and perseverance needed for consistent moral action come from a self that is not staged by advertisers but rather is rooted at its core in a set of values that do not change, values learned from parents, friends, religions, communities, art, and literature which still honor and participate in the Judeo-Christian and Greco-Roman guiding narratives.

Clinical psychologist Madeline Levine (2007) remarks that "pre-teens and teens from affluent homes have the highest rates of depression, anxiety disorders and substance abuse of any group of children in this country" (p. 33). Drawing from her experience treating privileged teenagers in wealthy Marin County, California, outside of San Francisco, she has noted how her clients often hide their cut wrists and forearms under designer clothes. She attributes their self-inflicted agony of "cutting" to their lacking "the things that are necessary to anchor a healthy sense of self: a sense of authenticity, of purpose, of being loved for who they are and not simply how they perform" (Levine, 2007, p. 34). Since young people mirror their parents' behavior, they have often become expert consumers of goods, but they are inexpert at hiding their inner emptiness. Levine recommends that privileged parents "learn some of the basic tenets of child development: that a sense of self is crafted from the inside out; that parental love cannot be conditional on performance; and that emotional availability—not simply ear-time racing from one activity to the next—is what helps kids develop a robust sense of self as well as a reliable repertoire of coping skills that help them to navigate through the inevitable challenges of life" (Levine, 2007, p 35). She adds, "We need to be teaching emotional resilience and self-management skills, not consumerism.

... Teaching skills for managing unhappy feelings are good for a lifetime; designer outfits are only good for a season" (Levine, 2007, pp. 35-36).

Her testimony as a therapist suggests that children are being dehumanized because their human need for unconditional love from their parents is being deflected to earning that love via external expert performances which gain products as their awards rather than authentic love. Perhaps the parents themselves have also missed being truly loved by their parents. Thus, consumerism's invasion of the sacred space of the family is being passed on from generation to generation. It is significant that these children lacking core selves authenticated by unconditional love seek such authentication in their favorite teachers. Levine (2007) notes, "When I asked a large group of my sons' friends what single thing would lessen the stress in their life, they told me—without prompting—that they wanted to spend fifteen minutes with their favorite teacher, just hanging out. That's what quality time means—it's human being, not human doing" (p. 60). Perhaps the teachers still value parts or all of the Judeo-Christian and Greco-Roman narratives; they authentically love their students, following the examples of Jesus and Socrates, and understand that spending quality time with them nurtures both their spirits and their intellects. Levine (2007) concludes, "Children need places where people value them for being who they are, not for what they do or how they perform" (p. 60). Parents can provide far more than fifteen minutes with their offspring. Unconditional, authentic love for one's children should endure a lifetime.

Levine's example of her patients desiring to spend even only fifteen minutes of "quality time" with their teachers suggests that education, besides cultivating and defending one's own "inner sanctum," may be another bright spot in the dark abyss of consumerism. However, Benjamin Ginsberg (2011) persuasively argues that "corporatization has successfully, and almost fatally, overtaken both public and private institutions of higher education in the United States. Professors are encouraged to help "customers (aka students)" (Ginsberg, 2011, p. 198) achieve predetermined student learning outcomes, not spend "quality time" outside of the classroom with their students. The achievement of these objectives seemingly can be measured by quantifiable instruments, but life changing enhancement of character is immeasurable and may not be evident until decades after the rich encounters between professor and student.

Thus, students are to consume distinctly measurable parts of their education while educators may even be penalized for spending too much "quality time" with students when they should be preparing their classes, correcting the diagnostic instruments that supposedly demonstrate that "slo's" (student learning outcomes) have been achieved, and producing professional articles and books, the number of which "scholarly products" can be quantitatively measured, although such counting up of the "products" may ignore their intellectual quality. Ginsberg (2011) explains, "As one prominent higher education accreditation official and former college administrator recently put it, though once seen as a route to 'personal growth and development,' higher education today should be understood more as, [sic] 'a strategic investment of resources to produce benefits for business and industry by leveraging fiscal and human capital to produce a direct, immediate and positive financial return on those investments'" (Ginsberg, 2011, p. 175).

Hence, the American university is becoming "a knowledge factory, offering more or less sophisticated forms of vocational training to meet the needs of other established institutions" (Ginsberg, 2011, p. 3), not an institution that cultivates critical thinking, including of "other established institutions" such as those found in the consumerism industry. Further, the American university no longer exists primarily to foster the moral character established through careful understanding of the Judeo-Christian and Greco-Roman heritages still to be found in Western culture and, as shown above, essential for guarding the sacred human space, be it within the person, the home, or the community, that can refuse to be violated by the onslaught of consumerism's tactics.

Researcher Benjamin R. Barber (2007) concurs with Ginsberg: "In higher education and elsewhere, the commercializing ethos of infantilization encourages and is encouraged by a political ideology of privatization that delegitimizes adult public goods such as critical thinking and public citizenship (once the primary objectives of higher education) in favor of self-involved private choice and narcissistic personal gain. A college marketing specialist thus sees students first of all as 'voracious consumers who use self-gratification to offset the rigors of academics and the stress of an uncertain future'" (Barber, 2007, p. 15). Barber notes that in the past higher education did act "as a counterpoint to commercial culture" (14), but its "corporatization" (Barber, 2007, p. 14), which he believes began in the 1960s, has subsequently yielded to "the forces of vocationalism" (Barber, 2007, p. 14). Critiquing marketers' ploys to sell products and services to customers, and even resolving not to work in the "consumption" industry itself, are definitely not student outcomes that manipulative marketers and their employers want.

Preceding their arrival at a college or university, young people have already been educated to be consumers via marketers' "kid empowerment" (Barber, 2007, p. 31) strategies noted above. Barber shrewdly observes that, for this type of consumer education to succeed, marketers realize that children must "be separated from [their] protective environment. . . uprooted from the homes and habits that initially protect [them] from predatory marketers and commercial exploitation" (Barber, 2007, p. 30). Hence, "adult-free zones" for shopping are established in the Disney and Warner Brothers stores (2007, p. 30), and specialty shops for youth are "on different shopping floors (or wings) so that the young will shop separately from their parents" (Barber, 2007, p. 30). As much as marketers want to free the young of paternal control when shopping, Barber affirms that an "invisible paternalism" is occurring by which, although "claim[ing] to be 'freeing' children from parental bonds in the name of autonomy. . . in fact they themselves are taking the parents' place as taste-and trendsetters" (Barber, 2007, p. 113). Vincent J. Miller (2003) reiterates Barber's concerns: "The rise of generational marketing niches further erodes the intergenerational mediation of culture. . . . Culture is thus constructed as something one learns from peers' appropriations of commercial popular culture, not wisdom handed down from elders" (p. 53). Sadly, many youth are totally unaware of this shift in loyalty and in role modelling; critical thinking and in-depth studies can give them new awareness and decision making power. Barber (2007) is not totally pessimistic: "Nevertheless, resistance is possible. . . it depends on. . . the reenergized citizen" (p. 54).

Miller (2003) echoes Barber's affirmation: "The only way forward is through consumer culture, by embracing grassroots agency" (p. 9). This type of agent can refuse to use products or services which he or she does not desire or need. Since consumerism is motivated by gaining profits, if producers and marketers cannot make money on a product or service because it is not used, then, according to their own logic, it should be discontinued. Barber (2007) remarks that historically "[c]onsumer boycotts have generally worked best when used in conjunction with government action" (p. 299). Thus, political action may accompany refusal to buy certain products and services. Indeed, currently food producers are having to change their strategies as their consumers are demanding healthier products, and tobacco manufacturers are having to consolidate with each other since people are choosing to smoke less or not at all.

Curiously, a danger is that the consumer industry appropriates even actions against it by making tee shirts proclaiming boycotts and suggesting profitable alternatives to smoking. Miller (2003) states, "Advanced capitalism has shown itself to be strangely immune to ideological criticism. It seems capable of selling anything, including the values of its most committed opponents" (p. 18). Hence, those encouraging boycotts must beware of falling into a consumerism trap even while doing so. Marketers and their bosses place profits above moral messages; they will activate their forces wherever money is potentially to be made, regardless of what ethic is being espoused: "Marketing latches onto any value. . . to sell merchandise" (Miller, 2003, p. 113).

In addition to negative tactics such as boycotts, consumers can follow positive plans. Barber (2007) nicely proclaims, "The challenge is to demonstrate that as consumers we can know what we want and want only what we need; and that, with the rest of our lives we intend to live as lovers or artists or learners or citizens in a plethora of life worlds in which consumption need play no role" (p. 292). He hopes the result of such strong action will be the creation of "a satisfying pull economy of real products and services meeting genuine human needs, or at least reasonable human wants" (Barber, 2007, p. 293). A "pull economy" means that the consumers control what is marketable and needed rather than the current "'push marketing' economy" (Barber, 2007, p. 293) that creates and sells superfluous products to consumers who do not need these products but are persuaded by advertisers of their seeming necessity. The "pull economy" could demand that consumers of necessary items receive truthful information about these instead of advertising "auras" and "myths" attached to them. In the past, before the onslaught of twentieth century consumerism and its accompanying creative advertising, this was the norm. Clapp (1998) notes, "Until the late nineteenth century, advertising had been mainly informational" (p. 184).

Accompanying that practice was the acceptance of frugality as a virtue. Miller (203) remarks that "[a]n excess of productive capacity changed frugality from a virtue to a vice and made consumption a social responsibility" (p. 42). This is perhaps the most dangerous myth of all: one is wrong not to voraciously consume what is being sold. Wiser voices need to counter this myth. For example, David G. Myers (2003) astutely notes, "Happiness is less a matter of getting what we want than of wanting what we have" (p. 48). The American Friends Service Committee advocates "simple living. . . a 'non-consumerist life-style based upon being and becoming, not having'" (Elgin & Mitchell, 2003, p. 147). Such messages liberate and energize consumers to become compassionate, reflective choosers of necessary products not narcissistic, unconscious consumers of unneeded items, ones who feel guilty if they do not "shop until they drop."

CONCLUSION

Thus consumerism, omnipresent in the Western world and particularly American culture, assaults subliminally as well as overtly the human being who, by definition, must consume some items to survive. It might be easier to stop the violence of consumerism by just no longer consuming, but this is impossible if one is to not only sustain life but also flourish. If one truly understands the numbing, illusory, irrational effects wrought by consumerism, then one has the possibility of becoming sensitive, clear-sighted, and rational about one's responses to its attempt to dehumanize its victims. This wise understanding could well turn into a "vocation." Miller (2003) explains, "Vocation involves commitment to a particular form of life and to the transformation of the self in order to sustain that commitment" (p. 137). He speaks of a "reformation of desire" (p. 138) which is actualized for the rest of one's life. In contrast to "[c]onsumer desire" (p. 141), which "is constantly enticed to go beyond what has been acquired to consider something new" (p. 141), a vocation that intends to thwart "[c]onsumer desire" would do just the opposite: be constantly enticed to be satisfied with what one has acquired and to consider something new only if it is determined by the consumer to be useful and desirable for his greater good and the good of those he loves (Miller, 2003).

For example, should parents on a limited income purchase a chemistry set that would definitely enhance their child's love of this science, particularly if the child has expressed a desire to eventually become a doctor? Should financially strapped newlyweds use money received as wedding gifts for a short honeymoon when, before opening those envelopes, such an important journey had been out of the question? Should a family buy a new car when they know their current one is dangerous to drive? These are the concrete dilemmas that confront people with the vocation to thwart "consumer desire" and not be seduced by it. Responses to these questions require a solid self, one rooted in positive core values and willing to take financial and emotional risks for a greater good; this action is called "agency": choosing to exert one's personal power. Thus, the agent has the power to choose to buy or not to buy after careful reflection (and often prayer, too). This agent has not been overly influenced, much less dehumanized, by a violent and violating consumer culture but rather has chosen what, for many reasons, seems best for him or her, not for the producers and marketers of products. Miller (2003) affirms, "The path [of deepening agency] lies forward, through this explosion of agency, by embracing and forming it" (p. 226).

REFERENCES

Achebe, C. (1988). *Things fall apart*. New York, NY: Fawcett.

Barber, B. (2007). *Consumer: How markets corrupt children, infantilize adults, and swallow citizens*. New York, NY: W. W. Norton & Company.

Beabout, G. R., & Echeverria, E. J. (2002). The culture of consumerism: A Catholic and personalist critique. *Journal of Markets & Morality*, *5*(2), 339–383.

Berman, R. (1981). *Advertising and social change*. Beverly Hills, CA: Sage.

Campbell, C. (2010). What is wrong with consumerism? An assessment of some common criticisms. *Anuario Filosofico*, *43*(2), 279–296.

Camus, A. (1955). *L'Etranger*. New York, NY: Appleton-Century Crofts.

Clapp, R. (1998). *The consuming passion: Christianity & the consumer culture*. Downers Grove, IL: InterVarsity Press.

Descartes, R. (2006). *A discourse on the method of correctly conducting one's reason and seeking truth in the sciences*. New York, NY: Oxford University Press.

Elgin, D., & Mitchell, A. (2003). Voluntary simplicity: A movement emerges. In D. Doherty & A. Etzioni (Eds.), *Voluntary simplicity: Responding to consumer culture* (pp. 145–171). Lanham, MD: Rowman & Littlefield.

Faulkner, W. (1956). *The sound and the fury*. New York, NY: Vintage Books.

Fromm, E. (1976). *To have or to be?* New York, NY: Harper & Row.

Ginsberg, B. (2011). *The fall of the faculty: The rise of the all-administrative university and why it matters*. New York, NY: Oxford University Press.

Hill, J. (2011). Endangered childhoods: How consumerism is impacting child and youth identity. *Media Culture & Society*, *33*(3), 347–362. doi:10.1177/0163443710393387

Kavanaugh, J. F. (1991). *Following Christ in a consumer society: The spirituality of cultural resistance*. Maryknoll, NY: Orbis Books.

Levi, P. (1996). *Survival at Auschwitz* (S. Woolf, Trans.). New York, NY: Simon & Schuster.

Levine, M. (2007). How materialism hurts our kids privilege. *Tikkun*, *22*(1), 33–36, 60.

Lewis, C. T., & Short, C. (1980). *A Latin dictionary*. Oxford, UK: Oxford UP.

Miller, V. J. (2003). *Consuming religion: Christian faith and practice in a consumer culture*. New York, NY: Bloomsbury.

Myers, D. G. (2003). Wealth and happiness: A limited relationship. In D. Doherty & A. Etzioni (Eds.), *Voluntary simplicity: Responding to consumer culture* (pp. 41–51). Lanham, MD: Rowman & Littlefield.

Wells, D. F. (1998). *Losing our virtue: Why the Church must recover its moral vision*. Grand Rapids, MI: Eerdmans.

Wiesel, E. (2006). *Night* (M. Wiesel, Trans.). New York, NY: Hill and Wang.

KEY TERMS AND DEFINITIONS

Agency: The individual's choice to exert his or her personal power in thoughts, words, and actions.

Consumerism: A preoccupation with the consumption of goods and services.

Dehumanization: A decreasing or depriving of human qualities or attributes.

Metanarrative: An influential, pervasive, and ongoing story that explains occurrences in a culture and governs people's thoughts and actions. Examples of metanarratives in Western culture are the Judeo-Christian beliefs and the Greco-Roman emphasis on rationalism.

Objectifying: Mentally turning human beings into objects to be acted upon.

Sacred: Holy, sanctified, or set apart from the normal usage or routine habits.

Secular: That which is not sacred: the mundane, routine, and typical.

Violence: Intentionally and forcefully injuring, dishonoring, outraging, or violating someone or something.

Section 4
Consumer Culture From a Global Perspective

Chapter 12
Turkey's Experience of Modern Consumer Culture

Elif Kıran
Tekirdağ Namık Kemal University, Turkey

ABSTRACT

This chapter adresses the issue of consumption from a sociological perspective and focuses primarily on the emergence of consumer society in Turkey by making use of the historical data in the literature as well as of arguments of some prominent thinkers on the subject, such as Baudrillard, Simmel, and Veblen. Following this general point of view, the author goes further, delving into the significant points of modern consumer culture in Turkey. To this aim, the rise of consumer culture in the country and the unique role of mass media and of the places of consumption in the spreading of this new lifestyle are discussed.

INTRODUCTION[1]

Consumption is one of the basic needs of humanity and is regarded as an indispensable element of life. Regardless of time and location, individuals have always engaged in consumption in the course of all stages of their lives. A new-born baby as well as an adult lives to consume; low-wage families as well as members of high-society are conditioned to consume; our ancestors having lived in very different physical and socio-economic environments had to consume and our descendants will continue to consume.

Being such a common behavior to all eras and places, consumption is frequently highlighted in most disciplines, especially in the social sciences. Economics, management, sociology, psychology are examples of such areas that contain a rich literature on consumption. The studies address the issue from different perspectives, ranging from the pyschological motivation behind consumer behavior to changing trends in free time activities.

This chapter addresses the issue of consumption from a sociological perspective, focusing on the socio-economic changes that Turkey has undergone since 1980. The paper consists of four main parts, the first addresses the general marks of consumer society and culture in Turkey. The second is about the evolution of consumer culture in the country. This part includes the core reasons behind the country's adopting consumer culture, and the importance of the period after 1980 in this transformation. Next, the

DOI: 10.4018/978-1-5225-6120-0.ch012

chapter explores the impact of mass media on individuals' consuming habits in Turkey, and the fourth and last part examines the influence of shopping places on the rise of consumer culture in Turkey. Through these four main parts, the main objectives of the chapter are 1) presenting a broad idea of the rise of modern consumer culture, 2) highlighting the issue of consumer culture from a sociological point of view, 3) emphasizing the historical background of modern consumerism, and examining the influence of communication tools, and 4) examining shopping centers in Turkey – put under the spotlight in detail.

BACKGROUND

Turkey's journey into the world of modern consumption has been an issue of interest for researchers from various disciplines. Sociology is a major study area among those in which the issue of consumption in Turkey is a recurrent concern, being addressed in several studies from different standpoints. As an example, Orçan's study (2014) handles the issue as a long timeline and examines Turkish consumer culture experience from Ottoman period to the 21st century. Additionally, Sandıkçı and Ger published several works focusing on the birth and development of consumer society in Turkey. In one of their papers, the researchers studied the consumptionscape of Turkey in general (2002) and in another one, they grouped Turkish consumer practises in four main categories as Islamist, spectacularist, nationalist, and historical (2005). In addition to these studies, Başfırıncı (2011) and Zorlu (2003) focus on the emergence and development of modern consumer habits in Turkish society in their research and highlight the importance of the years starting with 1980 in this social transformation.

Consumer Culture in Turkish Society

The notion of consumption has evolved into a culture. Societies adopting this culture have been addressed as consumer societies. This highly effective system acts as one of the vital components of capitalism since it provides the consumption levels needed to drive needed production. Despite the emphasis solely on production in the beginning years of industrialization, the subsequent years experienced a shift in emphasis towards consumption. Moreover, the importance of free time apart from labour time became an issue of concern.

The rise of the importance of consumption has affected almost every nation, aided by the help of communication tools and globalization. Although differences exist, a pervasiveness of a consumer focus has evolved – the rise of the so-called modern life of individuals. Modernism has assumed a common experience among most societies, although it is manifested differently depending on each country's own circumstances. Turkey is a nation that has met modernization via a nonwestern orientation and has adopted the system over time. From the very beginning of the Republic, laws were enacted with the purpose of determining and quickening modernization, serving the aim of cultural change and institutionalizing social reconciliations with Western countries (Gencer, 2008). Modern values that are idealized and determined to be goals to be achieved have entered into Turkish culture via consumer culture. The adoption of consumer culture values meant another step in the way of modernization for Turkish people. Despite the tendency to define consumption as an immoral cultural crime in Ottoman novels (Mardin, 1992), consumption depicts a dramatic change that has accompanied the path of modernization.

The Evolution of Consumer Culture in Turkey

The period after the last years of the Ottoman Empire and the first years of the new Republic, witnessed significant transformations in Turkey. Following foreign intervention, wars, political migrations, and the economic crisis in the 19th century and the first 20 years of the 20th century, Turkish society managed its largest stuctural developmental step in its history. This period formed an effective substructure with a new style in many areas, including law, politics, education, and individual lifestyles. The development of an urbanized, industrialized, organized, and professional environment, however, would not begin until the 1950s. It is important to note that modernization occured quickly after this time (Kıray, 2006). One of the most important factors was the restructuring of daily lifestyles of individuals. Changes in individuals' consumer habits was one of the primary changes resulting from a the adoption of a new modernized Westernized life. Turkish society underwent an enormous change in adopting Western style of consumption, which was portrayed as some of the vital aims of the new Republic.

As it is noted above, the history of the changes in the consumption habits of Turkish society dates back to the beginning of the new Republic. However, the most significant changes would not take place before the 1980s as the pace of change significantly quickened thereafter. This chapter concentrates on the period after 1980 addressing the consumer culture in Turkey. To this aim, it would be better to have a look at the situation worldwide. During the post-WW II time period, the marketing of goods based on the values and symbols associated with them became the norm for most products. This also occurred in Turkey, but beginning at a later time and at a quicker pace. The goods that were introduced into the market become primary tools for the developing individual identities (Dağtaş & Dağtaş, 2009). Accompanying this change, there was a shift in emphasis from future happiness to happiness at present. Consequently, the residents of Turkey changed their lifestyles to ones where gaining status from present purchases became the norm (Göle, 2002). The 1980s, which are known as the years with Özal, constituted a unique place in today's Turkey in many ways including the rise of a consunmer-based lifestyle which was significantly different from traditional consumption habits and lifestyles (Orçan, 2014).

The changing experiences in Turkey resulted in part from the policies of Turgut Özal led to a social transformation of Turkish society, from a nation characterized by limited consumption in daily life, to one characterized by plenty of alternatives of products and the desire to purchase them. Turgut Özal had a very different agenda than previous leaders of Turkey. He was known to be a follower of Nakshibendi tariqa resulting in a conservative worldview. However, he is also known for his strong inclination towards innovation and technology. He used visits to the US to keep abreast of current trends, a perspective that was also held by other Turkish leaders of that era. By blending these two different aspects together, Özal managed to gain the support of people from different wings. Moreover, he was the leading figure in the introduction of international products into Turkey (Orçan, 2014).

The changes in consumption habits and the rise of consumption acivities was a result of the country's entrance into the world market economy, which opened the way to globalization in Turkey. That period of time was an important one in the country's political history because the decisions to follow this route were made during the years of social uneasiness after the 1980 coup. With this new road map, known as 24th January 1980 decisions, a market economy was determined as the system for Turkey's industrial development. Imports and exports were supported, and, to this aim, banks were founded and credit opportunities were presented. In parallel with these developments, progress towards accepting a capitalist system was observed in Turkey (Boratav, 2014). Turkish individuals had no difficulty in adapting to this new system since these goods promised to simplify and enhance their daily lives. In other words, this entry into a new economic system posits a lively example of the influence of economy on the social atmosphere of a nation. The changes in the everyday life habits of Turkish people went hand in hand with those in economy.

Together with these changess, a new middle class, with a rise in its economic status, emerged. The consumer culture highly influenced the members of this class and, consequently, Turkish society after the 1980s had a strong inclination towards symbol-infused branded goods imported from Europe consistent with Baudrillard's (1998) ideas of symbolic consumption and Veblen's (2001) conspicious consumption. In direct proportion with the economic developments in the country, the amount of demand also rose. As the developing industrial institutions were producing goods, the social changes required new needs and the symbolism associated with products became vital components of objects of everday life. In other words, economic changes paved the way for a transformation from a traditional lifestyle to a modern one in Turkey. In the framework of this changing atmosphere, the concept of equality that emerged after the Industrial Revolution and the revolutions of the 19th century left its place to the notion of happiness. That is to say, the ultimate goal of individuals changed from equality to happiness. Happiness started to be viewed as goal in life (Baudrillard, 1998) and the ultimate way to happiness is the path of modern consumption.

The rise of an open economy and the accompanying entrance of foreign goods into the country informed Turkish residents of the innovation occurring not only in their homeland but also in other parts of the world, especially in the West. Significant relationships started between international organizations such as World Bank, IMF, and World Trade Organization, which were developed with the aim of becoming an international actor. One of its essentials was determined to be a developed economy, and, in order to reach this aim, market economy was put into action. As an outcome of this, individuals tended to adopt Western lifestyles. Moreover, the 24 January 1980 decisions reflected a determination that the capital class and industrialization in Turkey had developed enough to compete with the West. This was a guiding point indicating that the country was ready to be integrated in the rest of the world (Kongar, 1994). This idea of integration would not remain restricted to the economic realm and it started to be felt via the changes in daily life practises.

The social transformation was facilitated by the politics of modernization. Inclination to capitalism was in the core of this political system. To support the transition, credit cards were introduced to the public. Until that time, credit card ownership was a sign of eliteness in Turkish society and were only available to a select group. However, in tandem with the adoption of market economy, credit cards started to be offered to different social classes to increase consumption. Individuals who desired to shop but did not possess adequate cash were also added to the system of modern consumption via credit cards (Bali, 2011). This changed the transformation from a traditional future-oriented point-of-view to a modern one focusing on present happiness as a reflection of the idea of "today without future" (Ergur, 2002, pp. 128-141). Credit opportunities and credit cards were instrumental to creating consumers increasing prosperity.

In the light of this historical data, the 1980s, years starting with the ones of Turgut Özal's administration are evaluated as the most influential time phase in the transformation of Turkish habits of consumption. This changes were facilitated by a quickly developing mass media that mirrored the developments in political and economic life.

The Role of Mass Media in Consumption Culture of Turkey

Significant changes in mass media tools occurring in combination with changes in technology played a prominent role in the changes discussed above. These tools prompted cultural interchange among different places and people, regardless of the distances between them. Mass media takes a different function in modernism leading to differentiation of roles and functions, urbanization, social disintegration, and alienation, all of which weaken organic bonds (Tekinalp, 2002). In parallel with the developments in these tools, individuals' attention towards them also increased with mass media starting to be evaluated as a prominent item in individuals' daily lives. Consequently, individuals started to increasingly build their daily lives on the basis of consumption, and, in accordance with the developments in mass media, consumption behaviors in daily life started to be influenced by communication tools to a great extent. As an outcome of migration dynamics and global communication technologies, the public sphere gained its liberty from state control and evolved into international communication flows, paving the way for building close relationships across different cultures and civilizations (Göle, 2012, p. 24). The role of consumption in individuals' lives grew as a result, bringing more and more people into contact with mass media and advertising and the products that are available (Bocock, 1993). Communication tools, therefore, played a unique role in the spread of products and the growing strength of consumer culture in Turkey.

Mass media tools proved to be very powerful in the expanding role played by consumption in the daily lives of the Turkish people. The consumer culture spread by mass media started to change individuals' life styles after 1980s. With the change, Turkish media presented mostly the consuming habits of individuals belonging to the highest social classes, particularly in the newspaper sector. Arguably, the press adopted a focus on lifestyle by focusing on the activities of upper-class individuals (Dağtaş & Dağtaş, 2009). Moreover, media organisations were encouraging consumption and acted as mechanisms of support to the growing consumer culture to such an extent that they were heavily criticized by Frankfurt School members. Using mass media tools became the easiest and fastest way of creating and spreading a consumer lifestyle that was viewed favorably by the country's economic and political powers of that time (Tuna, 2005, p. 98). Mass media proved to be very successful in manipulating the public and creating a homogenous society in line with the hegemony of consumer society. Mass culture that is cultivated under the control of media is no longer under the control of society, which is the producer and protector of culture, but it is created by industry as something artificial and identical (Mora, 2008).

Mass media proved to be very successful. A clothing style depicted in a movie or a magazine, for instance, quickly becomes successful in the marketplace (Debord, 1994). Depending on the media, this process leads to a level of homogeniety in many areas, including fashion. This is a concrete example of Simmel's (1957) argument on fashion. Free time activities, clothing styles, special usages of speech and so on easily and quickly transfer among individuals of different social classes forming a flood of consumerism. Indeed, the unreal worlds depicted in media were viewed to quickly gain individuals' attention and their trust. Frankfurt School members, however, criticized the effects of mass media on individuals. They assert that, for the sake of media ownership, news are subjected to misinformation, disinformation and manipulation and via this way, worldly realities are transformed into mediatic realities (Mora, 2008).

If one is to go back to the starting point of the influence of communication tools on daily life in Turkey, one will find that Turkish people were introduced to TV broadcast in 1968, as a vital step into the world of communication. After the years with radio, TVs brought the country into a totally different atmosphere of mass media habits. These years were not only important for the entrance of TVs, but also for being the peak point of radio production. Moreover, following 1968, the year of 1980 stands as another prominent year, which is significant in the growth of consumer culture in Turkey. The 1980s are known as the years where more and more people started to have TVs in their homes. TV broadcast continued with state channel and limited programme alternatives for some time and in the following years, it became to be viewed as an indispensable source of information and attraction with the private channels and increasing number of programmes. Together with the private channels starting to broadcast in the 1990s, TVs started to evolve into a commodificated market good from a communication tool. Both with the objects sold and introduced on advertisements and shows, TVs become a new lucrative market for goods (Orçan, 2014). Goods marketed via TV advertising promise individuals an atttractive lifestyle that they are able to adapt only if they buy the advertised goods. They do not aim to empower the use-value of goods but their display value. TV viewers become advertisement followers and began to watch TV not only for the sake of programmes but also the advertisements shown. Ads are "the elixirs of life" (Adorno & Horkheimer, 1972) and act as the complementary items in consumption culture with their power of positing lifestyles (Gürbilek, 2007) directed towards consuming and are idealized by the economic and politic system in power.

Besides TV programmes and advertisements that are prominent due to their visual power, the printed media, especially newspapers and newspaper supplements, were also highly influential mass media tools directing Turkish society towards modern consumption habits. As it is the case of other communication tools, a consumer lifestyle started to be presented to Turkish audience via the printed media, together with the marketing of goods that are targeted as indispensable objects needed in order to maintain those idealized lifestyles. The consumer was not only affected by the advertisements in printed media but were also affected by the opinions expressed by columnists and media managers who willingly informed their readers about the imported goods, the moments and places they consume these goods, cultural and art activities, and luxurious tastes that entered Turkish social atmosphere upon the developments during the 1980s. Turkey started to see modern lifestyles on printed media in parallel with the ones on visual media, reinforcing the message. In addition to this, the differences between the past and the present were frequently emphasized via newspapers, praising the new style of that era. This also led Turkish people to evaluate the era of modern consumption and the new life styles in accordance with new consuming habits as aims to be sought (Bali, 2011).

Besides newspapers, the promotions included with newspapers further reinforced the consumer message. Promotions before the rise of consumer culture, tended to mostly focus on objects related to education and culture. However, after the 1980s, all types of consumer goods, even houses and cars, started to be given by newspaper coupons (Orçan, 2014). This role of newspaper promotions can be evaluated in an analogy with the emergence of credit cards. As it was highlighted before, credit cards played a significant role in forming modern consumers by helping ndividuals to spend money even if they do not have cash avaialble. Also, the promotions gave individuals the hope of possessing the objects they are dreaming of regardless of the ability to pay.

Magazines also played a key role in furthering consumer culture. Magazines changed as society changed. Manuscripts which were sold as magazine supplements and were used to elaborate subjects, such as travel, decoration, history or diet, started to be sold as separate magazines in the 1990s. Apart from women's magazines, which were very popular, there was an increase in the number of men's magazines, too. These tools of communication also promoted new lifestyles in Turkey based on consumption. Moreover, advertisements in magazines played a significant role in informing the audience of consumption alternatives, such as Western clothes and daily life activities, places, and modern consumption-based portrails of man and woman (Özdemir, 2009).

In the light of the arguments above, it can be deduced that mass media has played a prominent role in Turkey's encounter with and adaptation to modern consumer culture. By both the visual and printed media, Turkish people have been subjected to a dense amount of information and elaboration of a limitless number of consumption alternatives.

New Places of Consumption in Turkey

When Turkey's footsteps in the world of consumption are followed, it becomes clear that besides the significant effects of mass media tools, the occurrence of new places of consumption constitutes a vital place in this journey. This part of the chapter focuses on the binding points between space and consumption in Turkey.

One of the major requirements that emerged from increasing industrialization is the need for reorganization of the urban space. The new sites of living that had been built far from the city centers have caused various problems, one of which is the issue of accessibility to socio-cultural activities. As a result of this problem, urban settlers' demand for new places has emerged. Modern shopping centers have been constructed as solutions to problems revolving around issues of consumption and accessibility. Individuals in consumer culture are manipulated to feel that they can acquire the consuming goods promoted via mass media tools and, as a result, they feel the need for new places that are "embellished" with goods of all kinds (Bauman, 2009, p. 97). Shopping centers can be viewed as lively examples of the perfect combination of these two core elements of a consuming society.

Urban spaces resemble living organisms that form a common identity and places of trade for their residents. In traditional cities, bazaars or open places in the city centers were used to fullfill these roles. However, they are replaced by the modern shopping centers, and malls in modern urban settings. These places of shopping, which are also referred to as "consumption cathedrals" (Ritzer, 2010), are perceieved as holy (separate or special) places full of holy things. Individuals attribute holiness to material goods and they feel the need to visit these places of shopping regularly. Shopping malls are on top of the list of the notions that trigger individuals in consumer society that are surrounded by plenty of things (Baudrillard, 1998) to consume. These places are organized in every detail with the aim of making people to consume more and more. Music, lights, odours, campaigns and so on used in their atmosphere are neatly selected in order to arouse the need to consume in the modern individuals' minds.

New requirements of modern times gave birth to new needs in Turkey. Shopping centers were added as an indication of the new daily livestyles highlighted above and given special attention. A rise in the number of these places, which appeal to masses, has been witnessed since the liberalisation policies of the 1980s (Kandiyoti, 2005). The adventure of shopping malls started with "Galleria" which was built in 1988 in a central area of Istanbul and in the course of time the habit of going to shopping centers has been adopted very quickly. These places have started to act as meeting points of individuals of different socio-economic classes, as recreation areas, as shopping places, and so on and so forth. Since 1988, shopping malls have become indispensable elements of cities and of the daily life of urban settlers in Turkey. The number of shopping centers has increased through these years and these places have led to changes in the consuming habits of Turkish people. That is to say, people started to be more inclined to fashionable goods, and, as it is noted by Simmel (1957), in his argument on fashion, and by Veblen (2001), in his argument of conspicious consumption, individuals have become fashion followers in order to be a member of a certain socio-economic status and, moreover, to show off to others. Shopping centers give the opportunity to be among a great amount of people from different backgrounds and, in such an atmosphere, Turkish people have had the chance of witnessing others and following new trends in fashion. Moreover, they have been enjoying the chance of displaying their style of living to others, too. Therefore, just as the communication tools have been doing, these places have been acting as the channels of being a part of the modern consumer world for Turkish society.

SOLUTIONS AND RECOMMENDATIONS

This chapter has aimed to examine the issue of consumption from a sociological point of view and highlighted some significant points in the evolution and implementation of modern consumer culture in Turkey. The depiction reveals that, especially after the 1980s, a significant inclination towards consumption started as a vital aspect of social life. Moreover, individuals have been directed to build their identities via the goods they possess, the places they spend their free times, the movies they watch, etc. Moreover, this current theme seems to continue with an increasing pace. The solution and recommendation to be given here can somehow be related with coping with the components of modern life without totally characterizing oneself via consumption. That is to say, individuals of the 21st century are without doubt surrounded by consumer culture and it seems almost inevitable to escape from it. Therefore, people need to find a way to live a life balanced in terms of production and consumption, even though they are living in one focusing solely on consumption. Besides the ones of consumption, creating alternative ways of production in daily life should be an effective road map for individuals of consumer society. Additionally, trying to be aware of the fact that the consumption ideas are shaped and served by the economic powers of the current era in order to increase their benefits more than the ones of the consumers can be some recommendations here.

FUTURE RESEARCH DIRECTIONS

Although there are many studies which analyze the consumer culture in Turkey, there still exists a gap in terms of comparing and contrasting the evolution of consumer culture in Turkey with that in other countries. Therefore, future studies delving into this issue should be produced in order to overcome this weakness.

The experience of the rapid rise of consumer culture in Turkey indicates that consumer culture is not strictly a Western phenomenon. The appeal of consumer culture, particularly when it is promoted by the media, is very attractive to individuals and can be adopted very quickly even in cultures that have been traditionally opposed to consumption. Additional research into this attractiveness of consumer culture is warranted. Are there any cultures in which consumer culture would not be seen as attractive and would be rejected regardless of the promotion by government and mass media?

CONCLUSION

Consumption is a vital aspect of humans' daily lives. It embodies several submeanings which also carry the subject into different aspects of individuals' lives. This chapter has addressed the issue from the framework of sociology using the example of Turkey. To this aim, the periods in Turkish history that played a significant role in the country's embodying modern consumer culture characteristics have been examined. Additionally, mass media and the evolving of the places of consumption have been noted as two higlighting factors in Turkish society's daily life consumption dynamics.

In summary, it can be deduced that modern consumption which came into the picture after the rise in production, has a long history of development. Through many factors including mass media, shopping centers, and urbanization, consumption has evolved into its present status. The depiction of Turkey's modern consumption trends reflects a similar situation. Therefore, it can be concluded that consumer culture is a widespread phenomenon with significant power. Individuals that are bound to live in the atmosphere of a consumer culture should be aware of this power. Following this awareness, a number of solutions to this issue may be posited. As an example, the close relationship between consumer culture, media, and the economic powers can be taught at schools in classes, such as media literacy. In addition to that, there may be political issues. The government can convey messages to the public about the importance of being frugal, being productive, and can open places for free time activities rather than focusing solely on consumption in their free time. By the help of daily life steps such as these, individuals can reach a life balanced in production and consumption.

REFERENCES

Adorno, T. W., & Horkheimer, M. (1972). *Dialectic of enlightenment*. New York, NY: Continuum.

Bali, R. N. (2011). *Tarz-ı hayattan life style'a*. İstanbul, Turkey: İletişim Publications.

Başfırıncı, Ç. (2011). Modern Türk tüketim kültürüne yönelik bir araştırma. *Milli Folklor, 23*(91), 115–129.

Baudrillard, J. (1998). *The consumer society*. London, UK: Sage Publications.

Bauman, Z. (2009). *Does ethics have a chance in a world of consumers?* Boston: Harvard University Press.

Bauman, Z. (2009). *Does ethics have a chance in a world of consumers?* Boston: Harvard University Press.

Bell, D. (1976). *The cultural contradictions of western capitalism*. London, UK: Heineman.

Bocock, R. (1993). *Consumption*. London, UK: Routledge. doi:10.4324/9780203313114

Boratav, K. (2014). *Türkiye iktisat tarihi (1908-2009)*. Ankara, Turkey: İmge Bookstore.

Dağtaş, B., & Dağtaş, E. (Eds.). (2009). *Medya, tüketim kültürü ve yaşam tarzları: Türkiye medyasından örüntüler*. Ankara, Turkey: Ütopya Publications.

Debord, G. (1994). *The society of the spectacle*. New York, NY: Zone Books.

Ergur, A. (2002). Kredi kartı kullanımında zaman algılaması ve borçlu yaşam. *Toplum ve Bilim, 102*, 128–141.

Gencer, B. (2008). *İslam'da modernleşme*. Ankara, Turkey: Lotus Publications.

Göle, N. (2002). *Melez desenler: İslam ve modernlik üzerine*. İstanbul, Turkey: Metis Publications.

Göle, N. (2012). *Seküler ve dinsel: Aşınan sınırlar*. İstanbul, Turkey: Metis Publications.

Gürbilek, N. (2007). *Vitrinde yaşamak: 1980'lerin kültürel iklimi*. İstanbul, Turkey: Metis Publications.

Kandiyoti, D. (2005). Parçaları yorumlamak. In D. Kandiyoti & A. Saktanber (Eds.), *Kültür Fragmanları Türkiye'de Gündelik Hayat* (pp. 15–36). İstanbul, Turkey: Metis Publications.

Kıray, M. B. (2006). *Toplumsal yapı, toplumsal değişme*. İstanbul, Turkey: Bağlam Publications.

Kongar, E. (1994). *İmparatorluktan günümüze Türkiye'nin toplumsal yapısı*. İstanbul, Turkey: Remzi Bookstore.

Mardin, Ş. (1992). *Türk modernleşmesi*. İstanbul, Turkey: İletişim Publications.

Mora, N. (2008). *Medya çalışmaları, medya pedagojisi ve küresel iletişim*. İstanbul, Turkey: Alt Kitap Publications.

Orçan, M. (2014). *Osmanlı'dan günümüze modern türk tüketim kültürü*. Ankara, Turkey: Harf Publications.

Özdemir, İ. (2009). Türkiye'de popüler kadın magazin dergileri: yeni kadın kimliği ve sunulan yaşam tarzları. In M. Dağtaş & E. Dağtaş (Eds.), *Medya, Tüketim Kültürü ve Yaşam Tarzları- Türkiye Medyasından Örüntüler* (pp. 205–243). Ankara, Turkey: Ütopya Publications.

Ritzer, G. (2010). *Enchanting a disenchanted world: continuity and change in the cathedrals of consumption*. Los Angeles, CA: Sage Publications. doi:10.4135/9781483349572

Sandikci, O., & Ger, G. (2002). In-between modernities and postmodernities: theorizing Turkish consumptionscape. In S. M. Broniarczyk & K. N. Valdosta (Eds.), Advances in consumer research (pp. 465-470). Provo UT: Association for Consumer Research.

Sandikci, O., & Ger, G. (2005). Contemporary Turkish consumptionscape: polarity and plurality. *7th. Portoroz Business Conference*.

Simmel, G. (1957). Fashion. *American Journal of Sociology*, *62*(6), 541–558. doi:10.1086/222102

Tekinalp, Ş. (2002). İletişim araştırmalarında ideoloji ve küreselleşme: Eleştirel bir bakış. *Kocaeli University Journal of Communication Research*, *1*, 9–32.

Tuna, K. (2005). Batılı bilginin eleştirisi üzerine. İstanbul, Türkiye: Ufuk Books.

Veblen, T. (2001). *The theory of the leisure class*. New York, NY: Modern Library.

Zorlu, A. (2003). Batılı bir yaşam tarzı olarak tüketim: Türkiye'de tüketim ürünlerinin ve kültürünün tarihi gelişimi. *Hacettepe University Journal of Sociological Research*. Retrieved October 10, 2017, from: www.sdergi.hacettepe.edu.tr/zorlu_makale.htm

ADDITIONAL READING

Bauman, Z. (1998). *Globalization*. New York, NY: Polity Press.

Best, S., & Kellner, D. (1991). *Postmodern theory*. New York, NY: Guilford Press. doi:10.1007/978-1-349-21718-2

Campbell, C. (2005). The craft consumer: Culture, craft and consumption in a postmodern society. *Journal of Consumer Culture, 5*(1), 23–42. doi:10.1177/1469540505049843

Corrigan, P. (1997). *The sociology of consumption: an introduction*. London, UK: Sage Publications.

De Certeau, M. (1988). *The practice of everyday life*. Los Angeles, CA: University of California Press.

Douglas, M. (Ed.). (2003). *The world of goods: towards an anthropology of consumption* (6th ed.). London, UK: Routledge.

Featherstone, M. (2007). *Consumer culture and postmodernism*. London, UK: Sage.

Fırat, F. A., & Venkatesh, A. (1995). Liberatory postmodernism and the reenchantment of consumption. *The Journal of Consumer Research, 22*(3), 239–267. doi:10.1086/209448

Fiske, J. (1989). *Understanding popular culture*. London, UK: Routledge.

Gerro, T. K. (2004). Cultural consumption research: Review of methodology, theory, and consequence. *International Review of Sociology, 14*(1), 11–29. doi:10.1080/0390670042000186743

Göle, N. (2002). *Melez desenler: İslam ve modernlik üzerine*. İstanbul, Turkey: Metis Publications.

Gronow, J., & Warde, A. (Eds.). (2001). *Ordinary consumption*. London, UK: Routledge.

Illich, I. (2011). *Tüketim Köleliği*. İstanbul, Turkey: Pınar Publications.

Köse, H. (2010). *Medya ve tüketim sosyolojisi*. Ankara, Turkey: Ayraç Publications.

Lefebvre, H. (2002). *Everyday life in modern world*. New York, NY: Continuum.

Maigret, E. (2011). *Medya ve iletişim sosyolojisi* (H. Yücel, Trans.). İstanbul, Turkey: İletişim Publications.

McCracken, G. (1986). Culture and consumption: A theoretical account of the structure and movement of the cultural meaning of consumer goods. *The Journal of Consumer Research, 13*(1), 71–84. doi:10.1086/209048

Miller, D. (Ed.). (1995). *Acknowledging consumption*. London, UK: Routledge.

Nicosia, F. M., & Mayer, R. N. (1976). Toward a sociology of consumption. *The Journal of Consumer Research, 3*(2), 65–75. doi:10.1086/208653

Ritzer, G. (2001). *Explorations in the sociology of consumption: fast food, credit cards, and casinos*. London, UK: Sage Publications.

Shields, R. (Ed.). (2004). *Lifestyle shopping: the subject of consumption*. London, UK: Routledge.

Storey, J. (1999). *Cultural consumption and everyday life*. London, UK: Bloomsbury Academic.

Tuna, K. (2005). *Batılı bilginin eleştirisi üzerine*. İstanbul, Turkey: Ufuk Books.

Wagner, P. (1994). *A sociology of modernity: liberty and discipline*. London, UK: Routledge.

KEY TERMS AND DEFINITIONS

Conspicious Consumption: A kind of consumption which refers to the consuming of goods for the sake of showing off.

Consumer Culture: A form of culture which indicates to the emphasis on consumption.

Consumer Society: A society which is ruled by consumer culture.

Consumption: A term referring to possessing or using concrete or abstract things.

Mass Media: Media that addresses to the general public.

Social Interaction: A term referring to the daily relationships among individuals.

Symbolic Consumption: A consumption type in which consumers' choices depend on the symbolic values of goods not their functional ones.

ENDNOTE

1. This chapter is based on a part of the author's Phd dissertation.

Chapter 13
Advertising and Consumerism in Nigeria:
A Study of Unethical Promos by Telecom Operators

Floribert Patrick C. Endong
University of Calabar, Nigeria

ABSTRACT

Nigeria-based telecom companies yearly generate revenues that surpass their returns in other countries due to their growing number of subscribers. In spite of this development, the consumer has, in various ways, remained exploited by telecom companies. Two ways in which such exploitation has been perpetrated include misleading promotions and unsolicited commercial calls. This chapter examines these two anti-consumer paradigms under three principal research questions: What is the state of consumerism in the Nigerian telecom sector? What are some of the anti-consumer cultures prevailing in this sector? And how do consumer protection associations come to terms with these anti-consumer practices? The chapter is thus divided into three main parts. The first part provides a conceptual definition of consumerism. The second part explores consumerism in the Nigerian telecom sector, and the last part deals with misleading advertisements and unsolicited commercial calls as forms of anti-consumer practices.

INTRODUCTION

It is an accepted premise that consumers occupy a key position in business. As a popular aphorism puts it, the client is boss or king in business; without him or her, there cannot be business. "The consumer supplies the blood line that keeps the [manufacturer, producer or entrepreneur] in business and churning out more service. If the consumer is satisfied, the revenue belt increases" (Danbatta in Folarin, 2017). The plausibility of this position is further revealed by the fact that effective demand is defined as desire backed by purchasing power. In view of this, most businesses have been compelled by governmental or other relevant arbiters to regard their clients and consumers as important social entities with rights which must be respected, notably in such areas as advertising and marketing campaigns. Some of these

DOI: 10.4018/978-1-5225-6120-0.ch013

consumer rights to be respected by businesses or advertisers in their campaigns include (i) the right to choose from different brands of goods and services, (ii) the right (for the consumer) to be informed of important facts about products and services (notably durability and side effects) and (iii) the right to be heard by businesses, to ask questions or make complaints and suggestions. Despite modern and global movements to protect consumers, issues such as harmful or exploitative advertising continue to be observable – if not rampant – in most countries (Bishop, 1997; Endong, 2015; Najeeb & Mustansar, 2005; Radio Vatican, 2015). No doubt, many observers – particularly puritanical religious schools of thought – continue to arguably view advertising as a veritable art of deception, and a mere capitalist tool aimed at spurring consumers into excessive or inordinate consumption (Radio Vatican, 2015).

In recent times, Nigerian advertisers have been resorting to such exploitative advertising campaigns in a bid to increase sales or patronage. From religious institutions (such as churches) to video film marketers, some Nigerian advertisers have, of recent, circumstantially employed questionable communications to sell their products and services. The presence of advertising and communication regulatory organizations such as the Advertising Practitioners Council of Nigeria (APCON), the Nigerian Broadcasting Commission, and Nigerian Communications Council (NCC) has not really deterred the tradition of hyperbolic or harmful advertising campaigns by manufacturers and institutions in the country.

Some of the perpetrators of these questionable forms of advertising campaigns have been telecommunication operators which, through techniques such as advertised promotions and unsolicited commercial calls and text messages, have created potential sources of nuisance to consumers, as well as opportunities to exploit. Nigerian telecom operators have, for instance, entrenched the tradition of placing these unsolicited commercial calls and text messages at odd times of the day and at a high frequency. As reviewed by Oregbemhe (2015), such approaches may be frustrating and annoying to consumers. In some cases, many of the promises made by these telecommunications operators to their subscribers in the course of their promotional campaigns have turned out to be well-organized deceptions, scams or well calculated moves to exploit subscribers (Etukodo, 2008; Monye, Umoh & Chinyere, 2014; Piwuna, 2016).

This chapter critically explores the ways in which the Nigerian telecom operators often fail to give a modicum of attention to consumer rights and the extent to which advertising regulatory bodies and other consumer protection associations/initiatives operating in the country come to term with this anti-consumer culture. The chapter is structured in three principal sections. The first section provides a conceptual definition of consumerism. The second section explores consumerism in the Nigerian telecom sector, while the last section deals with misleading advertisements and unsolicited commercial calls as forms of anti-consumer practices in the Nigerian telecom sector.

CONCEPTUAL AND THEORETICAL ISSUES

The term consumerism has no universally accepted conceptualization. At least two definitions can be highlighted here to show the varied prisms from which theorists, policy designers and academics have been looking at the concept. The first is relatively pejorative: it associates consumerism with the culture of inordinate consumption of goods and services; that is, the continual expansion of consumers' want and need for goods and services. Viewed from this prism, a consumer culture, policy or ideology is one that encourages consumption or the acquisition of goods and services in an increasing – and sometimes disproportionate – amount. Still viewed from this angle, the concept could refer to the ideology that the free choice of consumers should guide or dictate production in a society; this in terms of what is produced and how it is produced. This way of conceiving the economy has been criticized by some conservative schools of thought, notably Pope Benedict who describes consumerism as a culture that has little to do with modesty and human relationships. In his words, the spectacular globalization of consumerism has "turned our society into a huge multicultural showcase tied only to the tastes of certain 'consumers,' while so many others only 'eat the crumbs which fall from their masters' table'" (cited in Radio Vatican, 2015). In the same line of thought, Ndukwe (2010) contends that, as a policy or modern ideology, consumerism often creates situations wherein "approach to life, issues and projects are [...] built around consumer choices rather than work ethics, development, necessary skills or jobs. A consumer society creates a mirage of social consequences that are rooted in ideological poverty" (p.29).

The second definition of consumerism is rather positive (humanist). It construes consumerism as a consumer protection paradigm or a form of consumer activism. Viewed from this angle, the concept refers to organized movements aimed at promoting, protecting and enforcing the rights of consumers in their exchange relationship with any social entity or institution in a country. Consumerism is thus a form of well-structured activism involving both citizens and the government and aimed principally at protecting the rights of consumers in their dealings with businesses or manufacturers. Kolter (cited in Mukhtar, 2012) defines it as a social movement seeking to augment the rights and powers of the consumer vis-à-vis the seller. This brings to the fore the idea that both the seller and the buyer have rights which can be schematized as follows:

1. The seller's rights consist of: (a) the right to introduce any new product provided it does not represent a health or safety threat to the consumer. In the case where the product is hazardous for the health and safety of the consumer, the seller has the right to include proper warnings in his/her advertising campaigns; (b) the right to charge any price for the product, provided no discrimination exists among similar kinds of buyers; (c) the right to invest any amount in guise of advertising the product; this is provided that the investment does not amount to unfair competition, (d) the right to formulate his advertising messages to his liking, provided these messages are not misleading, harmful and dishonest in terms of content and execution and (e) the right to deploy any buying incentive scheme provided it is not misleading or unfair.
2. The buyer's rights on the other hand, include the following: (a) the right not to buy a product on sale, (b) the right to expect the product to be safe and (c) the right to expect the product to perform as claimed (Kehinde, 2014; Ndu, 2013; Oguchukwu, 2013).

It is popularly believed that the consumerist ideology has its root in the U.S. The movement actually followed President John Kennedy's identification of four basic rights of the consumer in 1962. These four basic rights include the following: (i) the right to safe products, (ii) the right to be informed about all relevant aspects of a product; (iii) the right to be heard and (iv) the right to choose what to buy (Ijewere & Obeki, 2011). This chapter will principally hinge on the second definition of consumerism.

CONSUMERISM IN THE NIGERIAN TELECOMMUNICATION SECTOR

Since the beginning of the year 2000, the Nigerian telecommunications sector has seen tremendous growth. This has mainly been due to the introduction of the Global System of Mobile Communications (GSM) in the country and a phenomenal growth in the number of subscribers. The Nigerian telecom sector has become one of the most burgeoning telecommunications sectors in Africa today. The sector has spectacularly jumped from less than a million connected lines in 2000 to over 130 million active GSM mobile subscriptions in 2014 and about 150 million active lines in 2017 (Nigerian Communications Commission, 2017). This constant growth is equally evidenced in the increasing revenues generated yearly by Nigerian-based telecom companies. In 2012 alone, the sector generated N1.5 trillion ($9.3 billion) in terms of revenue, out of a total of N6.7 trillion ($41 billion) generated in sub-Saharan Africa (Akintaro, 2017a; Comms Week, 2014). As the telecom sector continues to grow, issues bordering on the quality of service provided by its four main players (MTN, Airtel, Globacom and Etisalat) to consumers continually fuel public debate. As shall be discussed in the subsequent sections of this chapter, the quality of service offered by these telecom operators and their marketing/advertising campaigns have most often frustrated consumers in different ways, pushing various consumer protection associations and government institutions (particularly telecom regulatory organizations) to advance and/or put in place various mechanisms to advance consumerism in the telecom sector.

Before delving into the task of exploring consumerism in the Nigerian telecommunication sector in particular, it will be expedient to do a brief incursion into the issue of consumerism in Nigeria in general. This will help provide an overview of the phenomenon in the country.

Consumerism in Nigeria

A number of consumer protection initiatives or movements have, since the 1980s, sprung up in Nigeria. These initiatives have been driven by both governmental and non-governmental entities and have, so far, had relatively palpable impact on the promotion and protection of consumer rights in various sectors of the Nigerian economy. Government's efforts have, from many indexes, been the most visible, vocal and publicized. In effect, as early as in the 1980s, the Nigerian government has created many agencies and adopted various legal tools, dedicated to furthering the cause of consumers in the country. Some of these agencies include the Consumer Protection Agency (CPC), the Service Compact with all Nigerians (Servicom), the National Association for Food and Drugs Administration and Control (NAFDAC) and the Federal Environmental Protection Agency (FEPA) among others. Other agencies and legal instruments designed to address the issue of unwholesome dealings between manufacturers, suppliers, marketers, service providers and consumers include the following:

1. The Standards Organization of Nigeria (SON)
2. The National Lottery Regulatory Commission
3. The Civil Aviation Act (2006)
4. The National Insurance Commission
5. The Central Bank of Nigeria Act (2007)
6. The National Drug Law Enforcement Agency (NDLEA)
7. The Economic and Financial Crime Commission (EFCC)
8. The Independent Corrupt Practices Commission (ICPC)
9. The National Communication Commission (NCC)
10. The Counterfeit and Fake Drugs Decree No 21 of 1988
11. The Food and Drugs Act Cap 150 of 1990 and
12. The Poison and Pharmacy Act Cap 366 of 1990, among others.

It goes without saying that the creation of these various government agencies has followed at least two logics. The first is that any consumer activism conducted without the support of government or government legislation is bound to either be ineffective or futile. The second logic is that there has always been an imbalance in the power relationship between the consumer and the manufacturer/producer in Nigeria. Such imbalance has most often made the consumer to be vulnerable, hence the necessity for government to intervene in favor of the interest of the buyer or consumer. Ify Umenyi, the General Director of the CPC (the Apex Consumer Protection Agency of Nigeria) underscores this reality when she contends that:

Due to consumers' lack of knowledge of the characteristics and technical components of goods and services, the superior bargaining power of the supplier of goods or services over the consumer, and the fact that producers of products and services are much more endowed in terms of resources, the consumer is considered as the weaker of the two in power relations. This makes it imperative for the existence of a third party, particularly a government agency that will help to balance the power relations between consumers and producers by assisting the former in his dealings with the latter (Cited in Ijewere & Obeki, 2011, p.189).

A number of nongovernmental initiatives (consumer associations) have, at one point or another, sought to supplement the efforts of government agencies. A good case in point is the Consumer Protection Association of Nigeria (CPAN) which was created in September 1980 with the five following objectives:

1. Promote and stimulate consumers' interest and awareness of the goods they buy and the services they consume.
2. Ensure that the goods and services sold to the consumers are of good quality and merchantable.
3. Provide a suitable platform for dialogue between producers, marketers, middlemen and consumers.
4. Cooperate with government or any other association/initative to defend the interest and rights of the consumer.
5. Provide serious assistance to consumers who seek redress in an advent of dispute related to good or services purchased.

Other similar consumer associations include the Enugu Consumer Movement, the Lagos Consumer's Movement, the Tenants' Association and the Association of Market Women in Lagos among others. These indexes pointing to the availability of non-governmental consumer movements in the country have, however, not meant that the Nigerian buyer or consumer's right has always been respected. Neither have these indexes meant that the Nigerian consumer has always been able to enjoy all his or her rights. As noted by a plurality of observers, the activities of these entities have not only been restricted to small communities but have equally not received the kind of publicity that could enable them to have greater – or a national – impact (Ijewere & Obeki, 2011). It is no surprise that many Nigerians are not aware of the consumer associations that claim to defend their rights. Many citizens of Nigeria do not know the procedure they can follow to seek redress in the advent of victimization by a business enterprise. Nigerians' lack of knowledge of the existence and activities of specific consumer associations has, over the years, made many victimized Nigerian consumers to suffer in silence and not to report cases of exploitative practices. This has been a serious challenge faced by the consumer protection movement in Nigeria.

Consumer Protection Movements in the Nigerian Telecom Sector

As in other sectors of the Nigerian economy, traces of consumer activism are visible in the telecommunication sector. It will be helpful here, to mention the activities of the Nigerian Communication Commission (NCC), the main regulatory body within the sector. Created by the Nigerian Communications Act of 2003, the NCC has been designed to protect the interests of the telecom consumer among many other prerogatives. Some of its consumer centric objectives include the following:

1. To promote the provision of modern, universal, efficient, reliable, affordable and easily accessible communications services and the widest coverage throughout Nigeria.
2. To encourage local and foreign investment in the Nigerian Communications industry and the introduction of innovative services and practices in the industry in accordance with international best practices and trends.
3. To protect the rights and interests of service providers and consumers within Nigeria; and
4. To ensure that the needs of disabled and elderly persons are taken into consideration in the provision of communications services (Nigerian Communication Commission, 2003).

It is evident that, the Nigerian Communications Commission has, these last years, increasingly given greater attention to the promotion and protection of consumers' rights. This modicum of attention given to consumerism is evidenced in the fact that, since 2001, the NCC has embarked on various forms of regulatory activism aimed at (i) raising the quality of service consciousness among service providers (telecom operators), (ii) increasing the potentials in Nigeria's ICT market, and (iii) ultimately protecting the interest of telecom consumers in the country. In September 2001, the NCC established the Consumer Affairs Bureau (CAB) whose mandate has been to protect the rights, privileges and interests of consumers against unfair practices by telecom operators. Since its creation, the Bureau has been operating under the motto "Take advantage of us, so that no one takes advantage of you" – a strong recommendation addressed to consumers. This motto in theory, shows how important the telecom consumer is to the NCC.

The Commission's pro-consumer activism has also been seen in the creation of such intellectual and technical forums as the Monthly Consumer Parliament which has enabled consumers to voice their complaints or critiques of various practices among telecom operators, and to be heard by both the telecommunications operators and the regulator. The Parliament has, in effect, created a platform through which major stakeholders within the sector (operators, associations of telecommunications consumers and regulators) systematically rub minds for the ultimate development of the sector and the benefit of the consumer. It (The Parliament) has also permitted the telecom operators to have a real appreciation of the quality of service delivered to subscribers/consumers, besides subtly informing some of the major policies adopted by the NCC to deal with tariffs charged to subscribers for calls made to customer care lines, for the purpose of making their complaints. Online magazine *Comms Week* (2010) underscores the ways in which this "Parliament" has been novel and beneficial to both telecom consumer and operators. It succinctly notes that:

[Multiple] sessions of Telecom Consumer Parliament [have] helped in no small measure in creating awareness of the rights of consumers and the obligations of the service providers in the resolution of their problems and concerns. It has enabled operators to clarify issues pertaining to service delivery for the benefit of their subscribers and also to publicly give account of their stewardship to the people. Useful

feedback has emanated from the programme which culminated in far-reaching regulatory interventions by the commission (para 13).

It is important here to note that the innovative and actionable nature of the Telecom Consumer Parliament has earned the Nigerian Communications Commission acclaim, not only from national critics but equally from a wide range of international observers including the International Telecommunications Union (ITU) and ICT professionals across the globe (Monye, Umoh, & Chinyere, 2014; Piwuna, 2016).

Another consumer centric scheme adopted in recent times by the NCC has been the Industry Consumer Advisory Forum (ICAF). The establishment of this forum has been completed with the cooperation of many other consumer protection agencies, some of which include the Consumer Protection Council, the Nigerian Bar Association, the National Lottery Regulatory Commission and many other telecom advocacy bodies. The forum has been conceived to function in an advisory capacity and to make recommendations to the telecommunication regulatory agency regarding the concerns and interests of consumers of telecom products in the countries. It is purported that the creation of the ICAF is one of the consequences of various investigations which provided serious evidences of sharp anti-consumer practices by many telecom operators. NCC's commitment to curtail such sharp anti-consumer practices among telecom operators has equally pushed it to design a number of processes to review the 2007 Consumer Code of Practice Regulation. This has enabled the Code to become a reference document for both the telecom consumer and the operator. The revised version of the code stipulates a number of issues among which should be mentioned the Service Level Agreement, the responsibilities and rights of each party and procedures for resolving disagreements whenever they arise.

The NCC's growing enthusiasm for consumer protection is further seen in the fact that, on May 15 2017, it declared 2017 the year of the telecom consumer; that is a year set aside to concentrate on the welfare of the Nigerian telecom subscriber. This highly symbolic gesture has been accompanied by varied campaigns aimed to educate telecom consumers on their rights and proffer actionable (legal) strategies to seek redress in the event of violation of their rights by telecom operators. According to its General Director, Garba Dambatta, consumer sensitization is key to consumer protection in the Nigerian context. He specifically notes that the education and empowerment of the consumer constitute one of the pre-requisites for consumer protection and healthy development in the telecom sector. As he puts it: "We intend to come down to the level of the consumers in order to get him to buy into the various regulations that are consumer centric and so in the process of trying to accomplish this objective, I think the university system has important role to play" (cited in Ugochukwu, 2017, p.23).

In spite of these various mechanisms put in place by the NCC to ensure a nationwide protection of the telecom consumer, many anti-consumer practices continue to prevail in the sector, calling for more drastic, repressive and corrective measures from the regulatory agency and consumer protection associations. Some of these anti-consumer cultures include unsolicited messages, illegal deductions from customers' credit, the disruption of Internet services without prior notice to consumers, the lack of compensation for down times, the persistence of unfavourable data roll-over terms, the non-provision of detailed billing information on used data, the prevalence of unfavourable customer care centres, the ineffectiveness of customer care lines, and the existence of non-transparent sales promotion terms and conditions among others. Some of these practices – particularly those bordering on Nigeria based telecoms' advertising campaigns – will be discussed in detail in the subsequent section of this discourse.

Many consumer associations have, at different points in time, sought to complement the efforts of the NCC towards consumer protection. A case in point is the National Association of Telecommunications Subscribers (NATCOMS) which, in several instances, has appealed to telecom firms to conceive better marketing policies notably fair compensatory plans for their subscribers. Recently, the Association took the major Nigerian-based telecom operators to court for violation of consumer rights. The Association wanted 10,000 Naira worth of credit to be allocated as compensation to consumers in 2013 and 15,000 Naira worth of credit for subsequent years until the quality of service is improved. Though NATCOMS' action has so far been unfruitful, the activities of this association have constituted a good symbol of consumer activism in the burgeoning Nigerian telecom sectors.

ANTI-CONSUMER PRACTICES IN THE MARKETING/ADVERTISING CAMPAIGNS OF NIGERIAN-BASED TELECOMS

Although there exist multiple forms of anti-consumer practices in the marketing and advertising campaigns designed by Nigerian-based telecom operators, this section of the discourse will specifically give attention only to two typologies, namely unsolicited commercial calls and deceitful promotions. This selective attention may be rationalized by the fact that, firstly, it will be herculean in a study like this to exhaustively cover all anti-consumer practices by these telecom operators. Secondly, the two selected forms of anti-consumer practices have arguably been the most decried by consumer associations (Comms Week, 2010; Oregbemhe, 2015; Ugochuckwu, 2017).

Unsolicited Commercial Calls

Over the years, Nigeria-based telecom companies have entrenched the culture of deploying various forms of unsolicited commercial SMS or calls to advertise their products and services. This commercial strategy has most often been geared towards out-smarting one another. In line with this aggressive commercial approach, Nigerian telecom subscribers have most often been bombarded with all manner of advertising messages urging them to participate in telecom promotions; this, sometimes at odd periods of the day, and in total disregard of the consumer's right to privacy. Some of these unsubscribed marketing messages are "covert" methods designed by telecom networks to "force their products and services on consumers for a fee deducted from their airtime" (Akintaro, 2017, pp. 34-35). They often take the form of unsubscribed calls, beauty and health tips, and airtime borrowing among others. With this, the commercial paradigm of unsolicited commercial calls has mostly been perceived by the Nigerian intelligentsia and even large pockets of the Nigerian populace as a serious source of nuisance. According to Oregbembe (2015), these unsolicited marketing calls are in violation of telecom consumers' right to privacy as they have high potential to disturb and be frustrating. This is especially due to the fact that they are sometimes sent at odd periods of the day and care less about the consumer's free will.

The oddity and prevalence of this harmful commercial strategy have recently caught the attention of the NCC. The latter has designed a number of more or less muscled measures to deal with the situation. However, these measures have only contributed to slightly mitigate and not totally eradicate the practice. In effect, the Nigerian Communications Commission started by recognizing the harmful nature of these unsolicited messages. In its *Guidelines on Advertisements and Promotion*, it notes that:

Mobile Messages/ Mobile information, Personal and corporate information dissemination via bulk SMS is a useful service and is beneficial to the economy of the nation. However the frequency and timing of the messages have become annoyingly disturbing, leading to public apathy and resentment. In order to protect consumers from flood-like messages, the following rules shall apply (Nigerian Communications Commission, 2005, p. 42).

In addition to questioning the culture of unsolicited advertising messages, the NCC introduced and popularized a number of Do Not Disturb (DND) directives aimed at enabling telecom subscribers to control or discontinue their reception of unsubscribed messages originating from the telecom operators. The DND directives have also been designed to help consumers submit their complaints about unsatisfactory services. This DND system is conceived to be activated by subscribers by simply dialling 2442 to warn operators against unsolicited messages. The NCC also introduced the 622 code to be dialled by consumers to make complaints. Still in line with its movement against the reckless use of unsolicited advertising messages by telecom operators, the NCC has banned all messages sent to telecom subscribers who have opted out of such service. The NCC notes that:

All advertisements, product information, marketing messages and other unsolicited messages from companies, businesses and commercial houses and advertising agencies that are to be broadcasted via the mobile network can only be sent as an END-OF-CALL notification.

Such messages need not be accompanied by sender identity. A message sent as an end-of-call attachment can include contact information of sender in case the receiver is interested in the advert and wants more information. [...] Operators will be held responsible for any scam, subversive, inciting mobile advertisement sent via end-of-call notification.

All other forms of unsolicited mobile adverts are hereby barred on the mobile network, these include IVR-based adverts, SMS-based adverts and voice call based adverts (including robot calls). Also a subscriber who has given a 'do-not-disturb' notice must not be sent any form of advert (Nigerian Communications Commission, 2005, p. 51).

Despite these laudable measures, unsolicited commercial calls continue to be a sad reality in the Nigerian telecommunications sector. Many recent studies and magazine articles have reviewed interesting cases of Nigerian telecom consumers who received such unsolicited messages and whose efforts to warn operators against the practice have been in vain (Akintaro, 2017; Coms Week, 2017; Folarin, 2017; Ugochuckwu, 2017). In effect, the telecom operators have literally defied the DND directives instituted by the NCC. As Akintaro (2017b) surmises:

[Unsolicited advertising messages continuing to come] is a form of beast that seems to respect no one. Both the rich and the poor in the country suffer from its pangs, yet [their] menace [...] has refused to be tamed, as series of regulatory efforts fail to end the suffering. And as those behind the messages reject the regulator's attempt to bring them under control, there seems to be no hope that this suffering by the mass of telecom customers will go away anytime soon (p.32).

Akintaro buttresses his position with a number of testimonials from victims of this illegal practice of sending unsolicited SMS commercials. He quotes a victim (shuaib Abdulkadir) as purporting that:

I have sent the word 'STOP' to the said code several times, they never stopped sending or making unsolicited text and messages to my phone number. Last time, I received an unsolicited call from 54881, later that same day I received a message telling me that 50 naira has been deducted from my account for a subscription I never made. So I decided to unsubscribe just to avoid future deduction from my credit (Cited in Akintaro, 2017a).

The persistence of unsolicited commercial messages by Nigerian telecom operators has motivated the NCC to envisage more punitive measures. In some of their public or mediatised communications, some executive members of the NCC – notably the NCC's Vice Chairman Umaru Danbatta – have revealed the Commission's plan to introduce a five million Naira penalty for any breach of the DND code option for subscribers. This penalty is to be deployed as a last resort to bring defaulters to order. Speaking at the Academia on ITU Study Group Participation held at the Digital Bridge Institute, NCC's Vice Chairman pointedly promised that:

We are at the stage of imposing the Do Not Disturb (DND) code direction, meaning that any breach of this direction will attract a fine of ₦5 million. If a consumer lodges complaint to NCC that a MNO sent unsolicited text messages and the complaint from the consumer gets to us, we will ensure that credit deducted from the consumers for this unsolicited text messages is returned to the consumer and will also invoke provision of the fine on the MNO which is N5 million. This is to ensure total compliance and this is a measure of last resort. The NCC impose this regulation as a measure of last resort, after we have given the MNO time to ensure compliance and we have monitored them to ensure compliance to ensure that the compliance is not selective (Cited in Onynye, 2017, para 4).

This punitive measure or "threat" of extreme punitive actions has generated various reactions from the Nigerian public. Some observers have interpreted these measures as a move that may be very detrimental to such providers of value added services as bulk SMS, premium SMS, and ring back tunes. In spite of their potential "collateral damages," these extreme measures – used as last resort to bring recalcitrant Nigeria-based telecoms to order – remain a step in the right direction. They represent greater engagement to defend telecom consumers' rights in Nigeria.

Misleading and Deceptive Advertised Promotions by Telecom Companies

Another serious anti-consumer practice in the Nigerian telecom sector has been the prevalence of misleading promotions. These misleading promotions have most often taken the forms of puffing and fluffing. Through these two questionable approaches, most Nigerian telecommunications operators have embarked on giving partial or incomplete descriptions of their products, visibly to conceal their "negative" sides (the bad sides of their products). It should be noted here that an incomplete description generally consists in stating some and not all the contents of a product; while a partial description highlights what a product can do but not what it cannot do (Ozoh, 2007).

A good example of misleading advertisement is Airtel's "Unlimited Data" campaign which, among other things, expressed the operator's promise of offering its customers unlimited data and unhindered speed for upload and download at a time when Nigerian telecom consumers frequently complained about the poor quality services offered by telecom operators. At first glance, such a campaign appeared to be a real technological breakthrough that could give Airtel a clear competitive advantage. However, scratching beneath the surface reveals that the campaign happened to be a form of puffery. In effect, a check at Airtel's site clearly reveals that, far from being unlimited, the data plan advertised by the operator is limited by Fair Usage Policies (FUP). These policies state that when the consumption of Unlimited 10 reaches 40 GB, the speed will be throttled to 256 kbps. The Unlimited 15 and Unlimited 20 will both also throttle to a speed of 256 kbps when consumption gets to 65 GB and 100 GB respectively. Meanwhile the television advertisement used for this unlimited data campaign does not inform the consumers of the existence of such terms and conditions. Babalogbon (2017) rightly observes that CSG Network's download speed calculator indicates that a 100 MB file would take 51 minutes and 19 seconds to get downloaded at the speed of 256 kbps. This reveals that Airtel's offering cannot be totally unlimited. Therefore, even the name used to christen the product is outrageously misleading or at least, likely to mislead the average subscribers in their decision-making.

Like Airtel, Etisalat (another Nigeria-based telecom company) has in some of its promotional campaigns, deployed misleading advertising messages. Etukodo (2008) highlights such an anti-consumer culture when he notes that:

Recently I was attracted to a centre-spread advertisement of Etisalat Mobile Telecommunications about to be introduced into the Nigerian market, the catcher in the advertisement was a promise of free airtime for life once a consumer calls to reserve a number. As a good Nigerian, I did not waste time before calling to book my special number, after about seven minutes' conversation with the customer service representative of the company, I was informed of my success of having a reserved number that will guarantee free air time for life. The euphoria did not last after the Etisalat representative opened-up on the hidden deception by informing me that my special number will cost me N10, 000 only (p. 11).

Like Etukodo cited above, many other Nigerians have been victims of various misleading and deceptive advertising campaigns designed by Nigerian telecom operators. Some of these victims have attempted to seek redress or compensation through legal means (lawsuits). Unfortunately, their attempts have mostly been to no avail. A good example is Mr. Ozioko Pascal's suit initiated in July 2012, to seek a court order compelling Etisalat to publish the names of the winners of one of its promotions in national dailies. Ozioko's legal action also aimed at obtaining an award of N100 million as damages against the defendant (Etisalat) for allegedly misleading him in its promotion. In effect, the suit had its origin in the fact that, Etisalat allegedly launched a promotion based on unsolicited SMS messages in November 2011 which promised its customers lofty prizes to be won monthly and daily (Premium Times, 2014). The advertisements deployed by the telecom company stated that Range Rover jeeps were to be won monthly and a daily cash prize of N500,000 if subscribers answered daily questions sent to them. Each text was to cost N100 and each correct answer was to attract points to the subscriber to qualify him for the prize. In spite of its pertinence, the suit did not yield the awaited dividends.

Individual telecom users and consumer protection associations have initiated several court actions against Nigerian telecom companies for various violations of customers' rights. These actions have mostly been unfruitful or partial successes, creating the spectre of virtually untouchable telecom operators in the country. It is observable that only a few legal moves initiated by the NCC have so far yielded a number of positive fruits. In 2014, the NCC compelled three elite telecom companies in the country (MTN Nigeria, Globacom and Airtel) to pay fines of N647 million as compensation for poor services provided to Nigerian consumers between July 2013 to January 2014 (Comms Week, 2014). Such muscled actions have been lauded in many pro-consumerism quarters in the countries. However, it must be highlighted that such corrective actions – leading to the compensation of consumers by telecom operators – are very rare. As noted by an observer cited in *Comms Week* (2014), seeking compensation from Nigerian telecom operators for poor services amount to "asking the Sahara desert to bring forth ice-cold water."

FURTHER RESEARCH DIRECTIONS

This study has specifically focused on how advertising (in the form of advertised promos and unsolicited commercial calls) is used by Nigeria-based telecom operators as a tool to systematically exploit Nigerian consumers and how consumer protection movements have been fighting against such exploitation. Further research may focus on how other Nigeria-based business organizations such as banks, insurances companies, and the like violate consumers' rights in the country and how consumer protection initiatives have been organising to mitigate this situation. Other research efforts may focus on how the consumer protection movement has evolved in the country and how bodies such APCON have, these last five years, supported the movement. Another interesting research axis may have to do with exploring the extent to which consumerism is promoted in religious circles or institutions in Nigeria.

CONCLUSION

Consumers have been very central to the growth of telecom companies in Nigeria. Indeed, on a yearly basis, Nigeria-based telecom companies have been generating revenues that surpass their returns in other countries; and this has mainly been thanks to their growing number of subscribers. In spite of this positive development, the consumer has, in various ways, remained exploited by telecom companies. Two ways in which such exploitation has been perpetrated include misleading promotions and unsolicited commercial calls. This chapter has examined these anti-consumer paradigms under three principal research questions: what is the state of consumerism in the Nigerian telecom sector? What are some of the anti-consumer cultures prevailing in this sector? And how is the telecom regulatory body (the Nigerian Communications Commission) coming to terms with these anti-consumer practices?

This chapter has argued that unsolicited SMS messages and misleading and deceptive advertising represent two of the most decried anti-consumer cultures among Nigeria based telecom companies. They represent a growing menace for the Nigerian telecom user. Unsolicited SMS messages in particular have been serious sources of nuisance to most Nigerian telecom consumers particularly as they have sometimes been sent during odd periods of the day and have been used to advertise promotional schemes that are highly exploitative to the consumers. The growth in the two above mentioned practices is one of the multiple indexes pointing to the fact that most Nigerian telecoms are still largely bent on outdoing one another and on making profit even to the detriment of consumers (subscribers) – consumers who are at the base of their success or survival in the Nigerian economy.

The high prevalence of these practices has motivated the NCC and many other consumer protection associations to design some mechanisms and initiate moves to strategically deal with these challenges. This chapter has reviewed some of these mechanisms and moves, highlighting their limitations. Measures taken by the NCC – notably the introduction of the DND code/directives and the fine imposed on some elite telecom companies for poor quality of services – have to an extent reduced the issues of unsolicited SMS commercials and other anti-consumer cultures in the sector. However these cultures continue most often in some insidious ways. It could therefore be concluded that although a growing attention is given to consumerism in the Nigerian telecom sector, more actionable solutions are still to be envisaged to ameliorate the situation of the consumer.

REFERENCES

Akintaro, S. (2017a, December 14). Unsolicited messages: Subscribers lament as telcos defy "NDN" rule. *Oracle News*, 12-17.

Akintaro, S. (2017b). Consumers' plight and regulatory confusion over value added service. *IT Telecom Digest*, 32-37.

Babalogbon, O. (2017, October 13). Airtel's Unlimited Data campaign: A case of puffery. *The Nation*, 23-26.

Bishop, N. (1997). Advertising overload. *Marketing Magazine*, *15*, 42.

Comms Week. (2010, May 24). Consumer advocacy in a liberalized telecom sector. *Communications Week*. Retrieved December 12, 2017 from http:www.consumer-advocacy-in-a-liberalized-telecom-secrtor/commsweek/com

Comms Week. (2014). How telcos cheat, frustrate subscribers. *Communications Week*. Retrieved December 17, 2017, from http:www.how-telcos-cheast-frustrate-subscribers/commsweek/com

Comms Week. (2017). How telcos cheat, frustrate subscribers. *Communications Week*. Retrieved December 17, 2017, from http:www.how-telcos-cheast-frustrate-subscribers/commsweek/com

Endong, F. P. C. (2015). How ethical is print advertising by religious organizations in Nigeria. *International Journal of Media Journalism and Mass Communication*, *1*(2), 5–13.

Etukodo, M. (2008). Advertising and consumerism in Nigeria. *The Control Tower*, *2*(3), 11–24.

Folorin, B. (2017). NCC 2017 year of telecom consumer: Minister calls for adoption of made in Nigeria software. *World Stage*. Retrieved December 11, 2017 from http://worldstagegroup.com/worldstagenew/index.php?active=news&newscid=34954&catid=31

Ijewere, A. A., & Obeki, O. S. (2011). Consumerism in Nigeria. *JORIND: Journal of Research in Development*, *9*(2), 186–192.

Kehinde, O. J. (2014). Consumerism and its influences on food and drug marketing in Nigeria. *Multi-disciplinary Journal of Research Development*, *8*(5), 53–67.

Monye, F., Umoh, B., & Chinyere, C. (2014). Research report on the state of consumer protection in Nigeria: A review of consumer protection in the telecommunications sector in Nigeria. Lagos, Nigeria: Consumer International & Open Society Initiative for West Africa (OSIWA)

Mukhtar, H. (2012). The development of consumerism in Nigeria: Prospects and challenges. *International Journal of Art and Commerce*, *1*(4), 274–285.

Najeeb, U., & Mustansar, H. (2005). Impact of unethical advertising, misleading information or deceptive advertising on customer purchasing intention with mediating effect of word of mouth: Case of Pakistan. *International Journal of innovation and Economic Development, 1*(4), 49-69.

Ndu, O. A. E. (2013). Consumerism, the Nigerian experience: Study of the food and drink industries 1980-2012. *Business and Management Horizons*, *1*(2), 18–48. doi:10.5296/bmh.v1i2.4162

Ndukwe, O. (2010). Consumerism: The backbone of ideological poverty in Nigeria. *Bassey Andah Journal*, *3*, 29–47.

Nigerian Communication Commission. (2003). *The Nigerian Communication Commission Act*. Abuja, Nigeria: Government Printers.

Nigerian Communication Commission. (2017). *Guidelines on advertisements and promotion*. Abuja, Nigeria: Government Printers.

Nigerian Communications Commission. (2015). *Guidelines on advertisements and promotion*. Abuja, Nigeria: Government Printers.

Ogechuckwu, A. D. (2013). Consumerism the shame of marketing in Nigeria. Challenges to cooperate practices. *IPBJ: International Policy and Business Journal*, *5*(1), 1–30.

Onynye, U. (2017). Your network will pay a ₦5m fine if they don't stop sending you unwanted messages. *Techpoint*. Retrieved May 19, 2018 from https://techpoint.ng/2017/01/18/networks-unwanted-message-5-million-fine/

Oregbemhe, B. (2015). *Consumers Protection in Advertised Promotion and unsolicited Commercial Calls and Text Messages in Nigeria*. Retrieved September 14, 2017 from http://www.spaajibade.com/resources/consumers-protection-in-advertised-promotion-and-unsolicited-commercial-calls-and-text-messages-in-nigeria/

Ozoh, C. H. (2007). *Principles and practice of advertising*. Lagos, Nigeria: Macmillan.

Piwuna, M. G. (2016). Examination of the consumer protrection under the Nigerian Communications Commission Act 2003. *Journal of Education and Social Policy*, *3*(4), 101–111.

Premium Time. (2014). Fraudulent promo: Court grants Etisalat more time. *Premium Times*. Retrieved December 17, from https://www.premiumtimesng.com/news/163085-fraudulent-promo-court-grants-etisalat-time.html

Radio Vatican. (2015). Pope deplores consumerism and running after the latest fad. *Radio Vatican*. Retrieved December 5, 2017 from http://en.radiovaticana.va/

Ugochuckwu, U. (2017, January 18). NCC to impose N 5 Million fine on telecom that breach unsolicited SMS directives. *The Will Newspaper*, 34-35.

ADDITIONAL READING

Ajibola, A. (2014). Nigerian telecoms firm frustrate subscribers. *The Guardian*, (December), 43-62.

Chidiebere, N. C. (2017). Addressing the plight of the telecoms subscribers. *Punch*, April 11, 32-33.

Donovan, K. P., & Aaron, K. M. (2014). The rive of African SIM registration: The dynamics of regulatory change. *First Monday: Peer Reviewed Journal on the Internet*, *19*(2), 103–132. doi:10.5210/fm.v19i2.4351

KEY TERMS AND DEFINITIONS

Consumer Protection Associations: Institutions or groups involved in the protection of the consumer's rights.

Consumerism: Organized movement geared towards the protection and/or promotion of the interest of the consumer. This movement can be initiated or supported by government or individuals or groups.

Do Not Disturb Code: A code designed by the Nigerian Communication Commission (NCC) to enable the Nigerian consumer to unsubscribe from unsolicited commercial calls.

Fluffing and Puffery: A relatively questionable—though not illegal—technique of advertising product which consist in making vague claims about a product or service which cannot be proved or disproved. By this technique, the advertiser "puffs up" its product or service, to make it appear more than what it is.

MNO: Acronym used for mobile network operator.

Nigerian Communication Commission: Body responsible for regulating the telecommunications sector in Nigeria.

Unethical Advertising: A reprehensible type of advertising which often distorts or misrepresents a product or service, and which used questionable (secretive) ways of influencing audiences or readers.

Unsolicited Commercial Communications: Commercial communications sent by an operator to its customers without their request. These communications include voice mails or SMS made via telecommunications service for the purpose of informing about, soliciting or promoting commercial transaction bordering on product, service, or investment.

Section 5

Alternatives to Consumer Culture

Chapter 14
Waking Up:
Consumerism and Plato's *Republic*

C. P. Ragland
Saint Louis University, USA

ABSTRACT

Three motifs from Plato's Republic are summarized and related to contemporary consumer culture: the allegory of the cave, the three-part model of the soul, and the discussion of wage-earning. Reflection on these motifs supports the anti-consumerist educational program called for by Pope Francis in his environmental encyclical Laudato Si. Studying Plato can encourage people to think of consumerism as a waking dream, and to identify with their rational, altruistic desires. Such identification discourages thoughtless, environmentally destructive consumption.

INTRODUCTION

In his recent encyclical *Laudato Si*, Pope Francis connects the looming environmental crisis of climate change with "today's self-centred culture of instant gratification" (2015, 162/120).[1] "The present world system is certainly unsustainable," he declares, because "we have stopped thinking about the goals of human activity" (61/44), instead reveling in "extreme . . . consumerism" (50/36): "a throwaway culture which affects the excluded just as it quickly reduces things to rubbish" (22/17). This consumerism springs from what Francis calls the "technocratic paradigm" which "exalts the concept of a subject who, using logical and rational procedures, progressively approaches and gains control over an external object" (106/79), and culminates in "a technocracy which sees no intrinsic value" in non-human life (118/88).

If humans are to avoid catastrophe, Francis suggests, they must develop "a distinctive way of looking at things, a way of thinking, policies, an educational programme, a lifestyle and a spirituality which together generate resistance to the assault of the technocratic paradigm" (2015, 111/84). This new way of thinking "would necessarily have to take into account . . . philosophy and social ethics" (110/83).

This paper aims to contribute in a small way to the educational program Francis calls for. It does so by turning to a very old source of philosophical inspiration: Plato's *Republic*. Such an ancient book might seem irrelevant to a modern phenomenon like consumerism. However, ancient Athens

DOI: 10.4018/978-1-5225-6120-0.ch014

is often credited with becoming not only the world's first democracy but concurrently the world's first proper or 'full-fledged' 'money economy.' . . . Athenians were also amongst the first people in recorded history familiar with a central permanent marketplace, centred on the agora and filled with a range of goods offered by competing retailers/producers, with the experience not only of shopping—in a sense not totally dissimilar to the way it might be understood today—but of shopping around (Davidson, 2012, p. 24).

This was the economic and political environment in which Socrates and Plato lived. Socrates spent most of his time questioning people in the *agora*, and his disciple Plato penned a marvelous reflection on the basic human dynamics at work there. The *Republic* can shed considerable light both on the nature of the consumerist mentality and on the education required to escape it.

Three motifs from the work are particularly relevant: the allegory of the cave, the three-part model of the soul, and the discussion of wage-earning. This paper will first summarize and interpret the cave story, and then relate it to consumerism. From there it will move on to show how Plato's general theory of motivation and specific analysis of workplace motivations can help people begin to wake up from the consumerist dream.

BACKGROUND

Probably the most famous image in Plato's corpus, the allegory of the cave appears in Book 7 of the *Republic*. The character Socrates uses it to illustrate "the effect of education and . . . the lack of it on our nature" (2004, p. 514a). Socrates asks his interlocutors to

Imagine human beings living in an underground, cavelike dwelling, with an entrance a long way up that is open to the light and as wide as the cave itself. They have been there since childhood, with their necks and legs fettered, so that they are fixed in the same place, able to see only in front of them . . . Light is provided by a fire burning far above and behind them. Between the prisoners and the fire, there is an elevated road stretching . . . along this road a low wall has been built—like the screen in front of people that is provided by puppeteers, and above which they show their puppets. (2004, p. 514a-b5)[2]

On the other side of this wall from the prisoners are the "puppeteers": people walking on the road "carrying multifarious artifacts that project above [the wall]—statues of people and other animals" made of various materials (Plato, 2004, p. 514c-515a). With the fire behind them, these puppets or statues cast shadows onto the wall in front of the prisoners. When the puppeteers speak, their voices echo off the wall, so that the shadows themselves seem to be speaking (Plato, 2004, p. 515b7).

The prisoners are aware only of the apparently self-moving, noisy shadows. They know nothing about how these images are produced. Therefore, "what the prisoners take for true reality is nothing other than the shadows of those artifacts" (Plato, 2004, p. 515b11), and they assume that words apply "to the things they see passing in front of them" (Plato, 2004, p. 515b5). For example, they think the word "horse" refers to a certain kind of shadow before them on the wall. They think the shadow *is* a horse.

Because they take an image (the shadow) to be the very thing it represents (a horse), the prisoners are *dreaming*. For according to Socrates, to dream is "to think—whether awake or asleep—that a likeness is not a likeness, but rather the thing itself that it is like" (Plato, 2014, p. 476c4). This definition of dreaming captures what literally happens when people wake up from a very vivid dream: they realize that the events they took to be really happening during the dream were merely their own subjective images of such events. When they were "taken in" by the dream, they confused these private sensations with the sorts of real events that normally cause such sensations.

For Plato, education involves being awakened from this dream-state. It has two stages. In the first, a prisoner is "freed and suddenly compelled to stand up, turn his neck around, walk, and look up toward the light" (2004, p. 515c6) and is presented with "the things whose shadows he had seen before" (p. 515c9)—i.e. the puppets, and perhaps also the fire and the puppeteers. At first, he would consider "the things he saw earlier [i.e., the shadows] more truly real than the ones he was [now] being shown" (p. 516d5), but after adjusting (p. 516a4) to the initially dazzling and disorienting light (p. 515c7), he could grasp that the shadows are merely effects of the statues and the fire, merely images of the statues—which he would now consider to be the real things. The newly freed prisoner would now think that "horse" refers to a statue. But remaining in the cave, he would be unaware that the statue is itself merely an image of an above-ground animal. He would still be dreaming.

His full education requires a second awakening, in which someone drags him "by force away from there, along the rough, steep, upward path . . . into the light of the sun" (Plato, 2004, p. 515e6). Once his eyes have sufficiently adjusted, he will be able to see "the things themselves" (p. 516a6), that move on the surface of the earth, but also heavenly bodies, including the sun. Now fully in touch with reality, he realizes that "horse" refers to an animal outside the cave and so can finally point to the right thing if asked "what is a horse?" (whereas before, he would have pointed not to a horse but to a shadow or statue). He now knows "precisely what each image is, and also what it is an image of" (p. 520c4).

Socrates' story of liberation from the cave illustrates movement through the four levels of awareness in the divided line analogy at the end of *Republic* Book Six. These levels of awareness are individuated by their objects (Murdoch, 1993, p. 320). First, there are "visible" objects—those revealed by the senses. Of these, there are two kinds: images, such as "shadows . . . reflections of bodies in water . . . and everything of that sort" (Plato, 2004, p. 510a), and the physical objects of which those things are images (p. 510a4). Second, there are "intelligible" objects also divided into two classes: the many general forms or essences of which particular physical things are instances (e.g. the definition of "couch" which all particular couches exemplify), and the one "unhypothetical . . . first principle of everything" (Plato 2004, p. 511b6): the form of the Good.

Socrates explains the meaning of the cave story as follows:

The realm revealed through sight should be likened to the prison dwelling, and the light of the fire inside it to the sun's power. And if you think of the upward journey and the seeing of things above as the journey of the soul to the intelligible realm, you won't mistake my intention (Plato, 2004, p. 517b; see also p. 532b5-d).

Education is progress from preoccupation with the objects of the senses to an understanding of eternal realities. This movement from illusion to truth is helpfully illustrated as motion from the bottom to the top in Table 1.

In depicting this cognitive ascent, the cave story also illustrates the nature of education, for education *just is* this (difficult) process of ascent. It is not putting sight into blind eyes, but turning the eyes of the mind away from images and toward the most real thing—the Good (Plato, p. 2004, 518b5-d). Rather than teaching people to think, the true educator changes *what* they think about,[4] and so enables them

Table 1. Movement from illusion to truth

Level of Awareness	Object(s)	Analogous Object(s) in Cave Story
Noésis (understanding)	Form of the Good[3]	The Sun
Dianoia (reasoning)	Forms	Terrestrial Objects
Pistis (belief)	Physical Objects	Puppets
Eikasia (imagination)	Images	Shadows

to make progress up towards the highest form of consciousness. Because all forms—but especially the form of the Good—are standards against which their physical instances can be measured, education is a normative enterprise: it aims to help us see not only how things actually are, but also how they *ought* to be (see Plato, 2004, pp. 476a-d; 478d-480).[5] It gives us a perspective from which to criticize the injustices and deficiencies of the status quo.

For present purposes, the distinction between the top two levels in the chart is not especially important. Focus instead on the two experiences of "waking up" or perspective-shift the prisoner experiences in his educational process.[6] In the first, he realizes that shadows, which he thought were real things, are merely dream-like images (i.e. copies or representations) of the puppets. In the second, he realizes that the puppets are merely copies of above-ground things. Here, the story represents the perspective-shifts that occur when people realize that images are not real physical objects (as when they literally awake from a vivid dream), and again when they realize that physical objects are merely spatial-temporal appearances of the Forms, which are the true things themselves.

These perspective shifts divide human cognitive states into three ascending levels: preoccupation with images, awareness of physical objects, and knowledge of forms. These three levels map onto three states that modern people occupy in mentally escaping consumer culture: (1) the stage of ideology and the commodity fetish, (2) an awareness of the true sources of products and their meanings, and (3) an awareness of values not dependent on those sources.

CONSUMERISM AS LIFE IN THE CAVE

In her book *Carried Away,* Rachel Bowlby (2000) notes:

Consumer culture lends itself to images of unconscious imprisonment. The deluded are unaware that their desires are for worthless or superfluous things, or that they are shaped—if not entirely created—by the skills and tricks of advertising and other forms of presentation. They do not know that there is a better and freer world than the shopping world in which they find themselves; for them it has no exit, nor do they seek one (p. 3).

As Bowlby depicts them, hapless modern consumers are in roughly the same position as the prisoners in Plato's cave. Most know next to nothing about the origins of the products they buy, nor do they stop to consider how such products get their value.

Modern consumers are accustomed to buying products without knowing much about how they are made. Sitting on their store shelves, these products

. . . speak for themselves, calling out to us . . . to buy them and take them home. They say little, however, of how they were produced: bright sweaters tell us nothing of the well-lit garment factories or dark sweatshops where they were produced; the glistening steaks in the meat counter are silent about the open plains or cramped feedlots where the cattle from which they were butchered lived; our electronics are mum about whether the tantalum in their capacitors was mined in Australia or in a way that perpetuated violent conflict in the Democratic Republic of Congo (Miller, 2014, pp. 2-3).

In their ignorance of how these products are made, consumers exactly resemble Plato's cave prisoners, who see the shadows but have no inkling of how they are produced.[7]

Even if their mode of production is hidden, the *value* of products seems obvious. But what exactly is this value, and where does *it* come from? Reflection on these questions reveals something illusory about the value of products (or at least reveals that their value is much more complex than it first seems to be). As Miller (2004) notes, "the commodity appears to us as intrinsically valuable, when in fact its true value is dependent on a number of factors that do not appear with it" (p. 36).

The commodity illusion that Miller points to is similar to a familiar illusion regarding color. It is natural for people (especially children) to think that physical objects have a property, color, which exactly resembles their sensations of color. They think, to put it somewhat simplistically, that the yellow *color they see* is really in the daffodils even when no one is looking at them. But that is an illusion. A more reflective, modern-scientific approach to the world concedes that *color as seen* is mind-dependent, varying in its experienced quality according to variations in the perceiver (the same stop sign does not have the same color appearance to a color-blind person as to a non-color-blind person). The quality of color requires a *relation* between viewer and object, even though it *appears*—this is the illusion—to be intrinsic to the object alone.

Similarly, just a little reflection reveals that the economic value of commodities cannot be inherent in them. Consider diamonds. Would they be worth anything if no one cared about them or wanted to buy them? Surely not. Their value is a function of supply and demand, and the more fundamental creator of value there is the demand. Economic value is a function of human desire. It is a relative value, and insofar as people experience it as absolute or intrinsic to commodities, they are deluded.[8] And yet this is precisely how most people unreflectively think about commodity value: they see it as inherent in the things themselves, just as they unreflectively think that color *as experienced* belongs to objects independently of experience. They see the value of products, but not the hidden sources of this value (indeed, the illusion is that this value *has* no other sources). In this respect, most people resemble the cave prisoners.

Among these hidden sources lie the powerful associations created in people's minds by advertisements and other media images. These images create an artificial context for the product, a vivid story giving it meaning and value (what Jean Baudrillard calls the "sign value" of products) (Miller, 2004, pp. 60-63).[9] Thanks to the near omnipresence of advertising in modern life, people remain keenly aware of this made-up story even as they are usually almost completely ignorant of the product's *real* story (of production, distribution, etc.).

The advertisers who create this sign-value resemble the puppeteers in Plato's story of the cave. The shadows on the cave wall have *meaning* for the cave prisoners only in relation to one another and to the voices of the puppeteers bouncing off the wall. Only when the prisoners can begin to discern patterns in those relations can they be said to *understand* what they are seeing (for example, if a cow-shadow is always or usually followed by a lion-shadow, the prisoners will come to understand that the presence of a "cow" *means* that a lion is likely coming next). Because the puppeteers control the patterns exhibited by the shadows, they also control what the shadows will mean to the prisoners. In the same way (though clearly not to the same extent), advertisers control the meanings people assign to products by creating associations in ads. It can be difficult to gauge the extent to which one's evaluation of any *particular* product depends on the influence of any particular ad or marketing strategy (just as it is difficult to trace the history of any particular product), but the general influence of advertising seems obvious. Otherwise, why would U.S. Corporations spend over $180 billion on advertising in one year alone? (eMarketer, 2014).

Advertising exemplifies a more general similarity between modern consumers and the cave prisoners: a large part of people's contact with the world is mediated rather than direct. According to one interpreter, Plato uses the term "imagination" (exemplified by the cave prisoners staring at shadows) to denote "the sorts of second-hand, uninformed views that people hold, not finding out for themselves about the world, but just believing what they are told, e.g. in the newspapers" (Lacewing, n.d., p. 1). Because it is impossible to find out many facts directly for themselves, people cannot escape relying on "imagination" in this sense for much, if not most, of their factual knowledge. But what *sense* or *meaning* do they make of these facts, and to what extent is that controlled by the nature of the media that bring the messages? Noting this parallel between modern people and the cave dwellers, Iris Murdoch (1993) once wrote: "The technical excellence of television (the Cave) leads us to accept vivid scrappy images and disconnected oddments of information as insight into truth" (p. 13).

More importantly, for those awash in images like no people before in human history, media play a very large role in defining behavioral conventions. And as C.D.C. Reeve puts it in his introduction to the *Republic*, "it is these conventions that largely determine a subject's conception of justice and the other virtues. By being trained to follow or obey them, therefore, a subject is unwittingly adopting an ideology" (Plato, 2004, p. xiii). In short, media powerfully shape people's sense not only of facts but also of values, of who they *ought* to be and what kind of world they *ought* to live in, of what questions are worth asking and which are not. And though it is paranoid to fear a dark cabal of business barons pulling the strings of the media machine, there can be no doubt that the impersonal market forces of global capitalism act as puppeteers in the contemporary situation. In the repeated practices of everyday life (e.g. buying food and eating it), people reinforce the norms they have been taught, "valuing things without asking" (Miller, 2004, p. 38) where they came from or where they are going, because those questions do not seem *worth* asking.

Advertisers and media images (and the corporations behind them) wield power over people largely by shaping their desires. They control what people value by training them to want some things and not others. Consumers act as they wish and so are free in a sense, but their desires themselves have been manipulated. As Pope Francis notes,

Since the market tends to promote extreme consumerism in an effort to sell its products, people can easily get caught up in a whirlwind of needless buying and spending. Compulsive consumerism is one example of how the techno-economic paradigm affects individuals. This paradigm leads people to believe that they are free as long as they have the supposed freedom to consume. But those really free are the minority who wield economic and financial power (2015, 203/149-50).

Economic value is a creature of desire, a point that will be important to keep in mind in exploring what it might look like for people to "wake up" from their contemporary state of consumerist "imagination."

Waking up requires growing up to some extent. A great deal of research "documents that children evaluate marketing communications less critically than adults because they have not yet developed the advertising knowledge and cognitive skills necessary to cope effectively with advertising messages" (Connell, Brucks, & Nielson, 2014, p. 120). In other words, children are easily persuaded and so are in some ways ideal consumers from a marketer's point of view (not to mention the fact that they form a crucial bridge between marketers and parents' pocketbooks (see Schor, 2004). Children lack the reflective capacity to grasp how their own desires (as shaped by the images and cultural habits around them) inject value into the products they crave. They simply see the value as intrinsic to the products. Waking up and shattering the power of this illusion requires first developing adult cognitive capacities. But it also requires *using* those capacities—something that people in today's culture are rarely urged to do. As Benjamin Barber (2008) has noted, market forces conspire both to sell things to children and to "infantilize" adults (pp. 5-7)—to keep them more childlike—so that "Shakespeare's seven ages of man are in danger of being washed away by lifelong puerility" (p. 3).[10]

If they swim against the tide and awake from childlike imagination, if they realize that economic value is relative to our desires, people are bound to raise some crucial philosophical questions: (1) Is *all* value economic, or are there sources of value that lie outside the system of exchange? (2) If there are other kinds of value, are they *like* economic value? Is there any goodness intrinsic to things, or is it all relative to the pleasure people take in it?

Plato clearly answers both these questions in the affirmative. The Good is not relative to human thoughts or desires, but rather absolutely real and independent of any human systems of exchange or ideology—just as the sun shines above-ground regardless of the goings-on in the cave. Plato would say that people can—and should—ask whether the economy is just, whether media images are accurate or misleading, whether their desires themselves are appropriate. The entire economy and consumer culture are the cave, and to "wake up" for the second time is to realize that one is capable of standing outside them (if only briefly in moments of reflection) and evaluating them by holding them against absolute standards. In light of this evaluation, one can work to change the respects in human culture that fall short.

But it is possible to criticize consumer culture without agreeing with Plato on both these points. The "second awakening" that enables criticism does not depend on non-economic standards being absolute (not relative to desires). Though many religious thinkers more-or-less identify God with Plato's form of the good[11] and hence believe in absolute standards, others hold that moral standards are relative to God's desires. Non-religious people might hold that moral standards are relative to altruistic desires in human beings. All these meta-ethical positions are consistent with the possibility of a second awakening—a coming to awareness that *economic* values do not define moral goodness, but are accountable to more fundamental or important non-economic values (in roughly the same way that the person who gets out of Plato's cave comes to understand that the puppets do not define the natures of animals, but are merely more-or-less accurate approximations of the real natures existing above ground). The key question is whether a realm of value exists outside the economy. If so, then criticism of the status quo is possible.

It might seem obvious that there *are* more fundamental non-economic values rooted in the nature of human relationships and love. But it is possible to think of even these in economic terms. Miller (2004) recounts an example of such thinking:

Commodity logic is insidious. It preinterprets dimensions of our existence that we consider separate from economic calculus. I once overheard a young man's response to a criticism of his fiancée's appearance. In defense of his choice of spouse, he noted the many other things that she offered: intelligence, psychological depth, compatiblility, companionship, and so on . . . the response shared with the challenge the same crass logic of exchange. Physical attractiveness and psychological compatibility are of course perennial factors in romantic desire, but this logic transforms them. Love is reduced to a calculus of maximum returns, relationship to an exchange of emotional commodities . . . This logic is our cultural default, the form in which we are most likely to cast our deliberations. The question of why we love someone is reflexively translated into a question about what we love about them (p. 37).

Few would *say* that they think all value is economic, but do their actions betray them?

Those who think that all value is created by the system of exchange (and the human desires behind it) will not be able to "wake up" a second time, but will be like a prisoner who comes to the see how the shadows are produced, but never learns about the world outside the cave. Such a person would be in a position to see that the puppeteers dominate the lives of the prisoners, but would lack any standards for assessing the truth or falsehood of the puppeteer's depictions of things. Plato's character Thrasymachus in the *Republic* seems to be in this position. He realizes that by controlling the system of education, rulers instill moral convictions and conventional practices in those they rule. But he does not believe in any higher standards by which the ruler's practices can be assessed. So he reaches the cynical conclusion that the best sort of life is that of a tyrant (2004, p. 344a-d), who can do whatever he wants and make it legal (and perhaps even "right" in the opinion of the people). Similarly, the cynical person in our day would probably conclude that the best life is one of greatest economic power, which would allow one to manipulate the system that manipulates the minds of the masses. Such a person would naturally seek to exploit the system rather than tear it down or try to "wake up" other people. As Pope Francis puts it: "When human beings place themselves at the centre, they give absolute priority to immediate convenience and all else becomes relative" (2015, 122/90).

The key to emerging from the consumerist cave is to focus and act on our desires for *non-economic* goods, things that do not get their value through exchange. Plato's tripartite theory of the soul offers a helpful way of understanding such desires by situating them within a larger theory of human motivation.

THE THREE PARTS OF THE SOUL

In *Republic* 435b through 442, Plato depicts the human psyche as composed of three basic parts: the "irrational and appetitive element" with which the soul "feels passion, hungers, thirsts, and is stirred by other appetites"; the rational part "with which it calculates"; and the "spirited element . . . with which we feel anger" (2004, p. 439d-e5). Elsewhere, each of the three parts is defined in terms of the kind of thing it desires, loves, and enjoys. The appetitive part is called the "money-loving" part of the soul, because its intense "appetites for food, drink, sex, and all the things that go along with them . . . are most easily satisfied by means of money," (2004, p. 580e-581a) and hence "its pleasure and love are for profit" (p. 581a3). The spirited part aims wholly at "mastery, victory, and high repute" and so is called the "honor-loving" part of the soul (2004, p. 581b, see also p. 550b7). The rational part "is always wholly straining to know where the truth lies" and so is called the "learning-loving and philosophic" element of the soul (p. 581b-c).

Cooper (1984) helpfully clarifies some important aspects of these three distinct motivational systems. First, while desires for food, drink and sex are the *clearest* examples of appetitive motivation, they are by no means the only appetitive motivations. The drives of the appetitive part are those that "have their ultimate origin simply in facts of experience, in the fact that the person in question happens to get a certain pleasure from doing these things" (p. 12). In other words, appetite pursues pleasant feelings, whether of the body or the mind. It is even possible to appetitively dabble in philosophy for the fun of it (Cooper, 1984; Plato, 2004).

According to Cooper (1984), the spirited part is

that wherein one feels a) the competitive drive to distinguish oneself from the run-of-the-mill person, to do and be something noteworthy within the context provided by one's society and its scheme of values; b) pride in oneself and one's accomplishments, to the extent that one succeeds in this effort; c) esteem for noteworthy others and (especially) the desire to be esteemed by others and by oneself (p. 14).

It expresses itself in the desire "to be effective both in one's own private life and in the community's" (Cooper, 1984, pp. 12-13).

Finally, the rational part concerns itself not merely with a theoretical search for truth (though it *is* concerned with that), but also with the practical pursuit of goodness. According to Cooper, "what is inherent in reason is the desire for good as such—not the desire for any particular good;" in other words, this is "the desire on the part of reason to work out the ends of life on its own and to achieve them" (1984, p. 8). So the rational part seeks to know truth in order to live well (but also seeks truth for its own sake because simply knowing the truth about certain questions is *part* of living well).

Interestingly, these three parts of the soul map onto the three stages of awareness discussed above in connection with the allegory of the cave. The appetitive part is fundamentally concerned with good *feelings*, which are subjective perceptual states much like the sensations and mental images by means of which people perceive the world. Plato would surely include all such images and feelings as part of "imagination" since they can (at least in principle) be experienced in vivid dreams. So, the appetitive part is at home at the level of images, and would be unfazed by thought that the good feelings it enjoys might be illusory—produced by computers as in *The Matrix*,[12] say, or by Descartes' evil demon—for veridical or not, such sensations still *feel* the same.

The spirited part is concerned with real physical things—the objects of Plato's second level of awareness (belief). When people desire to have a good reputation, they are not just looking to *feel like* other people appreciate them; they want others *actually* to hold them in high regard. This requires that the world outside one's mind be a certain way (the other people need to really exist, to be thinking about one, to have positive feelings in so thinking, etc.). Nevertheless, the spirited part's concern with social reality is fundamentally self-regarding: the concern is with how one appears to others (love of honor) and with how dominant one is in the social order (love of victory and control). The only motivation here is to climb in the current social system (as mentioned above in the discussion of Thrasymachus); there is no capacity to evaluate that system.

For Plato, only the rational part is capable of getting in touch with the Forms or objective values, and so reaching the highest levels of consciousness (see Plato (2004, p. 585d-587)). This awareness of forms—especially that of the Good—puts it into a position to see what is best for the soul as a whole and to exercise foresight on its behalf (this is why Plato thinks the rational part both wants to and should "rule" the soul—i.e., determine how one behaves) (p. 441e). But more importantly, the rational part also enables a person to grasp the common good not just of oneself but also of *society*. Through it, one can understand how to "contribute [one's] own work for the common use of all" (p. 369e), to make one's life a gift to others. Through it, one can see where current social arrangements undermine the common good, and can begin to work to change them.

The three parts of the soul, then, fall on a scale from most self-centered (appetitive part) to most altruistic (the rational part), a "series with egoistic fantasies at one end and . . . mystical selflessness" at the other (Murdoch, 1993, p. 320). Plato sees education as the gradual empowerment of the rational part, and hence as a turning away from egoism toward altruism.

Modern marketing largely seeks to exploit the appetitive and spirited motivational systems. It might seem that marketing—since it is trying to get us to spend money—targets only the appetitive or "money-loving" part. But as (Davidson, 2012) notes, ancient Athenians associated spending money almost exclusively with ephemeral bodily pleasures. They did not engage, as modern people do, in purchasing goods in order to project social status (or at least, they did not do this to nearly the same extent). Noting this fact of modern society in 1759, Adam Smith remarked in his *Theory of Moral Sentiments* that the only true advantages of wealth are "to be observed, to be attended to, to be taken notice of with sympathy, complacency, and approbation" (Smith, 2002, p. 61). And as Juliet Schor (1998) emphasizes, in today's society, people use clothes and all sorts of other purchased products and services to communicate their social status (pp. 25-64). In modern times, money has become an easy means for satisfying the desires of *both* the appetitive part and spirited parts.

To a certain extent, it is possible to purchase social status (or at least the *signs* of it), and this social function of products has arguably eclipsed their role of giving physical satisfaction. Consumer desire is driven by fantasy, and "our fantasies . . . reveal the centrality of gaining others' esteem" (Schor, 1998, p. 71). As Burns and Warren (2008) note, in today's world "the importance attributed to products arises not from the physical needs they fulfill, but from their ability to establish one's identity or one' self—to display who we are to others" (p. 45). In this competition for social position, "others are viewed as 'enemies,' being the target selves to which one's self is compared" (p.45). Consumers are at war with one another, and "products become the weapons used" (p.45). Marketers become arms dealers, relentlessly appealing to our competitive social desires (for connection and status) to motivate us to purchase products (Burns & Warren, 2009).

So one key to waking up from the consumerist dream is to check one's own motivations. What is one's predominant goal? To *feel* good? Or to get status? Or rather to be one's best self, contributing to the common good? Does that best self really need the product here on offer? Plato's insightful breakdown of the types of motivation can help people get clear insight into themselves on these points.

The *Republic* also teaches that because the rational part of the soul is essential to human nature—and is indeed the most truly human part of the soul[13]—no way of life that frustrates it can be deeply satisfying. If people act only on the basis of selfish appetite or concern for our reputation, they miss the deepest pleasures in life (Plato, 2004). This point becomes abundantly clear in Plato's discussion of wage-earning.

WORK VS. WAGE-EARNING

In book I of the *Republic*, Plato (2004) draws an important distinction between the practice of an art or craft, and the practice of earning a wage (see pp. 346-347). Each art or job aims at some particular benefit, and this benefit defines the function of the job. So for example, the function of medicine is to produce health, the function of housing construction is to produce and house, and the function of wage-earning is to get money. Now suppose someone constructs a house, and through the prolonged strenuous physical activity involved, becomes more healthy. He has produced health in himself by building a house. Does this mean that he is now a doctor and that house-building is medicine? Certainly not. For even if house-building produces health, that is not its *function*—its principal intended aim, the thing that only it can do, or that it does better than anything else (Plato, 2004, p. 353b). In the same way, wage-earning is not medicine even if one becomes healthy in the process of earning one's wages.

Most importantly for Plato's argument, the converse is also true: medicine is not wage-earning, "even if someone earns pay while healing" (p. 346b9). In most situations, the doctor plays two distinct roles. In the role as doctor, patient health is promoted. In the role as wage-earner, money is acquired from this activity. The wage-earning is not essential to medicine, as is clear from the example of *pro bono* treatment. If the doctor is not paid, no benefit is derived from the activity, but the patient gets the benefit of health, which is medicine's aim. The doctor is still a doctor, but not a wage earner.

Notice that wage-earning is egoistic: it is about getting benefits for oneself. Most other arts or jobs are, according to Plato's analysis, altruistic: they benefit someone else (e.g. the patient). In their work life, most people are simultaneously seeking to serve others (by doing a job for them) and to serve themselves (by earning wages).

But which of these two roles do they view as primary or more fundamental? Do they seek first to live in a way that does good for others, and enjoy wages as a kind of side-effect of this activity, or do they primarily seek for wages and serve others only as a means to this end? In other words, do they see helping others as intrinsically valuable, as worth doing for its own sake, or only valuable as a means to money (and ultimately, consumption)?

To take consumption as one's ultimate end is to embody what Homer Warren (2014) calls "consumer consciousness," working "for the sole purpose of making money to buy things" (p. 5). Consumer consciousness alienates people from their work. The work is not something they do because they want to do it, not a free expression of themselves. It has no intrinsic value for them, only extrinsic value insofar as it produces a wage that they can spend in consumption, when they are "really alive." Consumer consciousness produces "the estrangement of workers from self-realization in their labor" (Miller, 2004, p. 34).

If, on the other hand, people see intrinsic value in doing something for others, if they have what Warren calls "producer consciousness," then work will not be drudgery but a form of creative self-expression. A recent research review showed that "you're more likely to like your job if you focus on the work itself, and less likely to enjoy it if you're focused on money" (Chamorro-Premuzic, 2013). Aware of this, the management expert Peter Drucker once delared: "Most people need to feel that they are here for a purpose, and unless an organization can connect to this need to leave something behind that makes this a better world, or at least a different one, it won't be successful over time" (*The Drucker Institute*, 2013). Drucker saw that employees' sense of purpose is crucial for the health of organizations. But it is also crucial to each employee's *own* wellbeing.

Based on their "comprehensive global study of more than 150 countries," (Rath & Harter, 2010, p. 4) and over fifty years of polling, Gallup developed an assessment of overall wellbeing that involves five essential elements: "Career Wellbeing, Social Wellbeing, Financial Wellbeing, Physical Wellbeing, and Community Wellbeing" (Rath & Harter, 2010, p. 6). Career Wellbeing is essentially enjoyment of one's work, and it flows from the worker's sense of purpose and intrinsic value of the work. "People with high Career Wellbeing wake up every morning with something to look forward to doing that day .

. . [they] have a deep purpose in life and a plan to attain their goals" (Rath & Harter, 2010, p. 28). Gallup's analysis found that

Career Wellbeing is arguably the most essential of the five elements. If you don't have the opportunity to regularly do something you enjoy—even if it's more of a passion or interest than something you get paid to do—the odds of your having high wellbeing in other areas diminish rapidly. People with high Career Wellbeing are more than twice as likely to be thriving in their lives overall (p. 16).

Enjoying one's work is probably so important to overall wellbeing because people get much of their sense of identity from work (this is evidenced by the fact that prolonged unemployment is "the only major life event from which people do not fully recover within five years" (Rath & Harter, 2010, p. 16); life satisfaction can rebound much more easily from the death of a spouse than from prolonged unemployment (p. 17)).

This research demonstrates a practical paradox of consumer consciousness. The more one values things only insofar as they maximize one's own pleasure and happiness, the less joy one will find in work. Gallup found that "engaged workers [i.e. those who saw their work as intrinsically meaningful] had similar happiness levels on working and nonworking days . . . However, disengaged workers experienced dramatic drops in happiness and interest—as well as major increases in stress—during working days (Rath & Harter, 2010, p. 21). But, out of necessity, most people have to spend at least half their waking lives working, and the lack of joy in working corrodes well-being in other areas. So when people see only their own pleasure and happiness as intrinsically valuable, they inevitably *bring down* their overall pleasure and happiness! St. Francis was right: it is in *giving* that we receive. People are better off when focusing their attention primarily on the well-being of *others*.

FUTURE RESEARCH DIRECTIONS

Further development of an anti-consumerist educational program (such as the one called for by Pope Francis) would benefit from research along several lines, posed here as questions. What is nature of the "technocratic paradigm," and what are its historical and psychological origins? What concepts and narratives, if any, are most effective at actually reducing consumption among people exposed to them? Are the Platonic motifs studied here translatable to non-Western cultural contexts, especially in regions (e.g. Africa, Southeast Asia) where development is rapidly underway? If not, are similarly effective motifs available in local culture (religion, philosophy, etc.)? Answers to such questions would aid implementation of an educational program that militates against the technocratic paradigm.

CONCLUSION

It is fitting to close by returning to some words from Pope Francis. *Laudato Si* contains a reference to Plato's rational part of the soul and its orientation toward the objective, non-economic values of truth, goodness, and beauty:

. . . all is not lost. Human beings, while capable of the worst, are also capable of rising above themselves, choosing again what is good, and making a new start, despite their mental and social conditioning. We are able to take an honest look at ourselves, to acknowledge our deep dissatisfaction, and to embark on new paths to authentic freedom. No system can completely suppress our openness to what is good, true and beautiful, or our God-given ability to respond to his grace at work deep in our hearts. I appeal to everyone throughout the world not to forget this dignity which is ours. (Francis, 2015, 205/151)

Let us hope that Pope Francis is right, and that a deep dissatisfaction with consumerism will motivate people to wake up—before it is too late.

ACKNOWLEDGMENT

The research and writing of this paper were made possible by a stipend from the Lilly Fellows Program and a Mellon summer research grant from the Saint Louis University College of Arts and Sciences. The author is grateful for their support.

REFERENCES

Anselm. (2001). *Proslogion with the replies of Gaunilo and Anselm* (T. Williams, Trans.). Indianapolis, IN: Hackett.

Barber, B. (2008). *Consumed: How markets corrupt children, infantilize adults, and swallow citizens whole*. New York, NY: W. W. Norton & Company.

Bowlby, R. (2000). *Carried away: The invention of modern shopping*. London, UK: Faber and Faber.

Burns, D. J., & Warren, H. B. (2008). Consumer warfare: Implications for marketing strategy. *The Journal of Business Strategy*, *29*(6), 44–52. doi:10.1108/02756660810917237

Burns, D. J., & Warren, H. B. (2009). Are marketers nothing more than arms dealers? *Journal of Business Management and Change*, *4*(1), 9–26.

Chamorro-Premuzic, T. (2013). Does money really affect motivation? A review of the research. *Harvard Business Review*. Retrieved June 18, 2015 from https://hbr.org/2013/04/does-money-really-affect-motiv

Connell, P. M., Brucks, M., & Nielsen, J. H. (2014). How childhood advertising exposure can create biased product evaluations that persist into adulthood. *The Journal of Consumer Research*, *41*(1), 119–134. doi:10.1086/675218

Cooper, J. M. (1984). Plato's theory of human motivation. *History of Philosophy Quarterly*, *1*(1), 3–21.

Cornford, F. M. (1965). Mathematics and dialectic in the Republic VI-VII. In Studies in Plato's metaphysics (pp. 61-96). London, UK: Routledge & Kegan Paul.

Davidson, J. (2012). Citizen consumers: The Athenian democracy and the origins of Western consumption. In The Oxford handbook of the history of consumption (pp. 23-46). Oxford, UK: Oxford University Press.

Dixsaut, M. (1997). What is it Plato calls thinking? *Proceedings of the Boston Area Colloquium in Ancient Philosophy*, *13*(1), 1–27. doi:10.1163/2213441797X00037

eMarketer. (2014). Total US ad spending to see largest increase since 2004. *eMarketer*. Retrieved June 15, 2015, from http://www.emarketer.com/Article/Total-US-Ad-Spending-See-Largest-Increase-Since-2004/1010982

Francis. (2015). *Encyclical Letter Laudato Si' of the Holy Father Francis on Care for our Common Home*. Retrieved from https://theyear2015.wikispaces.com/file/detail/papa-francesco_20150524_enciclica-laudato-si_en.pdf/554210024

Hyland, D. A. (1995). *Finitude and transcendence in the Platonic dialogues*. Albany, NY: State University of New York Press.

Lacewing, M. (n.d.). *Plato's similes of the cave and the divided line*. Retrieved January 15, 2018 from http://documents.routledge-interactive.s3.amazonaws.com/9781138793934/A2/Plato/PlatoSimilesLineCave.pdf

Marx, K. (1990). *Capital: A critique of political economy* (B. Fowkes & D. Fernbach, Trans.). London, UK: Penguin Books.

Miller, V. J. (2004). *Consuming religion: Christian faith and practice in a consumer culture*. New York, NY: Continuum.

Miller, V. J. (2014). Slavery and commodity chains: Fighting the globalization of indifference. *America: The National Catholic Review*. Retrieved January 15, 2018 from http://americamagazine.org/issue/slavery-and-commodity-chains-fighting-globalization-indifference

Murdoch, I. (1993). *Metaphysics as a guide to morals*. New York, NY: Penguin Press.

Plato. (2004). *Republic* (C. D. C. Reeve, Trans.). Indianapolis, IN: Hackett.

Pope Francis. (2015). *Laudato Si*. Vatican City: Libreria Editrice Vaticana.

Rath, T., & Harter, J. K. (2010). *Wellbeing: The five essential elements*. New York, NY: Gallup Press.

Schor, J. (1998). *The overspent American: Upscaling, downshifting, and the new consumer*. New York, NY: Basic Books.

Schor, J. (2004). *Born to buy: The commercialized child and the new consumer culture*. New York, NY: Scribner.

Smith, A. (2002). *The theory of moral sentiments*. Cambridge, UK: Cambridge University Press. doi:10.1017/CBO9780511800153.005

The Drucker Institute. (2013). *The purpose of purpose*. The Drucker Institute. Retrieved January 14, 2018, from http://www.druckerinstitute.com/2013/04/purpose-of-purpose/

Wallace, D. F. (2009). *This is water: Some thoughts, delivered on a significant occasion, about living a compassionate life*. New York, NY: Little, Brown, and Company.

Warren, H. (2014). *Replacing consumer consciousness with producer consciousness*. Unpublished.

ADDITIONAL READING

Browning, B. (2013). What price, the soul?: Examining consumerism through Plato, Aristotle and the Stoics. *Hohonu 11* [online]. Retrieved April 7, 2018 from https://hilo.hawaii.edu/campuscenter/hohonu/volumes/documents/WhatPricetheSoulExaminingConsumerismThroughPlatoAristotleandtheStoicsBenjaminBrowning.pdf

Corner, J., & Pels, D. (2003). *Media and the restyling of politics: Consumerism, celebrity, and cynicism*. London, UK: Sage.

Davidson, A. (2001). *Technology and the contested meanings of sustainability*. Albany, NY: State University of New York Press.

Dobson, A. (1999). *Fairness and futurity: Essays on environmental sustainability and social justice*. New York, NY: Oxford University Press. doi:10.1093/0198294891.001.0001

Harris, D. (2000). *Cute, quaint, hungry, and romantic: The aesthetics of consumerism*. New York, NY: Da Capo Press.

Newton, L. H. (2003). *Ethics and sustainability: Sustainable development and the moral life*. Upper Saddle River, NJ: Prentice-Hall.

Trentmann, F. (2016). How humans became 'consumers:' A history. *The Atlantic* [online]. Retrieved April 7, 2018 from https://www.theatlantic.com/business/archive/2016/11/how-humans-became-consumers/508700/

Trimble, R. (2014). The desire for "more" is killing us: Lessons from Plato's Republic. *Refine the Mind* [online]. Retrieved April 7, 2018 from http://www.refinethemind.com/desire-killing-us-lessons-platos-republic/

KEY TERMS AND DEFINITIONS

Allegory: A story or image that carries a hidden meaning.

Appetitive: Characteristic of or pertaining to appetite.

Association: A link or connection between two states of mind, such as the tendency to think of a word's meaning upon seeing the word.

Commodity: An item of trade or commerce.

Illusion: An appearance that makes things seem different from how they actually are.

Intelligible: Able to be understood by the intellect.

Rational: Characteristic of or pertaining to reason.

ENDNOTES

1 References to Pope Francis (2015) use the following system: (paragraph number/page number of the pdf version found at https://theyear2015.wikispaces.com/file/detail/papa-francesco_20150524_enciclica-laudato-si_en.pdf/554210024).

2 References to the *Republic* refer to the standard "Stephanus" page numbers. Line numbers, when included, are approximate. All quotations are from the translation by C. D. C. Reeve in Plato (2004).

3 The claim here that understanding involves awareness of the Good is controversial. Lacewing, for example, implies that *dianoia* and *noesis* are distinguished by a difference not of object (both get us in touch with the Good along with all the other forms) but rather of how the mind relates to the object. This reading is not implausible. However, the following three passages suggest that understanding involves a grip on the Good in a way that reasoning does not. First, at the close of the allegory of the cave, Socrates says:

In the knowable realm, the last thing to be seen is the form of the good, and it is seen only with toil and trouble. Once one has seen it, however, one must infer that it is the cause of all this is correct and beautiful in anything, that in the visible realm it produces both light and its source, and that in the intelligible realm it controls and provides truth and understanding; and that anyone who is to act sensibly . . . must see it (Plato, 2004, pp. 517b5-c5).

Second, Socrates earlier claims that just as the sun "not only gives visible things the power to be seen but also provides for the coming-to-be, growth, and nourishment," so also the form of the Good is responsible for not only for "the objects of knowledge . . . being known," but also for their "existence and being." (Plato, 2004, p. 509b5). Together, these passages seem to imply that the Good is the source of being not only for the sun and all its products, but also for the many other forms. It is, in short, the first principle of everything, and so it seems to be the key object Socrates mentions in this (third) passage describing the difference between reasoning and understanding:

by [understanding] I mean what reason itself grasps by the power of dialectical discussion, treating its hypotheses, not as first principles, but as genuine hypotheses (that is, stepping stones and links in a chain), in order to arrive at what is unhypothetical and the first principle of everything. Having grasped this principle, it reverses itself and, keeping hold of what follows from it, comes down to a conclusion . . ." (Plato 2004, 511b-c).

Taken all together, these three passages suggest that "the supreme power, which unifies the Forms, is the Form of the Good" (Murdoch, 1993, p. 10), and that understanding involves a grasp of this unity behind all plurality in a way that reasoning alone does not. As Dixsaut (1997) puts it: "What is being described here is the need to join together *all* types of knowledge if we are ever to become philosophers" (p. 17). The reading here largely agrees with Cornford (1965, pp. 75-77), but also points out that there no single sense in which Plato uses the terms "dainoia" and "noiesis." For another good discussions of the dianoia vs. noiesis distinction, see Hyland (1995, p. 181). Readers wishing to study this distinction further would do well to carefully examine *Republic* pp. 532-534d.

4 For an interesting contemporary discussion on the same theme, see David Foster Wallace's commencement address to Kenyon College (Wallace (2009)), in which he says "the fact that you even got admitted to a college this good seems like proof that you already know how to think. But I'm going to posit to you that . . . the really significant education in thinking that we're supposed to get in a place like this isn't really about the capacity to think, but rather about the choice of what to think about."

5 According to Murdoch (1993), Forms . . . are models, archetypes: universals, general concepts as distinct from particular entities, and, in their ethical role, moral ideals active in our lives, radiant icons, images of virtue (p. 10).

6 *Republic (Plato 2004, p.* 533b-c5) suggests that there is yet another awakening in moving from "reasoning" to "understanding," but that move is not important for our purposes in relating the cave story to consumerism.

7 This ignorance has disturbing ethical implications, because some common products (e.g. pig iron) are produced by slave-labor; consumers are thus perhaps unwitting supporters not only of sweat-shops and child labor, but even of slavery.

8 Karl Marx (1990) explains this phenomenon in his discussion of the "commodity fetish." He declares:

A commodity is . . . a mysterious thing, simply because in it the social character of men's labour appears to them as an objective character stamped upon the product of that labour . . . In the same way the light from an object is perceived by us not as the subjective excitation of our optic nerve, but as the objective form of something outside the eye itself (Pt I, Ch I, §4, ¶4).

According to Marx, a commodity's value, is actually a *projection* of human subjective mental states onto the commodity. People see as intrinsic to the product a value that it *actually* gets from them as buyers, from its producers and their labor, and from the system of exchange that links everyone together. As Marx puts it, "a definite social relation between men . . . assumes, in their eyes, the fantastic form of a relation between things" (Marx, 1990, Pt I, Ch I, §4, ¶4). Marx calls this a commodity "fetishism" because of the similarity he saw between it and religious fetishes. In both cases, Marx (an atheist) insists, "the productions of the human brain appear as independent beings endowed with life, and entering into relation both with one another and the human race" (Marz, 1990, Pt I, Ch I, §4, ¶4).

9 As Miller (2004) puts it, "the commodity appears naked in the marketplace, shorn of all the communal references that would give it meaning. . . this systematic evacuation of meaning provides the void that advertising fills" (p. 38).

10 For example, in *Proslogion*, chapter 22, Anselm (2001) says to God: "you are nothing other than the one supreme good, utterly self-sufficient, needing nothing, whom all things need for their being and their well-being" (p. 21).

11 *The Matrix* trilogy of films is in fact a kind of science-fiction retelling of the allegory of the cave.

12 At pp. 588b-589c, Plato (2004) uses pictures to represent the parts of the soul: for the appetitive part, a many-headed monster; for the spirited part, a lion; and for the rational part, a human. By choosing to represent it as a human, Plato clearly identifies with the rational part, considering it "the inner human being" (2004, p. 589b) or true self.

Chapter 15
A Producer Mindset as an Alternative to a Consumer Mindset

Homer Warren
Youngstown State University, USA

Linette Stratford
Youngstown State University, USA

ABSTRACT

Consumer mindset (or consciousness) promotes childlike behaviors and inhibits intelligent decision making needed for human wellbeing. Producer mindset (consciousness), on the other hand, promotes intelligent decision making, autonomy, self-efficacy, individual empowerment, and overall wellbeing. This chapter gives an overview of the difference between the two types of consciousness, provides language to nurture a producer consciousness, and illustrates the benefits of replacing consumer consciousness with producer consciousness.

INTRODUCTION

Who Am I is a powerful question. It's a question that likely dates to the first moments of contemplation by early humans. It's the heart of spirituality and has motivated philosophical ideas. Scratch the surface of science and you find it behind the search for truth. Scratch the surface of all notions of love and happiness and you will find that the ability to love another and be happy relate directly to how the Who Am I question is answered. At the material level, efforts to answer this question have resulted in many human achievements (e.g., medical advances, academic citadels, highways, 10,000 square foot homes, stainless steel appliances, smartphones, the Internet, virtual reality video games). Though humans have experienced many comforts and pleasures from these achievements, ancient wisdoms to modern social critiques suggest that unfettered movements toward material wealth and possessions tend to usurp dignity, moral development, wellbeing, and human potential. Indeed, today's commercialized, commodified, and consumerized world has been correlated highly with major lapses in dignity and moral development.

DOI: 10.4018/978-1-5225-6120-0.ch015

Chapters in this book have addressed consumerism and its relationship to violence, nihilism, disrespect, identity, and other individual and cultural issues. That's the bad news. The good news is that humans have a natural ability to experience material comforts with dignity, self-efficacy, moral development, and wellbeing. Understanding and nurturing our natural ability starts by exposing how being a consumer has framed the answer to the Who Am I question.

THE CONSUMER

Words are powerful. Words used in conversation with others and in self-talk affect the quality of one's life and relationships. Though words can enlighten, they have the power to make people feel worthless, helpless, hopeless, insignificant, fearful, and childlike. The authors propose that the word *consumer* be at the top of the list of powerful words. In many developed cultures around the world, people effectively live 24/7 under the word *consumer*. If we are not in the physical or electronic marketplace buying things, we are thinking about buying things, having conversations about buying things, having conversations about the things we've bought, subjecting ourselves to a media filled with persuasive messages to buy things, or using the things we've bought. The profound American ideas of freedom, liberty, justice, and equality have been reduced to the freedom to choose and buy things in the marketplace. The word *consumer* has morphed America's pursuit of happiness into pursuing emotional pleasures from material possessions.

Neuropsychologist Antonio Damasio (1994) says that people are driven by emotions before rational thinking kicks in. When higher thinking powers do operate, they mostly rationalize and justify desires, greed, envy, fear, and other manifestations of the lower reptilian and mammalian brain functions that operate purely on the basis of pleasure/pain, approach/avoidance, and fight/flight. Though classical economics sees the "rational man" as the antecedent of capitalism and our consumer culture, Damasio is saying the rational part of buying products is secondary to the emotional attachment to the products.

Damasio raises an interesting idea. Emotion before thinking is how infants operate. Could it be that an adult's product buying decisions are no more than an infant's disposition and decision-making based upon Wow-Ugh? Are consumers navigating marketplaces with a child's "I Like – I Don't Like" decision-making? Are the millions of advertisements on cable programs, websites, billboards, magazines, newspapers, and in-store promotions playing to the infant within? Benjamin Barber (2007) thinks so. Barber calls it infantilization (adults made to act childlike).

In *Theory of the Leisure Class* Thorstein Veblen (1957) wrote about conspicuous consumption, the activity of buying products to reflect one's higher status in society. Most observers presume Veblen was only being critical of how wealthy people were showing off their luxurious material possessions. His book, however, gives a lesser known look at the power of the word *consumer*. Veblen's conspicuous consumption charges higher income groups with functioning in history's barbaric period of primitive tribal warfare. To Veblen (1957), luxury goods were nothing more than weapons of choice in the battle against other tribal members for tribal power and, more importantly, for keeping tribes with lower wealth and income at bay. Along these lines, David Burns and Homer Warren (2008, 2009) expanded Veblen's primal warfare and positioned all consumer products as weapons and armament manufactured by corporations to facilitate the warfare. In a consumer culture, all people, no matter their socio-economic situation, use products as signifiers and identifiers of relative status, power, and position. In a vulgar way, people are saying "I own this Mercedes Benz (new or used), Gucci bag (authentic or knockoff), or Titleist golf driver (new or used) and it's a badass product that makes me better than you."

If one person is to be blamed for the power of the word *consumer* in our modern time it would have to be Sigmund Freud's nephew, Edward Bernays. At the start of the 1900's, corporations were dramatically improving their mass production capabilities, resulting in supply-demand imbalances. To alleviate their overproduction and oversupply problems, corporations relied on sales and advertising to get people to buy more goods. Before these industrial developments, the average American household was a self-sufficient production unit producing many of the day-to-day life needs. Products bought in the marketplace (e.g., tools, ingredients, or raw materials) were used primarily for the purpose of producing the household unit's own final products (e.g., clothing, meals, and furniture). Bernays (1955) helped corporations devise public relation schemes and persuasive emotional advertising to transform autonomous household production units into consumption platforms desiring finished products made by corporations. Bernays effectively transformed the selling of products on the basis of functionality into buying products based on emotions, resulting in the full-blown consumer culture known today.

CONSUMERISM

Webster's New Collegiate Dictionary defines consumerism as the promotion of the consumer's interests. At first brush the definition implies advocacy for the production and marketing of products that serve the consumer's physical and mental wellbeing. The opposite holds more truth. There's quite a long list of the products proven to have less than beneficial consequences for human wellbeing (e.g., cigarettes, alcohol, pharmaceuticals, processed foods, household cleaning agents, violent video games).

Andrew Gibson (2011) provides an informative continuum of the many commentaries on consumerism. At one end is Charles Taylor, who sees "the problems of consumerism in relation to cultural ideas of selfhood; that we face a crisis of 'self-determining freedom' and the diminishing ability for 'individual self-discovery and personal development.'" (as cited in Gibson, 2011). At the other end is Joseph Heath who looks at consumerism in the context of structural failures in the market. Heath argues that "markets are structurally geared toward products that fall under the category of 'medium-sized dried goods' (e.g., clothing, cars, and TV sets). Markets are much less apt at responding to demands for other types of goods (e.g., large goods such as bridges or water filtration plants, intangible goods such as knowledge, or natural goods such as clean air)" (as cited in Gibson, 2011). To Heath, markets often ignore including the positive and negative externalities (spillovers or side effects) of the production and selling of medium-sized dried goods; which "reduces the incentive for citizens to invest in public goods such as education, health care, and clean air and water" (as cited in Gibson, 2011). **Consumer Consciousness**Though there is a large collection of books, journal articles, essays, and documentaries critiquing consumerism in conjunction with issues of social justice, corporate ethics, individual power and control, self-efficacy, and overall cultural development, Benjamin Barber's infantilization of adults, Thorstein Veblen's view of conspicuous consumption, Antonio Damasio's emotion driven decision-making, and Andrew Gibson's continuum of consumerism give sufficient support to what the authors will call **Consumer Consciousness**. Consumer Consciousness will be defined as the way being a consumer shapes the quality or state of being aware, especially of something within oneself; shapes the state or fact of being conscious of an external object, state, or fact; and even shapes one's state of being as characterized by sensation, emotion, volition, and thought. *[Webster's New Collegiate Dictionary's definition of consciousness was used to construct this definition (Merriam Webster, 2018). Consumer Consciousness will be capitalized to emphasize its power over our state of being.]* As defined, Consumer Consciousness is not relegated to shopping and buying behaviors. Consumer Consciousness affects how people see themselves, how people see the world, and how people interact with one another. In light of the literature on consumerism, Consumer Consciousness has interfered with the ability to effectively address personal and interpersonal problems and limited the imagination needed to deal with many of the current societal, economic, political, and ecological issues. In short, Consumer Consciousness has been answering the Who Am I question.

THE PRODUCER

The great irony is that human beings are not consumers by any physical design feature. Biologically, there is nothing that even comes close to supporting any notion of being a consumer and, therefore, needing to operate under Consumer Consciousness. Every cell, every tissue, every organ, and every major system of the human body is a production operation producing life and the ability to survive and flourish in the world. There are approximately 20 trillion cells in the human body; 20 trillion little production units. The brain alone contains hundreds of billions of neurons and supporting cells operating in a phenomenal interconnectivity to produce the feelings, actions, reactions, and thoughts that allow humans to physically and mentally navigate relationships, activities, interest, and opinions. Even eating food should not be viewed in terms of consumption. Foods are raw materials used by the body to produce the energy to navigate our world. Chewing food is the body's first production activity in the digestive operation. *[Chewing food slower and longer helps the digestive system maximize productivity. Unfortunately, there are foods on the market that inhibit productivity.]*

Metaphysically, humans are not consumers. Many traditional religions and spiritual schools propose the existence of a universal energy (higher power) from which humans were created (produced) and by which we function in space and time. Using the Judeo-Christian religion as an example, right from the opening of the Bible (Genesis 1:27) it states that humans are "made" in the image and likeness of God, the Creator (i.e., the "Big Producer"). From Genesis to Revelation there are instructions about the behaviors and responsibilities the Big Producer expects us "little producers" to produce (e.g., the production of love and compassion for others). Relative to divine production, biblical references to materialism are often presented negatively (e.g., Matthew 19:24 – "Again I say to you, it is easier for a camel to go through the eye of a needle, than for a rich man to enter the kingdom of God").

Clearly, science supports the notion that humans are little producers. From the universe down to the quantum level, the laws of nature have forces at work vibrating, wiggling, moving, shaping, making, and maintaining both inert and living entities. Each organic life form on this planet is a unique production story. Preferring the evolutionary story over the idea of being a little producer made in the image of a Big Producer doesn't change the fact that humans are producers composed of 20 trillion cellular production units that follow the physical laws of nature.

Biologically, neurologically, spiritually, and by the laws of nature, humans are PRODUCERS! The full scope of the human experience has nothing to do with anything related to being a consumer. Therefore, without hesitation, the authors offer that the word *consumer* be eliminated from the vocabulary. Say it loud, shout it out: Humans are not consumers. We are PRODUCERS!

Hence, operating with a Consumer Consciousness is not natural. Metaphorically, Consumer Consciousness is like a virus that has invaded the brain in the same way that a flu virus infects the body or a software virus corrupts a computer. Consumer Consciousness takes the brain out of sync and corrupts its natural productive capabilities for life-sustaining, life-enhancing, and life-flourishing information processing, decision-making, and problem solving. Taking the metaphor a step further, the body has natural restorative operations that fight a flu virus. The results of the battle are fever, nausea, coughing, and full body aches and pains. It may well be that the brain has natural restorative operations triggered to fight the Consumer Consciousness virus. We experience this battle as stress, anxiety, alienation, fear, anger, tension, frustration, boredom, and overall (dis)ease.

PRODUCER CONSCIOUSNESS

For humans to live according to the biological, neurological, and spiritual designs to be Producers, Consumer Consciousness and the language of consumer and consumerism must be replaced by a consciousness and language compatible with being Producers. The alternative consciousness will be called Producer Consciousness (see Warren & Stratford, 2016). Producer Consciousness is defined as the way being a Producer shapes the quality or state of being aware, especially of something within oneself; shape the state or fact of being conscious of an external object, state, or fact; and even shape one's state of being as characterized by sensation, emotion, volition, and thought. *[For emphasis, Producer and Producer Consciousness will be capitalized.]*

The language of Producer Consciousness starts with the economic input-output model (inputs → producer → outputs) that is fundamental to the operation of corporate, entrepreneurial, governmental, and nonprofit organizations. For many corporations, the inputs are raw materials, raw resources, energy, supplies, labor, component parts, financial resources, and public goods (water, sewage removal, roadways, law enforcement, etc.). Most corporations have departments, units, and/or divisions set up to use inputs to produce the outputs of goods, services, and ideas.

Interestingly enough, the input-output model that is foundational to organizations has been used since our hunter-gatherer and agrarian methods of survival. Our distant and recent ancestors were Producers who, from scratch, produced the human outputs of meals, clothing, equipment, and furniture. As stated earlier, in America's not so distant past, humans bought few finished goods. *[One of the authors thinks back to the ingredients, simple tools, and cooking skills (all inputs) that grandma used to produce her delicious German chocolate cake (the output).]* People marvel at the inventory systems, assembly line systems, equipment systems, maintenance systems, inspection systems, and information systems used by the likes of General Motors, Apple, Amazon, Walmart, and Monsanto. But human beings are Producers no less than major corporations. In fact, far more sophisticated are the human Producer's **phenomenal production systems**:

- Circulatory system
- Respiratory system
- Skeletal system
- Muscular system
- Cranial system
- Endocrine system
- Digestive system
- Lymphatic system
- Reproductive system
- Dermatological system

If we can marvel at a corporation's input-output model, we can surely marvel at our own **Human Input-Output Model** (Inputs → Human Producer → Human Outputs). Indeed, as the word *consumer* should never be used to identify human beings, the word *producer* should never be used to identify organizations of any type (especially, corporations). Humans, along with the other nonhuman life forms, are the only entities on Earth that should be called Producers. All organizations (especially, corporations) should be viewed as playing an important role as suppliers of the goods and services that human Producers use as inputs to produce human outputs.

Important note: Humans, as Producers operating under a Producer Consciousness, can still shop and buy things. The difference is that, unlike functioning with the childlike behaviors of Consumer Consciousness, people see corporations and retailers as suppliers of the inputs (goods and services) that are used to produce desired human outputs. The next three sections will illustrate inputs used to produce desired human outputs; the chapter will end with a discussion of how Producer Consciousness can benefit corporate business models by seeing markets as a collection of Producers.

Human Outputs

Under Producer Consciousness, everything each person does is a human output produced by the phenomenal production systems (especially, the brain-mind). The following is a catalog of human outputs: All physical movements and actions of the body

- Interpersonal skills
- Personality characteristics
- Emotions, motives, and values
- Beliefs, customs, and conventions
- Artifacts (objects made by humans)
- Techniways (the way humans use artifacts)
- Activities, interests, and opinions
- Work skills
- Literacy and verbal communication
- Self-concepts
- Morality and ethics

Last, but not least, children (little Producers)Even excluding physical movements and actions, over a lifetime a human Producer can produce hundreds of thousands of human outputs. The following is a very short list of the human outputs the authors currently enjoy producing: playing golf, playing the piano, exercising, quieting the chattering mind, cooking vegetarian meals, communicating with our children, teaching business ethics, laughing at clever and clean jokes, and discussing Producer Consciousness with anyone who will listen. Human outputs the authors choose not to produce are smoking, drinking alcohol, hatred, gossiping, driving fast, canoeing, skydiving, and mountain climbing *[although producing the last three items may be tried one day]*.

Inputs

Inputs used by human Producers to produce human outputs come from other people, organizations, places, things, ideas, and even from the Producer her/himself. Inputs come in the form of sights, sounds, tastes, smells, and touches picked up by the five senses. The following is a catalog of inputs:

- Workplace
- Corporations
- Spiritual Organizations
- Educational Institutions
- Nonprofit Organizations
- Governments
- Household
- Supplies (formally known as consumer products)
- The Media
- History
- Nature
- Activities, Interests, and Opinions
- Loved Ones
- Other People
- Words
- Ideas

Yourself (your outputs become your inputs)To illustrate inputs and human outputs the golfing experience is used. *[The authors enjoy golfing. Apologies to non-golfers.]* From a long straight drive to a missed short putt, each golf shot is a single human output that's produced from many inputs. Inputs include selecting the right golf club, having golf equipment suited to one's physical type, taking practice swings, proper swing techniques, physical fitness *[there is a fatigue factor in golfing]*, good mental approach to the game *[golf can be very frustrating]*, and good natured golfing partners *[some golfers can be a bit trying]*. Also, the layout and design of each golf hole (e.g., bunkers, water, hills, slopes, length, and trees) are inputs in the production of a good shot.

Admittedly, the conspicuous consumption items of fashionable golf shoes and clothing and the latest high tech golf equipment are also inputs. Using Producer Consciousness, arguably, the human outputs being produced with these inputs are things like social status, individuality, competitiveness, self-esteem, and ideal social self. At this time, there doesn't seem to be much research showing how these inputs actually contribute to the production of a good golf shot; there may well be some psychological link between the two. The key point is that under Producer Consciousness one is aware that these items are inputs to produce social and symbolic human outputs and not for the production of a successful golf shot.

Human Production Chains

The above illustration leads to the idea of **human production chains**, wherein a human output becomes an input that is used to produce another human output which becomes an input used to produce another human output which becomes an input used to produce another human output, etc., etc. The following is a general production chain scheme:

Input → Producer → Human Output (Input) → Producer → Human Output (Input) → Producer → Human Output (Input) → etc.

Human production chains operate in relationships. As an example, let's suppose Earl produces the human output of hard work to get a raise. Earl's output becomes an input encountered (picked up) by a work associate, Ted. Ted uses this input (Earl's hard work) to produce his own human output of guilt for not working as hard as Earl. Ted's guilt becomes an input encountered by his partner Lisa. Lisa uses this input (Ted's guilt) to produce her human output of compassion for Ted. Lisa's compassion for Ted's guilt becomes an input encountered by Lisa's mother, who produces her human output of anger towards Lisa for "marrying a bum." Lisa's mother's human output of anger towards Lisa becomes an input encountered by Lisa's sister Mary, who produces her human output of frustration with her mother. *[Note how the narrative can be continued. Also, imagine how other people may be brought into this production chain.]*

Humans have many personal production chains. An example is getting an education degree. The degree is a human output produced by way of a long string of inputs that become human outputs that, in turn, become inputs, etc. One input needed to produce the degree (human output) is passing a course. But note that passing a course is itself a produced human output that has a number of inputs; one of which is attending classes for the course. In turn, attending classes is a produced human output that has a number of inputs; one of which is the physical act of going to class (e.g., walking, biking, driving, or taking a bus). In turn, the physical act of going to class (let's use walking) is itself a produced human output that has a number of inputs (e.g., physical ability and energy, time, the terrain, type of shoes, the ambition value, the fact that other students walk, and desire to be ecologically concerned and reduce carbon footprints). In turn, the physical ability and energy is itself a produced human output that has a number of inputs (e.g., proper sleep, proper eating, and exercise routine). In turn, the input of an exercise routine is itself a produced human output that has a number of inputs (e.g., exercise equipment, time, safety need, sense of accomplishment value, etc.). In turn, the input of having an ambition value is itself a produced human output with a number of inputs (e.g., a demanding parent, strong self-esteem need, strong need to compete with others, etc.). The personal production chain for education is depicted as:

(A demanding parent) Input → Producer → Output (increased ambitiousness) becomes Input → Producer → Output (exercise routine) becomes Input → Producer → Output (physical ability – increased energy) becomes Input → Producer → Output (ability to walk to class) becomes Input → Producer → Output (attending classes) becomes Input → Producer → Output (passing the course) becomes Input → Producer → Output (attaining degree)

Obviously, this production chain doesn't end with attaining a degree. The degree (output) becomes an input in the production of other human outputs (e.g., income, occupation, sense of accomplishment value, family security value, status). In turn, each of these human outputs becomes an input producing other human outputs (e.g., income becomes an input used to produce purchasing a nice car). In turn, the nice car becomes an input used to produce other human outputs (e.g., getting to work, taking the kids to dance classes, taking the kids to soccer practice, going to the grocery store, taking a long vacation drive).

It goes without saying that human production chains can be complex. Starting from birth one's entire life is an unimaginable number of long and interconnecting human production chains. Arguably, change any one input in any one production chain and life turns out differently. *[Sort of like the "butterfly effect". A butterfly flapping its wings in one part of the world generates a major weather condition in another part of the world.]* In lieu of the complexities, it's quite obvious that simply recognizing the existence of human production chains in one's own life and in others promotes mindfulness of behaviors, introspection, intelligent decision-making, and critical thinking.

The Phenomenal Cranial Production System (Brain-Mind)

Before presenting the Producer Consciousness language for the brain-mind, a little disclaimer is needed. The word *brain* is used to reference brain components; otherwise, the term *brain-mind* will be used. The scientific study of the brain-mind falls under the amazing fields of neuroscience and neuropsychology. The authors are not scientists or psychologists. The authors have read a number of books, journals, and websites about the neuronal components of the brain, how the brain operates to navigate the world of inputs, and how the brain-mind produces feelings, actions, reactions, and thoughts. In no way does this qualify the authors as learned minds on the subject. The authors, however, do propose that the technical jargon and scientific narratives of neuroscience and neuropsychology are beyond the conceptual and application reach of the masses of human Producers who need to understand the brain-mind's production of human outputs. Because neuroscience and its psychology siblings are advanced explorations into the Who Am I question, why not make the technical jargon and scientific narratives user friendly for the human Producers who live with consequences of not knowing Who Am I and/or improperly answering the Who Am I question? To this end, the following sections offer Producer Consciousness language that people can use in self-reflection, decision-making, and conversation with others about the phenomenal production activities of the brain-mind.

Production of Feelings, Actions, Reactions, and Thoughts

The human outputs listed earlier can be captured under four dominant aspects of human behavior: feelings, actions, reactions, and thoughts (**FARTs**). *[Yes, FARTs. A distasteful acronym for some but a great way to teach Producer Consciousness to young people.]* When a Producer encounters an input the phenomenal cranial production system (brain-mind) produces a FART (feeling, action, reaction, and thought). **Feelings** will be defined as physiological (bodily) sensations. To identify, analyze, describe, rationalize, justify, and/or give meaning to their feelings, people tend to use words like anger, disgust, sadness, pity, nervousness, love, hate, disappointment, joy, and fear. For many people, putting feelings into words is not easy. It is suggested that people refrain from relying on words to talk about or deal with feelings. Instead of words, use the currently popular **"emoji"** or **"emoticon"** (the little round faces expressing a range of feelings from anger to joy). Emojis are straightforward, easy to create, and, because pictures speak a thousand words, they are a powerful way to express feelings.

Actions will be defined as specific physiological activities (actual body movements) produced upon encountering an input. Actions have the appearance of being instinctive but are to be considered intentional, often leading to habitual behaviors. Examples of near instinctive and automatic actions are facial expressions (uncontrolled emojis), posture changes, head movements, hand gestures, running from a fight, and throwing a punch. Many actions, however, are out of habit and training (e.g., the physiological activities attached to sports, hobbies, recreation, work, getting an education degree, and everyday activities like walking, taking a shower, driving). Actions can occur very quickly or be performed over a long period of time. Throwing a punch when angry happens quickly. It takes time to run a marathon or study for an examination.

Reactions are purely instinctual and autonomic (automatic) functions of the phenomenal cranial production system. The brain's autonomic reactions to inputs are primarily electro-chemical processes involving neurotransmitters such as dopamine, noradrenaline, adrenalin, serotonin, oxytocin, cortisol and GABA (gamma-aminobutyric acid). *[Note that electro-chemicals are also behind the operation of feelings and actions.]* Whereas actions are observable physical movements that can be manipulated, reactions are the genetically programmed physiological operations behind the physical movements. Reactions can be experienced as changes in the respiratory system (breathing), the circulatory system (blood flow and heart rate), and the various states of central nervous system (sensations of stress and relaxation). Reactions can also be experienced as uncontrollable muscle reflexes, jumping when startled, dilatation of the pupils, sweating, crying, butterflies in the stomach, gnashing of the teeth, tightening in the chest, lump in the throat, shoulder and neck tension, tingling in the face, and even primal sounds (e.g., screams, grunts, squeals, sighs).

Thoughts are produced by the cognitive components of the brain-mind. Producer Consciousness views all thoughts in terms of a collection and arrangement of words to identify, analyze, describe, rationalize, justify, and/or give meaning to the feelings, actions, and reactions that have been produced for inputs. Producer Consciousness also includes as thoughts the pictures and images seen inside the head; pictures do speak a thousand words.

Important note: The brain-mind is a tremendously complex production system. The acronym *FART* implies a sequence of production from feelings to actions to reactions to thoughts. Complicating matters is how FARTs can appear to be produced simultaneously. But as everyone knows, thoughts can trigger feelings, actions, and reactions. Actions can trigger feelings. Reactions (by the above definition) can happen far quicker than feelings, actions, and thoughts. Again, the authors are simply providing a language to accompany a new mindset. At this juncture, no matter which sequence is operating, how they are produced, and how fast they are produce, the key point is that humans are Producers and the brain-mind is producing FARTs for inputs.

Road Rage Example

The human output of anger will be used to illustrate the operation of the Human Input-Output Model (Inputs → Human Producer → Human Outputs) and the brain-mind's production of FARTs (feeling, actions, reactions, and thoughts). In many cases, we tend to accuse other people or situations for causing our anger. That's wrongheaded. That's the childlike "wow/ugh" behavior of Consumer Consciousness. No matter what or who you point to as the cause of your anger, the fact is that you, the Producer, used inputs to produce your human output of anger. As an example, let's say that while Tom is driving, Jerry unexpectedly pulls out in front of him. Jerry's driving (an output) is Tom's input. As a reaction to the input, the electro-chemical processes of Tom's brain produces automatic alarm sensations (i.e., adrenaline, heart rate change, respiratory change, and even a primal scream). Tom's immediate actions are to swerve the car to avoid hitting Jerry's car. Tom produces feelings of being intruded upon and threatened (remember, because feelings are difficult to verbalize, the authors recommend using emojis). Tom's subsequent actions are to honk the horn and give Jerry the finger. After the immediacy of the FARs (feelings, actions, and reactions), Tom thinks about how drivers like Jerry are idiots who shouldn't be allowed to drive and are always messing up his day. Tom is blaming Jerry for his feelings, actions, reactions, and thoughts when the fact is **Tom is a Producer and he produced the FART!**

Taking a closer Producer Consciousness look at this situation, Jerry's driving behavior may only be one of many inputs contributing to Tom's production of anger. Yes, Jerry is clearly a dominant and current input but using the production chain there may be a number of recent and/or past inputs that are also contributing to Tom's production of anger. Examples of other inputs are: A near car accident he recently experienced

- Jerry is driving a luxury car (a little wealth envy by Tom)
- He just finished fighting with friend
- He had a bad day at work
- He got little sleep last night
- There was too much sugar in the large piece of cake he had for lunch
- The extra glass of wine he had with lunch

Tom's anger toward Jerry's output (i.e., Tom's input) can be identified as a negative (-) FART (feelings, actions, reactions, and thoughts). Equally, each of the above seven past inputs can be discussed in terms of a positive (+) or negative (-) FART produced at the time the inputs occurred. Producer Consciousness proposes that all inputs result in the brain-mind producing some degree of positive or negative FART; as a reference, the range can be from very weak to very strong. Obviously, many inputs encountered throughout a day are taken for granted, ignored, or below the threshold of attention; these inputs are considered to produce neutral FARTs. For purpose of discussion, Tom's past inputs of a similar near car accident, being envious of wealthy people, fighting with a friend, having a bad day at work, and getting little sleep likely resulted in his production of strong negative (-) FARTs. The piece of cake and glasses of wine were inputs that resulted in Tom producing positive (+) FARTs. The cake and wine are production chain examples of inputs that, in and of themselves, immediately produced positive (+) FARTs but became inputs contributing to the production of negative (-) FART towards Jerry. In a broader context this shows how past inputs and +/-FARTs play a role in the production of +/-FARTs for currently encountered inputs. In short, current +/-FARTs are influenced by past +/-FARTs and current +/-FARTs can shape future +/-FARTs.

Memory

The human memory will be viewed as the storage system of a lifetime of inputs and the +/-FARTs produced for the inputs. Producer Consciousness uses the word **Vector** to detail the storage of inputs and their +/-FARTs. The sights, sounds, smells, tastes, and/or touches of each object (i.e., person, place, thing, and idea) encountered in a lifetime is assigned a Vector that stores all of the object's inputs and +/-FARTs produced for the inputs. Hence, humans have a Vector for each person, a Vector for each good and service, a Vector for each geographic place, a Vector for each aspect of nature, a Vector for each organization, a Vector for each idea, and a Vector for each word ever encountered in one's lifetime. There's even a Vector for oneself (i.e., a Me Vector). Over an adult's lifetime, the brain has developed tens of thousands of Vectors storing hundreds of millions of inputs and their accompanying +/-FARTs. Wow!

The following outlines the characteristics of Vectors:

- A Vector arranges inputs from or about a specific person, place, thing, or idea in a timeline from the very first to the most recent encounter with the person, place, thing, or idea. The touch, taste, smell, sound, and visual aspects of an input are stored in the Vector. A Vector is literally a virtual reality show of the person, place, thing, and idea.

- A Vector can be dominant or recessive. Dominant Vectors have strong impact on a person's life (e.g., a school teacher Vector, a parent or guardian Vector, a sibling Vector, a pet Vector, an ex-girl(boy)friend Vector). Recessive Vectors are far less impactful (e.g., a paper clip Vector, a safety pin Vector, a curtain rod Vector, and an eating utensil Vector).
- A Vector can contain a few to a huge number of inputs and FARTs. Most people have little or no inputs in the String Theory Vector. On the other hand, many people have hundreds of thousands of inputs in the Mommy Vector
- Vectors are everlasting. One may not be able to recall a particular Vector, but it still exists.
- Vectors can be real or imagined. Children often have imaginary Vectors. Arguably, Hollywood, Madison Avenue, and social media feed the adult brain a lot of imaginary Vectors.
- Vectors are interconnected (wired together). The inputs and +/-FARTs in a Daddy Vector and/or Mommy Vector can influence the inputs and +/-FARTs in the Vector for a current partner.

To appreciate the huge number of inputs and +/-FARTs stored in Vectors, consider the following thought exercise. Focus on the Mommy Vector, Daddy Vector, Guardian Vector, Sibling Vector, Relative Vector, Close Friend Vector, and/or Ex-girl/boyfriend Vector. Recall every single sight, sound, smell, taste, and touch (inputs) in the selected Vector(s). *[Of course that's impossible. Long term relationships will have hundreds of thousands, if not millions, of inputs in the Vector.]* To make the exercise easier, choose a few of the most memorable inputs in the selected Vector(s). Now, recall the +/-FARTs produced for the memorable inputs. In Producer Consciousness terms, this memory exercise has the reader do a "ride-down" the Vector of the selected person (as in ride down memory lane), stop at the time that the memorable inputs occurred, and revisit the +/-FARTs produced for those inputs. A companion exercise is for the reader to "ride-down" his/her own Me Vector containing things that the reader has said and done (i.e., human outputs). Here, the reader can revisit the +/-FARTs that the reader produced for his/her own human outputs. Essentially, a "ride-down" the Me Vector is an act of self-reflection that entails reviewing past behaviors and +/-FARTs relative to the behavior.

For both exercises note that a "ride-down" a Vector effectively makes current the past inputs and +/-FARTs in the Vector, just as if they were happening, again. Once past inputs and +/-FARTs are made current, the brain-mind can produce a subsequent +/-FART. In short, when reviewing past life events one can produce a current +/-FART for something (inputs) that happened years ago. In many cases, a "ride-down" a Vector produces neutral FARTs. In worse cases, people can't let go of troubling events of the past and keep rehashing the old negative (-) FARTs; and, by making the past current, keep adding negative FARTs to the Vectors involved in the events *[**Note**: Producer Consciousness has a method to deal with troubling past events that one keeps chattering about in the head, it is called the Quiet. The method is beyond the scope of this chapter. Full details can be found in* "Producer Consciousness" *by Warren and Stratford (2016).]*

As human Producers have individual memories, communities and nations can be viewed as having historical memory. In the same manner that Vectors hold the memories of human Producers, Vectors can be used as a language to explore historical memory (i.e., the inputs, outputs, and +/-FARTs) that shape communities and nations. In the same way that Vectors serve individual self-reflection, Vectors for a community can serve a critical thinking approach to the political, social, economic, and cultural spaces of a community. he following section illustrates how Vectors and other Producer Consciousness language can be used to critique a few individual and community issues. Given the intent of this chapter, the illustrations will be framed in terms of Producer Consciousness being an alternative to Consumer Consciousness.

PRODUCER CONSCIOUSNESS VS. CONSUMER CONSCIOUSNESS

Whereas Consumer Consciousness is like a viral infection that takes the brain out of sync with its natural design to be a Producer, Producer Consciousness brings the brain in sync with its natural design. Whereas Consumer Consciousness channels intelligence through infantile and childlike defensiveness, rationalizations, and justifications, the natural Producer Consciousness nurtures critical thinking and intelligent decision-making for human wellbeing (which is correlated with the wellbeing of ecosystems). hereas Consumer Consciousness results in stress, anxiety, alienation, fear, tension, frustration, boredom, and (dis)ease, the natural Producer Consciousness produces a sense of self-efficacy, central locus of control, long-lasting joy, serenity, peace, and an ease. To illustrate how Producer Consciousness can be used to critique individual and community issues and highlight the benefits of replacing Consumer Consciousness with Producer Consciousness, food buying, education, relationships, and the workplace are used.

Food Buying

Under Consumer Consciousness corporate food processors recognize the market's childlike decision-making and use additives, preservatives, and marketing methods to make food inputs attractive and appealing. This has resulted in people having food Vectors filled with adulterated and processed smell, touch, taste, and sight inputs. With the childlike "I Like – I Don't Like", "Wow-Ugh" decision-making, people ignore evidence (inputs) that the adulterated and processed foods may be contributing to poor health and reduced wellbeing. Consumer Consciousness is having people produce positive FARTs for food inputs when negative FARTs would be more appropriate and productive. In the end, by creating unnecessary healthcare costs, Consumer Consciousness is bankrupting the nation both economically and morally (the September 2012 report from the Institute of Medicine states that the U.S. healthcare system annually wastes $750 billion).

On the other hand, a human Producer operating under Producer Consciousness views each food item as having a collection of inputs to be used by the phenomenal production systems (body) to produce the energy needed to produce desired human outputs. The food inputs of smell, touch, taste, sight, and labelled ingredients are assessed for their potential harm (or benefit) to the phenomenal production systems and the production of desired physical, personal, intellectual, societal, political, economic, and spiritual human outputs. Food inputs that are harmful will receive negative FARTs. Food inputs that are a contribution to the production of desired human outputs will receive positive FARTs. Over time, all food Vectors will come to contain food inputs with +/-FARTs directly related to the healthfulness and productiveness of the food item. *[Clearly, Producer Consciousness could transform the food processing and healthcare industries.]*

Education

Under Consumer Consciousness students (K-12 and higher education) turn classroom inputs (e.g., books, courses, studying, classroom architect, administrative practices and policies, and the teacher's looks, personality, character, presentation methods) into "commodities" to be liked or disliked. Seemingly, negative FARTs for these education inputs have become the norm. But unlike the physical and electronic marketplaces where any dissatisfaction (negative FARTs) is freely expressed by not buying and leaving the store or website, students are stuck in the classroom. Students are expected to tolerate their negative FARTs and sit quietly in their classroom seats of stress, boredom, anxiety, and alienation. Unfortunately, for many teachers, the students' negative FARTs are expressed in many undesirable classroom behaviors (human outputs); which become inputs to which teachers produce negative FARTs. In the end, students move from grade to grade accumulating a huge number negative FARTs in their Vectors for books, courses, teachers, studying, classroom architect and artifacts, and administrative practices and policies.

Added to the classroom dilemma caused by Consumer Consciousness is how teachers tend to revert to entertaining students to get "Wow's" and "I-Like" (+FARTs). Some teachers (especially, those not skilled at standup comedy) come to dislike their job and, if they don't quit, simply mentally shutdown and wait for retirement. This indicates that, in some cases, teachers may have Vectors for students, parents, administrators, other teachers that are filled with far more negative than positive FARTs. In addition, many school systems motivate students with the idea that education leads to a good job that in turn leads to affording nice material things (this is the education human production chain discussed earlier). This practice only feeds Consumer Consciousness and moves the student further away from developing positive FARTs for the ideas of learning for learning's sake and for the overall educational process. Equally unproductive is how education administrators use business models that encourage the treatment of students as consumers. This clearly serves to perpetuate the Consumer Consciousness that's contributing to classroom problems.

Under Producer Consciousness a student sees her/himself as a Producer who takes personal responsibility for producing education outputs. The student comes to recognize that he/she produces his/her classroom behaviors (e.g., I produce learning, I produce studying, I produce going to class, I produce listening to the teacher, I produce anger, I produce moodiness, and I produce +/-FARTs for all inputs encountered in the classroom). As a Producer, the student sees books, courses, teachers, studying, the classroom, administrative practices and policies as inputs in a human production chain that contributes to the production of her/his desired human outputs. Under Producer Consciousness teachers (along with administrators and parents) encourage students to be Producers, show them the importance of having positive FARTs in their Vectors for books, courses, teachers, studying, classroom architect, administrative practices and policies, and help them understand and develop human production chains to reach their desired current and future human outputs. *[Yes, even in the best Producer Consciousness classroom, students can still produce negative FARTs for inputs; but they are taught to understand their Vectors and how Vectors store negative FARTs for inputs.]*

Producer Consciousness also helps teachers and administrators see themselves as Producers producing the human outputs of classroom information, personality characteristics, body language, interpersonal skills, values, etc. Teachers and administrators recognize that their human outputs become inputs to which students will produce +/-FARTs. Teachers and administrators recognize that each student brings

Vectors to the classroom, some often filled with negative FARTs for inputs encountered in their life experiences. Recognizing a student's FARTs for the classroom, teacher's human outputs, and for the life experiences brought to the classroom is a key component in many theories of pedagogy.

Relationships

Under Consumer Consciousness people exhibit childlike behaviors in their relationships. As if dealing with a commodity, both parties act as if they were "buying" or "not buying" the human outputs of the other. As an example, Joe and Mary are in a relationship. Without any contemplation, Joe simply produces +/-FARTs for Mary's outputs (which are Joe's inputs) and Mary simply produces +/-FARTs for Joe's outputs (Mary's inputs). Joe has a Mary Vector filled with inputs with +/-FARTs and Mary has a Joe Vector filled with inputs with +/-FARTs. Both, using childlike decision-making (lying, being selfish, easy to cry, needy, and lacking compassion) produce a lot of +/-FARTs that are unproductive to the relationship. Joe and Mary have other Vectors (e.g., the Mommy Vector, Daddy Vector, Ex's Vector, Vectors for in-laws, and Vectors for close friends) filled with inputs and +/-FARTs that are impacting their relationship. Going to a relationship counselor can be problematic because even the best of counselors can never know the huge number of inputs, human outputs, human production chains, and +/-FARTs produced in the relationship. Counselors cannot know the effect of the other Vectors on the relationship.

Under Producer Consciousness a relationship becomes a dynamic interaction with both parties being mindful of inputs, human outputs, +/-FARTs, and human production chains (especially, other people influencing the relationship). Joe is more aware of his human outputs becoming inputs to which Mary will produce +/-FART and store in her Joe Vector. Mary is more aware of her human outputs becoming inputs to which Joe will produce +/-FART and store in his Mary Vector. Joe and Mary are also mindful of how the human outputs of other people can influence their relationship. The language of Producer Consciousness also facilitates effective communication (especially, the production of listening), a very important aspect of a relationship,

Workplace

Consumer Consciousness thrives in the workplace. The first thing of note is that most people work for the purpose of making money to buy things or to pay for the things they have bought. Secondly, a lot of decision-making and interpersonal situations in the workplace are based on childlike feelings, actions, and reactions (FARs). Of all places, you would think that corporations would naturally operate under a Producer Consciousness with administrators and employees treating each other as Producers. Instead, in hierarchical (vertical) organization charts, management tends to treat employees as commodities no different than the raw materials and component parts used to make the company's goods and services. Management literature is filled with examples and cases of unproductive management-employee relations that interfere with the organization's profitability.

Under Producer Consciousness, all members of the organization see each other as Producers producing human outputs that contribute to the productivity and profitability of the organization. Management recognizes and appreciates each employee as having multiple Vectors (e.g., family Vectors, work policy Vectors, a company Vector, management Vectors, the Me Vector) containing +/-FARTs that directly affect the employee's productivity. Whereas, under Consumer Consciousness the classic vertical organization block chart effectively has the members standing on one another's head to climb the corporate ladder, under Producer Consciousness there would be a tacit horizontal chart representing how each member stands as equal Producers contributing to the survival and flourishing of all the organization's production chains (both human and operational). A shift to Producer Consciousness in the workplace facilitates greater respect, cooperation, engagement, responsibility, and value creation among all of the Producers.

ARGUMENTS

This chapter is proposing that people make a dramatic shift in the way they see themselves, see others, and see the world. Because unique proposals like this will have challenges, it is helpful to present five reoccurring arguments raised against Producer Consciousness.

- **Argument 1:** *People have always seen themselves as consumers and many love shopping. It will be very difficult to transition people to thinking of themselves in such a counterintuitive way.*

There's quite a bit of evidence of people who have voluntarily moved from consumerism and Consumer Consciousness (e.g., ascetics, artists, minimalists, people who practice meditation and mindfulness, successful people who simply dropped out of the "rat race"). Admittedly, changing any one person's mindset (consciousness) is problematic but such changes are often a function of the difficulty and reasonableness of the task. Consumer Consciousness causes infantilization of intelligence and many people are cognitive misers of different degrees. The authors think a large number of people will be persuaded by some of the benefits of Producer Consciousness outlined earlier. Producer Consciousness matures the cognitive processes, increases mindfulness, and opens the door to a healthful self-introspection that leads to real self-awareness, self-actualization, and self-efficacy. By recognizing that all goods and services supplied on the market have inputs used by human Producers to produce desired human outputs, people become more efficient and productive shoppers. As stated earlier, adopting Producer Consciousness will not stop people from shopping and buying things But, given the organic qualities of Producer Consciousness, once a person is aware of his/her true nature as a Producer they can't go back to being a consumer.

- **Argument 2:** *Social movements often peter out or they don't fully benefit the people they are designed to help. Why would Producer Consciousness be any different?*

A common theme of discussions, lectures, debates, presentations, movies, and podcasts dealing with social movements is the powerful idea that the individual has to seek the truth for him/herself, see her/his intrinsic worth, and independently overcome being marginalized. Furthermore, to counter systemic abuses of natural and human resources, people must first change self-perceptions and recognize the interconnectedness of all humans. Social movements have done a good job exposing Consumer Consciousness and how it has made us dependent, made us zombies of electronic screens, made us desire "toys", made us "consume" foods destructive to our phenomenal production systems, made us wasteful, and made us act like children fighting over silly things. But movements haven't done a great job of transitioning people out of Consumer Consciousness. In this vein, Producer Consciousness is not a social movement. In the critique of consumerism, Producer Consciousness is the individual transformation social movements implicitly call for. Producer Consciousness offers a language for all individuals to independently explore how Consumer Consciousness controls behaviors. It assists individuals in answering the Who Am I question; out of which come self-worth, resistance to marginalization, productive self-perception, and an awareness of the human production chains that integrate all of humanity.

- **Argument 3:** *Producer Consciousness is just another fashionable self-help idea.*

There are many religious, spiritual, psychology, and philosophy books, magazines, and websites designed to help people understand themselves, improve their personal wellbeing, and contribute to the wellbeing of others and the world. But given the huge amount of money, time, and effort the general public spends in the self-help industry, the payoffs are not much to brag about. *[According to a study published by Marketdata Enterprise, Inc. titled The U.S. Market for Self-Improvement Products and Services, in 2015 the self-help business was worth $9.84 billion.(Cision PRWeb, 2018)]* Individuals continue to experience fear, anger, angst, depression, despair, hopelessness, nihilism, and violence of all types. Relationships continue to collapse.

The teachers of the older spiritual traditions (e.g., Judaism, Christianity, Islam, Buddhism, and Hinduism) present an abundance of methods, instructions, and practices that their followers must use to overcome worldly problems and attain salvation. But giving instructions to follow a particular path out of one's (dis)ease is not the same as empowering the individual with instructions on how to independently evaluate, judge, create, and follow his/her own path. Interestingly enough, if you scratch the surface of many of the older spiritual traditions, you will find the often overlooked fundamental wisdom instructing people to not follow the teacher but discover the truth for themselves. As addressed in Argument 3, Producer Consciousness provides a language of self-discovery that fits our natural biological, neurological, and spiritual design to be Producers. The Producer Consciousness language of inputs, human outputs, human production chains, Vectors, and +/-FARTs is not a fashionable self-help idea, it's a powerful natural framework that facilitates individual and, thereby, societal flourishing.

- **Argument 4:** *Producer Consciousness will cause corporations that promote and profit from consumerism to make major changes in their business and marketing practices.*

This is not such a bad thing. There are a number of corporations that will have to change their business models (food processing and healthcare industries come to mind). Well-meaning corporations are always looking for productivity and profitability advantages. The current predictions are that stakeholders will play an increasingly integral role in corporate decision-making. Two currently prominent ideas are **prosumer** and **co-creation**. The term prosumer was first presented in the The Third Wave by Alvin Toffler (1980) and advanced in the marketing world by Phillip Kotler (1986). The foundation of the prosumer is that technology is advancing to the point where communication, energy development, and the physical movement of people and things will allow the individual to "produce" his/her own information, energy, and things (e.g., solar energy systems, 3-D printing, auto-drive transportation, drones, etc.). Co-creation was first introduced by Prahalad and Venkat (2004). The gist of co-creation involves collaboration with stakeholders in the design, development, and distribution of goods and services.

The research and literature on prosumption and co-creation indicate that corporate leaders are likely familiar with the notion of involving human Producers (stakeholders) in construction and operationalization of their business models. The authors speculate that prosumption and co-creation under Consumer Consciousness will only continue old patterns of childlike decision-making, class divisions, ethnic conflicts, wealth inequalities, and resource abuses. The advocates of prosumption and co-creation would do well to see stakeholders as Producers and use Producer Consciousness as the framework for including Producers in business models. One example, as stated earlier, is for corporations to see targeted market members as human Producers and, in turn, see themselves as suppliers of goods and services (inputs) used by human Producers to produce desired human outputs.

- **Argument 5:** *What empirical work supports Producer Consciousness?*

As of this date, Producer Consciousness hasn't been subjected to research designs; only the results of a pilot project and a lot of antidotal evidence exist. These results have been overwhelmingly supportive of the understanding, ease of application, and benefits from adopting Producer Consciousness. One individual said he stopped smoking; another said her parenting skills improved once she treated her children as little Producers; another experienced improvements in a personal relationship; another sees his educational experience in a totally different light; another indicated a total change in the way he approached shopping for food and eating. In short, Producer Consciousness has naturally endowed characteristics that have self-evident inherent and intuitive qualities. As the authors continue to advance the idea of Producer Consciousness there will be opportunities for employing more sophisticated research.

CONCLUSION

Over the past decades, there have been many people arguing for a change in consciousness to correct the ills of the world. The original opening lines of *New Dimensions Radio*, an internet radio program created by Michael and Justine Toms to discuss traditional and modern ideas about consciousness, captures these voices:

It's only through a change in human consciousness that the world will be transformed. The personal and the planetary are connected. As we expand our awareness of mind, body, psyche, and spirit and bring that awareness actively in the world as also will the world be changed.(New Dimensions Radio, 2018)

This chapter has argued for the abolition of all notions of the consumer and the Consumer Consciousness that perpetuates it. In its place should be a human consciousness that springs from the fact that humans are naturally endowed Producers. Being Producers, humans need a language and narratives sufficient to live by and communicate our ubiquitous production processes. Taking liberties with the Toms' quote, the authors propose that it is only through a change to Producer Consciousness that the world will be transformed.

REFERENCES

Barber, B. R. (2007). *Consumed: How markets corrupt children, infantilize adults, and swallow citizens whole*. New York, NY: W.W. Norton & Company.

Bernays, E. (1955). *The engineering of consent*. Norman, OK: University of Oklahoma Press.

Burns, D. J., & Warren, H. B. (2008). Consumer warfare: Implications for marketing strategy. *The Journal of Business Strategy*, *29*(6), 56–70. doi:10.1108/02756660810917237

Burns, D. J., & Warren, H. B. (2009). Are marketers nothing more than arms dealers? *Journal of Business Management and Change*, *4*(1), 9–25.

Cision PRWeb. (2018). *$10.4Billion Self-Imporvement Marktet Survives Scandals & Recession*. Retrieved from http://www.prweb.com/releases/2013/1/prweb10275905.htm

Demasio, A. (1994). *Descartes' error: Emotions, reason, and the human brain*. New York, NY: Avon Books.

Gibson, A. (2011). Ideas and practices in the critique of consumerism. *Environmental Philosophy*, *8*(2), 171–188. doi:10.5840/envirophil20118219

Kotler, P. (1986). The prosumer movement: a new challenge for marketers. In R. J. Lutz (Ed.), *Advances in Consumer Research* (pp. 510–513). Provo, UT: Association for Consumer Research.

Merriam Webster. (2018). *Consciousness*. Retrieved from https://www.merriam-webster.com/dictionary/consciousness

New Dimensions Radio. (2018). Retrieved from https://newdimensions.org/

Prahalad, C. K., & Venkat, R. (2004). *The future of competition*. Boston, MA: Harvard Business School Press.

Toffler, A. (1980). *The third wave: The classic study of tomorrow*. New York, NY: Bantam Books.

Veblen, T. (1957). *The theory of the leisure class*. New York, NY: New American Library.

Warren, H., & Stratford, L. (2016). *Producer consciousness*. San Francisco, CA: Blurb.

KEY TERMS AND DEFINITIONS

Actions: The Specific physiological activities (actual body movements) produced relative to inputs from objects (people, places, things, and ideas) one encounters. Many actions result from habit and training.

Consciousness: The quality or state of being aware of something within oneself and of the inputs from/about objects (people, places, things, or ideas) in the world.

Consumer: The party who exchanges monetary value for the goods and services provided by organizations.

Feelings: Physiological (bodily) sensations produced by the cranial system relative to inputs from objects (people, places, things, and ideas) one encounters. Feelings run from negative to positive (e.g., anger, disgust, hatred, love, compassion).

Human Outputs: All behaviors and what humans do (e.g., activities, interests, opinions).

Human Producer: The human being that uses his/her brain, body, and mind to make, construct, develop, and carry out all behaviors, activities, interests, and opinions.

Human Production Chain: The process of producing a human output that in turn becomes an input that is used to produce another human output that becomes an input used to produce another human output, etc.

Inputs: The outputs of humans, nature, and organizations that are encountered by the five senses (sight, sound, taste, smell, and touch).

Reactions: The instinctual and autonomic biological (e.g., respiratory, circulatory, dermatological) changes produced by the cranial system relative to inputs from objects (people, places, things, and ideas) one encounters.

Thoughts: The collection and arrangement of words produced by the cognitive components of the brain-mind to identify, analyze, describe, rationalize, justify, and/or give meaning to feelings, actions, and reactions for inputs.

Vector: A memory timeline that contains all of the inputs from/about a specific object (person, place, thing, or idea).

Compilation of References

(2013). Fetishistic disorder, 302.81 (F65.0). InAmerican Psychiatric Association (Ed.), *American Psychiatric Association. Diagnostic and statistical manual of mental disorders* (5th ed.; p. 700). Washington, DC: American Psychiatric Association Publishing.

Aaker, J. L., & Williams, P. (1998). Empathy versus pride: The influence of emotional appeals across cultures. *The Journal of Consumer Research*, *25*(3), 241–261. doi:10.1086/209537

Acemoglu, D., & Robinson, J. (2012). *Why nations fail: The origins of power, prosperity, and poverty*. New York, NY: Crown Business.

Achebe, C. (1988). *Things fall apart*. New York, NY: Fawcett.

Adorno, T. W., & Horkheimer, M. (1972). *Dialectic of enlightenment*. New York, NY: Continuum.

Agarwal, R., & Gort, M. (2002). Firm and product life cycles and firm survival. *The American Economic Review*, *92*(2), 184–190. doi:10.1257/000282802320189221

Ahponen, P. (1990). Signifying the signs – Simulating cultural political subjectivity in postmodernity. *Acta Sociologica*, *33*(4), 341–357. doi:10.1177/000169939003300406

Ahuvia, A. C. (2005). Beyond the extended self: Loved objects and consumers' identity narratives. *The Journal of Consumer Research*, *32*(1), 171–184. doi:10.1086/429607

Ajzen, I., & Fishbein, M. (1980). *Understanding attitudes and predicting social behavior*. Ann Arbor, MI: Prentice Hall.

Akerlof, G. A., & Shiller, R. J. (2015). *Phishing for phools: The economics of manipulation and deception*. Princeton, NJ: Princeton University Press. doi:10.1515/9781400873265

Akintaro, S. (2017a, December 14). Unsolicited messages: Subscribers lament as telcos defy "NDN" rule. *Oracle News*, 12-17.

Akintaro, S. (2017b). Consumers' plight and regulatory confusion over value added service. *IT Telecom Digest*, 32-37.

Albert, E. (1968). Value systems. In D. Sills (Ed.), *International encyclopedia of the social sciences* (Vol. 16, pp. 287–291). New York, NY: Cromwell Collier and Macmillan.

Albert, T. C. (2003). Need-based segmentation and customized communication strategies in a complex-commodity industry: A supply chain study. *Industrial Marketing Management*, *32*(4), 281–290. doi:10.1016/S0019-8501(02)00204-3

Albinsson, P. A., Wolf, M., & Kopf, D. A. (2010). Anti-consumption in East Germany: Consumer resistance to hyperconsumption. *Journal of Consumer Behaviour*, *9*(6), 412–425. doi:10.1002/cb.333

Alden, D. L., Steenkamp, J. B. E., & Batra, R. (1999). Brand positioning through advertising in Asia, North America, and Europe: The role of global consumer culture. *Journal of Marketing*, *63*(1), 75–87. doi:10.2307/1252002

Alicke, M. (1983). Philosophical investigations of values. In L. Kahle (Ed.), *Social values and social change: Adaptation to life in America* (pp. 3–23). New York, NY: Praeger Publishers.

Allen, R. (1993). *The structure of value*. Aldershot, UK: Avebury.

Altemeyer, B. (2004). Perspectives: The decline of organized religion in Western civilization. *The International Journal for the Psychology of Religion*, *14*(2), 77–89. doi:10.120715327582ijpr1402_1

Andreasen, A. R. (1984). Life status changes and changes in consumer preferences and satisfaction. *The Journal of Consumer Research*, *11*(3), 784–794. doi:10.1086/209014

Ang, C.-S., Mansor, A., & Tan, K.-A. (2014). Pangs of loneliness breed material lifestyle but do not power up life satisfaction of young people: The moderating effect of gender. *Social Indicators Research*, *117*(2), 353–365. doi:10.100711205-013-0349-0

Angeles, P. (Ed.). (1992). *HarperCollins dictionary of philosophy*. New York, NY: HarperCollins.

Ansari, A., & Mela, C. F. (2003). E-customization. *JMR, Journal of Marketing Research*, *40*(2), 131–145. doi:10.1509/jmkr.40.2.131.19224

Anselm. (2001). *Proslogion with the replies of Gaunilo and Anselm* (T. Williams, Trans.). Indianapolis, IN: Hackett.

Appadurai, A. (Ed.). (1986). *The social life of things*. Cambridge, UK: Cambridge University Press. doi:10.1017/CBO9780511819582

Aroean, L., & Michaelidou, N. (2014). Are innovative consumers emotional and prestigiously sensitive to price? *Journal of Marketing Management*, *30*(3/4), 245–267. doi:10.1080/0267257X.2013.811094

Arvidsson, A. (2005). Brands: A critical perspective. *Journal of Consumer Culture*, *5*(2), 235–258. doi:10.1177/1469540505053093

Aschenbrenner, K. (1971). *The concepts of value: Foundations of value theory*. Dordrecht, The Netherlands: D. Reidel Publishing. doi:10.1007/978-94-010-3093-9

Ashforth, B. E., & Mael, F. (1989). Social identity theory and the organization. *Academy of Management Review*, *14*(1), 20–39. doi:10.5465/amr.1989.4278999

Atwal, G., & Williams, A. (2009). Luxury brand marketing–the experience is everything! *Journal of Brand Management*, *16*(5), 338–346. doi:10.1057/bm.2008.48

Babalogbon, O. (2017, October 13). Airtel's Unlimited Data campaign: A case of puffery. *The Nation*, 23-26.

Bagozzi, R. P. (1980). *Causal models in marketing*. New York, NY: John Wiley & Sons.

Bagozzi, R. P., & Dholakia, U. M. (2006). Antecedents and purchase consequences of customer participation in small group brand communities. *International Journal of Research in Marketing*, *23*(1), 45–61. doi:10.1016/j.ijresmar.2006.01.005

Bahl, S., Milne, G. R., Ross, S. M., Mick, D. G., Grier, S. A., Chugani, S. K., & Schindler, R. M. (2016). Mindfulness: Its transformative potential for consumer, societal, and environmental well-being. *Journal of Public Policy & Marketing*, *35*(2), 198–210. doi:10.1509/jppm.15.139

Bahm, A. (1993). *Axiology: The science of values*. Amsterdam, The Netherlands: Editions Rodopi.

Bailey, C., Baines, P. R., Wilson, H., & Clark, M. (2009). Segmentation and customer insight in contemporary services marketing practice: Why grouping customers is no longer enough. *Journal of Marketing Management*, *25*(3-4), 227–252. doi:10.1362/026725709X429737

Bailie, G. (2002). *Violence unveiled: Humanity at the crossroads*. New York, NY: Crossroad.

Bali, R. N. (2011). *Tarz-ı hayattan life style'a*. İstanbul, Turkey: İletişim Publications.

Bandura, A., & Walters, R. H. (1977). *Social learning theory* (Vol. 1). Englewood Cliffs, NJ: Prentice-Hall.

Barakat, H. (1969). Alienation: A process of encounter between utopia and reality. *The British Journal of Sociology*, *20*(1), 1–10. doi:10.2307/588995 PMID:5771898

Barbash, J. (1972). *The tensions of work*. Madison, WI: Industrial Relations Research Institute.

Barber, B. (2007). *Consumer: How markets corrupt children, infantilize adults, and swallow citizens*. New York, NY: W. W. Norton & Company.

Barber, B. (2008). *Consumed: How markets corrupt children, infantilize adults, and swallow citizens whole*. New York, NY: W. W. Norton & Company.

Barni, D., Knafo, A., Ben-Arieh, A., & Haj-Yahia, M. M. (2014). Parent–child value similarity across and within cultures. *Journal of Cross-Cultural Psychology*, *45*(6), 853–867. doi:10.1177/0022022114530494

Başfırıncı, Ç. (2011). Modern Türk tüketim kültürüne yönelik bir araştırma. *Milli Folklor*, *23*(91), 115–129.

Baudrillard, J. (1981). *For a critique of the political economy of the sign* (C. Levin, Trans.). Candor, NY: Telos Press Publishing.

Baudrillard, J. (1996). *The System of Objects*. New York, NY: Verso.

Baudrillard, J. (1998). *The consumer society: Myths and structures*. Thousand Oaks, CA: Sage.

Baudrillard, J. (2017). *The consumer society* (C. Turner, Trans.). London, UK: Sage.

Baudrillard, J., & Petit, P. (1998). *Paroxysm: Interviews with Philippe Petit*. London, UK: Verso.

Bauman, Z. (2001). Consuming life. *Journal of Consumer Culture*, *1*(1), 9–29. doi:10.1177/146954050100100102

Bauman, Z. (2009). *Does ethics have a chance in a world of consumers?* Boston: Harvard University Press.

Baumeister, R. F. (1987). How the self became a problem: A psychological review of historical research. *Journal of Personality and Social Psychology*, *52*(1), 163–176. doi:10.1037/0022-3514.52.1.163

Baumeister, R. F. (1997). The self and society: Changes, problems, and opportunities. In R. D. Ashmore & L. Jussim (Eds.), *Self and identity* (pp. 191–217). New York, NY: Oxford University Press.

Beabout, G. R., & Echeverria, E. J. (2002). The culture of consumerism: A Catholic and personalist critique. *Journal of Markets & Morality*, *5*(2), 339–383.

Bearden, W., & Haws, K. (2012). How low spending control harms consumers. *Journal of the Academy of Marketing Science*, *40*(1), 181–193. doi:10.100711747-011-0282-1

Beaubot, G., & Echeverria, E. (2011). The culture of consumerism: A Catholic and Personalist critique. *Journal of Markets & Morality*, *5*(2), 339–383.

Beaudoin, T. (2003). *Consuming faith: Integrating who we are with what we buy*. Lanham, MD: Rowan & Littlefield.

Beckett, S. (1954). *Waiting for Godot*. New York, NY: Grove Press, Inc.

Beck, U., & Beck-Gernsheim, E. (1996). Individualization and 'precarious freedoms': Perspectives and controversies of a subject-oriented sociology. In P. Heelas, S. Lash, & P. Morris (Eds.), *Detraditionalization: critical reflections on authority and identity* (pp. 23–48). Cambridge, MA: Blackwell.

Belk, R. W. (1985). Materialism: Trait aspects of living in the material world. *The Journal of Consumer Research, 12*(3), 265–280. doi:10.1086/208515

Belk, R. W. (1988). Possessions and the extended self. *The Journal of Consumer Research, 15*(2), 139–168. doi:10.1086/209154

Belk, R. W. (2015). Frontiers of culture and psychology. In S. Ng & A. Y. Lee (Eds.), *Handbook of culture and consumer behavior* (pp. 290–323). New York, NY: Oxford University Press.

Belk, R. W., Ger, G., & Askegaard, S. (2003). The fire of desire: A multisited inquiry into consumer passion. *The Journal of Consumer Research, 30*(3), 326–351. doi:10.1086/378613

Bell, D. (1976). *The cultural contradictions of western capitalism*. London, UK: Heineman.

Bennett, A. (2005). In defence of neo-tribes: A response to Blackman and Hesmondhalgh. *Journal of Youth Studies, 9*(2), 255–259. doi:10.1080/13676260500149402

Berger, A. (2005). *Shop 'til you drop: Consumer behavior and American culture*. New York, NY: Rowman & Littlefield.

Berkowitz, L. (1989). Frustration-aggression hypothesis: Examination and reformulation. *Psychological Bulletin, 106*(1), 59–73. doi:10.1037/0033-2909.106.1.59 PMID:2667009

Berleant, A. (1973). The experience and judgement of values. In E. Laszlo & J. Wilbur (Eds.), Value theory in philosophy and social science (pp. 24-37). London: Gordon and Breach Science Publishers.

Berman, R. (1981). *Advertising and social change*. Beverly Hills, CA: Sage.

Bernays, E. (1955). *The engineering of consent*. Norman, OK: University of Oklahoma Press.

Bernstein, R. (1983). *Beyond objectivism and relativism*. Philadelphia, PA: University of Pennsylvania Press.

Berridge, K. C., Robinson, T. E., & Aldridge, J. W. (2009). Dissecting components of reward: 'Liking,' 'wanting,' and 'learning.'. *Current Opinion in Pharmacology, 9*(1), 65–73. doi:10.1016/j.coph.2008.12.014 PMID:19162544

Besley, T. A. (2009). Governmentality of Youth: Beyond Cultural Studies. *Contemporary Readings in Law & Social Justice, 1*(2), 36–83.

Bettany, S. (2007). The material semiotics of consumption or where (and what) are the objects in consumer culture theory? *Research in Consumer Behavior, 11*, 41–56.

Beverland, M. B., & Farrelly, F. J. (2009). The quest for authenticity in consumption: Consumers' purposive choice of authentic cues to shape experienced outcomes. *The Journal of Consumer Research, 36*(5), 838–856. doi:10.1086/615047

Bhatt, S. R. (2001). The Buddhist doctrine of universal compassion and quality of life. In R. P. Singh & G. F. McLean (Eds.), The Buddhist world view (pp. 111-120). Faridabad, India: Om.

Bhattacharya, C. B., & Bolton, R. N. (2000). Relationship marketing in mass markets. In J. N. Sheth & A. Parvatiyar (Eds.), *Handbook of relationship marketing* (pp. 327–355). Thousand Oaks, CA: Sage Publications. doi:10.4135/9781452231310.n12

Binswanger, M. (2006). Why does income growth fail to make us happier? Searching for the treadmills behind the paradox of happiness. *Journal of Socio-Economics, 35*(2), 366–381. doi:10.1016/j.socec.2005.11.040

Bishop, N. (1997). Advertising overload. *Marketing Magazine, 15*, 42.

Blackman, S. (2004). *Chilling out: The cultural politics of substance consumption, youth and drug policy*. London, UK: McGraw-Hill.

Blackman, S., & Kempson, M. (Eds.). (2016). *The subcultural imagination: Theory, research and reflexivity in contemporary youth culture (youth, young adulthood and society)*. Abington, UK: Routledge.

Blank, R. M., & Blinder, A. S. (1985). *Macroeconomics, income distribution, and poverty*. National Bureau of Economic Research working paper series, No. 1567. Retrieved May 15, 2018, from http://www.nber.org/papers/w1567

Blumer, H. (1969). Fashion: From class differentiation to collective selection. *The Sociological Quarterly, 10*(3), 275–291. doi:10.1111/j.1533-8525.1969.tb01292.x

Bocock, R. (1993). *Consumption*. London, UK: Routledge. doi:10.4324/9780203313114

Bond, E. (1983). *Reason and value*. Cambridge, UK: Cambridge University Press.

Boratav, K. (2014). *Türkiye iktisat tarihi (1908-2009)*. Ankara, Turkey: İmge Bookstore.

Bordo, S. (2000). Hunger as ideology. In J. B. Schor & D. B. Holt (Eds.), *The consumer society reader* (pp. 99–114). New York, NY: The New Press.

Borgerson, J. L. (2005). Materiality, agency, and the constitution of consuming subjects: Insights for consumer research. In G. Menon & A. R. Rao (Eds.), *Advances in consumer research* (pp. 439–443). Duluth, MN: Association for Consumer Research.

Bourdieu, P. (1984). *Distinction: A social critique of the judgement of taste*. London, UK: Routledge.

Bove, L. L., Nagpal, A., & Dorsett, A. S. (2009). Exploring the determinants of the frugal shopper. *Journal of Retailing and Consumer Services, 16*(4), 291–297. doi:10.1016/j.jretconser.2009.02.004

Bowlby, R. (2001). *Carried away: The invention of modern shopping*. New York, NY: Columbia University Press.

Bowles, S. (1998). Endogenous preferences: The cultural consequences of markets and other economic institutions. *Journal of Economic Literature, 36*(1), 75–111.

Bowles, S. (2008). Policies designed for self-interested citizens may undermine "the moral sentiments:" Evidence from economic experiments. *Science, 320*(5883), 1605–1609. doi:10.1126cience.1152110 PMID:18566278

Bowles, S. (2011). Is liberal society a parasite on tradition? *Philosophy & Public Affairs, 39*(1), 46–81. doi:10.1111/j.1088-4963.2011.01201.x

Bowles, S., & Gintis, H. (1976). *Schooling in capitalist America*. New York: Basic Books.

Brady, M. T. (2017). Subversiveness in adolescence. *Contemporary Psychoanalysis, 53*(3), 346–361. doi:10.1080/00107530.2017.1355693

Brakus, J. J., Schmitt, B. H., & Zarantonello, L. (2009). Brand experience: What is it? How is it measured? Does it affect loyalty? *Journal of Marketing, 73*(3), 52–68. doi:10.1509/jmkg.73.3.52

Bronfenbrenner, U. (1986). Alienation and the four worlds of childhood. *Phi Delta Kappan, 67*(6), 430–436.

Bronfenbrenner, U. (1994). Ecological models of human development. In *International encyclopedia of education* (2nd ed.; Vol. 3). Oxford, UK: Elsevier.

Brooks, D. (2008, May 13). The neural Buddhists. *The New York Times*, p.13.

Brown, B., & Merritt, R. (2002). *No easy answers: The truth behind death at Columbine*. New York, NY: Lantern Books.

Brownlie, D., Saren, M., Wensley, R., & Whittington, R. (1999). Marketing disequilibrium: On redress and restoration. In D. Brownlie, M. Saren, R. Wensley, & R. Whittington (Eds.), *Rethinking marketing: Toward critical marketing accounting* (pp. 1–22). Thousand Oaks, CA: Sage Publications. doi:10.4135/9781446280058.n2

Brown, M. R., Higgins, K., Pierce, T., Hong, E., & Thoma, C. (2003). Secondary students' perceptions of school life with regard to alienation: The effects of disability, gender and race. *Learning Disability Quarterly*, *26*(4), 227–238. doi:10.2307/1593636

Burnham, T. A., Frels, J. K., & Mahajan, V. (2003). Consumer switching costs: A typology, antecedents, and consequences. *Journal of the Academy of Marketing Science*, *31*(2), 109–126. doi:10.1177/0092070302250897

Burns, D. (2014). *Identity through consumption activities: A review and critical analysis*. Unpublished paper.

Burns, D. (n.d.). *Identity through consumption activities: A review and critical analysis*. Unpublished manuscript.

Burns, D. J. (2002). *Identity through consumption activities: A review and critical analysis*. Unpublished Manuscript, Xavier University.

Burns, D. (2011). Consumption in consumer culture: The role of fear and internal longings. *Proceedings of the Colleagues in Jesuit Business Education Conference*.

Burns, D. J. (2006). Self-construction through consumption activities: An analysis and review of alternatives. In P. C. Vitz & S. M. Felch (Eds.), *The self: Beyond the postmodern crisis* (pp. 149–167). Wilmington, DE: Intercollegiate Studies Institute.

Burns, D. J. (2010). Mimeticism and the basis of value: Toward a theory of fashion marketing. *Journal of Global Fashion Marketing*, *1*(1), 40–50. doi:10.1080/20932685.2010.10593056

Burns, D. J., & Warren, H. B. (2008). Consumer warfare: Implications for marketing strategy. *The Journal of Business Strategy*, *29*(6), 44–52. doi:10.1108/02756660810917237

Burns, D. J., & Warren, H. B. (2009). Are marketers nothing more than arms dealers. *Journal of Business Management and Change*, *4*(1), 9–26.

Burns, D. J., & Warren, H. B. (2009). Are marketers nothing more than arms dealers? *Journal of Business Management and Change*, *4*(1), 9–26.

Burns, D., & Fawcett, J. (2012). The role of brands in a consumer culture: Can strong brands serve as a substitute for a relationship with God? *Journal of Biblical Integration in Business*, *15*(2), 28–42.

Butters, C. (2010). *An examination of arousal in experienced skydivers*. Fullerton, CA: California State University.

Calabrese, R. L. (1989). The effects of mobility on adolescent alienation. *High School Journal*, *73*(1), 41–46.

Callero, P. L. (2003). The sociology of the self. *Annual Review of Sociology*, *29*(1), 115–133. doi:10.1146/annurev.soc.29.010202.100057

Calvin, J. (1960). Institutes of the Christian religion (J. T. McNeill, Ed.; F. L. Battles, Trans.). Philadelphia, PA: Westminster Press.

Camacho, L. A. (1998). Consumption as a topic for the north-south dialogue. In D. A. Crocker & T. Linden (Eds.), *Ethics of consumption: The good life, justice, and global stewardship* (pp. 19–27). Lanham, MD: Rowman and Littlefield Publishers, Inc.

Campbell, C. (1987). *The romantic ethic and the spirit of modern consumerism.* Cambridge, MA: Blackwell.

Campbell, C. (2010). What is wrong with consumerism? An assessment of some common criticisms. *Anuario Filosofico, 43*(2), 279–296.

Camus, A. (1955). *L'Etranger.* New York, NY: Appleton-Century Crofts.

Camus, A. (1955). *The myth of Sisyphus and other essays* (J. O'Brien, Trans.). New York, NY: Vintage Books.

Case, J. M. (2008). Alienation and engagement: Development of an alternative theoretical framework for understanding student learning. *Higher Education, 55*(3), 321–332. doi:10.100710734-007-9057-5

Catalano, J. S. (1986). A commentary on Jean-Paul Sartre's critique of dialectical reason: Vol. 1. *Theory of practical ensembles.* Chicago, IL: University of Chicago Press.

Chamorro-Premuzic, T. (2013). Does money really affect motivation? A review of the research. *Harvard Business Review.* Retrieved June 18, 2015 from https://hbr.org/2013/04/does-money-really-affect-motiv

Chancellor, J., & Lyubomirsky, S. (2011). Happiness and thrift: When (spending) less is (hedonically) more. *Journal of Consumer Psychology, 21*(2), 131–138. doi:10.1016/j.jcps.2011.02.004

Chang, S. J., van Witteloostuijn, A., & Eden, L. (2010). From the editors: common method variance in international business research. Journal of International Business Studies, 41(2), 178-184.

Chang, P. L., & Chieng, M. H. (2006). Building consumer–brand relationship: A cross-cultural experiential view. *Psychology and Marketing, 23*(11), 927–959. doi:10.1002/mar.20140

Chan, K., & Prendergast, G. P. (2008). Social comparison, imitation of celebrity models and materialism among Chinese youth. *International Journal of Advertising, 27*(5), 799–826. doi:10.2501/S026504870808030X

Chatterjee, A., & Hunt, J. M. (1996). Self-monitoring as a personality correlate of materialism: An investigation of related cognitive. *Psychological Reports, 79*(2), 523–528. doi:10.2466/pr0.1996.79.2.523

Chernev, A., Hamilton, R., & Gal, D. (2011). Competing for consumer identity: Limits to self-expression and the perils of lifestyle branding. *Journal of Marketing, 75*(3), 66–82. doi:10.1509/jmkg.75.3.66

Chewning, R. (2012). Augustine and Aquinas: Their theological progeny comes face to face with business as mission. *The Journal of Biblical Integration in Business, 15*(2), 64–83.

Chomsky, N., & Skinner, B. F. (1959). Review of Verbal Behavior by B. F. Skinner. *Language, 35*(1), 27–58. doi:10.2307/411334

Christman, J. (2003). Autonomy in moral and political philosophy. In E.N. Zalta (Ed.), *Stanford encyclopedia of philosophy.* Retrieved November 21, 2015 from http://plato.stanford.edu/archives/fall2003/entries/autonomy-moral/

Christman, J. (1991). Autonomy and personal history. *Canadian Journal of Philosophy, 21*(1), 1–24. doi:10.1080/00455091.1991.10717234

Chung, J. (1994). *Utility and production functions: Theory and applications.* Oxford, UK: Blackwell Publishers.

Cicourel, A. (1973). *Cognitive sociology: Language and meaning in social interaction.* Baltimore, MD: Penguin Books.

Cision PRWeb. (2018). *$10.4Billion Self-Imporvement Marktet Survives Scandals & Recession.* Retrieved from http://www.prweb.com/releases/2013/1/prweb10275905.htm

Clapp, R. (1998). *The consuming passion: Christianity & the consumer culture.* Downers Grove, IL: InterVarsity Press.

Clark, G. (2009). *A farewell to alms: A brief economic history of the world.* Princeton, NJ: Princeton University Press.

Cloninger, C. R. (1987). A systematic method for clinical description and classification of personality variants: A proposal. *Archives of General Psychiatry, 44*(6), 573–588. doi:10.1001/archpsyc.1987.01800180093014 PMID:3579504

Cloninger, C. R. (1991). Brain networks underlying personality development. In B. J. Carroll & J. E. Barrett (Eds.), *Psychopathology and the brain* (pp. 183–208). New York, NY: Raven Press.

Cloninger, C. R. (1994). Temperament and personality. *Current Opinion in Neurobiology, 4*(2), 266–273. doi:10.1016/0959-4388(94)90083-3 PMID:8038587

Cohen, J. B. (1967). An interpersonal orientation to the study of consumer behavior. *JMR, Journal of Marketing Research, 4*(3), 270–278. doi:10.2307/3149459

Cohen, P. (2016). From here to modernity. In S. Blackman & M. Kempson (Eds.), *The subcultural imagination: Theory, research and reflexivity in contemporary youth cultures* (pp. 19–32). New York, NY: Routledge.

Collins, C., & Yeskel, F. (2011). *Economic apartheid in America: A primer on economic inequality & insecurity.* New York, NY: The New Press.

Collins, N. L., & Read, S. J. (1990). Adult attachment, working models, and relationship quality in dating couples. *Journal of Personality and Social Psychology, 58*(4), 644–663. doi:10.1037/0022-3514.58.4.644 PMID:14570079

Comms Week. (2010, May 24). Consumer advocacy in a liberalized telecom sector. *Communications Week.* Retrieved December 12, 2017 from http:www.consumer-advocacy-in-a-liberalized-telecom-secrtor/commsweek/com

Comms Week. (2014). How telcos cheat, frustrate subscribers. *Communications Week.* Retrieved December 17, 2017, from http:www.how-telcos-cheast-frustrate-subscribers/commsweek/com

Comms Week. (2017). How telcos cheat, frustrate subscribers. *Communications Week.* Retrieved December 17, 2017, from http:www.how-telcos-cheast-frustrate-subscribers/commsweek/com

Connell, P. M., Brucks, M., & Nielsen, J. H. (2014). How childhood advertising exposure can create biased product evaluations that persist into adulthood. *The Journal of Consumer Research, 41*(1), 119–134. doi:10.1086/675218

Connor, S. (1992). *Theory and cultural value.* Oxford, UK: Blackwell Publishers.

Constantinople, A. (1969). An Eriksonian measure of personality development in college students. *Developmental Psychology, 1*(4), 357–372. doi:10.1037/h0027706

Cooper, J. M. (1984). Plato's theory of human motivation. *History of Philosophy Quarterly, 1*(1), 3–21.

Cooper, S., McLoughlin, D., & Keating, A. (2005). Individual and neo-tribal consumption: Tales from the Simpsons of Springfield. *Journal of Consumer Behaviour, 4*(5), 330–344. doi:10.1002/cb.17

Cornford, F. M. (1965). Mathematics and dialectic in the Republic VI-VII. In Studies in Plato's metaphysics (pp. 61-96). London, UK: Routledge & Kegan Paul.

Corrigan, P. (1997). *The sovereignty of consumption: An introduction.* Thousand Oaks, CA: Sage.

Cova, B. (1996). What postmodernism means to marketing managers. *European Management Journal, 14*(5), 494–499. doi:10.1016/0263-2373(96)00043-6

Cova, B. (1997). Community and consumption: Towards a definition of the 'linking value' of products or services. *European Journal of Marketing, 3*(3/4), 297–316. doi:10.1108/03090569710162380

Crane, D. (2010). Environmental change and the future of consumption: Implications for consumer identity. *Anuario Filosofico, 43*(2), 353–379.

Crotty, M. (1998). *The foundations of social research: Meaning and perspective in the research process.* Thousand Oaks, CA: Sage Publications.

Cryder, C. E., Lerner, J. S., Gross, J. J., & Dahl, R. E. (2008). Misery is not miserly: Sad and self-focused individuals spend more. *Psychological Science, 19*(6), 525–530. doi:10.1111/j.1467-9280.2008.02118.x PMID:18578840

Dağtaş, B., & Dağtaş, E. (Eds.). (2009). *Medya, tüketim kültürü ve yaşam tarzları: Türkiye medyasından örüntüler.* Ankara, Turkey: Ütopya Publications.

Dahlsgaard, K., Peterson, C., & Seligman, M. E. (2005). Shared virtue: The convergence of valued human strengths across culture and history. *Review of General Psychology, 9*(3), 203–213. doi:10.1037/1089-2680.9.3.203

Daly, H. E. (1998). Consumption: Value added, physical transformation, and welfare. In D. A. Crocker & T. Linden (Eds.), *Ethics of consumption: The good life, justice, and global stewardship* (pp. 19–27). Lanham, MD: Rowman and Littlefield Publishers, Inc.

Daly, H. E., & Cobb, J. B. (1994). *For the common good: Redirecting the economy toward community, the environment, and a sustainable future (2nd ed.).* Boston, MA: Beacon Press.

Daniels, J. (2008). Wanting nothing: Imitation and production in the economy of desire. *New Blackfriars, 90*(1025), 90–107. doi:10.1111/j.1741-2005.2008.00237.x

Dauvergne, P. (2010). *The shadows of consumption: Consequences for the global environment.* Cambridge, MA: The MIT Press.

Davidson, J. (2012). Citizen consumers: The Athenian democracy and the origins of Western consumption. In The Oxford handbook of the history of consumption (pp. 23-46). Oxford, UK: Oxford University Press.

De Graaf, J., Wann, D., & Naylor, T. H. (2005). *Affluenza: The all-consuming epidemic.* San Francisco, CA: Berrett-Koehler Publishers.

Dean, T., & Kanazawa, K. (1989). A model for reasoning about persistence and causation. *Computational Intelligence, 5*(2), 142–150. doi:10.1111/j.1467-8640.1989.tb00324.x

Debord, G. (1994). *The society of the spectacle.* New York, NY: Zone Books.

Deighton, J., & Barwise, P. (2000). Digital marketing communication. Future media working waper, No. 00-801. London UK: London Business School.

Demasio, A. (1994). *Descartes' error: Emotions, reason, and the human brain.* New York, NY: Avon Books.

Denzin, N. K. (1987). On semiotics and symbolic interactionism. *Symbolic Interaction, 10*(1), 1–19. doi:10.1525i.1987.10.1.1

Descartes, R. (2006). *A discourse on the method of correctly conducting one's reason and seeking truth in the sciences.* New York, NY: Oxford University Press.

Deshpande, R., Hoyer, W. D., & Donthu, N. (1986). The intensity of ethnic affiliation: A study of the sociology of Hispanic consumption. *The Journal of Consumer Research, 13*(2), 214–220. doi:10.1086/209061

Diamond, J. M. (1999). *Guns, germs, and steel: The fates of human societies*. New York, NY: W. W. Norton & Company.

Dibb, S. (2001). New millennium, new segments: Moving towards the segment of one? *Journal of Strategic Marketing, 9*(3), 193–213. doi:10.1080/713775742

Dichter, E. (2002). *The strategy of desire*. New Brunswick, NJ: Transaction.

Dittmar, H. (2007). The costs of consumer culture and the "cage within": The impact of the material "good life" and "body perfect" ideals on individuals" identity and well-being. *Psychological Inquiry, 18*(1), 23–31. doi:10.1080/10478400701389045

Dittmar, H., Bond, R., Hurst, M., & Kasser, T. (2014). The relationship between materialism and personal well-being: A meta-analysis. *Journal of Personality and Social Psychology, 107*(5), 879–924. doi:10.1037/a0037409 PMID:25347131

Dixsaut, M. (1997). What is it Plato calls thinking? *Proceedings of the Boston Area Colloquium in Ancient Philosophy, 13*(1), 1–27. doi:10.1163/2213441797X00037

Doherty, D., & Etzioni, A. (2003). *Voluntary simplicity: Responding to consumer culture*. Lanham, MD: Rowan and Littlefield.

Duncan, T., & Moriarty, S. E. (1998). A communication-based marketing model for managing relationships. *Journal of Marketing, 62*(2), 1–13. doi:10.2307/1252157

Dunn, R. G. (2000). Identity, commodification, and consumer culture. In J. E. David (Ed.), *Identity and social change* (pp. 109–134). Abington, UK: Routledge.

Durgee, J. (1986). Richer findings from qualitative research. *Journal of Advertising Research, 26*(4), 36–44.

Durkheim, E. (1974). Value judgements and judgements of reality. In E. Durkheim (Ed.), *Sociology and philosophy*. New York, NY: Free Press.

Dutt, R. C. (1983). *Buddhism & Buddhist Civilisation in India*. Delhi, India: Seema.

Duygu, F. (2011). The use of decision making styles as a market segmentation variable: A study in Turkey. *The Journal of American Academy of Business, Cambridge, 16*(2), 223–229.

Dworkin, G. (1988). *The theory and practice of autonomy*. Cambridge, UK: Cambridge University Press. doi:10.1017/CBO9780511625206

Easterbrook, M. J., Wright, M. L., Dittmar, H., & Banerjee, R. (2014). Consumer culture ideals, extrinsic motivations, and well-being in children. *European Journal of Social Psychology, 44*(4), 349–359. doi:10.1002/ejsp.2020

Eastman, J. K., Goldsmith, R. E., & Flynn, L. R. (1999). Status consumption in consumer behavior: Scale development and validation. *Journal of Marketing Theory and Practice, 7*(3), 41–51. doi:10.1080/10696679.1999.11501839

Eastman, J. K., & Iyer, R. (2012). The relationship between cognitive age and status consumption: An exploratory look. *The Marketing Management Journal, 22*(1), 80–96.

El-Bassiouny, N. (2016). Where is "Islamic marketing" heading?: A commentary on Jafari and Sandikci's (2015) "Islamic" consumers, markets, and marketing. *Journal of Business Research, 69*(2), 569–578. doi:10.1016/j.jbusres.2015.05.012

Elgendy, N., & Elragal, A. (2014). Big data analytics: a literature review paper. In *Industrial Conference on Data Mining* (pp. 214-227). Berlin, Germany: Springer. 10.1007/978-3-319-08976-8_16

Elgin, D., & Mitchell, A. (2003). Voluntary simplicity: A movement emerges. In D. Doherty & A. Etzioni (Eds.), *Voluntary simplicity: Responding to consumer culture* (pp. 145–171). Lanham, MD: Rowman & Littlefield.

Elliot, R., & Wattanasuwan, K. (1998). Brands as symbolic resources for the construction of identity. *International Journal of Advertising*, *17*(2), 131–144. doi:10.1080/02650487.1998.11104712

Elliott, A., & Lemert, C. (2009). *The new individualism: The emotional costs of globalization* (rev. ed.). Abington, UK: Routledge.

Elliott, R. (1997). Existential consumption and irrational desire. *European Journal of Marketing*, *31*(3/4), 285–296. doi:10.1108/03090569710162371

Elsbach, K. D., & Sutton, R. I. (1992). Acquiring organizational legitimacy through illegitimate actions: A marriage of institutional and impression management theories. *Academy of Management Journal*, *35*(4), 699–738.

eMarketer. (2014). Total US ad spending to see largest increase since 2004. *eMarketer*. Retrieved June 15, 2015, from http://www.emarketer.com/Article/Total-US-Ad-Spending-See-Largest-Increase-Since-2004/1010982

Emdin, C. (2007). Exploring the contexts of urban science classrooms. Part 2: The emergence of rituals in the learning of science. *Cultural Studies of Science Education*, *2*(2), 351–392. doi:10.100711422-007-9057-x

Emdin, C. (2010). Affiliation and alienation: Hip-hop, rap, and urban science education. *Journal of Curriculum Studies*, *42*(1), 1–25. doi:10.1080/00220270903161118

Emmons, R. A. (2005). Striving for the sacred: Personal goals, life meaning, and religion. *The Journal of Social Issues*, *61*(4), 731–745. doi:10.1111/j.1540-4560.2005.00429.x

Endong, F. P. C. (2015). How ethical is print advertising by religious organizations in Nigeria. *International Journal of Media Journalism and Mass Communication*, *1*(2), 5–13.

Ergur, A. (2002). Kredi kartı kullanımında zaman algılaması ve borçlu yaşam. *Toplum ve Bilim*, *102*, 128–141.

Erikson, E. H. (1994). *Identity: Youth and crisis*. New York, NY: WW Norton & Company.

Erikson, E. H., & Erikson, J. M. (1998). *The life cycle completed (extended version)*. New York, NY: WW Norton & Company.

Erwin, E. (Ed.). (2002). *The Freud encyclopedia: Theory, therapy, and culture*. New York, NY: Taylor & Francis.

Escalas, J. E., & Bettman, J. R. (2005). Self-construal, reference groups and brand meaning. *The Journal of Consumer Research*, *32*(3), 378–389. doi:10.1086/497549

Escalas, J., & Bettman, J. R. (2003). You are what they eat: The influence of reference groups on consumers' connections to brands. *Journal of Consumer Psychology*, *13*(3), 339–348. doi:10.1207/S15327663JCP1303_14

Etukodo, M. (2008). Advertising and consumerism in Nigeria. *The Control Tower*, *2*(3), 11–24.

Evans, F. B. (1959). Psychological and objective factors in the prediction of brand choice Ford versus Chevrolet. *The Journal of Business*, *32*(4), 340–369. doi:10.1086/294291

Faulkner, W. (1956). *The sound and the fury*. New York, NY: Vintage Books.

Featherstone, M. (1991). *Consumer culture and postmodernism*. London, UK: Sage Publications Limited.

Feick, L. F., & Price, L. L. (1987). The market maven: A diffuser of marketplace information. *Journal of Marketing*, *51*(1), 83–97. doi:10.2307/1251146

Ferguson, H. (1992). *Religious transformation in Western society: The end of happiness*. New York: Routledge.

Ferguson, H. (1992). Watching the world go round: Atrium culture and the psychology of shopping. In R. Shields (Ed.), *Lifestyle shopping: The subject of consumption* (pp. 21–39). London, UK: Routledge. doi:10.4324/9780203413074_chapter_2

Ferreira, M. C., & Scaraboto, D. (2016). 'My plastic dreams:' Towards an extended understanding of materiality and the shaping of consumer identities. *Journal of Business Research*, *69*(1), 191–207. doi:10.1016/j.jbusres.2015.07.032

Ferrell, J. (2006). *Empire of scrounge: Inside the urban underground of dumpster diving, trash picking, and street scavenging*. New York, NY: NYU Press.

Firat, A. F., & Venkatesh, A. (1995). Liberatory postmodernism and the reenchantment of consumption. *The Journal of Consumer Research*, *22*(3), 239–267. doi:10.1086/209448

Fitzmaurice, J., & Comegys, C. (2006). Materialism and social construction. *Journal of Marketing Theory and Practice*, *14*(4), 287–299. doi:10.2753/MTP1069-6679140403

Fleming, C. (2004). *Rene Girard: Violence and mimesis*. Malden, MA: Polity Press.

Floh, A., Zauner, A., Koller, M., & Rusch, T. (2014). Customer segmentation using unobserved heterogeneity in the perceived-value–loyalty–intentions link. *Journal of Business Research*, *67*(5), 974–982. doi:10.1016/j.jbusres.2013.08.003

Flynn, L. R., & Goldsmith, R. E. (2015). Introducing the super consumer. *Journal of Consumer Behaviour*, *15*(3), 201–207. doi:10.1002/cb.1535

Flynn, L. R., Goldsmith, R. E., & Kim, W.-M. (2000). A cross-cultural validation of three new marketing scales for fashion research: Involvement, opinion seeking, and knowledge. *Journal of Fashion Marketing and Management*, *4*(2), 110–120. doi:10.1108/eb022583

Flynn, L. R., Goldsmith, R. E., & Kim, W.-M. (2013). A cross-cultural study of materialism and brand engagement. *Journal of Multi-Disciplinary Studies*, *5*(3), 49–69.

Flynn, L. R., Goldsmith, R. E., & Pollitte, W. (2016). Materialism, status consumption, and market involved consumers. *Psychology and Marketing*, *33*(9), 761–776. doi:10.1002/mar.20915

Folorin, B. (2017). NCC 2017 year of telecom consumer: Minister calls for adoption of made in Nigeria software. *World Stage*. Retrieved December 11, 2017 from http://worldstagegroup.com/worldstagenew/index.php?active=news&news cid=34954&catid=31

Force, W. R. (2009). Consumption styles and the fluid complexity of punk authenticity. *Symbolic Interaction*, *32*(4), 289–309. doi:10.1525i.2009.32.4.289

Fortin, N. M., & Lemieux, T. (1997). Institutional changes and rising wage inequality: Is there a linkage? *The Journal of Economic Perspectives*, *11*(2), 75–96. doi:10.1257/jep.11.2.75

Foucault, M. (1980). *Power/knowledge: Selected interviews and other writings, 1972-1977*. New York, NY: Pantheon.

Foucault, M. (1984). *The Foucault reader*. New York, NY: Pantheon.

Fournier, S. (1998). Consumers and their brands: Developing relationship theory in consumer research. *The Journal of Consumer Research*, *24*(4), 343–373. doi:10.1086/209515

Fournier, S., & Avery, J. (2011). Putting the relationship back into CRM. *MIT Sloan Management Review*, *52*(3), 63–72.

Francis. (2015). *Encyclical Letter Laudato Si' of the Holy Father Francis on Care for our Common Home*. Retrieved from https://theyear2015.wikispaces.com/file/detail/papa-francesco_20150524_enciclica-laudato-si_en.pdf/554210024

Frankena, W. (1967). Value and valuation. In P. Edwards (Ed.), *The encyclopedia of philosophy* (Vol. 18, pp. 229–232). New York, NY: Macmillan Publishing Company.

Frankfurt, H. (1971). Freedom of the will and the concept of the person. *The Journal of Philosophy, 68*(1), 5–20. doi:10.2307/2024717

Frank, R. H. (2005). Positional externalities cause large and preventable welfare losses. *The American Economic Review, 95*(2), 137–141. doi:10.1257/000282805774670392

Freud, A. (1992). *The ego and the mechanisms of defence*. New York, NY: Karnac Books.

Freud, S. (1914). On narcissism: An introduction. In *The standard edition of the complete psychological works of Sigmund Freud* (J. Strachey, Trans.; vol. 14, pp. 67–102). London, UK: Hogarth Press.

Frohlich, M. T., & Dixon, J. R. (2001). A taxonomy of manufacturing strategies revisited. *Journal of Operations Management, 19*(5), 541–558. doi:10.1016/S0272-6963(01)00063-8

Fromm, E. (1956). *The art of loving: An enquiry into the nature of love*. New York, NY: Harper.

Fromm, E. (1976). *To have or to be?* New York, NY: Harper & Row.

Frondizi, R. (1971). *What is value?: An introduction to axiology*. La Salle, CA: Open Court.

Frost, R. O., Kyrios, M., McCarthy, K. D., & Matthews, Y. (2007). Self-ambivalence and attachment to possessions. *Journal of Cognitive Psychotherapy, 21*(3), 232–242. doi:10.1891/088983907781494582

Frymer, B. (2009). The media spectacle of Columbine: Alienated youth as an object of fear. *The American Behavioral Scientist, 52*(10), 1387–1404. doi:10.1177/0002764209332554

Fullerton, G. L. (1998). The marketing concept in a post-modern era. In P. J. Gordon & B. J. Kellerman (Eds.), *Enhancing knowledge development in marketing* (pp. 198–203). Chicago, IL: American Marketing Association.

Gabriel, Y., & Lang, T. (2015). *The unmanageable consumer*. London, UK: Sage.

Galbo, J. J. (1988). An exploration of the effects of the relationships of adolescents and adults on learning in secondary schools. *High School Journal, 71*(2), 97–102.

Galbraith, J. K. (1958/1998). The affluent society (40th anniversary ed.). New York, NY: Mariner Books.

Gambrel, J. C., & Cafaro, P. (2010). The virtue of simplicity. *Journal of Agricultural & Environmental Ethics, 23*(1/2), 85–108. doi:10.100710806-009-9187-0

Garðarsdóttir, R. B., & Dittmar, H. (2012). The relationship of materialism to debt and financial well-being: The case of Iceland's perceived prosperity. *Journal of Economic Psychology, 33*(3), 471–481. doi:10.1016/j.joep.2011.12.008

Gardner, B. B., & Levy, S. J. (1955). The product and the brand. *Harvard Business Review, 33*(2), 33–39.

Garfinkel, H. (1969). *Studies in ethnomethodology*. Englewood Cliffs, NJ: Prentice-Hall.

Garvey, J. (2008). *The ethics of climate change: Right and wrong in a warming world*. New York, NY: Bloomsbury Academic.

Gaus, G. (1990). *Values and justification: The foundations of liberal theory*. Cambridge, UK: Cambridge University Press. doi:10.1017/CBO9780511625046

Geertz, C. (1973). Thick description: Toward and interpretive theory of culture, the interpretation of culture. In C. Geertz (Ed.), *The interpretation of cultures: selected essays* (pp. 3–30). New York: Basic Books.

Geiger-Oneto, S., Gelb, B. D., Walker, D., & Hess, J. D. (2013). 'Buying status' by choosing or rejecting luxury brands and their counterfeits. *Journal of the Academy of Marketing Science*, *41*(3), 357–372. doi:10.100711747-012-0314-5

Gencer, B. (2008). *İslam'da modernleşme*. Ankara, Turkey: Lotus Publications.

George, D. (2004). *Preference pollution: How markets create the desires we dislike*. Ann Arbor, MI: University of Michigan Press.

Ghazzawi, I., & Smith, Y. (2009). Crafting the whole employee: Job satisfaction, job commitment, and faith. *Business Review (Federal Reserve Bank of Philadelphia)*, *12*(2), 300–309.

Gibson, A. (2011). Ideas and practices in the critique of consumerism. *Environmental Philosophy*, *8*(2), 171–188. doi:10.5840/envirophil20118219

Giddens, A. (1991). *Modernity and self-identity*. Cambridge, UK: Polity Press.

Ginsberg, B. (2011). *The fall of the faculty: The rise of the all-administrative university and why it matters*. New York, NY: Oxford University Press.

Girard, R. (1979). *Violence and the sacred* (P. Gregory, Trans.). Baltimore, MD: Johns Hopkins University.

Girard, R. (1997a). From mimetic desire to the monstrous double. In T. Murray (Ed.), *Mimesis, masochism and mime: The politics of theatricality in contemporary French thought* (pp. 87–111). Ann Arbor, MI: University of Michigan Press.

Girard, R. (1997b). *Resurrection from the underground: Feodor Dostoevsky* (J. G. Williams, Trans.). New York, NY: Crossroad.

Girard, R. (2001). *I see Satan fall like lightning* (J. G. Williams, Trans.). Maryknoll, NY: Orbis Books.

Gloege, T. (2015). *Guaranteed pure: The Moody Bible Institute, business, and the making of modern Evangelicalism*. Chapel Hill, NC: University of North Carolina Press. doi:10.5149/northcarolina/9781469621012.001.0001

Glover, T. D. (2003). Regulating the rave scene: Exploring the policy alternatives of government. *Leisure Sciences*, *25*(4), 307–325. doi:10.1080/714044493

Goldberg, L. R. (1993). The structure of phenotypic personality traits. *The American Psychologist*, *48*(1), 26–34. doi:10.1037/0003-066X.48.1.26 PMID:8427480

Goldin, C. D., & Katz, L. F. (2008). *The race between education and technology*. Boston, MA: Harvard University Press.

Goldman, R., & Papson, S. (2000). Advertising in the age of accelerated meaning. In J. B. Schor & D. B. Holt (Eds.), *The consumer society reader* (pp. 99–114). New York, NY: The New Press.

Goldsmith, R. E., Flynn, L. R., & Clark, R. A. (2014). The etiology of the frugal consumer. *Journal of Retailing and Consumer Services*, *21*(2), 175–184. doi:10.1016/j.jretconser.2013.11.005

Goldsmith, R. E., Flynn, L. R., & Kim, D. (2010). Status consumption and price sensitivity. *Journal of Marketing Theory and Practice*, *18*(4), 323–338. doi:10.2753/MTP1069-6679180402

Göle, N. (2002). *Melez desenler: İslam ve modernlik üzerine*. İstanbul, Turkey: Metis Publications.

Göle, N. (2012). *Seküler ve dinsel: Aşınan sınırlar*. İstanbul, Turkey: Metis Publications.

Golsan, R. J. (2002). *Rene Girard and myth*. New York, NY: Routledge.

González-Benito, Ó., Martos-Partal, M., & Fustinoni-Venturini, M. (2014). Retailers' price positioning and the motivational profiling of store-brand shoppers: The case of Spain. *Psychology and Marketing*, *31*(2), 115–125. doi:10.1002/mar.20680

Gordon, W. R., & Caltabiano, M. L. (1996). Urban-rural differences in adolescent self-esteem, leisure boredom, and sensation-seeking as predictors of leisure-time usage and satisfaction. *Adolescence*, *31*(124), 883–901. PMID:8970661

Goswick, R. A., & Jones, W. H. (1982). Components of loneliness during adolescence. *Journal of Youth and Adolescence*, *11*(5), 373–383. doi:10.1007/BF01540375 PMID:24310911

Grande, P. B. (2015). Desire in the Great Gatsby. *Anthropoetics*, *21*(1), 2–18.

Green, R. (1959). *Protestantism and capitalism: The Weber thesis and its critics*. Boston, MA: D. C. Heath and Company.

Grönroos, C. (1998). Marketing services: The case of a missing product. *Journal of Business and Industrial Marketing*, *13*(4/5), 322–338. doi:10.1108/08858629810226645

Gürbilek, N. (2007). *Vitrinde yaşamak: 1980'lerin kültürel iklimi*. İstanbul, Turkey: Metis Publications.

Gusfield, J. R. (2003). A journey with symbolic interaction. *Symbolic Interaction*, *26*(1), 119–139. doi:10.1525i.2003.26.1.119

Hall, E. (1952). *What is value? An essay in philosophical analysis*. London: Routledge & Paul.

Handa, M., & Khare, A. (2013). Gender as a moderator of the relationship between materialism and fashion clothing involvement among Indian youth. *International Journal of Consumer Studies*, *37*(1), 112–120. doi:10.1111/j.1470-6431.2011.01057.x

Hansson, R. O., Jones, W. H., Carpenter, B. N., & Remondet, I. (1986). Loneliness and adjustment to old age. *International Journal of Aging & Human Development*, *24*(1), 41–53. doi:10.2190/82XB-5L9T-JWKE-U6T8 PMID:3557646

Harber, C. (2008). Perpetrating disaffection: Schooling as an international problem. *Educational Studies*, *34*(5), 457–467. doi:10.1080/03055690802288445

Hartman, A. (2000). In search of subjugated knowledge. *Feminism, Community, and Communication, 11*(4), 19-23.

Hartman, R. (1973). Formal axiology and the measurement of value. In E. Laszlo & J. Wilbur (Eds.), *Value theory in philosophy and social science* (pp. 38–47). London: Gordon and Breach Science Publishers.

Hassan, S. S., & Craft, S. H. (2005). Linking global market segmentation decisions with strategic positioning options. *Journal of Consumer Marketing*, *22*(2), 81–89. doi:10.1108/07363760510589244

Hays, R. D., & DiMatteo, M. R. (1987). A short-form measure of loneliness. *Journal of Personality Assessment*, *51*(1), 69–81. doi:10.120715327752jpa5101_6 PMID:3572711

Heath, J., & Potter, A. (2004). *The rebel sell: Why the culture can't be jammed*. New York, NY: HarperCollins.

Heath, J., & Potter, A. (2005). *Nation of rebels: Why counterculture became consumer culture*. New York, NY: HarperCollins.

Heilbronner, R. (1953). *The worldly philosophers*. New York, NY: Simon & Schuster.

Hekma, G. (2007). Fetishism. In G. Ritzer (Ed.), *The Blackwell encyclopedia of sociology*. London: Blackwell Publishing. Retrieved May 19, 2018 from http://www.blackwellreference.com/public/tocnode?id=g9781405124331_chunk_g978140512433112_ss1-52

Herman, B. (1993). *The practice of moral judgment*. Cambridge, MA: Harvard University Press.

Hewitt, J. P. (1976). *Self and society: A symbolic interactionist social psychology*. Oxford, UK: Allyn & Bacon.

Hill, J. (2011). Endangered childhoods: How consumerism is impacting child and youth identity. *Media Culture & Society*, *33*(3), 347–362. doi:10.1177/0163443710393387

Hill, T. E. Jr. (1991). *Autonomy and self-respect*. Cambridge, UK: Cambridge University Press. doi:10.1017/CBO9780511609237

Hodkinson, A. (2015). *Key issues in special educational needs and inclusion*. London, UK: Sage.

Hoek, J., Gendall, P., & Esslemont, D. (1996). Market segmentation: A search for the Holy Grail? *Journal of Marketing Practice: Applied Marketing Science*, *2*(1), 25–34. doi:10.1108/EUM0000000000005

Hofstede, G. (2004). *Cultures and organizations: software for the mind*. London, UK: McGraw-Hill.

Holbrook, M. (Ed.). (1999). *Consumer value: A framework for analysis and research*. London: Routledge. doi:10.4324/9780203010679

Hollands, R. (2002). Divisions in the dark: Youth cultures, transitions and segmented consumption spaces in the night-time economy. *Journal of Youth Studies*, *5*(2), 153–171. doi:10.1080/13676260220134421

Holman, B., & Ziedenberg, J. (2006). *The dangers of detention: The impact of incarcerating youth in detention and other secure facilities*. Washington, DC: Justice Policy Institute.

Holmes, J. (2001). *The search for the secure base: Attachment theory and psychotherapy*. New York, NY: Routledge.

Holt, D. (1994). Consumers' cultural differences as local systems of tastes: A critique of the personality/values approach and an alternative framework. *Asia Pacific Advances in Consumer Research*, *1*, 178–184.

Holt, D. (1997). Poststructuralist lifestyle analysis: Conceptualizing the social patterning of consumption in postmodernism. *The Journal of Consumer Research*, *23*(4), 326–350. doi:10.1086/209487

Holt, D. B. (2005). An interview with Juliet Schor. *Journal of Consumer Culture*, *5*(1), 5–21. doi:10.1177/1469540505049847

Holt, D. B. (2006). Toward a sociology of branding. *Journal of Consumer Culture*, *6*(3), 299–302. doi:10.1177/1469540506068680

Horney, K. (1937). *The neurotic personality of our time*. New York, NY: W.W. Norton & Company.

Howe, L. A. (2008). Self and pretence: Playing with identity. *Journal of Social Philosophy*, *39*(4), 564–582. doi:10.1111/j.1467-9833.2008.00443.x

Huntington, S. P. (1993). The clash of civilizations? *Foreign Affairs*, *72*(3), 22–49. doi:10.2307/20045621

Hunt, S. D., & Vitell, S. (1986). A general theory of marketing ethics. *Journal of Macromarketing*, *6*(1), 5–16. doi:10.1177/027614678600600103

Hunt, S. D., & Vitell, S. J. (2006). The general theory of marketing ethics: A revision and three questions. *Journal of Macromarketing*, *26*(2), 143–153. doi:10.1177/0276146706290923

Hur, Y.-M., Jeong, H.-U., Schermer, J. A., & Rushton, J. P. (2011). Miserliness is heritable. *Personality and Individual Differences*, *51*(8), 1052–1055. doi:10.1016/j.paid.2011.08.005

Hyland, D. A. (1995). *Finitude and transcendence in the Platonic dialogues*. Albany, NY: State University of New York Press.

Ijewere, A. A., & Obeki, O. S. (2011). Consumerism in Nigeria. *JORIND: Journal of Research in Development*, *9*(2), 186–192.

Illouz, E. (2009). Emotions, imagination and consumption: A new research agenda. *Journal of Consumer Culture*, *9*(3), 377–413. doi:10.1177/1469540509342053

Jackson, S. E. (1981). Measurement of commitment to role identities. *Journal of Personality and Social Psychology*, *40*(1), 138–146. doi:10.1037/0022-3514.40.1.138

Jameson, F. (1991). *Postmodernism, or, the cultural logic of late capitalism*. Durham, NC: Duke University Press.

James, R. (2011). *Shiny objects: Why we spend money we don't have in search of happiness we can't buy*. New York, NY: Harper One.

Jardine, M. (2004). *The making and unmaking of technological society: How Christianity can save modernity from itself*. Grand Rapids, MI: Brazos Press.

Jones, W. H., Freeman, J. R., & Goswick, R. A. (1981). The persistence of loneliness: Self and other determinants. *Journal of Personality*, *49*(1), 27–48. doi:10.1111/j.1467-6494.1981.tb00844.x

Jones, W. H., Rose, J., & Russell, D. (1990). Loneliness and social anxiety. In H. Leitenberg (Ed.), *Handbook of Social and Evaluation Anxiety* (pp. 247–266). New York, NY: Plenum. doi:10.1007/978-1-4899-2504-6_9

Kahle, L. R., Beatty, S. E., & Homer, P. (1986). Alternative measurement approaches to consumer values: The list of values (LOV) and values and life style (VALS). *The Journal of Consumer Research*, *13*(3), 405–409. doi:10.1086/209079

Kaiser, S. B., Chandler, J., & Hammidi, T. (2001). Minding appearances in female academic culture. In A. Guy, E. Green, & M. Banim (Eds.), *Through the wardrobe: Women's relationships with their clothes* (pp. 117–136). New York, NY: Berg. doi:10.2752/9781847888921/THRWARD0012

Kamppinen, M. (Ed.). (1993). *Consciousness, cognitive schemata, and relativism: Multidisciplinary explorations in cognitive science*. Dordrecht, The Netherlands: Kluwer Academic. doi:10.1007/978-94-017-1141-8

Kandiyoti, D. (2005). Parçaları yorumlamak. In D. Kandiyoti & A. Saktanber (Eds.), *Kültür Fragmanları Türkiye'de Gündelik Hayat* (pp. 15–36). İstanbul, Turkey: Metis Publications.

Kant, I. (1978). *Anthropology from a pragmatic point of view*. Carbondale, IL: Southern Illinois University Press.

Kant, I. (1996). *The metaphysics of morals* (M. Gregor, Trans. & Ed.). Cambridge, UK: Cambridge University Press. doi:10.1017/CBO9780511809644

Kant, I. (1998). *Religion within the boundaries of mere reason* (A. Wood & G. di Giovanni, Trans. & Eds.). Cambridge, UK: Cambridge University Press.

Kaplan, G. (2016). *René Girard, Unlikely apologist: Mimetic theory and fundamental theology*. Notre Dame, IN: University of Notre Dame Press.

Kassarjian, H. H. (1981). Low involvement: A second look. In K. B. Monroe (Ed.), *ACR North American Advances in Consumer Research* (pp. 31–34). Ann Arbor, MI: Association for Consumer Research.

Kasser, T. (2002). *The high price of materialism*. Cambridge, MA: The MIT Press.

Kasser, T., & Ahuvia, A. (2002). Materialistic values and well-being in business students. *European Journal of Social Psychology*, *32*(1), 137–146. doi:10.1002/ejsp.85

Kasser, T., & Kanner, A. D. (2004). Where is the psychology of consumer culture? In T. Kasser & A. D. Kanner (Eds.), *Psychology and consumer culture: The struggle for a good life in a materialistic world* (pp. 3–7). Washington, DC: American Psychological Association. doi:10.1037/10658-001

Kasser, T., Ryan, M., Couchman, C. E., & Sheldon, K. M. (2003). Materialistic values: Their causes and consequences. In T. Kasser & A. D. Kanner (Eds.), *Psychology and consumer culture: The struggle for a good life in a materialistic world* (pp. 11–28). Washington, DC: American Psychological Association.

Kasser, T., & Ryan, R. M. (1993). A dark side of the American dream: Correlates of financial success as a central life aspiration. *Journal of Personality and Social Psychology*, *65*(2), 410–422. doi:10.1037/0022-3514.65.2.410 PMID:8366427

Kasser, T., & Ryan, R. M. (1996). Further examining the American dream: Differential correlates of intrinsic and extrinsic goals. *Personality and Social Psychology Bulletin*, *22*(3), 280–287. doi:10.1177/0146167296223006

Katz, M. L., & Shapiro, C. (1985). Network externalities, competition, and compatibility. *The American Economic Review*, *75*(3), 424–440.

Katz, M. L., & Shapiro, C. (1994). Systems competition and network effects. *The Journal of Economic Perspectives*, *8*(2), 93–115. doi:10.1257/jep.8.2.93

Kavanaugh, J. F. (1991). *Following Christ in a consumer society: The spirituality of cultural resistance*. Maryknoll, NY: Orbis Books.

Kehinde, O. J. (2014). Consumerism and its influences on food and drug marketing in Nigeria. *Multidisciplinary Journal of Research Development*, *8*(5), 53–67.

Kellner, D. (2015). *Guys and guns amok: Domestic terrorism and school shootings from the Oklahoma City bombing to the Virginia Tech massacre*. Abington, UK: Routledge.

Kennedy, R., Ehrenberg, A., & Long, S. (2000). Competitive brand's user-profiles hardly differ. In *Market Research Society: Annual Conference Brighton England* (pp. 15 – 22). London, UK: Market Research Society.

Kilby, R. (1993). *The study of human values*. Lanham, MD: University Press of America.

Kilsheimer, J. C. (1993). *Status consumption: The development and implications of a scale measuring the motivation to consume for status* (PhD Dissertation). Florida State University.

Kim, B.-D., & Rossi, P. E. (1994). Purchase frequency, sample selection, and price sensitivity: The heavy-user bias. *Marketing Letters*, *5*(1), 57–67. doi:10.1007/BF00993958

Kinnear, T. C., & Taylor, J. R. (1976). Psychographics: Some additional findings. *JMR, Journal of Marketing Research*, *13*(4), 422–425. doi:10.2307/3151034

Kıray, M. B. (2006). *Toplumsal yapı, toplumsal değişme*. İstanbul, Turkey: Bağlam Publications.

Kitch, M. J. (1967). *Capitalism and the Reformation*. London, UK: Longmans, Green & Co.

Klausmeier, H., & Harris, C. (Eds.). (1966). *Analyses of concept learning*. New York, NY: Academic Press.

Kleinberg, J., Papadimitriou, C., & Raghavan, P. (2004). Segmentation problems. *Journal of the Association for Computing Machinery*, *51*(2), 263–280. doi:10.1145/972639.972644

Kleine, R. E. III, Kleine, S. S., & Kernan, J. B. (1993). Mundane consumption and the self: A social-identity perspective. *Journal of Consumer Psychology*, *2*(3), 209–235. doi:10.1016/S1057-7408(08)80015-0

Klein, N., & Sawchuk, J. K. (2000). No Logo: Taking aim at the brand bullies. *Canadian Journal of Communication*, *25*(4), 576–578.

Klein, N., & Sawchuk, K. (2000). No logo: Taking aim at the brand bullies. *Canadian Journal of Communication*, *25*(4), 576–578.

Ko, E., Taylor, C. R., Sung, H., Lee, J., Wagner, U., Navarro, D. M. C., & Wang, F. (2012). Global marketing segmentation usefulness in the sportswear industry. *Journal of Business Research*, *65*(11), 1565–1575. doi:10.1016/j.jbusres.2011.02.041

Kongar, E. (1994). *İmparatorluktan günümüze Türkiye'nin toplumsal yapısı*. İstanbul, Turkey: Remzi Bookstore.

Koppl, R. (1996). Man has fallen and he can't get up: An essay on postmodernism and advertising. In M. Cross (Ed.), *Advertising and culture: Theoretical perspectives* (pp. 75–84). Westpoint, CT: Praeger.

Korman, A. K., Wittig-Berman, U., & Lang, D. (1981). Career success and personal failure: Alienation in professionals and managers. *Academy of Management Journal*, *24*(2), 342–360.

Kotler, P., & Keller, K. (2011), Marketing management (14th ed.). London, UK: Pearson International Edition.

Kotler, P. (1972). A generic concept of marketing. *Journal of Marketing*, *36*(2), 46–54. doi:10.2307/1250977

Kotler, P. (1986). The prosumer movement: a new challenge for marketers. In R. J. Lutz (Ed.), *Advances in Consumer Research* (pp. 510–513). Provo, UT: Association for Consumer Research.

Kottler, J. A. (1999). *Exploring and treating acquisitive desire: Living in the material world*. Thousand Oaks, CA: Sage Publications.

Kozinets, R. (2002). Can consumers escape the market? Emancipatory illuminations from burning man. *The Journal of Consumer Research*, *29*(1), 20–38. doi:10.1086/339919

Krueger, D., & Perri, F. (2006). Does income inequality lead to consumption inequality? Evidence and theory. *The Review of Economic Studies*, *73*(1), 163–193. doi:10.1111/j.1467-937X.2006.00373.x

Kruks, S. (1992). Gender and subjectivity: Simone de Beauvoir and contemporary feminism. *Signs (Chicago, Ill.)*, *18*(1), 89–110. doi:10.1086/494780

Kumar, S., & Krob, W. A. (2005). *Managing product life cycle in a supply chain context: A prescription based on empirical research*. New York, NY: Springer.

Kvale, S. (1996). *Interviews: An introduction to qualitative research interviewing*. Thousand Oaks, CA: Sage Publications.

Kymlicka, W. (2002). *Contemporary political philosophy: An introduction* (2nd ed.). Oxford, UK: Oxford University Press.

Lacewing, M. (n.d.). *Plato's similes of the cave and the divided line*. Retrieved January 15, 2018 from http://documents.routledge-interactive.s3.amazonaws.com/9781138793934/A2/Plato/PlatoSimilesLineCave.pdf

Laird, J. (1929). *The idea of value*. Cambridge, UK: Cambridge University Press.

Lane, R. E. (1998). The road not taken: Friendship, consumerism and happiness. In D. A. Crocker & T. Linden (Eds.), *Ethics in consumption: The good life, justice and global stewardship* (pp. 218–248). Lantham, MD: Rowman & Littlefield.

Lapoint, V. D., & Hambrick-Dixon, P. J. (2004). Consumerism's influence on black youth: The case of dress-related challenges. In T. Kasser & A. D. Kanner (Eds.), *Psychology and consumer culture: The struggle for a good life in a materialistic world* (pp. 233–250). Washington, DC: American Psychological Association. doi:10.1037/10658-013

LaRossa, R., & Reitzes, D. C. (2009). Symbolic interactionism and family studies. In P. C. Boss, W. J. Doherty, R. LaRosa, W. R. Schumm, & S. K. Steinmetz (Eds.), *Sourcebook of family theories and methods* (pp. 135–166). New York, NY: Springer.

Larsen, V., Sirgy, M. J., & Wright, N. D. (1999). Materialism: The construct, measures, antecedents and consequences. *Academy of Marketing Studies Journal*, *3*, 78–110.

Lasch, C. (1991). *The culture of narcissism: American life in an age of diminishing expectations*. New York, NY: WW Norton & Company.

Lastovicka, J. L., Bettencourt, L. A., Hughner, R. S., & Kuntze, R. J. (1999). Lifestyle of the tight and frugal: Theory and measurement. *The Journal of Consumer Research*, *26*(1), 85–98. doi:10.1086/209552

Lastovicka, J., & Sirianni, N. (2012). Truly, madly, deeply: Consumers in the throes of material possessive love. *The Journal of Consumer Research*, *38*(2), 323–342. doi:10.1086/658338

Latendresse, S. J., Rose, R. J., Viken, R. J., Pulkkinen, L., Kaprio, J., & Dick, D. M. (2008). Parenting mechanisms in links between parents' and adolescents' alcohol use behaviors. *Alcoholism, Clinical and Experimental Research*, *32*(2), 322–330. doi:10.1111/j.1530-0277.2007.00583.x PMID:18162066

LaValle, S., Lesser, E., Shockley, R., Hopkins, M. S., & Kruschwitz, N. (2011). Big data, analytics and the path from insights to value. *MIT Sloan Management Review*, *52*(2), 21.

Lee, M. (1993). *Consumer culture reborn: The cultural politics of consumption*. London, UK: Routledge. doi:10.4324/9780203359655

Leete, L., & Schor, J. B. (1994). Assessing the time-squeeze hypothesis: Hours worked in the United States, 1969-1989. *Industrial Relations*, *33*(1), 25–43. doi:10.1111/j.1468-232X.1994.tb00325.x

Lehmann, H., & Roth, G. (1993). *Weber's Protestant ethic*. Cambridge, England: Cambridge University Press. doi:10.1017/CBO9781139052467

Leippe, M. R., & Elkin, R. A. (1987). When motives clash: Issue involvement and response involvement as determinants of persuasion. *Journal of Personality and Social Psychology*, *52*(2), 269–278. doi:10.1037/0022-3514.52.2.269

Lemos, R. (1995). *The nature of value: Axiological investigations*. Gainesville, FL: University of Florida Press.

Leonard, A. (2011). *The story of stuff: The impact of overconsumption on the planet, our communities, and our health--and how we can make it petter (Reprint edition)*. New York, NY: Free Press.

Lerach, W. S. (2002). Plundering America: How American investors got taken for trillions by corporate insiders – The rise of the new corporate kleptocracy. *Stanford Journal of Law, Business & Finance*, *8*(1), 69–126.

Levine, M. (2007). How materialism hurts our kids privilege. *Tikkun*, *22*(1), 33–36, 60.

Levi, P. (1996). *Survival at Auschwitz* (S. Woolf, Trans.). New York, NY: Simon & Schuster.

Levy, S. J. (1959). Symbols for sale. *Harvard Business Review*, *37*(4), 117–124.

Lewis, C. T., & Short, C. (1980). *A Latin dictionary*. Oxford, UK: Oxford UP.

Liao, J., & Wang, L. (2009). Face as a mediator of the relationship between material value and brand consciousness. *Psychology and Marketing*, *26*(11), 987–1001. doi:10.1002/mar.20309

Limbu, Y. B., Huhmann, B. A., & Xu, B. (2012). Are college students at greater risk of credit card abuse? Age, gender, materialism and parental influence on consumer response to credit cards. *Journal of Financial Services Marketing*, *17*(2), 148–162. doi:10.1057/fsm.2012.9

Lindlof, T. (1995). *Qualitative communication research methods*. Thousand Oaks, CA: Sage Publications.

Linton, R. (1936). *The study of man: an introduction*. New York, NY: D. Appleton and Co.

Livingston, P. (1992). *Models of desire: Rene Girard and the psychology of mimesis*. Baltimore, MD: Johns Hopkins University Press.

Lopata, H. Z. (1991). Role theory. Social roles and social institutions. In J. R. Blau & N. Goodman (Eds.), *Essays in honor of Rose Laub Coser* (pp. 1–11). New Brunswick, NJ: Transaction Publishers.

Lovejoy, A. (1950). Terminal and adjectival values. *The Journal of Philosophy*, *47*(21), 593–608. doi:10.2307/2021804

Ludwig, T., & Myers, D. (1979). How Christians can cope with inflation. *The Christian Century, 96*, 609-613.

Luther, M. (2003). *On Christian liberty* (W. A. Lambert Trans. & Ed.). Minneapolis, MN: Augsburg Fortress.

Lyon, D. (1999). *Postmodernity*. Minneapolis, MN: University of Minnesota Press.

Machauer, A., & Morgner, S. (2001). Segmentation of bank customers by expected benefits and attitudes. *International Journal of Bank Marketing*, *19*(1), 6–17. doi:10.1108/02652320110366472

Mahoney, J. L., & Stattin, H. (2000). Leisure activities and adolescent antisocial behavior: The role of structure and social context. *Journal of Adolescence*, *23*(2), 113–127. doi:10.1006/jado.2000.0302 PMID:10831137

Maines, D. R. (2001). *The faultline of consciousness: A view of interactionism in sociology*. New York, NY: Aldine Transaction.

Makant, M. (2010). The pursuit of happiness: The virtue of consumption and the consumption of virtue. *Dialog: A Journal of Theology, 49*(4), 291-299.

Malhotra, N., & Birks, D. (2006). *Marketing research: An applied perspective*. Englewood Cliffs, NJ: Prentice Hall. doi:10.1108/S1548-6435(2006)2

Malmquist, C. P. (2007). *Homicide: A psychiatric perspective*. Washington, DC: American Psychiatric Publications.

Mandiberg, M. (Ed.). (2012). *The social media reader*. New York, NY: NYU Press.

Mardin, Ş. (1992). *Türk modernleşmesi*. İstanbul, Turkey: İletişim Publications.

Marriot T. V. Commercial. (2017). *Human: The golden rule*. Retrieved March 31, 2018 from https://www.ispot.tv/ad/w6rw/marriott-human-the-golden-rule

Martínez, E., & Montaner, T. (2008). Characterization of Spanish store brand consumers. *International Journal of Retail & Distribution Management*, *36*(4), 477–493. doi:10.1108/09590550810873947

Marx, K. (1867). *Capital: A critique of political economy*. Retrieved May 19, 2018 from https://www.marxists.org/archive/marx/works/download/pdf/Capital-Volume-I.pdf

Marx, K. (1964). *The Economic and Philosophic Manuscripts of 1844* (D. Struik, Ed.). New York, NY: International Publishers.

Marx, K. (1990). *Capital: A critique of political economy* (B. Fowkes & D. Fernbach, Trans.). London, UK: Penguin Books.

Marx, K., & Engels, F. (1992). *The communist manifesto*. New York, NY: Bantam Books. (Original work published 1848)

Maslow, A. H. (1954). *Personality and motivation*. Harlow, UK: Longman.

Masterman, L. (1983). Media education in the 1980s. *Journal of Educational Television, 9*(1), 7–20. doi:10.1080/0260741830090102

Masterman, L. (1993). The media education revolution. *Canadian Journal of Educational Communication, 22*(1), 5–14.

Masterman, L. (1997). A rationale for media education. In R. W. Kubey (Ed.), *Media literacy in the information age* (pp. 15–68). New Brunswick, NJ: Transaction Publishers.

Mathur, A. (2013). Materialism and charitable giving: Can they co-exist? *Journal of Consumer Behaviour, 12*(3), 149–158. doi:10.1002/cb.1404

Mau, R. (1992). The validity and devolution of a concept: Student alienation. *Adolescence, 27*(107), 731–741. PMID:1414583

Mau, R. Y. (1992). The validity and devolution of a concept: Student alienation. *Adolescence, 27*(107), 731–741. PMID:1414583

Maureen, M., & Sally, D. (1998). Implementing market segmentation strategies in UK personal financial services: Problems and progress. *Service Industries Journal, 18*(2), 45–63. doi:10.1080/02642069800000018

McAdams, D. P. (1996). Personality, modernity, and the storied self: A contemporary framework for studying persons. *Psychological Inquiry, 7*(4), 295–321. doi:10.120715327965pli0704_1

McAll, C. (1990). Structural seclusion: Making structural inequality possible. In C. McAll (Ed.), *Class, ethnicity, and social inequality* (pp. 203–215). Montreal, Canada: McGill-Queen's Press.

McCloskey, D. N. (2011). *Bourgeois dignity: Why economics can't explain the modern world.* Chicago, IL: University Of Chicago Press.

McClure, R. F. (1984). The relationship between money attitudes and overall pathology. *Psychology: A Quarterly Journal of Human Behavior, 21*(1), 4–6.

McCracken, G. (1986). Culture and consumption: A theoretical account of the structure and movement of the cultural meaning of consumer goods. *The Journal of Consumer Research, 13*(1), 71–84. doi:10.1086/209048

McCracken, G. (1988). *The Long Interview*. London, UK: Sage. doi:10.4135/9781412986229

McCrae, R. R., & Costa, P. T. Jr. (1997). Personality trait structure as a human universal. *The American Psychologist, 52*(5), 509–516. doi:10.1037/0003-066X.52.5.509 PMID:9145021

McDonald, M., & Wearing, S. (2013). *Social psychology and theories of consumer culture: A political economy perspective*. East Sussex, UK: Routledge.

McDonald, M., & Wearing, S. (2013). *Social psychology and theories of consumer culture: a political economy perspective*. London: Routledge.

McGonigal, K. (2012). *The willpower instinct: How self-control works, Why it matters, and what you can do to get more of it*. London, UK: Avery.

McGuigan, J. (2009). *Cool capitalism*. London, UK: Pluto Press.

McKeage, K. K., & Gulas, C. S. (2013). Relationships, Roleș, and Consumer Identity in Services Marketing. *Services Marketing Quarterly*, *34*(3), 231–239. doi:10.1080/15332969.2013.798198

McKendrick, N. (1982). Commercialization and the economy. In N. McKendrick, J. Brewer, & J. H. Plumb (Eds.), *The birth of a consumer society: The commercialization of eighteenth-century England* (pp. 9–194). Bloomington, IN: Indiana University Press.

McKnight, D. (1994). The theory value of the Austrian school. *The Appraisal Journal*, *62*(3), 465–469.

McLoughlin, W. (1959). *Modern revivalism: Charles Grandison Finney to Billy Graham*. New York, NY: The Ronald Press Co.

McMullen, S. (2015). Is capitalism to blame? Animal lives in the marketplacė. *Journal of Animal Ethics*, *5*(2), 126–134. doi:10.5406/janimalethics.5.2.0126

McMullen, S. (2016). *Animals and the economy*. London, UK: Palgrave Macmillan. doi:10.1057/978-1-137-43474-6

McRobbie, A., & Thornton, S. L. (1995). Rethinking 'moral panic' for multi-mediated social worlds. *The British Journal of Sociology*, *46*(4), 559–574. doi:10.2307/591571

Meadows, D. H. (1972). *Limits to growth*. New York, NY: Signet.

Meadows, D. H., Randers, J., & Meadows, D. L. (2004). *Limits to growth: The 30-year update* (3rd ed.). White River Junction, VT: Chelsea Green Publishing.

Meadows, M., & Dibb, S. (1988). Assessing the implementation of market segmentation in retail financial services. *International Journal of Service Quality Management*, *9*(3), 266–279.

Mean Girls. (2004). Paramount Pictures.

Meddin, J. (1975). Attitudes, values, and related concepts: A system of classification. *Social Science Quarterly*, *55*(4), 889–900.

Menor, L. J., Roth, A. V., & Mason, C. H. (2001). Agility in retail banking: A numerical taxonomy of strategic service groups. *Manufacturing & Service Operations Management: M & SOM*, *3*(4), 273–292. doi:10.1287/msom.3.4.273.9969

Merisavo, M., & Raulas, M. (2004). The impact of e-mail marketing on brand loyalty. *Journal of Product and Brand Management*, *13*(7), 498–505. doi:10.1108/10610420410568435

Merriam Webster. (2018). *Consciousness*. Retrieved from https://www.merriam-webster.com/dictionary/consciousness

Merton, R. K. (1957). Priorities in scientific discovery: A chapter in the sociology of science. *American Sociological Review*, *22*(6), 635–659. doi:10.2307/2089193

Merton, T. (1966). *Raids on the unspeakable*. New York, NY: New Directions Publishing.

Mick, D. G., Pettigrew, S., Pechmann, C., & Ozanne, J. (2012). *Transformative consumer research for personal and collective well-being*. New York, NY: Taylor & Francis.

Miller, V. J. (2014). Slavery and commodity chains: Fighting the globalization of indifference. *America: The National Catholic Review*. Retrieved January 15, 2018 from http://americamagazine.org/issue/slavery-and-commodity-chains-fighting-globalization-indifference

Miller, J. G., & Roth, A. V. (1994). A taxonomy of manufacturing strategies. *Management Science, 40*(3), 285–304. doi:10.1287/mnsc.40.3.285

Miller, M. J., Woehr, D. J., & Hudspeth, N. (2001). The meaning and measurement of work ethic: Construction and initial validation of a multidimensional inventory. *Journal of Vocational Behavior, 60*(3), 451–489. doi:10.1006/jvbe.2001.1838

Miller, V. (2004). *Consuming religion: Christian faith and practice in a consumer culture*. New York, NY: Continuum.

Mitchell, A. (1983). *The VALS typology*. Basingstoke, UK: Macmillan Publishing.

Moisio, R., Arnould, E. J., & Price, L. L. (2004). Between mothers and markets: Constructing family identity through homemade food. *Journal of Consumer Culture, 4*(3), 361–384. doi:10.1177/1469540504046523

Molnar, A. (1996). *Giving kids the business: The commercialization of America's schools*. Dunmore, PA: Westview Press.

Monye, F., Umoh, B., & Chinyere, C. (2014). Research report on the state of consumer protection in Nigeria: A review of consumer protection in the telecommunications sector in Nigeria. Lagos, Nigeria: Consumer International & Open Society Initiative for West Africa (OSIWA)

Moore, S., & Boldero, J. (1991). Psychosocial development and friendship functions in adolescence. *Sex Roles, 25*(9-10), 521–536. doi:10.1007/BF00290061

Mora, N. (2008). *Medya çalışmaları, medya pedagojisi ve küresel iletişim*. İstanbul, Turkey: Alt Kitap Publications.

Moschis, G. P., & Churchill, G. A. Jr. (1978). Consumer socialization: A theoretical and empirical analysis. *JMR, Journal of Marketing Research, 15*(4), 599–609. doi:10.2307/3150629

Moschis, G. P., & Moore, R. L. (1984). Anticipatory consumer socialization. *Journal of the Academy of Marketing Science, 12*(4), 109–123. doi:10.1007/BF02721803

Mukhtar, H. (2012). The development of consumerism in Nigeria: Prospects and challenges. *International Journal of Art and Commerce, 1*(4), 274–285.

Muller, H. (2006). Work and the conduct of life: Weber's legacy. *Max Weber Studies, 6*(1), 119–145. doi:10.15543/MWS/2006/1/6

Mulvey, L. (1993). Some thoughts on theories of fetishism in the context of contemporary culture. *October, 65*, 3-20.

Mulyanegara, R. C., Tsarenko, Y., & Mavondo, F. (2010). Church marketing: The effect of market orientation on perceived benefits and church participation. *Services Marketing Quarterly, 32*(1), 60–82. doi:10.1080/15332969.2011.533100

Murdoch, I. (1993). *Metaphysics as a guide to morals*. New York, NY: Penguin Press.

Myers, D. G. (2000). *The American paradox: Spiritual hunger in an age of plenty*. New Haven, CT: Yale University Press.

Myers, D. G. (2003). Wealth and happiness: A limited relationship. In D. Doherty & A. Etzioni (Eds.), *Voluntary simplicity: Responding to consumer culture* (pp. 41–51). Lanham, MD: Rowman and Littlefield.

Nahon, K. (2011). Network theoryl Fuzziness of inclusion/exclusion in networks. *International Journal of Communication, 5*, 756–772.

Najeeb, U., & Mustansar, H. (2005). Impact of unethical advertising, misleading information or deceptive advertising on customer purchasing intention with mediating effect of word of mouth: Case of Pakistan. *International Journal of innovation and Economic Development, 1*(4), 49-69.

Ndukwe, O. (2010). Consumerism: The backbone of ideological poverty in Nigeria. *Bassey Andah Journal, 3*, 29–47.

Ndu, O. A. E. (2013). Consumerism, the Nigerian experience: Study of the food and drink industries 1980-2012. *Business and Management Horizons, 1*(2), 18–48. doi:10.5296/bmh.v1i2.4162

Nepomuceno, M. V., & Laroche, M. (2015). The impact of materialism and anti-consumption lifestyles on personal debt and account balances. *Journal of Business Research, 68*(3), 654–664. doi:10.1016/j.jbusres.2014.08.006

Neubauer, G., & Hurrelmann, K. (Eds.). (1995). *Individualization in childhood and adolescence.* Berlin: Walter de Gruyter. doi:10.1515/9783110811001

New Dimensions Radio. (2018). Retrieved from https://newdimensions.org/

Newholm, T., & Hopkinson, G. C. (2009). I just tend to wear what I like: Contemporary consumption and the paradoxical construction of individuality. *Marketing Theory, 9*(4), 439–462. doi:10.1177/1470593109346896

Nietzsche, F. (2001). *The gay science* (B. Williams, Trans. & Ed.). Cambridge, UK: Cambridge University Press. doi:10.1017/CBO9780511812088.005

Nigerian Communication Commission. (2003). *The Nigerian Communication Commission Act.* Abuja, Nigeria: Government Printers.

Nigerian Communication Commission. (2017). *Guidelines on advertisements and promotion.* Abuja, Nigeria: Government Printers.

Nikolaus, F., Reisinger, H., & Hoppe, D. (2009). Remaining within-cluster heterogeneity: A mata-analysis of the "dark side" of clustering methods. *Journal of Marketing Management, 25*(3-4), 273–293. doi:10.1362/026725709X429755

Noerager, J. P. (1979). An assessment of CAD: A personality instrument developed specifically for marketing research. *JMR, Journal of Marketing Research, 16*(1), 53–59. doi:10.2307/3150874

Novak, T., Leeuw, J. D., & MacEvoy, B. (1992). Richness Curves for Evaluating Market Segmentation. *JMR, Journal of Marketing Research, 29*(2), 254–267. doi:10.2307/3172574

Nussbaum, M. C. (2001). *Women and human development: The capabilities approach.* Cambridge, UK: Cambridge University Press.

O'Shaughnessy, J. (1992). *Explaining buyer behaviour: Central concepts and philosophy of science issues.* Oxford, UK: Oxford University Press.

O'Shaughnessy, J., & O' Shaughnessy, N. J. (2002). Marketing, the consumer society and hedonism. *European Journal of Marketing, 36*(5/6), 524–547. doi:10.1108/03090560210422871

Office of Juvenile Justice and Delinquency Prevention. (2008). *Introduction to the survey of youth in residential placement.* Washington, DC: Author.

Ogechuckwu, A. D. (2013). Consumerism the shame of marketing in Nigeria. Challenges to cooperate practices. *IPBJ: International Policy and Business Journal, 5*(1), 1–30.

Onynye, U. (2017). Your network will pay a ₦5m fine if they don't stop sending you unwanted messages. *Techpoint.* Retrieved May 19, 2018 from https://techpoint.ng/2017/01/18/networks-unwanted-message-5-million-fine/

Orçan, M. (2014). *Osmanlı'dan günümüze modern türk tüketim kültürü.* Ankara, Turkey: Harf Publications.

Oregbemhe, B. (2015). *Consumers Protection in Advertised Promotion and unsolicited Commercial Calls and Text Messages in Nigeria.* Retrieved September 14, 2017 from http://www.spaajibade.com/resources/consumers-protection-in-advertised-promotion-and-unsolicited-commercial-calls-and-text-messages-in-nigeria/

Orlean, A. (1988). Money and mimetic speculation. In P. Dumouchel (Ed.), *Violence and truth: On the work of Rene Girard* (AnspaughM. A., Trans.; pp. 1–112). Stanford, CA: Stanford University Press.

Osborne, J. W., & Blanchard, M. R. (2011). Random responding from participants is a threat to the validity of social science research results. *Frontiers in Psychology*, *1*, 1–7. doi:10.3389/fpsyg.2010.00220 PMID:21833275

Ostrovskaya, L., & Sarabia-Sánchez, F. (2013). Effect of materialism on the use of the brand name in purchasing decisions from a cross-cultural perspective. *Esic Market Economic and Business Journal*, *44*(1), 91–115. doi:10.7200/esicm.144.0441.3i

Özdemir, İ. (2009). Türkiye'de popüler kadın magazin dergileri: yeni kadın kimliği ve sunulan yaşam tarzları. In M. Dağtaş & E. Dağtaş (Eds.), *Medya, Tüketim Kültürü ve Yaşam Tarzları- Türkiye Medyasından Örüntüler* (pp. 205–243). Ankara, Turkey: Ütopya Publications.

Ozoh, C. H. (2007). *Principles and practice of advertising*. Lagos, Nigeria: Macmillan.

Packard, V. O. (1980). *The hidden persuaders*. New York, NY: Pocket Books.

Pack, S. (2012). Keeping up with the Begays: Observations of competitive consumption in contemporary Navajo society. *Native Studies Review*, *21*(1), 83–101.

Panigyrakis, P., & Zarkada, A. (2014). A philosophical investigation of the transition from integrated marketing communications to metamodern meaning co-creation. *Journal of Global Scholars of Marketing Science*, *24*(3), 262–278. doi:10.1080/21639159.2014.911494

Parotta, J. L., & Johnson, P. J. (1998). The impact of financial attitudes and knowledge on financial management and satisfaction of recently married individuals. *Financial Counseling and Planning*, *9*(2), 59–75.

Paterson, M. (2006). *Consumption and everyday life*. New York, NY: Routledge.

Patrick, D. (2006). Customer segmentation. *ABA Bankers News*, *14*(9), 1.

Patterson, P. G., Cowley, E., & Prasongsukarn, K. (2006). Service failure recovery: The moderating impact of individual-level cultural value orientation on perceptions of justice. *International Journal of Research in Marketing*, *23*(3), 263–277. doi:10.1016/j.ijresmar.2006.02.004

Payutto, P. A. (2000). *Dictionary of Buddhism*. Bangkok, Thailand: Suetawan.

Penaloza, L., & Price, L. (1993). Consumer resistance: A conceptual overview. In L. McAlister & M. L. Rothschild (Eds.), *Advances in consumer research* (pp. 123–128). Provo, UT: Association for Consumer Research.

Pepper, M., Jackson, T., & Uzzell, D. (2009). An examination of the values that motivate socially conscious and frugal consumer behaviours. *International Journal of Consumer Studies*, *33*(2), 126–136. doi:10.1111/j.1470-6431.2009.00753.x

Peppers, D., & Rogers, M. (2004). *Managing customer relationships: A strategic framework*. New York, NY: John Wiley & Sons.

Perkin, H. (1969). *The origins of modern English society, 1780-1880*. New York, NY: Routledge.

Perlman, D., & Peplau, L. A. (1981). Toward a social psychology of loneliness. In S. W. Duck & R. Gilmour (Eds.), *Personal relationships in disorder* (pp. 31–56). London, UK: Academic Press.

Petty, R. E., & Cacioppo, J. T. (1979). Issue involvement can increase or decrease persuasion by enhancing message-relevant cognitive responses. *Journal of Personality and Social Psychology*, *37*(10), 1915–1926. doi:10.1037/0022-3514.37.10.1915

Pham, M. T., & Higgins, E. T. (2005). Promotion and prevention in consumer decision making: The state of the art and theoretical propositions. In S. Ratneshwar & D. G. Mick (Eds.), *Inside consumption: Consumer motives, goals and desires* (pp. 8–43). New York, NY: Routledge.

Pham, T. H., Yap, K., & Dowling, N. A. (2012). The impact of financial management practices and financial attitudes on the relationship between materialism and compulsive buying. *Journal of Economic Psychology*, *33*(3), 461–470. doi:10.1016/j.joep.2011.12.007

Pieters, R., Baumgartner, H., & Allen, D. (1995). A means-end chain approach to consumer goal structures. *International Journal of Research in Marketing*, *12*(3), 227–244. doi:10.1016/0167-8116(95)00023-U

Pietz, W. (1987). The problem of the fetish, II: The origin of the fetish. *Res: Anthropology and Aesthetics*, *13*, 23–45. doi:10.1086/RESv13n1ms20166762

Piketty, T. (2014). *Capital in the twenty-first century*. Cambridge, MA: Belknap Press. doi:10.4159/9780674369542

Piketty, T., & Saez, E. (2006). The evolution of top incomes: A historical and international perspective. *The American Economic Review*, *96*(2), 200–205. doi:10.1257/000282806777212116

Pipher, M. (1996). *The shelter of each other: Rebuilding our families*. New York, NY: Ballantine.

Piwuna, M. G. (2016). Examination of the consumer protrection under the Nigerian Communications Commission Act 2003. *Journal of Education and Social Policy*, *3*(4), 101–111.

Plato. (2004). *Republic* (C. D. C. Reeve, Trans.). Indianapolis, IN: Hackett.

Podoshen, J. S., & Andrzejewski, S. A. (2012). An examination of the relationships between materialism, conspicuous consumption, impulse buying, and brand loyalty. *Journal of Marketing Theory and Practice*, *20*(3), 319–334. doi:10.2753/MTP1069-6679200306

Pogge, T. W. (1998). A global resources dividend. In D. A. Crocker & T. Linden (Eds.), *Ethics of consumption: The good life, justice, and global stewardship* (pp. 19–27). Lanham, MD: Rowman and Littlefield Publishers, Inc.

Ponzetti, J. J. Jr. (1990). Loneliness among college students. *Family Relations*, *39*(3), 336–340. doi:10.2307/584881

Pooler, J. (2003). *Why we shop: Emotional rewards and retail strategies*. Westport, CT: Praeger.

Pope Francis. (2015). *Laudato Si*. Vatican City: Libreria Editrice Vaticana.

Poyntz, S. R. (2006). Independent media, youth agency, and the promise of media education. *Canadian Journal of Education/Revue canadienne de l'éducation*, *29*(1), 154-175.

Prahalad, C. K., & Venkat, R. (2004). *The future of competition*. Boston, MA: Harvard Business School Press.

Prasongsukarn, K. (2009). Validating the cultural value scale (CVSCALE): A case study of Thailand. *ABAC Journal*, *29*(2), 1–13.

Premium Time. (2014). Fraudulent promo: Court grants Etisalat more time. *Premium Times*. Retrieved December 17, from https://www.premiumtimesng.com/news/163085-fraudulent-promo-court-grants-etisalat-time.html

Pulkkinen, L. (1996). Impulse control in children. *Journal of Forensic Psychiatry*, *7*(2), 228–233. doi:10.1080/09585189608415008

Quinn, L. (2009). Market segmentation in managerial practice: A qualitative examination. *Journal of Marketing Management*, *25*(3-4), 253–272. doi:10.1362/026725709X429746

Radio Vatican. (2015). Pope deplores consumerism and running after the latest fad. *Radio Vatican*. Retrieved December 5, 2017 from http://en.radiovaticana.va/

Rath, T., & Harter, J. K. (2010). *Wellbeing: The five essential elements*. New York, NY: Gallup Press.

Redding, S. G. (1990). *The spirit of Chinese capitalism*. New York, NY: Walter de Gruyter. doi:10.1515/9783110887709

Reed, A. (2002). Social identity as a useful perspective for self-concept–based consumer research. *Psychology and Marketing*, *19*(3), 235–266. doi:10.1002/mar.10011

Reibstein, D. J., Day, G., & Wind, J. (2009). Guest editorial: Is marketing academia losing its way? *Journal of Marketing*, *73*(4), 1–3. doi:10.1509/jmkg.73.4.1

Reich, S. M. (2010). Adolescents' sense of community on myspace and facebook: A mixed-methods approach. *Journal of Community Psychology*, *38*(6), 688–705. doi:10.1002/jcop.20389

Reijntjes, A., Thomaes, S., Bushman, B. J., Boelen, P. A., de Castro, B. O., & Telch, M. J. (2010). The outcast-lash-out effect in youth: Alienation increases aggression following peer rejection. *Psychological Science*, *21*(10), 1394–1398. doi:10.1177/0956797610381509 PMID:20739674

Reinartz, W., Thomas, J. S., & Kumar, V. (2005). Balancing acquisition and retention resources to maximize customer profitability. *Journal of Marketing*, *69*(1), 63–79. doi:10.1509/jmkg.69.1.63.55511

Richins, M. L. (2004). The Material Values Scale: Measurement properties and development of a short form. *The Journal of Consumer Research*, *31*(1), 209–219. doi:10.1086/383436

Richins, M. L. (2011). Materialism, transformation expectations, and spending: Implications for credit use. *Journal of Public Policy & Marketing*, *30*(2), 141–156. doi:10.1509/jppm.30.2.141

Richins, M. L., & Dawson, S. (1992). Consumer values orientation for materialism and its measurement: Scale development and validation. *The Journal of Consumer Research*, *19*(3), 303–316. doi:10.1086/209304

Rick, S. I., Cryder, C. E., & Loewenstein, G. (2008). Tightwads and spendthrifts. *The Journal of Consumer Research*, *34*(6), 767–782. doi:10.1086/523285

Riesman, D., Glazer, N., & Denney, R. (1950). *The lonely crowd: A study of the changing American character*. New Haven, CT: Yale.

Rigby, D. K., Reichheld, F. F., & Schefter, P. (2002). Avoid the four perils of CRM. *Harvard Business Review*, *80*(2), 101–109. PMID:11894676

Ritzer, G. (2010). *Enchanting a disenchanted world: continuity and change in the cathedrals of consumption*. Los Angeles, CA: Sage Publications. doi:10.4135/9781483349572

Robbins, P. R. (2000). *Aggression and violence: An interdisciplinary approach*. Jefferson, NC: McFarland & Company.

Rojek, C. (1999). *Leisure and culture*. Berlin: Springer.

Rokach, A., Orzeck, T., Cripps, J., Lackovic-Grgin, K., & Penezic, Z. (2001). The effects of culture on the meaning of loneliness. *Social Indicators Research*, *53*(1), 17–31. doi:10.1023/A:1007183101458

Rokeach, M. (1968). A theory of organization and change within value-attitude systems. *The Journal of Social Issues*, *24*(1), 13–33. doi:10.1111/j.1540-4560.1968.tb01466.x

Rokeach, M. (1973). *The nature of human values*. New York, NY: Free Press.

Roper Starch Worldwide. (1994). *Survey of America's inner financial life*. New York, NY: Roper Starch Worldwide.

Rosato, D. (2012, January). Get happy in 2012. *Money,* 14-15.

Rose, P., Smith, S. T., & Segrist, D. J. (2010). Too cheap to chug: Frugality as a buffer against college-student drinking. *Journal of Consumer Behaviour*, *9*(3), 228–238. doi:10.1002/cb.314

Runes, D. (Ed.). (1983). *Dictionary of philosophy*. New York, NY: Philosophical Library.

Ryan, T. (2012). What is the new normal? *Retailwire*. Retrieved May 15, 2018, from http://www.retailwire.com/discussion/16192/what-is-the-new-normal

Sagiroglu, A., & Duygu, B. (2013). Big data: A review. Collaboration Technologies and Systems (CTS). *2013 International Conference on. IEEE.*

Samiee, S., & Jeong, I. (1994). Cross-cultural Research in Advertising: An Assessment of Methodologies. *Journal of the Academy of Marketing Science*, *22*(3), 205–217. doi:10.1177/0092070394223002

Sandel, M. (1982). *Liberalism and the limits of justice*. Cambridge, UK: Cambridge University Press.

Sandikci, O., & Ger, G. (2002). In-between modernities and postmodernities: theorizing Turkish consumptionscape. In S. M. Broniarczyk & K. N. Valdosta (Eds.), Advances in consumer research (pp. 465-470). Provo UT: Association for Consumer Research.

Sandikci, O., & Ger, G. (2005). Contemporary Turkish consumptionscape: polarity and plurality. *7th. Portoroz Business Conference*.

Sandlin, J., & Callahan, J. (2009). Deviance, dissonance, and détournement: Culture jammers' use of emotion in consumer resistance. *Journal of Consumer Culture*, *9*(1), 79–115. doi:10.1177/1469540508099703

Santamarina, J. C., & Chameau, J. L. (1987). Membership functions II: Trends in fuzziness and implications. *International Journal of Approximate Reasoning*, *1*(3), 303–317. doi:10.1016/S0888-613X(87)80004-X

Sartre, J. P. (2004). *Critique of dialectical reason: Theory of practical ensembles* (Vol. 1). New York, NY: Verso.

Schaefers, T. (2007). Standing out from the crowd: Niche product choice as a form of conspicuous consumption. *European Journal of Marketing*, *48*(9/10), 1805–1827. doi:10.1108/EJM-03-2013-0121

Schectman, M. (1996). *The constitution of selves*. Ithaca, NY: Cornell University Press.

Schindler, R. M., Lala, V., & Corcoran, C. (2014). Intergenerational influence in consumer deal proneness. *Psychology and Marketing*, *31*(5), 307–320. doi:10.1002/mar.20696

Schlegelmilch, B. B., & Öberseder, M. (2010). Half a century of marketing ethics: Shifting perspectives and emerging trends. *Journal of Business Ethics*, *93*(1), 1–19. doi:10.100710551-009-0182-1

Schlenker, B. R. (1980). *Impression management*. Pacific Grove, CA: Brooks/Cole Publishing Company.

Schor, J. (2000). The New Politics of Consumption. In J. Cohen & J. Rogers (Eds.), *Do Americans shop too much?* (pp. 3–35). Boston, MA: Beacon Press.

Schor, J. (2004). *Born to buy: The commercialized child and the new consumer culture*. New York, NY: Scribner.

Schor, J. (2008). *The overworked American: The unexpected decline of leisure*. New York, NY: Basic Books.

Schor, J. B. (1994). Decline of leisure time in America. *Vital Speeches of the Day*, *60*(24), 748–752.

Schor, J. B. (1998). *The overspent American: Upscaling, downshifting, and the new consumer.* New York, NY: Basic Books.

Schor, J. B. (1999). *The overspent American: Why we want what we don't need.* New York, NY: HarperPerennial.

Schor, J. B. (2004). The problem of overconsumption: Why economists don't get it. In D. Doherty & A. Etzioni (Eds.), *Voluntary simplicity: Responding to the consumer culture* (pp. 65–82). Lanham, MD: Rowman & Littlefield.

Schor, J. B. (2007). In defense of consumer critique: Revisiting the consumption debates of the twentieth century. *The Annals of the American Academy of Political and Social Science, 611*(1), 16–30. doi:10.1177/0002716206299145

Schor, J. B. (2014). *Born to buy: the commercialized child and the new consumer cult.* New York, NY: Simon and Schuster.

Schouten, J. W. (1991). Selves in transition: Symbolic consumption in personal rites of passage and identity reconstruction. *The Journal of Consumer Research, 17*(4), 412–425. doi:10.1086/208567

Schroeder, J. E., & Dugal, S. (1995). Psychological correlates of the materialism construct. *Journal of Social Behavior and Personality, 10*(1), 243–253.

Schulz, H. M. (2015). Reference group influence in consumer role rehearsal narratives. *Qualitative Market Research, 18*(2), 210–229. doi:10.1108/QMR-02-2012-0009

Schulz, L., & Rubel, D. (2011). A phenomenology of alienation in high school: The experiences of five male non-completers. *Professional School Counseling, 14*(5), 286–298. doi:10.5330/PSC.n.2011-14.286

Schwandt, T. (1997). *Qualitative inquiry: A dictionary of terms.* Thousand Oaks, CA: Sage Publications.

Schwartz, B. (2004). *The paradox of choice: Why more is less.* New York, NY: Harper Collins.

Schwartz, S. H. (1992). Universals in the content and structure of values: Theoretical advances and empirical tests in 20 countries. Cambridge, MA: Academic Press. doi:10.1016/S0065-2601(08)60281-6

Schweiker, W. (1994). Religion and the philosophers of mimesis. In M. I. Wallace & T. H. Smith (Eds.), *Curing violence* (pp. 25–44). Sonoma, CA: Polebridge Press.

Seeman, M. (1959). On the meaning of alienation. *American Sociological Review, 24*(6), 783–791. doi:10.2307/2088565

Sen, A. (1999). *Development as freedom.* New York, NY: Knopf.

Shantz, J. (2005). One person's garbage another person's treasure: Dumpster diving, freeganism, and anarchy. *VERB, 3*(1), 9–19.

Sher, S. (2011). A framework for assessing immorally manipulative marketing tactics. *Journal of Business Ethics, 102*(1), 97–118. doi:10.100710551-011-0802-4

Shildrick, T., & MacDonald, R. (2006). In defence of subculture: Young people, leisure and social divisions. *Journal of Youth Studies, 9*(2), 125–140. doi:10.1080/13676260600635599

Shimp, T. A. (1983). *A potpourri of consumer research methods. ACR North American Advances.* Ann Arbor, MI: Association for Consumer Research.

Shim, S. (1996). Adolescent consumer decision-making styles: The consumer socialization perspective. *Psychology and Marketing, 13*(6), 547–569. doi:10.1002/(SICI)1520-6793(199609)13:6<547::AID-MAR2>3.0.CO;2-8

Simmel, G. (1957). Fashion. *American Journal of Sociology, 62*(6), 541–558. doi:10.1086/222102

Simon, D. R. (2013). *Meatonomics: How the rigged economics of meat and dairy make you consume too much--and how to eat better, live longer, and spend smarter*. Newburyport, MA: Conari Press.

Simonson, I. (2005). Determinants of customers' responses to customized offers: Conceptual framework and research propositions. *Journal of Marketing*, *69*(1), 32–45. doi:10.1509/jmkg.69.1.32.55512

Singelis, T. M., Triandis, H. C., Bhawuk, D. P., & Gelfand, M. J. (1995). Horizontal and vertical dimensions of individualism and collectivism: A theoretical and measurement refinement. *Cross-Cultural Research*, *29*(3), 240–275. doi:10.1177/106939719502900302

Skerrett, K. R. (2003). Desire and anathema: Mimetic rivalry in defense of plenitude. *Journal of the American Academy of Religion*, *71*(4), 793–809. doi:10.1093/jaarel/lfg099

Slama, M. E., Williams, T. G., & Tashchian, A. (1988). *Compliant, aggressive and detached types differ in generalized purchasing involvement. In ACR North American Advances* (pp. 158–167). Ann Arbor, MI: Association for Consumer Research.

Slater, D. (1997). *Consumer culture and modernity*. Cambridge, UK: Polity Press.

Smart, W. (1891). *An introduction to the theory of value*. London: Macmillan.

Smith, A. (1816). *An inquiry into the nature and causes of wealth in nations*. Philadelphia, PA: D. Hanna.

Smith, A. (2002). *The theory of moral sentiments*. Cambridge, UK: Cambridge University Press. doi:10.1017/CBO9780511800153.005

Smith, A. (2012). *An inquiry into the nature and causes of the wealth of nations*. London, UK: Wordsworth. (Original work published 1776)

Smith, P. K., Ananiadou, K., & Cowie, H. (2003). Interventions to reduce school bullying. *Canadian Journal of Psychiatry*, *48*(9), 591–599. doi:10.1177/070674370304800905 PMID:14631879

Smith, V. O., & Smith, Y. S. (2013). Bias, history and the Protestant work ethic. *Journal of Management History*, *7*(3), 282–298.

Smith, W. R. (1956). Product differentiation and market segmentation as alternative marketing strategies. *Journal of Marketing*, *21*(1), 3–8. doi:10.2307/1247695

Smith, W. R. (1995). Product differentiation and market segmentation as alternative marketing strategies. *Marketing Management*, *4*(3), 63.

Snyder, C. R., & Fromkin, H. L. (1980). *Uniqueness: The human pursuit of difference*. New York, NY: Plenum Press. doi:10.1007/978-1-4684-3659-4

Solomon, M. R., Surprenant, C., Czepiel, J. A., & Gutman, E. G. (1985). A role theory perspective on dyadic interactions: The service encounter. *Journal of Marketing*, *49*(1), 99–111. doi:10.2307/1251180

Sommer, K. L., Williams, K. D., Ciarocco, N. J., & Baumeister, R. F. (2001). When silence speaks louder than words: Explorations into the intrapsychic and interpersonal consequences of social ostracism. *Basic and Applied Social Psychology*, *23*(4), 225–243. doi:10.1207/S15324834BASP2304_1

So, S. I., & Morrison, A. M. (2004). The repeat travel market for Taiwan: A multi-stage segmentation approach. *Asia Pacific Journal of Tourism Research*, *9*(1), 71–87. doi:10.1080/1094166042000199585

Speed, R., & Smith, G. (1992). Retail financial services segmentation. *Service Industries Journal, 12*(3), 368–383. doi:10.1080/02642069200000045

Spiggle, S. (1994). Analysis and interpretation of qualitative data in consumer research. *The Journal of Consumer Research, 21*(3), 491–503. doi:10.1086/209413

Sprotles, G. B., & Kendall, E. L. (1986). A methodology for profiling consumers' decision-making styles. *The Journal of Consumer Affairs, 20*(2), 267–279. doi:10.1111/j.1745-6606.1986.tb00382.x

Sprott, D., Czellar, S., & Spangenberg, E. (2009). The importance of a general measure of brand engagement on market behavior: Development and validation of a scale. *JMR, Journal of Marketing Research, 46*(1), 92–104. doi:10.1509/jmkr.46.1.92

Steenkamp, J. B. E., & Hofstede, F. (2002). International market segmentation: Issues and perspectives. *International Journal of Research in Marketing, 19*(3), 185–213. doi:10.1016/S0167-8116(02)00076-9

Steinfeld, H., Gerber, P., Wassenaar, T., Castel, V., Rosales, M., & de Haan, C. (2006). *Livestock's long shadow*. Rome, Italy: Food and Agriculture Organization of the United Nations.

Steinley, D., & Brusco, M. J. (2007). Initializing K-means batch clustering: A critical analysis of several techniques. *Journal of Classification, 24*(1), 99–121. doi:10.100700357-007-0003-0

Stirling, M. C. (2004). Violent religion: Rene Girard's theory of culture. In J. H. Ellenus (Ed.), *The destructive power of religion: Violence in Judaism, Christianity, and Islam* (pp. 11–50). Westport, CT: Praeger.

Stryker, S. (1980). *Symbolic interactionism: A social structural version.* Menlo Park, CA. Benjamin/Cummings Publishing Company

Stryker, S., & Serpe, R. T. (1982). Commitment, identity salience, and role behavior: Theory and research example. In W. Ickes & E. S. Knowles (Eds.), *Personality, roles, and social behavior* (pp. 199–218). New York, NY: Springer. doi:10.1007/978-1-4613-9469-3_7

Stryker, S., & Serpe, R. T. (1983). Toward a theory of family influence in the socialization of children. *Research in Sociology of Education and Socialization, 4*, 47–71.

Stuart, T. (2009). *Waste: Uncovering the global food scandal.* New York, NY: W. W. Norton & Company.

Sum, C.-C., Kow, L. S.-J., & Chen, C.-S. (2004). A taxonomy of operations strategies of high performing small and medium enterprises in Singapore. *International Journal of Operations & Production Management, 24*(3), 321–345. doi:10.1108/01443570410519051

Sunstein, C. R. (1991). Preferences and politics. *Philosophy & Public Affairs, 20*(1), 3–34.

Sunstein, C. R. (1993). Endogenous preferences, environmental law. *The Journal of Legal Studies, 22*(2), 217–254. doi:10.1086/468164

Sunstein, C. R. (1997). How law constructs preferences. *The Georgetown Law Journal, 86*, 2637.

Suzanne, S. (2002). The evolution of segmentation methods in financial services: Where next? *Journal of Financial Services Marketing, 7*(1), 67–74. doi:10.1057/palgrave.fsm.4770073

Tajfel, H., & Turner, J. C. (1985). The social identity theory of intergroup behavior. In S. Worchel & W. G. Austin (Eds.), *Psychology of intergroup relations* (2nd ed.; pp. 7–24). Chicago: Nelson-Hall.

Tanner, R. J., Ferraro, R., Chartrand, T. L., Bettman, J. R., & Van Baaren, R. (2008). Of chameleons and consumption: The impact of mimicry on choice and preferences. *The Journal of Consumer Research*, *34*(6), 754–766. doi:10.1086/522322

Tatzel, M. (2014). Value-seekers, big-spenders, non-spenders, and experiencers: Consumption, personality, and well-being. In M. Tatzel (Ed.), Consumption and well-being in the material world (pp. 75-108). Dordrecht, The Netherlands: Springer.

Tatzel, M. (2002). 'Money worlds' and well-being: An integration of money dispositions, materialism and price-related behavior. *Journal of Economic Psychology*, *23*(1), 103–126. doi:10.1016/S0167-4870(01)00069-1

Tatzel, M. (2003). The art of buying: Coming to terms with money and materialism. *Journal of Happiness Studies*, *4*(4), 405–435. doi:10.1023/B:JOHS.0000005770.92248.77

Taylor, C. (1989). *Sources of the self: The making of the modern identity*. Cambridge, MA: Harvard University Press.

Taylor, C. (1991). *The ethics of authenticity*. Cambridge, MA: Harvard University Press.

Taylor, C. (2007). Cultures of democracy and citizen efficacy. *Public Culture*, *19*(1), 117–150. doi:10.1215/08992363-2006-027

Taylor, R. (2000). The meaning of life. In E. D. Klemke (Ed.), *The meaning of life* (2nd ed.; pp. 167–175). Oxford, UK: Oxford University Press.

Tedeschi, J. T. (Ed.). (2013). *Impression management theory and social psychological research*. New York, NY: Academic Press.

Tekinalp, Ş. (2002). İletişim araştırmalarında ideoloji ve küreselleşme: Eleştirel bir bakış. *Kocaeli University Journal of Communication Research*, *1*, 9–32.

Terrero, R. (2007). Ultra-luxe Travel Trends. *Travel Agent*, *329*(11), 8.

The Drucker Institute. (2013). *The purpose of purpose*. The Drucker Institute. Retrieved January 14, 2018, from http://www.druckerinstitute.com/2013/04/purpose-of-purpose/

Thompson, C. (1997). Interpreting consumers: A hermeneutical framework for deriving Marketing insights from the texts of consumers' stories. *JMR, Journal of Marketing Research*, *34*(4), 438–455. doi:10.2307/3151963

Thompson, C., Locander, W., & Pollio, H. (1989). Putting consumer experience back into consumer research: The philosophy and method of existential-phenomenology. *The Journal of Consumer Research*, *16*(2), 133–146. doi:10.1086/209203

Thompson, C., Locander, W., & Pollio, H. (1990). The lived meaning of free choice: An existential-phenomenological description of everyday consumer experiences of contemporary married women. *The Journal of Consumer Research*, *17*(3), 346–361. doi:10.1086/208562

Thompson, C., & Troester, M. (2002). Consumer value systems in the age of postmodern fragmentation: The case of the natural health microculture. *The Journal of Consumer Research*, *28*(4), 550–571. doi:10.1086/338213

Thompson, S. A., & Loveland, J. M. (2015). Integrating identity and consumption: An identity investment theory. *Journal of Marketing Theory and Practice*, *23*(3), 235–253. doi:10.1080/10696679.2015.1032471

Thorlindsson, T., & Bernburg, J. G. (2006). Peer groups and substance use: Examining the direct and interactive effect of leisure activity. *Adolescence*, *41*(162), 321–339. PMID:16981620

Thornton, S. (1995). *Club cultures*. Cambridge, UK: Polity.

Tian, K. T., Bearden, W. O., & Hunter, G. L. (2001). Consumers' need for uniqueness: Scale development and validation. *The Journal of Consumer Research*, *28*(1), 50–66. doi:10.1086/321947

Toffler, A. (1980). *The third wave: The classic study of tomorrow*. New York, NY: Bantam Books.

Trainor, S., Delfabbro, P., Anderson, S., & Winefield, A. (2010). Leisure activities and adolescent psychological well-being. *Journal of Adolescence*, *33*(1), 173–186. doi:10.1016/j.adolescence.2009.03.013 PMID:19406463

Trainspotting. (1996). Miramax.

Troisi, J. D., Christopher, A. N., & Marek, P. (2006). Materialism and money spending disposition as predictors of economic and personality variables. *North American Journal of Psychology*, *8*(3), 421–436.

Trompenaars, A., & Hampden-Turner, C. (1998). *Riding the waves of culture: understanding diversity in global business*. London, UK: McGraw-Hill.

Tuna, K. (2005). Batılı bilginin eleştirisi üzerine. İstanbul, Türkiye: Ufuk Books.

Twenge, J. M., Baumeister, R. F., Tice, D. M., & Stucke, T. S. (2001). If you can't join them, beat them: Effects of social exclusion on aggressive behavior. *Journal of Personality and Social Psychology*, *81*(6), 1058–1069. doi:10.1037/0022-3514.81.6.1058 PMID:11761307

Twining, J. E. (1980). Alienation as a social process. *The Sociological Quarterly*, *21*(3), 417–428. doi:10.1111/j.1533-8525.1980.tb00622.x

Twitchell, J. B. (1999). *Lead us into temptation: The triumph of American materialism*. New York, NY: Columbia University Press.

Ugochuckwu, U. (2017, January 18). NCC to impose N 5 Million fine on telecom that breach unsolicited SMS directives. *The Will Newspaper*, 34-35.

Umemura, T., & Šerek, J. (2016). Different Developmental Pathways from Parental Warmth to Adolescents' Trust in Peers and Politicians: Mediating Roles of Adolescent–Parent Attachment and Belief in a Just World. *Social Justice Research*, *29*(2), 186–205. doi:10.100711211-016-0258-x

Urban, W. (1909). *Valuation: Its nature and laws*. London: S. Sonnenschein and Company.

Üstüner, T., & Holt, D. B. (2014). Toward a theory of status consumption in less industrialized countries. *The Journal of Consumer Research*, *37*(1), S248–S267.

Valsiner, J. (1992). Interest: a metatheoretical perspective. In K. Renninger, S. Hidi, & A. Krapp (Eds.), *The role of interest in learning and development* (pp. 27–42). Hillsdale, IL: Lawrence Erlbaum Associates.

Van Esch, P., Van Esch, L., & Cowley, J. (2013). The dimensions of religion as underpinning constructs for mass media social marketing campaigns: An emerging concept. *International Journal of Marketing Studies*, *5*(1), 96–106. doi:10.5539/ijms.v5n1p96

Vargo, S. L., & Lusch, R. F. (2004). Evolving to a new dominant logic for marketing. *Journal of Marketing*, *68*(1), 1–17. doi:10.1509/jmkg.68.1.1.24036

Vaughan, B. (2002). The punitive consequences of consumer culture. *Punishment & Society*, *4*(2), 195–211. doi:10.1177/14624740222228545

Veblen, T. B. (1897). *The theory of the leisure class*. New York, NY: Macmillan.

Venkatesh, A. (1999). Postmodernism perspectives for macromarketing: An inquiry into the global information and sign economy. *Journal of Macromarketing*, *19*(2), 153–169. doi:10.1177/0276146799192006

Veroff, J. (1983). Introduction. In L. Kahle (Ed.), *Social values and social change: Adaptation to life in America* (pp. xiii–xviii). New York, NY: Praeger Publishers.

Vriens, M., & ter Hofstede, F. (2000). Linking attributes, benefits, and consumer values. *Marketing Research, 12*(3), 4–10.

Wachtel, P. (1983). *The poverty of affluence: A psychological portrait of the American way of life*. Philadelphia, PA: New Society Publishers.

Waide, J. (1987). The making of self and world in advertising. *Journal of Business Ethics, 6*(2), 73–79. doi:10.1007/BF00382020

Wallace, D. F. (2009). *This is water: Some thoughts, delivered on a significant occasion, about living a compassionate life*. New York, NY: Little, Brown, and Company.

Wallace, M. I., & Smith, T. H. (1994). Religion as cure or religion as structure of violence. In M. I. Wallace & T. H. Smith (Eds.), *Curing violence* (pp. xvii–xx). Sonoma, CA: Polebridge Press.

Walsh, D. (1998). Subject/object. In C. Jenks (Ed.), *Core sociological dichotomies* (pp. 275–298). London: Sage Publications. doi:10.4135/9781446222041.n18

Walsh, G., Hennig-Thurau, T., Wayne-Mitchell, V., & Wiedmann, K.-P. (2001). Consumers' decision-making style as a basis for market segmentation. *Journal of Targeting. Measurement and Analysis for Marketing, 10*(2), 117–131. doi:10.1057/palgrave.jt.5740039

Walther, C. S., & Sandlin, J. A. (2013). Green capital and social reproduction within families practicing voluntary simplicity in the US. *International Journal of Consumer Studies, 37*(1), 36–45. doi:10.1111/j.1470-6431.2011.01050.x

Wang, J., & Wallendorf, M. (2006). Materialism, status signaling, and product satisfaction. *Journal of the Academy of Marketing Science, 34*(4), 494–505. doi:10.1177/0092070306289291

Ward, S. (1974). Consumer socialization. *The Journal of Consumer Research, 1*(2), 1–14. doi:10.1086/208584

Ward, S., & Robertson, T. S. (1973). *Consumer behavior: Theoretical sources*. Englewood Cliffs, NJ: Prentice-Hall.

Warren, H. (2014). *Replacing consumer consciousness with producer consciousness*. Unpublished.

Warren, H., & Stratford, L. (2016). *Producer consciousness*. San Francisco, CA: Blurb.

Warr, P. (2008). Work values: Some demographic and cultural correlates. *Journal of Occupational and Organizational Psychology, 81*(4), 751–775. doi:10.1348/096317907X263638

Watson, J. J. (1998). Materialism and debt: A study of current attitudes and behaviors. *Advances in Consumer Research. Association for Consumer Research (U. S.), 25*(1), 203–207.

Wearing, S. L. (2003). *Volunteer tourism: Experiences that make a difference*. New York, NY: Taylor & Francis.

Wearing, S. L., McDonald, M., & Wearing, M. (2013). Consumer culture, the mobilisation of the narcissistic self and adolescent deviant leisure. *Leisure Studies, 32*(4), 367–381. doi:10.1080/02614367.2012.668557

Wearing, S., & McGehee, N. G. (2013). Volunteer tourism: A review. *Tourism Management, 38*(October), 120–130. doi:10.1016/j.tourman.2013.03.002

Webb, D. (2000). Understanding customer role and its importance in the formation of service quality expectations. *Service Industries Journal, 20*(1), 1–21. doi:10.1080/02642060000000001

Webb, D., & Wong, J. (2014). Exploring antecedents of charitable giving and their impact on subjective well-being in Singapore. *Social Indicators Research, 117*(1), 65–87. doi:10.100711205-013-0331-x

Weber, M. (1930). *The Protestant ethic and the spirit of capitalism. (T. Parsons, Ttrans.).* London, England: Routledge.

Wedel, M., & Kamakura, W. (2002). Introduction to the special issue on market segmentation. *International Journal of Research in Marketing, 19*(3), 181–304. doi:10.1016/S0167-8116(02)00075-7

Wells, D. F. (1998). *Losing our virtue: Why the Church must recover its moral vision.* Grand Rapids, MI: Eerdmans.

Werkmeister, W. (1961). *Theories of ethics.* Lincoln, NE: Johnsen Publishing.

Werkmeister, W. (1967). *Man and his values.* Lincoln, NE: University of Nebraska Press.

Werkmeister, W. (1970a). Historical spectrum of value theories: Vol. I. *German language group.* Lincoln, NE: Johnsen Publishing.

Werkmeister, W. (1970b). Historical spectrum of value theories: Vol. II. *Anglo/American group.* Lincoln, NE: Johnsen Publishing.

Westfall, R. (1962). Psychological factors in predicting product choice. *Journal of Marketing, 26*(2), 34–40. doi:10.2307/1248434

Wharff, J. (2007). Bernard of Clairvaux and René Girard on desire and envy. *Cistercian Studies Quarterly, 42*(2), 183–207.

White, K., & Argo, J. J. (2009). Social identity threat and consumer preferences. *Journal of Consumer Psychology, 19*(3), 313–325. doi:10.1016/j.jcps.2009.03.007

Wiesel, E. (2006). *Night* (M. Wiesel, Trans.). New York, NY: Hill and Wang.

Wikipedia. (2018). *Bill Gates's House.* Retrieved from https://en.wikipedia.org/wiki/Bill_Gates%27s_house

Williamson, I., & Cullingford, C. (1997). The uses and misuses of 'alienation'in the social sciences and education. *British Journal of Educational Studies, 45*(3), 263–275. doi:10.1111/1467-8527.00051

Williams, R. (1949). Values. *Bulletin of the American Psychoanalytic Association, 5*(September), 40–51.

Winlow, S., & Hall, S. (2009). Living for the weekend: Youth identities in northeast England. *Ethnography, 10*(1), 91–113. doi:10.1177/1466138108099588

Winter, L., & Kron, T. (2009). Fuzzy thinking in sociology. In R. Seising (Ed.), *Views on fuzzy sets and systems from different perspectives* (pp. 301–320). Berlin, Germany: Springer. doi:10.1007/978-3-540-93802-6_14

Wolfe, T. (1996). Sorry, but your soul just died. *Forbes ASAP*, 210-219.

Wong, N. Y., & Ahuvia, A. C. (1998). Personal taste and family face: Luxury consumption in Confucian and Western societies. *Psychology and Marketing, 15*(5), 423–441. doi:10.1002/(SICI)1520-6793(199808)15:5<423::AID-MAR2>3.0.CO;2-9

Woodman, D., & Bennett, A. (2015). Cultures, transitions, and generations: The case for a new youth studies. In D. Woodman & A. Bennett (Eds.), *Youth cultures, transitions, and generations* (pp. 1–15). London, UK: Palgrave Macmillan UK. doi:10.1057/9781137377234_1

Woodruff, R. (1997). Customer value: The next source of competitive advantage. *Journal of the Academy of Marketing Science, 25*(2), 139–153. doi:10.1007/BF02894350

Woodside, A. G., & Andress, R. (1975). CAD eight years later. *Journal of the Academy of Marketing Science*, *3*(3-4), 309–313. doi:10.1007/BF02729291

Woodward, S. (2005). Looking good: Feeling right – Aesthetics of the self. In S. Küchler & D. Miller (Eds.), *Clothing as material culture* (pp. 21–39). Oxford, UK: Berg. doi:10.2752/9780857854056/CLMATCULT0005

Wrenn, B. (2010). Religious marketing is different. *Services Marketing Quarterly*, *32*(1), 44–59. doi:10.1080/15332969.2011.533095

Wuthnow, R. (1996). *Poor Richard's principle.* Princeton, NJ: Princeton University Press.

Yankelovich, D., & Meer, D. (2006). Rediscovering Market Segmentation. *Harvard Business Review*, *84*(2), 122–131. PMID:16485810

Yount, D. (1997). *Spiritual simplicity: Simplify your life and enrich your soul.* New York, NY: Simon & Schuster.

Zeithaml, V. (1988). Consumer Perceptions of Price, Quality, and Values: A Means-End Model and Synthesis of Evidence. *Journal of Marketing*, *52*(3), 2–22. doi:10.2307/1251446

Zorlu, A. (2003). Batılı bir yaşam tarzı olarak tüketim: Türkiye'de tüketim ürünlerinin ve kültürünün tarihi gelişimi. *Hacettepe University Journal of Sociological Research.* Retrieved October 10, 2017, from: www.sdergi.hacettepe.edu.tr/zorlu_makale.htm

Zukin, S. (2005). *Point of purchase: How shopping changes American culture.* New York, NY: Routledge.

Zukin, S., & Maguire, J. S. (2004). Consumers and consumption. *Annual Review of Sociology*, *30*(1), 173–197. doi:10.1146/annurev.soc.30.012703.110553

About the Contributors

David J. Burns, D.B.A. (1987, Kent State University), is Chair and Professor of Marketing and Professional Sales, Kennesaw State University. He has co-authored several books, published over 100 journal articles and book chapters, and presented over 200 papers. His research interests include retail location and atmospherics, ethics, higher education, and consumer culture. His teaching interests include retailing and other consumer-based areas, including Marketing and the Consumer Culture and Neuromarketing.

* * *

John Branch is Clinical Assistant Professor of Business Administration, and Co-Director of the Yaffe Digital Media Initiative, at the Stephen M. Ross School of Business, and Faculty Associate at the Center for Russian, East European, & Eurasian Studies, both of the Unviersity of Michigan. He is also a Visiting Fellow at Wolfson College at the University of Cambridge.

Michael Brusco's research interests include scheduling, facility layout, clustering, and variable selection in multivariate statistics. His work has been published in journals of several disciplines, including operations management, operations research, industrial engineering, marketing, and statistics.

Floribert Patrick C. Endong (PhD) is a research consultant in the humanities and social sciences. He is a reviewer and editor with many scientific journals in the social sciences. His current research interest focuses on advertising, cinema and globalization, international communication, gender studies, digital media, media laws, international relations, culture and religious communication. He is author of numerous peer-reviewed articles and book chapters in the above-mentioned areas of interest.

Leisa Reinecke Flynn, Ph.D., is BAC Research Professor of Marketing at the University of Southern Mississippi where she specializes in studying materialism in consumers.

Ronald E. Goldsmith, Ph.D., was the Richard M. Baker Professor of Marketing at Florida State University where he specialized in individual differences in consumer behavior. He is currently Emeritus Professor of Marketing.

Brad Hadaway is Professor of Philosophy and Director of Oxford Programs at Georgetown College in Georgetown, Kentucky.

Elif Kiran studied consumer society for her Phd thesis and she is currently an Asst. Prof. of Sociology at Namık Kemal University, Tekirdag, Turkey.

Eirini Koronaki is an academic in the field of marketing and holds a Ph.D. in Business Administration (Subject: Luxury Branding) from the Athens University of Economics and Business and an MSc in Marketing & Strategy from Warwick Business School. She currently works as a Part Time Faculty in Deree - The American College of Greece, has received an Academic Scholarship for teaching and research from Athens University of Economics and Business and is a Visiting Professor for ECS Rennes School of Business. Her research interests include luxury branding, marketing communications and cross-cultural research. She has co-authored chapters in books and has presented papers in several conferences. She has professional experience as a Business Development Manager for Eurodiet Med.

Carole J. Lambert is Professor of English at Azusa Pacific University in California. In addition to four National Endowment for the Humanities grants, she was awarded a Fulbright Fellowship to conduct research in Brussels, Belgium, and recently participated in the Lilly Fellows Program in Humanities and the Arts Seminar. She is the author of *The Empthy Cross: Medieval Hopes, Modern Futility in the Theater of Maurice Maeterlinck, Paul Claudel, August Strindberg, and Georg Kaiser; Is God Man's Friend? Theodicy and Friendship in Elie Wiesel's Novels; Ethics After Auschwitz? Primo Levi's and Elie Wiesel's Response; and Against Indifference: Four Christian Responses to Jewish Suffering During the Holocaust (C.S. Lewis, Thomas Merton, Dietrich Bonhoeffer, Andre and Magda Trocme).* She earned her Ph.D. in comparative literature from the University of California, Berkeley, and has been published widely in several journals.

Steven McMullen is an associate professor of economics at Hope College in Holland Michigan.

Vannie Naidoo is a senior staff member at the University of KwaZulu-Natal, South Africa. She is actively involved in teaching and research within the faculty. Dr Naidoo is actively involved in post graduate supervision of masters and PHD students. She has published in various local and international journals on various issues of management, workplace dynamics, marketing, education, ICT and culture. Dr Naidoo has also written various chapters on different contemporary issues in education, marketing and management. Dr Naidoo is a well established researcher well known to the international community- she has served as keynote speaker at Emerging Trends in Academic Research ETAR-2017, November 27-28, 2017 Bali, Indonesia and has shared her ideas and participated and chaired many sessions at many local and international conferences.

George G. Panigyrakis is a Professor of Marketing in the Department of Business Administration of Athens University of Economics and Business. He was the Director of the MBA program of the Athens University of Economics and Business for 12 years. He has served on the faculties of Groupe ESSEC and University of Stirling and has held visiting appointments at numerous Universities in Europe and in Asia. He is a member of the editorial board of international peer reviewed journals and has participated and coordinated national and international research projects. His research in the areas of Marketing, Integrated Marketing Communications, Brand Management and International Marketing, has appeared in numerous books and journals. He has extensive consultancy experience in companies and organizations.

C. P. Ragland is Associate Professor and Chair of the Philosophy Department at Saint Louis University. He is author of The Will to Reason: Theodicy and Freedom in Descartes (Oxford, 2016). His previous research has focused on the history of modern philosophy, the philosophy of religion, and the metaphysics of free will. However, he very much enjoys teaching Plato to undergraduates, and the ideas in his contribution to this volume arose from that experience.

Charles E. Stokes is Associate Professor of Sociology at Samford University.

Linette Stratford earned her Juris Doctor degree from The Ohio State University College of Law in 1990. Earned a Bachelor of Science in Business Administration from Youngstown State University, 1987. She is the Chief Assistant Prosecutor for Mahoning County, Ohio. Attorney Stratford is also an adjunct professor at Youngstown State University teaching Business Ethics . And she instructs attorneys in professional ethics for the Academy of Continuing Legal Education. In 2016 Attorney Stratford co-authored a book, advancing a new philosophy titled Producer Consciousness. She is currently writing a book advocating a shift to a producer consciousness for the criminal justice system.

Kent Van Til teaches Religion at Hope College. He has published in the area of Ethics and Economics. His works include: "Less than $2.00 a Day: a Christian View of Poverty and the Free Market," and "The Moral Disciple: an Introduction to Christian Ethics," both with Eerdmans.

Rahul R. Verma is a Lecturer in Management with Department of Training and Technical Education, Govt. of NCT of Delhi, India for the last 7 years and also pursuing Ph. D. in Commerce from Mewar University. His research interests include Digitalization and Cyber Spaces. He has attended more than 10 national and international conferences and has presented papers in more than 7 national and international conferences. He has published more than 5 research papers with prestigious publishers and edited one book on Digitalization published by IGI Global. He is also on editorial board of peer reviewed prestigious journals.

Homer Warren has a D.B.A. from Kent State University, 1986. He is an Emeritus Professor of Marketing at Youngstown State University. His recent research publications concern creative thinking methodologies in marketing management. His recent book is Producer Consciousness.

John Wilson is interested in the interfaces between philosophy, sociology and psychology plus all areas of 20th century thought including the 'analytical' and 'continental' traditions. He was Director of the Language Institute at Dhurakijpundit University in the early 2000s. He teaches Philosophy and English Literature at Assumption University of Thailand, is an elder member of the Guna Chakra Research group, publishes internationally and is a counselor for young people with mental health and adjustment problems.

Index

E

F

G

H

I

K

L

M

N

O

P

R

S

T

U

V

W

www.ingramcontent.com/pod-product-compliance
Lightning Source LLC
LaVergne TN
LVHW060421300926
849162LV00006B/1487